Coal-Mining Women in Japan

In the years between the Meiji Restoration in 1868 and the beginning of Japan's war mobilization boom in 1930, collieries in Europe and America embraced new technologies and excluded women from working underground. In Japan, however, mining women witnessed no significant changes in working practices over this period. The availability of the cheap and abundant labor of these women allowed the captains of the coal industry in Japan to avoid expensive investments in new machinery and sophisticated mining methods; instead, they continued to exploit workers and markets intensively, making substantial profits without the burdens of extensive mechanization.

This unique book explores the lives of the thousands of women who labored underground in Japan's coal mines in the years 1868 to 1930. It examines their work, their family lives, their aspirations, and their achievements and disappointments. Drawing heavily on interview material with the miners themselves, W. Donald Burton combines translations of their stories with features of Japanese society at the time and coal-mining technology. In doing so, he presents a complex account of the women's lives and provides a keen insight into gender relations and the industrial and labor history of Japan.

Coal-mining Women in Japan will be welcomed by students and scholars of Japanese history, gender studies, and industrial history alike.

W. Donald Burton has taught in Canada at the University of British Columbia, St. Mary's University, McGill University, and the Open University of British Columbia.

Asia's transformations
Edited by Mark Selden
Cornell University, USA

The books in this series explore the political, social, economic, and cultural consequences of Asia's transformations in the 20th and 21st centuries. The series emphasizes the tumultuous interplay of local, national, regional, and global forces as Asia bids to become the hub of the world economy. While focusing on contemporary issues, it also looks back to analyze the antecedents of Asia's contested rise.

This series comprises several strands:

Asia's Transformations
Titles include:

1. Debating Human Rights*
Critical essays from the United States and Asia
Edited by Peter Van Ness

2. Hong Kong's History*
State and society under colonial rule
Edited by Tak-Wing Ngo

3. Japan's Comfort Women*
Sexual slavery and prostitution during World War II and the US occupation
Yuki Tanaka

4. Opium, Empire and the Global Political Economy*
Carl A. Trocki

5. Chinese Society*
Change, conflict and resistance
Edited by Elizabeth J. Perry and Mark Selden

6. Mao's Children in the New China*
Voices from the Red Guard generation
Yarong Jiang and David Ashley

7. Remaking the Chinese State*
Strategies, society and security
Edited by Chien-min Chao and Bruce J. Dickson

8. Korean Society*
Civil society, democracy and the state
Edited by Charles K. Armstrong

9. The Making of Modern Korea*
Adrian Buzo

10. The Resurgence of East Asia*
500, 150 and 50 Year perspectives
Edited by Giovanni Arrighi, Takeshi Hamashita and Mark Selden

11. Chinese Society, second edition*
Change, conflict and resistance
Edited by Elizabeth J. Perry and Mark Selden

12. Ethnicity in Asia*
Edited by Colin Mackerras

13. The Battle for Asia*
From decolonization to globalization
Mark T. Berger

14. State and Society in 21st Century China*
Edited by Peter Hays Gries and Stanley Rosen

15. Japan's Quiet Transformation*
Social change and civil society in the 21st century
Jeff Kingston

16. Confronting the Bush Doctrine*
Critical views from the Asia-Pacific
Edited by Mel Gurtov and Peter Van Ness

17. China in War and Revolution, 1895–1949*
Peter Zarrow

18. The Future of US–Korean Relations*
The imbalance of power
Edited by John Feffer

19. Working in China*
Ethnographies of labor and workplace transformations
Edited by Ching Kwan Lee

20. Korean Society, second edition*
Civil society, democracy and the state
Edited by Charles K. Armstrong

21. Singapore*
The state and the culture of excess
Souchou Yao

22. Pan-Asianism in Modern Japanese History*
Colonialism, regionalism and borders
Edited by Sven Saaler and J. Victor Koschmann

23. The Making of Modern Korea, 2nd Edition*
Adrian Buzo

24. Re-writing Culture in Taiwan*
Edited by Fang-long Shih, Stuart Thompson, and Paul-François Tremlett

25. Reclaiming Chinese Society*
The new social activism
Edited by You-tien Hsing and Ching Kwan Lee

26. Girl Reading Girl in Japan*
Edited by Tomoko Aoyama and Barbara Hartley

27. Chinese Politics*
State, society and the market
Edited by Peter Hays Gries and Stanley Rosen

28. Chinese Society, third edition*
Change, conflict and resistance
Edited by Elizabeth J. Perry and Mark Selden

29. Mapping Modernity in Shanghai
Space, gender, and visual culture in the Sojourners' City, 1853–98
Samuel Y. Liang

30. Minorities and Multiculturalism in Japanese Education
An interactive perspective
Edited by Ryoko Tsuneyoshi, Kaori H Okano and Sarane Boocock

31. Japan's Wartime Medical Atrocities
Comparative inquiries in science, history, and ethics
Edited by Jing-Bao Nie, Nanyan Guo, Mark Selden and Arthur Kleinman

32. State and Society in Modern Rangoon
Donald M. Seekins

33. Learning Chinese, Turning Chinese*
Becoming sinophone in a globalised world
Edward McDonald

34. Aesthetic Constructions of Korean Nationalism
Spectacle, politics and history
Hong Kal

35. Popular Culture and the State in East and Southeast Asia
Edited by Nissim Otmazgin and Eyal Ben Ari

36. Japan's Outcaste Abolition
The struggle for national inclusion and the making of the modern state
Noah Y. McCormack

37. The Market and Temple Fairs of Rural China
Red fire
Gene Cooper

38. The Role of American NGOs in China's Modernization
Invited influence
Norton Wheeler

39. State, Society and the Market in Contemporary Vietnam
Property, power and values
Edited by Hue-Tam Ho Tai and Mark Sidel

40. East Asia Beyond the History Wars
Confronting the ghosts of violence
Tessa Morris-Suzuki, Morris Low, Leonid Petrov and Timothy Yun Hui Tsu

41. China
How the empire fell
Joseph W. Esherick and C. X. George Wei

42. The Political Economy of Affect and Emotion in East Asia
Jie Yang

43. Remaking China's Great Cities
Space and culture in urban housing, renewal, and expansion
Samuel Y. Liang

44. Vietnam's Socialist Servants
Domesticity, class, gender, and identity
Minh T. N. Nguyen

Asia's Great Cities

Each volume aims to capture the heartbeat of the contemporary city from multiple perspectives emblematic of the authors own deep familiarity with the distinctive faces of the city, its history, society, culture, politics and economics, and its evolving position in national, regional, and global frameworks. Whereas most volumes emphasize urban developments since the Second World War, some pay close attention to the legacy of the longue durée in shaping the contemporary. Thematic and comparative volumes address such themes as urbanization, economic and financial linkages, architecture and space, wealth and power, gendered relationships, planning and anarchy, and ethnographies in national and regional perspective. Titles include:

1. Bangkok*
Place, practice and representation
Marc Askew

2. Representing Calcutta*
Modernity, nationalism and the colonial uncanny
Swati Chattopadhyay

3. Singapore*
Wealth, power and the culture of control
Carl A. Trocki

4. The City in South Asia
James Heitzman

5. Global Shanghai, 1850–2010*
A history in fragments
Jeffrey N. Wasserstrom

6. Hong Kong*
Becoming a global city
Stephen Chiu and Tai-Lok Lui

Asia.com is a series that focuses on the ways in which new information and communication technologies are influencing politics, society, and culture in Asia. Titles include:

1. Japanese Cybercultures*
Edited by Mark McLelland and Nanette Gottlieb

2. Asia.com*
Asia encounters the Internet
Edited by K. C. Ho, Randolph Kluver and Kenneth C. C. Yang

3. The Internet in Indonesia's New Democracy*
David T. Hill and Krishna Sen

4. Chinese Cyberspaces*
Technological changes and political effects
Edited by Jens Damm and Simona Thomas

5. Mobile Media in the Asia-Pacific
Gender and the art of being mobile
Larissa Hjorth

6. Online@AsiaPacific
Mobile, Social and Locative Media in the Asia–Pacific
Larissa Hjorth and Michael Arnold

Literature and Society

Literature and Society is a series that seeks to demonstrate the ways in which Asian Literature is influenced by the politics, society, and culture in which it is produced. Titles include:

1. The Body in Postwar Japanese Fiction
Douglas N. Slaymaker

2. Chinese Women Writers and the Feminist Imagination, 1905–1948*
Haiping Yan

3. Okinawan War Memory
Transgenerational trauma and the war fiction of Medoruma Shun
Kyle Ikeda

Routledge Studies in Asia's Transformations

Routledge Studies in Asia's Transformations is a forum for innovative new research intended for a high-level specialist readership.
Titles include:

1. The American Occupation of Japan and Okinawa*
Literature and memory
Michael Molasky

2. Koreans in Japan*
Critical voices from the margin
Edited by Sonia Ryang

3. Internationalizing the Pacific
The United States, Japan and the Institute of Pacific Relations in war and peace, 1919–1945
Tomoko Akami

4. Imperialism in South East Asia*
'A fleeting, passing phase'
Nicholas Tarling

5. Chinese Media, Global Contexts*
Edited by Chin-Chuan Lee

6. Remaking Citizenship in Hong Kong*
Community, nation and the global city
Edited by Agnes S. Ku and Ngai Pun

7. Japanese Industrial Governance
Protectionism and the licensing state
Yul Sohn

8. Developmental Dilemmas*
Land reform and institutional change
in China
Edited by Peter Ho

**9. Genders, Transgenders and
Sexualities in Japan***
*Edited by Mark McLelland and
Romit Dasgupta*

**10. Fertility, Family Planning and
Population Policy in China***
*Edited by Dudley L. Poston, Che-Fu Lee,
Chiung-Fang Chang, Sherry L. McKibben
and Carol S. Walther*

11. Japanese Diasporas*
Unsung pasts, conflicting presents and
uncertain futures
Edited by Nobuko Adachi

12. How China Works*
Perspectives on the twentieth-century
industrial workplace
Edited by Jacob Eyferth

**13. Remolding and Resistance among
Writers of the Chinese Prison Camp**
Disciplined and published
Edited by Philip F. Williams and Yenna Wu

**14. Popular Culture, Globalization and
Japan***
*Edited by Matthew Allen and Rumi
Sakamoto*

15. medi@sia*
Global media/tion in and out of context
*Edited by Todd Joseph Miles Holden and
Timothy J. Scrase*

16. Vientiane*
Transformations of a Lao landscape
*Marc Askew, William S. Logan and
Colin Long*

**17. State Formation and Radical
Democracy in India**
Manali Desai

18. Democracy in Occupied Japan*
The U.S. occupation and Japanese politics
and society
*Edited by Mark E. Caprio and
Yoneyuki Sugita*

**19. Globalization, Culture and Society
in Laos***
Boike Rehbein

20. Transcultural Japan*
At the borderlands of race, gender,
and identity
*Edited by David Blake Willis and
Stephen Murphy-Shigematsu*

**21. Post-Conflict Heritage, Post-Colonial
Tourism**
Culture, politics and development at Angkor
Tim Winter

22. Education and Reform in China*
Emily Hannum and Albert Park

**23. Writing Okinawa: Narrative Acts of
Identity and Resistance**
Davinder L. Bhowmik

24. Maid in China*
Media, morality, and the cultural politics
of boundaries
Wanning Sun

**25. Northern Territories, Asia-Pacific
Regional Conflicts and the Åland
Experience**
Untying the Kurillian knot
Edited by Kimie Hara and Geoffrey Jukes

26. Reconciling Indonesia
Grassroots agency for peace
Birgit Bräuchler

27. Singapore in the Malay World*
Building and breaching regional bridges
Lily Zubaidah Rahim

28. Pirate Modernity*
Delhi's media urbanism
Ravi Sundaram

29. The World Bank and the post-Washington Consensus in Vietnam and Indonesia
Inheritance of loss
Susan Engel

30. China on Video
Smaller Screen Realities
Paola Voci

31. Overseas Chinese, Ethnic Minorities and Nationalism
De-centering China
Elena Barabantseva

32. The Education of Migrant Children and China's Future
The urban left behind
Holly H. Ming

Critical Asian Scholarship

Critical Asian Scholarship is a series intended to showcase the most important individual contributions to scholarship in Asian Studies. Each of the volumes presents a leading Asian scholar addressing themes that are central to his or her most significant and lasting contribution to Asian studies. The series is committed to the rich variety of research and writing on Asia and is not restricted to any particular discipline, theoretical approach, or geographical expertise.

1. Southeast Asia*
A testament
George McT. Kahin

2. Women and the Family in Chinese History*
Patricia Buckley Ebrey

3. China Unbound*
Evolving perspectives on the Chinese past
Paul A. Cohen

4. China's Past, China's Future*
Energy, food, environment
Vaclav Smil

5. The Chinese State in Ming Society*
Timothy Brook

6. China, East Asia and the Global Economy*
Regional and historical perspectives
Takeshi Hamashita
Edited by Mark Selden and Linda Grove

7. The Global and Regional in China's Nation-Formation*
Prasenjit Duara

8. Decoding Subaltern Politics*
Ideology, disguise, and resistance in agrarian politics
James C. Scott

9. Mapping China and Managing the World*
Culture, cartography and cosmology in late Imperial times
Richard J. Smith

10. Technology, Gender and History in Imperial China*
Great transformations reconsidered
Francesca Bray

* Available in paperback

Coal-Mining Women in Japan

Heavy burdens

W. Donald Burton

LONDON AND NEW YORK

First published 2014
by Routledge
2 Park Square, Milton Park, Abingdon, Oxon OX14 4RN

and by Routledge
711 Third Avenue, New York, NY 10017

Routledge is an imprint of the Taylor & Francis Group, an informa business

© 2014 W. Donald Burton

The right of W. Donald Burton to be identified as author of this work has been asserted by him in accordance with sections 77 and 78 of the Copyright, Designs and Patents Act 1988.

All rights reserved. No part of this book may be reprinted or reproduced or utilised in any form or by any electronic, mechanical, or other means, now known or hereafter invented, including photocopying and recording, or in any information storage or retrieval system, without permission in writing from the publishers.

Trademark notice: Product or corporate names may be trademarks or registered trademarks, and are used only for identification and explanation without intent to infringe.

British Library Cataloguing in Publication Data
A catalogue record for this book is available from the British Library

Library of Congress Cataloging-in-Publication Data
Burton, W. Donald.
Coal mining women in Japan : heavy burdens / W. Donald Burton.
pages cm – (Asia's transformations ; 44)
Includes bibliographical references and index.
1. Women coal miners–Japan–19th century. 2. Coal mines and mining–Japan–19th century. 3. Women coal miners–Japan–20th century. 4. Coal mines and mining–Japan–20th century. I. Title.
HD6073.M62J32 2014
331.4'822334095209034–dc23
2014003830

ISBN: 978-0-415-74432-4 (hbk)
ISBN: 978-1-315-81306-6 (ebk)

Typeset in TimesNewRoman
by Cenveo Publisher Services

To E. Patricia (Paddy) Tsurumi, my mentor and inspiration

Contents

Acknowledgments	xvi
List of illustrations and tables	xviii
Maps	xx

Introduction   1

Plus ça change, plus c'est la même chose 7
Burakumin: the inconspicuous "others" 8
Miners all 9
Voices 10

1   Background   11

Number of women in mining 13
Age and marital status 14
Origins of coal miners 17
Gender disparity 19
Racial and social discrimination 20

2   Work and wages   28

Hewing and hauling 28
Little light on the subject 39
Obtaining and pushing out wagons 41
The competition for wagons 44
Piecework wages and deductions 46
Framing and tunneling 50
Blasting 54
Sorting and transporting 57

3   Working conditions   62

Darkness, wetness, heat, and grime 62
Disease 67
Fire and explosions 68
Cave-ins and other nasty accidents 75

xiv *Contents*

Dynamite! 78
Nonpunitive damages 80
In harm's way 83
What kind of treatment? 84
Relief programs 85
A dangerous occupation! 86
Epitaph 87

4   Their life trajectory 92

Oya no kao o miwasureru na yo
(Don't forget your mother's face!) 94
A single mother prototype? 96
Schooling (or not) 97
Child labor 98
Attitudes toward child labor 100
Courting and marriage 101
Choice of partners 105
The loose bonds of marriage 108
How wives dealt with the "big change" 110
The marital struggle 111
A revelation 114
Getten *117*
Reproduction and conflict 118
Debt: another source of marital friction 121

5   The daily routine 127

Early in the morning 127
The little hovel 127
Some improvements? 129
Water! 132
Preparation for yet another day 134
Going down 136
Inadequate clothing 137
Straw sandals 139
Hygiene and sanitation 141
Adornment 142
Eating underground 143
Long shifts 144
Late in the evening 145
The evening bath 148
A woman's work is never done 150
Not even a song at twilight 152

6   Solidarity, divisions, bondage, and resistance 160

A shared fate 160
Mutual aid 163

The Indomitables 164
Rivalry and conflict 165
Feisty termagants or subdued proletarians? 166
Recruitment by subterfuge 167
They owed their souls to the company and the boss 170
And to the company store 173
Subservience to the gang boss 173
Ketsuwari—*indirect resistance 175*
Repercussions 180
Brutality as a management strategy 183
The power of the boss 184
"Behavior modification" 185
"Subtle" and not-so-subtle forms of resistance 186
Regulatory and discriminatory regimes 188
The suppression of Korean miners 190
Divisions and solidarity 191
The Rice Riots and attempts at organized resistance 193
Epilogue—the potential for change 196

7   Common seams, common attitudes   **203**

Lacking a "nobler" cause 204
Spiritual strength, self-confidence, and survival 205
Self-esteem and indignities 206
Reactions to bondage 208
The limits of endurance 209
Gender differences and inequities 210
Changing rewards 212
"Work-Sharing" and the division of labor 213
The women's capabilities 214
Standing up to the men 215
Superstition and credulity 217
Accepting their lot 218
Fear 219
No place to call "Home" 220
Sexual abuse 223
Their unnatural environment 225
Perpetual night work 227
The "benevolence" of the bosses 229
The incredible brightness of being 231

Afterword	238
Glossary	241
Bibliography	246
Index	252

Acknowledgments

I owe abundant thanks to many colleagues and friends over such an extended period of time that I may have forgotten some of the most welcome contributions. Librarians and faculty at the School of Oriental and African Studies of London University, UK, helped me with my doctoral dissertation on a related topic, and librarians at the Japanese Diet Library in Tokyo and at the University of British Columbia in Vancouver assisted with more recent research. I would particularly like to thank Tsuneharu Gonnami, retired Asian librarian emeritus at the latter for his many indulgences and his assistance in obtainng permissions for the use of Japanese materials.

The illustrations and commentaries from the work of Yamamoto Sakubei have added greatly to my understanding and appreciation of the working lives of the coal-mining women, and I am grateful to the family of Yamamoto and the staff of the Tagawa City Coal Mining Historical Museum for allowing me to use these materials. Yamamoto's prolific work has recently been archived and is preserved in the Memory of the World Register of The United Nations Educational, Scientific and Cultural Organization.

My acknowledgment of Japanese mentors and colleagues would run to many pages, could I list them all by name. Particular thanks are due to Nimura Kazuo of the Ohara Social Research Institute, Hosei University, who advised me in the early stages of my research and who relinquished his own copy of Morisaki's interviews, which started me on the path to publication. I remember with nostalgia and gratitude the guidance of mentors at Hitotsubashi University, introduced by my colleague, Yasumaru Yasuo, including Nishinarita Yutaka, Nakamura Masao, and Watanabe Etsuji. My initiation into the language and complexities of modern Japanese history was undertaken at the Japanese History Research Room (the *Kokushi Kenkyu Shitsu*) of Kyoto University, where Noda Emi facilitated my studies and colleagues—including Asao Naohiro, Kawane Yoshiyasu, and Shibahara Takuji—tutored me assiduously. I also enjoyed the guidance and friendship of Sasaki Ryuji, Suzuki Ryo, and the Wakitas, Osamu and Haruko. My postgraduate classmate, Ohara Hidesaburo, was an inspiration to me, though it was difficult for me to respond adequately to his historical enthusiasm before I mastered certain elements of the Japanese language. Professor Kobata Atsushi, with great patience and generosity, provided me with factual knowledge of the historical background of Japanese feudalism and the mining industry. The tutelage of these mentors and colleagues did not extend to the later research on this book, and they cannot be blamed for any deficiencies herein.

Much gratitude is due to friends and colleagues who have helped with editing (and shortening) the manuscript. Katherine Howard, instigated by her grandmother, Irene, contended with my prolixity before Tom Wells did a thoroughly professional job on the whole manuscript and Ruth Hein helped streamline Chapter 4. Mark Selden scrutinized the manuscript and gave me judicious advice regarding publishable content and format. I am indebted to all of them, and to my late brother Neil and my brother-in-law David Carter who commented on parts of the text.

Many friends, academic and otherwise, have contributed to my scholarly endeavors. John Price of the University of Victoria was always supportive, while producing valuable publications on Japan's labor history and on Canada's relations with Japan and China with a much wider scope than this study.

My greatest debt, of course, is to the mining women whose reminiscences were only available to me through the interviews and biographies recorded in Japanese by Morisaki Kazue, Idegawa Yasuko, and Mashio Etsuko. I hope my translations and interpretations of the women's memoirs are faithful to the transcriptions of these authors and to the recollections of the mining women.

And finally, the study was initiated and inspired by Paddy (E. Patricia) Tsurumi, whose work on the silk-reeling and cotton-spinning women of Meiji Japan, was meant to be complemented by my work on coal-mining women. Many, including myself, who take an interest in early modern Japanese labor history will be forever indebted to her for her pioneering research and analysis.

W. Donald Burton
January 2014

List of illustrations and tables

Illustrations

2.1	Hewing and hauling	31
2.2	Hauling with the *sena*	32
2.3	Emptying *sena* at the pit mouth	33
2.4	Sieving and hauling from the pit mouth	34
2.5	Hauling with the *tebo*	35
2.6	With the basket *sura*	36
2.7	Two forms of *sura*	37
2.8	The *ukezura*	39
2.9	"Pit ponies"	41
2.10	Pushing wagons	42
2.11	Tallying output	48
2.12	Sounding out the roof	50
2.13	Framing in the haulageways	52
2.14	Man-and-wife frame	53
2.15	The use of dynamite	56
3.1	A dangerous occupation	78
3.2	Smoking at the *sasabeya*	81
4.1	Children underground	99
4.2	The men partying	112
4.3	Incessant conflict	115
4.4	Domestic violence	120
5.1	At the well	133
5.2	Woman hewing in *mabu-beko*	140
5.3	Lunch break underground	143
5.4	The common bath	149
5.5	Evening routine	153
6.1	"That will teach him a lesson!"	169
6.2	*Ketsuwari*—escaping	177
6.3	More exemplary punishment	179
6.4	*Rinchi*—"lynching"	182
6.5	"Moral correction"	183

List of illustrations and tables   xix

6.6	The officious staffer	186
6.7	*Uchikowashi*—house-wrecking	194
6.8	The state intervenes	195

Tables

1.1	Underground miners in major coal mines (1906)	15
1.2	Age and status of female workers (1924)	18
3.1	Deaths in various sectors of the Hōjō Mine, 1914	73
3.2	Major disasters in Japanese coal mines before 1930	74
3.3	Causes of injuries in Japanese coal mines (1924–6)	74
3.4	Casualties in Japanese coal mines (1917–26)	87

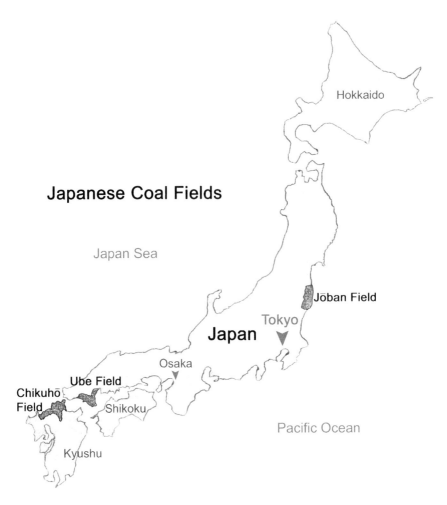

Map of Japan with locations of Chikuhō, Ube, and Jōban coalfields. (Sketched by author.)

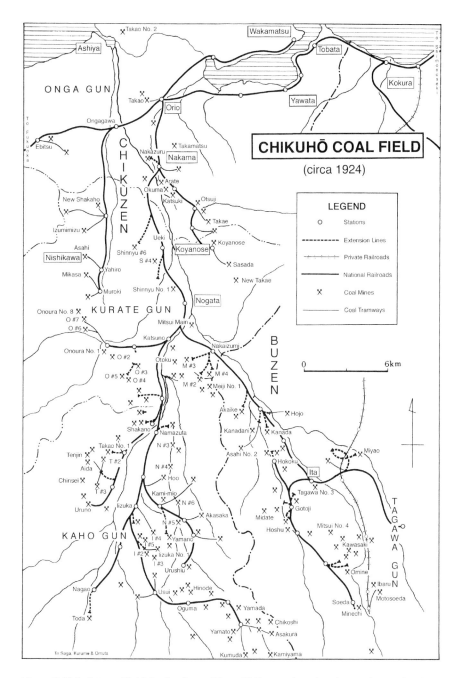

Map of Chikuhō coalfield in the Onga River Valley region showing major coal mines. (Adapted from Nakamura Masanori, *Rōdōsha to Nōmin, Nihon no Rekishi* series vol. 29, p. 134, and Tajima Masami, *Tankō Bijin*, p. i.)

Introduction

Hito ni kiite morau gena ii hanashi wa, hontō, nai bai.[1]
I certainly have none of the kind of stories that people would like to hear.

The story of the working lives of the coal-mining women of northern Kyushu in the period when the coal industry of Japan is thought to have been modernizing must be told. Between the Meiji Restoration in 1868 and the beginning of the war mobilization boom in 1930, new technology was being developed and used in the collieries of Europe and America, where women had long since been excluded from working underground. But the working methods of Japanese mining women did not change substantially in this period. Before the attempted exclusion of women from underground work in the late 1920s and the 1930s, the availability of the cheap and abundant labor of these women, in conjunction with the labor of their male partners, allowed the captains of the coal industry in Japan to avoid expensive investments in the new machinery and sophisticated mining methods that were being developed in the West. Instead, these Japanese "entrepreneurs" continued to reap substantial profits without the burdens of extensive mechanization.

This is a story about the exploitation of human labor, the back-bending labor of thousands of Japanese women, particularly those who worked underground. Most of these women were doing the hauling work done by the men and the boys in the West with more assistance from steam-driven windlasses, horse-driven railway equipment, and, later, electric-powered conveyors. Insofar as feasible, the story is told by the women themselves. Many told their stories to Morisaki Kazue and Idegawa Yasuko, sympathetic authors and interviewers who recorded their accounts faithfully and accurately while raising their own families in the coal-mining region of Fukuoka Prefecture.

This book aims to pay tribute both to the women who worked underground and to Morisaki and Idegawa, who became, after the publication of the two works used here, recognized scholars on the exploitation of women in the Japanese workforce. But neither they nor Mashio Etsuko, who lucidly recorded the life of underground haulier Fujisawa Maki in the Joban region of northeast Japan, regard the women's stories as merely an integral part of a larger history of modern development in the Japanese coal industry. In addition, this book

2 Introduction

attempts to show that what "modernization" did occur in the industry prior to the 1930s did not substantially affect the way the women worked and lived in the Japanese coalfields.

Because the women had few modern aids in the form of mechanized equipment, they were forced to rely upon their strength and wit to do the always-strenuous work of hauling in the most efficient manner available. And because their remuneration was in the form of piece rates—so much per wagon of coal put out by the team—they might work with little supervision from company representatives or gang bosses. However, because the piece rates were low, they could not take advantage of the absence of surveillance to "take it easy" or "goof off," although they often allege that their husbands did just that. The women had to work all-out to make a decent living. And because they had to try to keep up with the hewing, or cutting, of the coal from the coal face, which was mostly done by their male partners, they often worked harder and longer than the men. If the men took it easy or left after digging an amount of coal that they thought adequate but that the women could not haul out while the men were still there, the women were obliged to stay behind and work extra hours. Thus, they often worked very long days. The women invariably recall a harder workload for women than for men, even without the added burden of family care, in which the men did not take an active part.

The conditions in which the women worked were anything but salubrious. In the darkness of the underground caverns, carrying primitive lamps, they contended with moisture and uncontrolled running water, heat that varied from hot to unbearable, and coal or rock dust, which of course made breathing anything but easy. These conditions, endured over long periods of time, contributed to diseases and illnesses that could be fatal. The dangers of the work were omnipresent, and accidents and casualties often kept women from earning adequate sustenance for their families. Cave-ins, runaway coal wagons, congestion along narrow passageways, and slippery slopes all took their toll. Methane gas leaks and subsequent fires could be lethal, particularly if the fires set off an explosion of the pervasive coal dust in the air. Less frequent, but always dangerous nonetheless, were leaks of carbon monoxide. Even if the women were not close to the leaks, they could still suffer painful burns or asphyxiation. Given all these perils, it is not surprising that there was a higher incidence of casualties in Japanese coal mines than in the mines in England. And even with mechanization later there remained many dangers.

In addition to physical dangers, there were conditions that made it difficult for the women to maintain their dignity and self-respect. Because of the oppressive heat they were obliged to work half-naked, stripping to the waist and wearing only the miner's skirt, or *mabu-beko*, which revealed more of their "private parts" than they would have liked. Of course, they got used to the lack of clothing over time and even made jokes about it later, but when new recruits were first confronted with both naked men and women, they felt uncomfortable working alongside them. The reputation of coal miners as unsavory characters who might have criminal backgrounds also made newcomers leery of their new workmates.

Introduction   3

Their wariness contributed to friction and misunderstandings in the new milieu. Furthermore, the characterization of coal miners as a lower class, often labelled "vermin" by their bosses, colored the self-perceptions of the women as well as the men. In their reminiscences, they often attempted to overcome their feelings of unworthiness by claiming expertise at their work and success at raising their families. But the bosses did little, if anything, to promote these positive self-perceptions and in fact more often castigated and denigrated them in harsh terms, echoing the unfavorable perception of them by the outside world.

Uprooted from their rural homes in order to work in the mines, the women suffered a displacement that could be particularly hard for Japanese people, who strongly identified with their birthplaces and communal villages. Because the many smaller mines in the Chikuho region closed often because of flooding, cave-ins, or the working out of easily accessible seams, the rudimentary housing at the pit mouths inevitably had a temporary quality that did not persuade the women that it made good homes for their families. At larger mines the housing was not much better, and the constant attempts of miners to find better working conditions at other mines—rarely satisfied, it should be noted—could not promote a feeling of belonging to a colliery home. The women expressed some nostalgia for their rural birthplaces and feelings of rootlessness in the northern Kyushu mountains and plains. The physical separation between rural towns/villages and mining camps, which managements worked to preserve, also helped to divide miners and farmers and impeded any solidarity in what had previously been a relatively homogenous agrarian class.

In addition to being displaced from their homes and estranged from their relatives, the women also found themselves in a competitive work situation, contending for hauling equipment, good coal faces and haulage ways, and better working conditions. Some nurtured hard feelings toward other miners who were members of the same gang but who strove to best their rivals in putting out more coal. At times, the women felt obliged to please overseers who had the power to assign them to good faces, and this too could lead to abuse and friction in inter-personal relations. Although not subjected to the same degree of abuse as female textile workers by male overseers in the burgeoning textile mills because they usually worked in family groups, the mining women had to rely on their wits to gain favors in working conditions without offering favours in return. And single women, although still protected to some extent by their families, were nevertheless vulnerable in the underground world, where machismo men tried to assert their superiority.

In this competitive world, some of the women declared their independence by proclaiming that if their husbands proved incapable of working hard and efficiently enough to contribute sufficient income for their families, they would take up with someone who could. And sometimes they did. Others worked harder to compensate for inadequate mates, complaining but making the best of bad situations. By many of their accounts, their husbands were lazy wastrels who spent as little time as possible at work and wasted precious family resources on drinking, gambling, and whoring. Yet while the women endured much frustration and

4 Introduction

anxiety, they often related incidents both above and below ground with humour, acceptance, or quiet resignation. Only one woman indicated that she fully understood the source of her husband's frustration and indolence: the harsh conditions of the work underground. But any empathy she may have felt was tempered by the fact that she was subjected to the same working conditions and was not expected to react in the same way.

Although the underground work often put the women into competition with each other, life above ground, although much shorter because of the length of working days, was somewhat better in that it involved considerable sharing of limited resources and a modicum of social exchange. Although the women's recollections may have been shaped by the post-World War II ethos when they were interviewed, they remembered sharing food, cooperating in the preparation of meals, looking after neighbors' children, and even lending money back and forth, often without expectation of reimbursement and always without charging interest. For people with such few resources, many were remarkably generous and charitable. This mutuality was expressed more prominently among people recruited from the same prefecture, often to the same labor gangs, but it seems to have extended to others as well because they were considered to have come from similar circumstances of poverty and alienation.

Recruitment, for most of our period at all but the largest mines, was a matter of induction into a labor gang rather than employment by a mining company. The women did not join the gang except as adjuncts of their husbands or fathers, however, so their sense of belonging and being subservient to a gang boss was not as strong as the men's. At the same time, since the gangs were often the successors of family teams led by a skilled miner with contractual connections to mine operators, the women's sense of parity with male gang members could create expectations for equal treatment at work and an equitable division of wages. The gang boss received the whole wage packet for the gang and took a cut for his "services" (recruitment loans, other debt servicing, room and board for bachelors, provision of household goods and bedding for families, working tools, lamps, etc.). The women did not know the amount of the rakeoff and had to make do with the amounts passed on to them from their husbands, often after their husbands' accounts for drinking and gambling had been settled, at least partially. Although they recalled average rates for wagon loads of coal and sometimes claimed to have received pay equal to that of the men in the earlier period (Meiji and early Taisho), they do not divulge information about the division of the wage packets between hewer and haulier to support their claim.

While their incomes were claimed by the mine operators and bosses to be sufficient to provide adequate, even plentiful, food for their families, during frequent illnesses or injuries when they could not work or economic downturns when rates of pay were arbitrarily cut, they could only sustain themselves with loans from the gang boss. Their incomes were, on average, better than those of agrarian workers and laborers on construction and public works, although such workers were notoriously underpaid in the initial stages of modern capital accumulation in Japan. And women working underground earned substantially more than the mostly female sorters or "pickers" at the pit mouth. But sorters were predominantly single women without families to support (although many no doubt helped families they left behind in rural areas). Nearly all of the underground workers spoke of difficulties in making ends meet and of constant indebtedness to the gang boss or the company store. It was unusual for a woman to be able to set aside a nest egg—even in good times. And when she did succeed in accumulating modest savings, the bigger companies often required that they be deposited in company accounts that acted as security against the women's families quitting.

If coal miners had enough to eat during most of the period under consideration, they were never sheltered in adequate housing. Japanese scholars have labeled the labor gang system in Kyushu the *naya-seido* after the shanties and dormitories in which the families and bachelors were accommodated. Elsewhere in Japan it was called the *hamba-seido*, referring to the dormitory halls where unmarried gang members were fed. In both cases accommodation was rudimentary. The women all complained about the lack of living and storage space, the permeability of walls and roofs to inclement weather, the drifting of cooking fire smoke between family units, and the difficulty of keeping the *naya* clean. Although some bureaucrats, journalists, and scholars supported management claims that housing had been improved in the Taisho period, the women speak of no substantial improvements.

Outsiders from the elite establishment also claimed that childcare facilities improved over time, but it was only the large companies that provided for preschool children. At other companies, there might be a simple shack at the pit mouth where infants could be breastfed by mothers coming out between stints underground. And creches for weaned infants and toddlers might be staffed by caregivers at the *zaibatsu* mines. But caring for children was always taxing, and at most collieries preschool children were left with grandparents, older siblings, or others not employed underground. For the siblings, this could mean large gaps in their schooling, and the vaunted literacy and education programs of the modernizing government were not effective in most coal-mining areas. Since many girls went underground to help their parents at early ages and started work as adults at around age 14, their education was sorely deficient. Many of the girls had been "farmed out" as child-minders and maids to better-off farmers or townspeople for a couple of years before age 14; child labor was accepted as a fact of life among coal miners the same as it had been and was among farmers. The children of miners could be described as being schooled in tradition and custom rather than in the new "enlightenment."

Courting and coupling were certainly haphazard matters that were in no way subject to the careful matchmaking of middle-class Japanese society. Although parents and even some of the young girls themselves tried to arrange engagements with males who could make a decent living at mining, other liaisons were made casually and did not always turn into marital relations. It seems that many young men were recommended to parents as sober and hardworking prospects, only to turn out to be hard-drinking gamblers after marriage and the advent of

6 *Introduction*

children. Their deterioration was no doubt the result of disillusionment with the hard life of miners and the lack of other job prospects. Marital relations in many cases were anything but harmonious.

Although the women's relations with their spouses varied according to situation and temperament, they all reveal the difficulties created by the stresses and strains of work underground. And there was usually no escape from an unhappy relationship after the arrival of children; the women were simply forced to make the best of difficult situations. Moreover, to be widowed at the coal mines was a serious misfortune. The company and bosses would not provide for families not led by a male member of a gang. The gang boss and his wife would often fulfill the role of matchmaker for widows and single women in the camps, oftentimes ignoring the requirements of compatibility while forming the very teams on which the production process was based. Companies promoted family production to limit turnover, ensure application to the work, and promote harmony in the workforce—goals that were never, in fact, achieved.

The women had serious reason to be aggrieved by a situation that required so much of their labor, made life such an unrelenting struggle, and put their health and the welfare of their families at risk. But they did not rebel or abandon the industry, for they were "weak at the hands of those who fed them." After their families had been driven from their rural homes, often by bankruptcy, there were few respectable alternatives for employment. Some girls went into service at urban "tea houses," becoming prostitutes and leading lives not much better than those of slaves. Few were recruited for the textile mills, as competition for recruits from mining areas was suppressed by agents of the coal companies. For most young women, therefore, there was no choice but to "go down the pit." And once under the control of a gang boss, there could be no demands for improvements in working conditions, no appeals for better coal faces, no petitions for better wages, no requests for relief from assigned duties. Talking back to a boss or company official was considered insubordination, punishable by a beating or "dressing-down." Only occasionally would a group of younger women unite to take on the most arrogant and abusive superior, and only at the largest mines where women worked in close proximity to one another. Otherwise the women had to take what little satisfaction they could by damaging the reputations of bosses surreptitiously, singing scurrilous songs behind their backs or calling into question the supposedly "superior" education and behavior of these "almighty ones."

Above ground, the women could not organize for change. They were hard-pressed with family duties in addition to exhausting labor in the mines. Moreover, in camps where the bullies of the companies and labor gangs held sway, even the men were limited in what they might do to organize against exploitation and repression. In the early Taisho period dating from 1912, however, wildcat strikes, although apparently unorganized, sometimes achieved minor concessions from profitable companies. In the 1920s, early attempts at organization relied on the distribution of leaflets by the men and on clandestine meetings, sometimes facilitated by the women but always opposed and interdicted by the bosses. Later in the decade, women sometimes played subordinate roles in better-organized strikes. But the mine owners and managers had considerable success in preventing major actions or the development of working class solidarity extending beyond individual mines.

Women who had achieved some respect for carrying so much of the burden of coal hauling and family sustenance could not be expected to continue to be satisfied with carrying tea to men participating in sit-ins and offsite assemblies. But the beginnings of union organization and agitation from the 1920s still assigned minor roles to women at a time when a new paternalism came to be practiced by coal companies as they began removing women from underground work and attempting to prevent them from participating in "matters which should not concern them." Fewer jobs for women because of mechanization did not change working conditions substantially and did not release them from poverty and hardship. Only production demands during the war mobilization of the 1930s restored the women's indispensable positions in the industry. But by then all-out indoctrination had put them back into "their place" as adjuncts of skilled males or replacements for men who filled the more "honorable roles" of warriors for the Emperor.

Plus ça change, plus c'est la même chose

Most of the changes in the women's lives over the last decades of the nineteenth century and the first several decades of the twentieth were not so great as to change their mode of production or even the relationships within it. The differences in their reports of their conditions can be most often ascribed to their level of interest in recollecting their past, their ability to recall events and situations, and their degree of reliance on hearsay. Some reinforce what they believe to be true, and, no doubt, some embellish their narrative for the benefit of the interviewer and even possibly for the enlightenment of Japanese readers. While filtering out some of their few questionable statements, I came to believe in the honesty of these women in telling the stories of their lives and believe that there is very little embellishment in their accounts that might detract from their veracity and integrity. But while their stories show continuities in their working lives and their attitudes over time, the differing details in their accounts nonetheless provide an inkling of how the few mechanical innovations affected changes in their work and their lives, when the reorganization of the gang boss system brought them, at least theoretically, under the direct management of the larger companies, and when provision of some facilities for the improvement of worker welfare ameliorated, however modestly, their living conditions, at least at the bigger coal mines.

The accounts of the women also demonstrate that changes in working methods took place at different times at various mines. These changes depended primarily upon the size and location of the mine, on the market for coal, in the attitudes of management, the introduction of planned exploitation of coal seams, improvements in technique initiated by workers or bosses, and even, occasionally,

8   *Introduction*

pressures put upon managements by the threat of worker organization. Modest changes in life above ground also resulted from a variety of pressures or stimuli. The degree to which managers responded to requests or complaints about operational procedures and working and living conditions depended to a large degree upon markets and "the bottom line." Although they might or might not respond positively in boom times, they would not improve working conditions and wages in bad times, even if recession meant only the reduction, rather than elimination, of profits.

Before the 1920s, and even up to 1930 in many cases, management was unresponsive to worker needs—a passivity wrought directly by company executives protecting themselves from knowing the needs and conditions of their workforces by relying on middlemen, the gang bosses, to deal with the recruitment of labor and to set the conditions under which the miners worked and lived. But later the management system was unresponsive to worker needs largely because of a tendency to favor traditional ways of working and customary restraints imposed upon workers. The inelasticity in the labor market created by the Japanese management system and the lack of freedom of workers ensured that their responses to external changes were limited. The result was a lack of substantial improvement in the lives of the miners, hence a tendency among them to remember their lives as undifferentiated over time.

Burakumin: the inconspicuous "others"

Readers should be forewarned that many of my generalizations about the working lives of the female miners may not fully apply to the many outcaste women (*burakumin*) among them—nor to the much smaller number of Korean women living with their families at the collieries of North Kyushu. While often wondering which of the women interviewed by Morisaki and Idegawa may have been outcastes, aside from references to "*chigau-tachi*" (those who are different) or "*buraku no hito*" (people of the *buraku)* by a couple of them, and one who clearly identified herself as an outcaste,[2] the editors give very few clues for determining their caste origins. In part, this probably reflects a reasonable desire to show that the working experiences of the women were common to those of both "ordinary" and outcaste backgrounds. But it does make it difficult to delineate variations in life experience.

Burakumin were used and abused along with convicts in the early stages of large-scale coal mining in northern Kyushu. This association contributed to the stigmatization of mining labor as fit only for *sennin* (nonpeople—another label for the outcastes). Although discrimination against *burakumin* had been legally prohibited in 1871, informal discrimination continued throughout the pre-1945 era and, despite government efforts at elimination, still persists today. This discrimination resulted in early attempts by *burakumin* men and women who came to the collieries from other parts of Japan to hide their origins. Their successes in doing so unfortunately prevent us from discerning their numbers and hence the precise scope of their contributions to coal production and their unique role in the Kyushu mines.

Korean men, on the other hand, could not hide their ethnic differences. The numbers of these men, most of whom had been forcibly compelled into labor and wrenched from their homeland, were relatively small before 1930, and thus they could be integrated into the production system without a substantial impact on the Japanese workforce. The emotional and psychological difficulties that Korean wives endured while their mates worked at the most difficult and demeaning jobs underground is part of another story that has significance in Japanese working class history.[3]

The retired mining women do not evince all of the discriminatory attitudes of their agrarian and industrial sisters in other sectors of the Japanese population. While the relative absence of discrimination toward *burakumin* and Koreans could have been the result of solidarity engendered among the different groups of workers because of their common fate as exploited coal miners, such solidarity had to contend with the divide-and-rule tactics of mine managements and bosses that tended to exacerbate differences between ordinary, outcaste, and Korean workers.

The women do not claim any role in helping to integrate Koreans or *burakumin* into the workforce. Although they sometimes seemed to recognize the legitimacy of the needs and aspirations of Korean miners in Japan, they did not openly promote such rights for their fellow countrywomen, the *burakumin* with whom they worked.[4] But just as it would be a mistake to expect that female miners could have been leaders in labor organizations or antidiscrimination campaigns before 1930, it is impossible to tar them with the biases and prejudices that Japanese males in positions of some discretion evinced.

Miners all

The miners were, of course, also differentiated by the nature of the work they performed underground. In the Meiji period, however, even those Japanese people involved in mining failed to make a distinction between underground workers in general and those who actually separated the coal from the seam. This lack of distinction between miners who hewed and dug the coal and those who did the hauling and various forms of auxiliary work underground is common to Britain and North America as well. In Japan, all were called by the generic term *kōfu*—or miner—although, as Sumiya Mikio says, in matters of job classification, as well as being called miners the hewers might be termed *horifu*, digger, or *saitanfu*, getter of coal, by officials and managers.[5]

Although it was natural for female hauliers to consider themselves miners, they were engaged mainly in the work of hauling coal from the face. They will thus be termed *hauliers* here where it seems useful to distinguish their work from that of their hewer mates or where the nature of their work is emphasized. Intimately involved in the whole process of getting out the coal from the bowels of the earth, they quite rightly did not consider themselves to be doing jobs of any less importance than those of the predominantly male hewers. When they boasted about being able to do all the jobs that the men did, it is obvious they considered themselves

10 *Introduction*

to be interchangeable with the men as far as work was concerned, even if they did not regularly switch jobs with their mates. It seems reasonable, therefore, to call them miners when their hauling work is not emphasized and to think of them as full partners in the work of extracting the coal from the pits.

Voices

In their interviews the mining women often express doubts that nonminers, even sympathetic Japanese women such as Morisaki and Idegawa, can understand what work in the mines was really like. But although their voices may lack some variety in terms of their modes of expression, the women invariably do their best to describe their lives and effectively employ evocative language and intimate details. Particularly effective is their use of onomatopoeia to convey the atmosphere and sounds underground, adding life and rhythm to their descriptions of their work.

Although their earlier lives were dissimilar, often because of different geographic and social origins, their situations at the mines were remarkably similar. I have tried to find the common denominators by letting them speak in detail of as many aspects of their lives as possible. I hope that I have nonetheless retained some impression of their individuality while recounting their common struggle for dignity, self-esteem, and, ultimately, their very existence.

Notes

1 Retired woman coal miner, in Idegawa Yasuko, *Hi o Unda Haha-tachi* (Mothers Who Spawned the Fire), Ishobo, 1984, p. 174.
2 Morisaki, *Makkura*, p.167.
3 W. Donald Smith has told some of the Korean women's story in works cited in the bibliography.
4 See Yasukawa's analysis of the hierarchy of discrimination on which divide-and-rule management of the collieries was based. "*Hisabetsu Buraku to Josei*," in *Nihon Josei-shi*, vol. 4, pp.206–13.
5 *Nihon Sekitan Sangyō Bunseki*, pp.164–65. It will be noticed by those familiar with Japanese *kanji* that the suffix *fu* in *kōfu* is male in origin, but female miners were often designated *jokōfu*, adding the female prefix *jo* to the noun.

1 Background

Akai entotsu o meate de yukeba
Kome no manma ga abarekui.
    If you seek out the red chimney,
    You can feed on rice to your heart's content.[1]

Although many of the women came to the "red chimney" of the collieries from other parts of western Japan, we will deal here mainly with their working lives in the major coal-mining districts of the Chikuho region. This region comprises the traditional provinces of Chikuzen and Buzen in what is now Fukuoka Prefecture, Kyushu, in southwestern Japan. In the valleys and on the slopes of mountains drained by the tributaries and the main branch of the Onga River, production at the Chikuho coal mines increased through the Meiji period (1868–1912). Eventually these mines put out more coal than the other coal regions combined and employed up to half of all the coal miners in Japan.[2]

During the first two decades of Meiji, however, the Hizen region (particularly Takashima and other islands off Nagasaki Harbor and the northern part of what is now Saga Prefecture around Karatsu) produced more coal than Chikuho.[3] The location of the early Karatsu region coal mines on the slopes of the low mountains surrounding the coastal plains made mining relatively easy there, the evacuation of underground water being a simple matter of collecting and removing it at a level below the mining face.[4] Much of the water removal work was done by women. Easy access to the coal inhibited the application of modern methods of mining in the region, according to documents cited by Sumiya Mikio. In other regions, similar methods of hewing and hauling in "badger burrows" that exploited the poorer seams of the Karatsu and Chikuho region persisted into the post-Meiji era.

Even the best seams around Karatsu, reserved for the steamships of the new Imperial Navy, were poor in quality and size compared to those of the Chikuho region. In the era of the greatest expansion of the industry as a whole, the Karatsu seams were not able to sustain the large-scale production desired by the government and by entrepreneurs. Because of limitations on its size and coal reserves, the Ube field in Yamaguchi Prefecture (on the western end of

12   *Background*

Honshu—the mainland) would never yield much more than five per cent of Japan's output of coal, and this proportion would drop below four per cent in the latter half of Meiji (1890–1912).[5] Underground hauling methods developed in the Karatsu region and used by the female hauliers in the coal mines of Chikuho would continue to be used around Ube and at other small coalfields throughout the period of this study.

Sumiya argues that the development of more modern methods for dealing with underground water in the Chikuho region, as well as at the large Takashima and Miike coal mines, made possible the much faster expansion of coal mining after the late 1880s.[6] As they were more commonly at or below the water table than mines in the Karatsu region, the rich mines in the Chikuho valleys presented greater water removal problems.[7] In the feudal period before 1868, women had been involved in the manual winding of long wooden screws and bucket chains that brought water to the surface from drift shafts in copper, gold and silver mines.[8] In the few open-pit coal mines sunk in the early Meiji period, a balance-pole device called a *tsurube*, or, alternatively, a simple windlass such as that used in water wells in England and other countries, lifted buckets of water as well as coal from the mines. These too were often operated by women, though physical strength was essential for such work. It was not until the widespread application of steam power to windlasses and water pumps in the 1890s, however, that the more efficient removal of water and coal from vertical shafts at the Kyushu coal mines enabled a substantial increase in production at the bigger mines. Steam power also resulted in the loss of specialized jobs for women as well as outcaste people in the "water gangs."[9] In the smaller coal mines of Chikuho, the collection and removal of water continued to consume the manual labor of both men and women, at least until unmanageable accumulations closed them. Such closures were a frequent occurrence.[10]

At the same time that the Chikuho region became prominent in the production of coal—that is, the last half of the Meiji period—another region along the Pacific Coast in northeastern Japan was developing as a coal-producing center. This was the Joban region around the town of Hitachi, which much later generated the modern industrial giant of the same name. In a more constricted geographical area than the Chikuho mines, the Joban mines never produced the quantities of coal that their Kyushu counterparts put out, nor, consequently, employed such large numbers of women.[11] Although mining in the Joban coalfield had fewer problems with underground water than did the Chikuho fields, extraction methods in the smaller mines of the two regions were remarkably similar.

A third region of large-scale coal production, the northern island of Hokkaido, began development in the post-Restoration era after 1868. But labor had to be imported from the other main islands, and the number of women involved in underground work there was limited. The management of Mitsubishi and Hokutan (the Hokkaido Colliery and Steamship Company) acquired the captive labor of male convicts as a major "source of energy" for their initial ventures in southern and central Hokkaido. As limitations on the stamina and dedication of virtual slave labor became apparent, however, management recruited ever-larger numbers of migrant (*dekasegi*) workers from the impoverished northeastern region of the main island, Honshu, and gradually from even more distant locations. Although the administration of Hokkaido induced poor farm families to come to the island to open up less intensive cultivation than that on the mainland, the private coal companies did not recruit women for their coal-mining ventures on the same scale as they did elsewhere.[12] Hence, males did much of the underground hauling work. The dormitory housing of bachelors, inherited from the system for housing convicts, was cheaper than the housing and provisioning required for families. However, a small pool of female labor was created from immigrants to the island, and teams of sorting-women were organized for the surface labor of sorting and cleaning the coal. Although the work and contribution of sorters certainly deserve recognition, our story is mainly about the work and lives of female underground miners; therefore, female surface labor will not be dealt with here.[13]

Number of women in mining

Women in Japanese mining numbered fewer than those in textiles in the period of our study—from the 1880s to the 1930s. Textile mills used many more female workers than males.[14] In 1902, there were some 180,000 women working in cotton and silk mills throughout the country. By 1924, nearly 600,000 women worked in the textile factories. The number of women in mining, meanwhile, was relatively small—some 65,000 worked in the coal mines in 1924,[15] roughly one-tenth as many as in textile mills. But this represented a decline from earlier in that decade. Even after the recession of mid-1919 hit the coal industry of Kyushu particularly hard, there had been more than 97,000 women employed in Japanese mining in 1920.[16] This was more than a quarter of the number of men involved (about 328,000) or a little more than a fifth of the total mining workforce.[17] Female mining labor was concentrated at the coal mines; few women were involved in extraction at the precious and base metal mines.

Although women predominated in the newly mechanized and expanding textile mills, they also became a major force in coal mining, which tended to remain in an undeveloped state because of the very existence of this easily exploitable pool of cheap labor. Mining women were largely gathered in northern Kyushu (mainly the Karatsu and Chikuho regions), western Honshu, and the north-central Joban coalfields. In 1918 in Chikuho, 30 per cent of the coal mining workforce (some 69,000) was female—a substantial increase from the 46,000 women employed in 1916 before the late World War I boom.[18] The proportion of women in the coal mining workforce remained fairly stable into the 1920s; 29 per cent of Chikuho miners were women in the postwar years (up to 1924). In other words, women made up almost one-third of the workforce in the largest coal-producing region.

The numbers of women in coal mining grew in tandem with the growth of the industry and of the male workforce. In northern Kyushu, Yasukawa recalls, "By the time of the Russo-Japanese War (1904–05), the five districts of Chikuho in Fukuoka Prefecture were producing half of all the coal in Japan, and at the height

14 *Background*

of prosperity after the First World War, (female miners) in the Fukuoka Mines Bureau jurisdiction were almost two-thirds of those in the whole country."[19] Regine Mathias notes that out of 271,828 colliers in Fukuoka Prefecture, "81,861, or 30 per cent, were women in 1920."[20] In the Taisho period (1912–26) as a whole, the number of female miners ranged from 60,000 to 80,000, comprising almost one-third of all miners.[21]

Nishinarita Yutaka has presented a table to outline the composition of the underground coal-mining workforce in the late Meiji period (Table 1.1).[22] The statistics show that in 1906 almost 20,000 women worked at the major coal mines throughout Japan, compared to 62,000 men. Of the 20,000, some 13,500, or about two-thirds, worked underground.[23] Their numbers had been augmented as the result of improvements in powered winding gear, which increased coal output by larger numbers of both men and women. These statistics also show that relatively few women worked at the Hokkaido collieries and usually only outside at sorting (where a larger number of men than usual were employed) and hauling (where the women's role was minor compared to the number of men involved). However, the number of female underground hauliers (*kōnai unpanfu*) working at mines in regions other than Hokkaido in 1906 (only 36 in all) is grossly understated in the table—probably because company management was not much interested in differentiating between the functions of men and women underground. In Chikuho, as many as 8,316 women were designated *saitanfu* (the general classification for miners), almost half the number of men (17,570).

These statistics also suggest that in the early years of the century women were put in the category of framers (*shichūfu*) only in northern Kyushu. In the Chikuho region, where *saitanfu* originally did their own framing (or timbering) to prevent roof falls at the face, specialist framers in the mainways were known as *shikurifu*.[24] In later years, when specialist framers took over the work in larger rooms as well as in the main tunnels in most mines, some women participated in framing in the Joban coalfields; the classification of "auxiliary underground workers" in earlier statistics probably hides a number of women who worked at framing.[25] In any interpretation of the statistics, it should be noted that women played a prominent role throughout this period in regions other than Hokkaido, particularly in the arduous underground hauling and framing work.[26]

Age and marital status

Nishinarita notes that, in 1910, in the three major coalfields of Joban, Chikuho and Karatsu, married couples made up of a male hewer (*sakiyama*) and a female haulier (*atoyama* or *atomuki*) comprised, respectively, 38.3, 39.9, and 33.9 per cent of those involved directly in mining. When the considerable number of mining teams made up of unmarried pairs of men and women (both related and unrelated) is taken into account, we can say that a large part of the underground workforce was of mixed gender.[27]

Although the workforces at some large collieries (particularly those that had used convicts from the early Meiji period) were initially comprised predominantly

Table 1.1 Underground Miners in Major Coalfields (1906)

Coalfield	Hewers and Assistants	Framers	Underground Hauliers	Underground Technicians	Others	Total Underground
Hokkaido (6 mines)						
Males (no females or children)	3,076	188	1,733	49	1,408	6,454
Total	3,076 (28.6)	188 (1.7)	1,733 (16.1)	49 (0.5)	1,408 (13.1)	6,454 (60.0)
Jōban (7 mines)						
Males	2,226	246	441	129	297	3,339
Females	1,099	—	12	—	145	1,256
Children	—	—	—	—	13	13
Total	3,325 (54.4)	246 (4.0)	453 (7.4)	129 (2.1)	455 (7.4)	4,608 (75.4)
Chikuhō (25 mines)						
Males	17,570	2,418	1,224	949	1,646	23,807
Females	8,316	293	6	—	510	9,125
Children	115	—	—	—	1	116
Total	26,001 (57.4)	2,711 (6.0)	1,230 (2.7)	949 (2.1)	2,157 (4.8)	33,048 (73.0)
Miike (1 mine)						
Males	1,906	269	738	285	553	3,751
Females	997	28	—	—	222	1,247
Children	3	—	—	—	—	3
Total	2,906 (35.3)	297 (3.6)	738 (9.0)	285 (3.5)	775 (9.4)	5,001 (60.8)
Karatsu (6 mines)						
Males	3,153	1,343	288	106	279	5,169
Females	1,561	248	18	—	34	1,861
Children	144	12	—	—	4	160
Total	4,858 (49.8)	1,603 (16.4)	306 (3.1)	106 (1.1)	317 (3.2)	7,190 (73.7)
Nishisonoki (1 mine)						
Males (no females or children)	1,111	—	69	153	56	1,389
Total	1,111 (49.9)	—	69 (3.1)	153 (6.9)	56 (2.5)	1,389 (62.4)

N.B. Nishisonoki is in Nagasaki Prefecture, as is the (untabled) Takashima Mine in Nagasaki Bay, and the large Miike Mine is adjacent to the Chikuho region.

(*Source:* Nishinarita, "*Sekitan Kōgyō no Gijutsu Kakushin to Joshi Rōdō*," in Nakamura, ed., *Gijutsu Kakushin to Joshi Rōdō*, pp. 78–9, adapted from Ogino Yoshihiro, "*Nihon Shihon-shugi Kakuritsu-ki ni okeru Tankō Rōdō Kankei no 2 Ruikei*" [Two Types of Labor Relations at the Collieries in the Formative Stage of Japanese Capitalism], in *Enerugi Shi Kenkyū Nōto* [Research Notes on the History of Energy], no. 10, Kyushu Daigaku Sekitan Kenkyu Shiryo Senta, 1981.)

16   *Background*

of males, the family working unit persisted in the small- and medium-sized mines which made up the majority of coal mines in northern Kyushu.[28] In discussing the operations of a mine (probably a typical medium-sized one) in Matsuura, the "Enquiry Into the Development of Mines" (*Kōzan Enkaku Shirabe*) carried out in the Meiji period says that agreements signed and sealed on the hiring of any miner were assumed to apply to his family and, for pay purposes (presumably including accounts for provisions received), the family would be treated as a unit.[29]

At the large Miike Mine, where thicker seams allowed larger teams to work at the face (in bigger "rooms"), early statistics show that only 12.5 per cent of those actually engaged in mining per se were married couples.[30] On the other hand, the persistent working of many smaller mines with narrow seams ensured that family labor would continue to be a norm in the industry. Even at the Miike Mine, operated by Mitsui, family labor joined single males in the workforce when management moved away from the use of convict labor in the Taisho period. In 1914, 63 per cent of all workers at the mine were married.[31] And as the number of married couples was increasing, the number of convicts employed at Miike decreased, from 70 per cent of all hewers at the time of the take-over by Mitsui in 1889 to only 7 per cent in 1918.[32] The mixed gender underground working unit proved much more effective in keeping "free" men on the job, or at least in keeping them at the mines. It also kept productivity relatively high. Thus, most of the large mines in all regions except Hokkaido adopted the family work system before the end of the nineteenth century.[33]

One retired female miner argued, "If a married couple went down as a working team, they would work in accord. The results were good, and unfortunate incidents of people falling for a stranger or getting carried away, of escaping or running off, didn't occur. ... Everything said and done, women are very patient. Mines bosses make good use of that patience."[34] Although Sumiya Mikio suggests that the family team sustained morale underground[35] and thus might have been favored by the miners themselves, his own quotations from contemporary records show that management chose the family system because such teams were seen to have greater incentives to work harder in order to sustain their offspring. The relative cheapness of a family wage based on piece rates added to the profits of the company and improved "the bottom line." The inability of families to live on one man's wage, moreover, obliged miners to accept the necessity of taking their wives, daughters and other female relatives underground with them. Mathias notes that the increased size of the labor pool, with women participating and rearing future miners and men (hopefully) staying on the job due to the presence and needs of their families, gave a strong incentive to management to favor family labor.[36]

The large number of families living at and working in the coal mines meant that the average age of female coal miners was higher than that of cotton and silk spinners and weavers. Whereas 71 per cent of all female textile workers were under age 20 in 1924, only 24 per cent of female miners were, and 58 per cent were over 25.[37] Which is not to say that there were few young women in the mines. A survey by the Ministry of Agriculture and Commerce published in

1921 showed that there were at least 7,000 female miners under the age of 15 in the coal mines, and this referred only to the mines of Kyushu.[38] What is more, because of the traditional Japanese way of counting ages, a considerable number of 15 year olds may have been included in the 16- to 19-year-old category. Many female miners started work down in the pit at a very early age, and remained stuck in the job for most of the rest of their lives; female textile workers, on the other hand, tended to withdraw from the mills and return to their villages at marriageable age. (More than half of all female textile workers stayed less than three years at the mills, while a majority of the female miners worked more than five years at the mines.) Thus, although only 12 per cent of female textile workers were married, 75 per cent of female miners were registered as married in 1924 (Table 1.2).[39] This figure probably did not take into account a significant number of unregistered marriages. On the other hand, Nishinarita extracts from cabinet statistics the fact that more than one-third of coal-sorting women were under 20, and that fewer sorters were over 25 than among hewers, hauliers, and framers.[40] Of the underground women, about 80 per cent were married, while fewer than 58 per cent of sorters were wed. Sorters also tended to stay at their jobs for shorter periods than women working underground, partially because the latter did work in which their labor became more valuable as they gained skills and experience.

From the point of view of bigger mine operators, the ideal mining unit came to be that prescribed for recruitment at the Mitsui Tagawa mine in 1906: "'Three people comprised of a couple with a 12- or 13-year-old child, all working, and an elder to cook.'"[41] Later, children under 14 were prohibited by law from working in the pits. But managers in Meiji times were quite willing to use child labor underground, and the practice persisted.

The increasing preference for miners who, because of their attachments to wives and families, could be better "attached" (*dochaku sareru*) to the mines created a need for family housing. Families could not usually be kept in dormitories with bachelors, and separate living accommodations had to be provided.[42] A greater degree of privacy and independent living seems to have made family members feel much more independent of their gang bosses. The lack of amenities and comforts for families in the *nagaya*, however, echoed the dreary features of the bachelor quarters, and pressure from outside observers as well as the miners themselves (often indirectly) persuaded the bigger companies to gradually improve the amounts of space and built-in facilities in what could hitherto be best described as "hovels."[43] But as the housing improved, increasing surveillance and oppression were exerted by gang bosses at the behest of management in an undisguised attempt to foster discipline that would enhance exploitation of the workforce.

Origins of coal miners

The families of Chikuho miners originally came from other districts of northern Kyushu and from western parts of Japan, particularly Hiroshima. Eventually, some

Table 1.2 Age and Marital Status of Female Workers (1924)

	Coal Industry					Textile Industry
	Hewers	*Hauliers*	*Sorters*	*Framers*	*Miners*	*(Women)*
Under age 15	438 (6.1)	1,917 (6.3)	1,728 (14.0)	242 (4.5)	4,880 (7.5)	211,002 (35.7)
16–19 yrs	1,152 (16.0)	4,915 (16.3)	2,725 (22.0)	546 (10.2)	10,586 (16.3)	206,715 (35.0)
20–24 yrs	1,476 (20.5)	5,834 (19.3)	1,996 (16.1)	864 (16.1)	11,530 (17.7)	99,332 (16.8)
25–29 yrs	1,303 (18.1)	5,383 (17.8)	1,355 (11.0)	1,090 (20.4)	10,463 (16.1)	29,149 (4.9)
30–39 yrs	1,850 (25.7)	7,876 (26.1)	2,105 (17.0)	1,571 (29.3)	16,023 (24.7)	24,371 (4.1)
40–49 yrs	888 (12.3)	3,922 (13.0)	1,870 (15.1)	952 (17.8)	9,761 (15.0)	14,010 (2.4)
Over age 50	91 (1.3)	352 (1.2)	591 (4.8)	90 (1.7)	1,717 (2.6)	6,596 (1.1)
Total	7,198 (100)	30,199 (100)	12,370 (100)	5,355 (100)	64,960 (100)	591,175 (100)
With families	5,695 (79.1)	23,964 (79.4)	7,193 (58.1)	4,549 (84.9)	48,655 (74.9)	71,123 (12.0)
Without families	1,503 (20.9)	6,235 (20.6)	5,177 (41.9)	806 (15.1)	16,305 (25.1)	520,052 (88.0)

(*Sources*: Nishinarita, "*Sekitan Kōgyō no Gijutsu Kakushin to Joshi Rōdō*," p. 81, from Cabinet Statistics Bureau, *Rōdō Tokei Jitchi Chōsa Hōkoku* [Summary Report of Labor Statistics], 1924.)

came from as far away as Tajima, the old province on the Japan Sea side of what is now Hyogo Prefecture. Sumiya cites Konoe's *Chikuhō Tankō Shi* (History of the Chikuho Collieries) of 1898 to show that families from outside the Chikuho region were working in large numbers at the coal mines there. At one mine, "Those born in Hiroshima were most numerous and next came those from the Miike district." At another, "Most of the miners were born in Oita and Hiroshima, but some are *dekasegi* people from various other prefectures." Those migrants with families outnumbered bachelors there by a ratio of about seven to three. At still another mine, "Those born in the Iyo region (western Shikoku) were most numerous and most brought their families with them." As Sumiya says, "It is clear that, at the major mines, miners were mainly *dekasegi* (workers) bringing their families from other districts."[44]

As families gave up their hopes of saving enough money to return to their former rural homes, they succumbed to the prospect of spending their lives as miners and even to raising their children to work in the mines with them. But throughout the period under study (to 1930), increased production and the growing demands for labor in the mines ensured that a continuous flow of migrants from western Japan would add to the diversity and instability of the mining population.

Gender disparity

Some of the retired women asserted that they had worked as hard as the men—if not harder—and that, in earlier periods at least (late Meiji into Taisho), they often enjoyed equal pay. Perhaps influenced by later ideals, one woman recounted that, at the Nishijin Mine, "If a man earned one yen, a woman earned the same one yen. Because we did the same work. But in fact, women worked harder."[45] The recollections show that the women regularly worked at least as hard as the men and with more consistency. Participation rates for women were slightly lower than for men at larger mines because women also had multiple household tasks and were often proscribed from going down into the mines during menstruation.[46] But at smaller mines, where participation rate records were not kept, women probably worked more shifts and longer hours than the men.

Sumiya suggests that, during the mid-Meiji period, in an age of wage parity for men in different jobs such as hewing, hauling and framing, wages for women working underground were 40 per cent lower.[47] If indeed female wages were 60 per cent of male wages in mining, the difference was less than in farm labor, where daily wages for women were between 40 and 55 per cent of male wages in Saga Prefecture in 1883. Sumiya also notes that in coal mining, "Working conditions being as bad as they were, wages were higher than those for daily labor on the farm, but about the same as for artisans like carpenters and masons of average skill." Where pay packets were made up as a family wage for piecework (so much for each unit—usually a wagonload—of coal put out), there could be no comparison of individual wages for men and women working together.[48] And where an *atomuki* worked with a *sakiyama* to whom she was not related, the

20   *Background*

wages had to be divided according to some formula, but an absence of references to any such formula in their recollections suggests that the women were not privy to the real nature of the division.

By 1930, significant disparities in the wages of male and female coal miners were entrenched based on the patriarchal and paternalist systems that had been accentuated in so-called "modern" industry. As a retired male put it, "Our wages were reduced and we couldn't do anything about it, so if the wife didn't go down, we couldn't manage. At the same time, women's wages went down by half. Until this time, if they did similar work, they'd receive half of the wages."[49]

Daily wages for auxiliary workers in framing, tunneling, brushing, and carrying were paid at common rates for men and lower rates for women. Women seem to have been unaware how much of the wage paid by the company went to the gang boss. There are some intimations that they worked too long and hard to have time to try to calculate the precise rates at which they were being paid.

Racial and social discrimination

Yasukawa Junosuke, following the memoirs of Matsumoto Kichinosuke, a coal miner and leader in the Suihei-sha movement of the 1920s aimed at liberating the outcaste *buraku*, tells how discrimination persisted in coal-mining areas in the Meiji and Taisho periods. It was particularly evident within the school system, where school teachers and principals still condoned the labeling of *buraku* children as *eta*, thus failing to set a nondiscriminatory standard for parents and others. In the mines, *burakumin* would often be referred to by bosses as *kono eta-goro*, meaning something like "this *eta* ruffian." They were also called *ganzume*, which, though a name for a widely used and highly valued mining rake, seems to have meant in this case the claws of a four-legged animal, thus demeaning the human qualities of the outcastes.[50]

In the Meiji period, those leaving a *buraku* village to seek employment and accommodation in a mining camp often tried to hide their origins. As a result, the number of *burakumin* miners was not known, and up to the time of the First World War, the extent of their contribution to the industry cannot be fully appreciated. Nor was their contribution acknowledged by mine management or by the Japanese public outside the coal-mining regions. Matsumoto says that even among *burakumin* working in the mines, it was common to use discriminatory language and pejoratives aimed at those who were "out" so that suspicions should not be aroused as to the outcaste background of those hurling the insults. In later days, with the advent of the Suihei-sha movement in the 1920s, some *burakumin* were emboldened to challenge serious affronts, setting precedents for modern-day "impeachments" (*kyūdan*) of those guilty of unacceptable discriminatory language or behavior. These challenges might lead to the revelation of the outcaste origins of the offenders and to appropriate apologies.[51] According to Shindo Toyo, in the Taisho period there were many formal apologies from women who had discriminated against female *burakumin* miners; after "fervent remonstrations," these women were required to sign pledges to refrain from such acts in the future.[52] But the general acceptance of prejudice and discrimination continued, along with an environment of insults and affronts and the continuing concealment of their origins by many *burakumin* miners.[53]

Matsumoto Kichinosuke, speaking of Shimo-Mio, the *buraku* village in which he grew up, says "All the women of my village were female miners (*jokōfu*). My older sisters, too, went into the depths of the earth as miners. Both Gen who was two years older and Yuki who was six years above me were miners."[54] His wife's uncle by marriage, Wada Kyokichi, a gang boss and father of two sons later prominent in the Suihei-sha movement, gave Matsumoto work as a miner at the Uruno Mine in the Kaho district when he married. *Burakumin* were obliged to live in *tokushu buraku*, designated sections of larger villages or in villages separated from others.[55] Thus *burakumin* miners were treated as outcastes, even after the antidiscrimination statutes of 1871. And the Suihei-sha was not successful in ending the separation of *burakumin* and "ordinary people," even in the 1920s when it was most active.

Yasukawa Junosuke reaches the following conclusion:

> In the Chikuho coalfields ... the majority of colliery workers were from among the oppressed people of the *buraku*, and even among female miners who made up about one-third of all miners in the Taisho period, the greatest number (*tasū*) were women from the oppressed villages.[56]

In the Tagawa district, one center of the Chikuho coalfields, Umahara Tetsuo noted, "It can be presumed that about 60 per cent of workers at the big collieries and up to 80 per cent at medium-sized and small collieries were from the (outcaste) *buraku*."[57] Using these percentages, Yasukawa suggests that "at the height of prosperity which culminated after the First World War," a majority of miners in the whole Chikuho region were *burakumin*.[58] Shindo recalls simply that there was a concentration of *buraku* and *burakumin* in the Tagawa district.[59] But though such concentrations may not have been unusual in coal-mining areas, they may have been higher in Tagawa than in the rest of the region.[60] Although Yasukawa has a legitimate interest in stressing the importance of the *burakumin* contribution to coal mining in Chikuho, his use of Umahara's percentages for *burakumin* participation in the Tagawa district, as if they applied to the whole region, is probably not justified.

Other evidence suggests that large numbers of *burakumin* walked to work in the coal mines every day from *buraku* villages or hamlets separated from other rural villages and the coalfield towns. Shindo Toyo goes so far as to say that "Those from the *buraku* had such a predominance that virtually all female miners who did not live in the *naya* (tenements in the mining camps) were from the *buraku*." He quotes Matsumoto, "In the case of Uruno Mine, those who commuted may have been about 30 to 40 per cent [of the workforce], and virtually all of them can be assumed to have been from unliberated *buraku*. The remaining 60 to 70 per cent were workers living in the *naya*, but among these, too, there were many from the *buraku*."[61] These recollections come from the

22   Background

1920s during the recovery from the post–World War I recession, and although the percentages must be treated as conjectural, commuting on foot by *burakumin* was certainly a significant aspect of the North Kyushu coal-mining industry.

The already large number of *buraku* villages in northern Kyushu increased as miners came from outcaste villages in regions such as that around Hiroshima.[62] Migrants from prefectures in other regions likely found it relatively easy to hide their *burakumin* origins, and it may have been only in later years (after 1921) that the success of the Suihei-sha movement for liberation, ironically, encouraged migrant miners to openly congregate in villages of their peers rather than attempt to mingle with the commonality of mine workers. Shindo asserts that just as *burakumin* were only given "poor land in the mountain recesses" to cultivate on behalf of their landlords, "at the collieries as well, they were not admitted to the good coal mines of the big companies, but in most cases were obliged to work at small and medium-sized mines."[63] This statement tends to contradict Umahara's concerning the large percentage of *burakumin* at major collieries, but as I have argued earlier, collieries other than those at Tagawa may not have had similar numbers of *burakumin*. At the smaller mines, Shindo recounts, "They were usually assigned to work at faces where conditions were bad. In such circumstances, people from the *buraku* had to make the best of it, and endure their suffering."[64]

With regard to the qualitative contribution of *burakumin*, there is an interesting discussion among Japanese scholars of the origins of coal miners' songs. Shindo adduces substantial circumstantial evidence to support Ueno Eishin's claim that many *tankō-bushi* (colliers' songs) gained voice originally as *eta-bushi*, songs of the outcastes who worked at the mines, particularly the women at the sorting tables.[65] As well as dealing with the transference of lyrics and melodies from one status group to another (one woman reported that *Nihonjin* [Japanese people] were forbidden to sing outcaste songs at the mines), this evidence supports the thesis that the numbers of *burakumin* miners were indeed large, if not a majority.

In light of the fact that commuters provided their own housing, discriminatory wages for *burakumin* would have been especially harsh. According to Yasukawa, *burakumin* tended to be given "work for which wages were low." However, because they were either required to provide their own housing or were given inferior *tokushu naya* at the mines, it seems likely that they would not have been discriminated against to any major extent in matters of wages as well. Indeed, Yasukawa makes no mention of a separate wage scale for *burakumin* but says that Korean miners were paid 40.7 per cent of what other miners earned.[66] Discrimination against *burakumin* took other overt forms described by Yasukawa, such as special *eta-buro* baths and *tokushu naya* lodgings, which "put them in their place." Sakamoto Yuichi makes a rather convincing argument that management, which in a situation of labor shortage was keen to obtain *buraku* workers, could not impose obviously discriminatory conditions on these legally liberated *heimin* (commoners). It is less certain that the managers, as he claims, were merely reflecting the attitudes of their labor forces in keeping *burakumin* separated above ground.[67] Their propensity to use divide-and-rule methods to control and exploit their workers on the job suggests that a nondiscriminatory wage regime would be more a device for recruiting than a policy of enlightened management.

Ironically, because of their ethnic distinctiveness, the numbers of Koreans involved in the prewar coal industry is easier to ascertain than the much larger numbers of *burakumin*. Matthew Allen says that the first Koreans inducted into labor in the coal mines were brought to Japan after the annexation of Korea in 1910.[68] But one of the retired women remembered that as early as the aftermath of the Russo-Japanese War—that is, around 1906—"there were many Koreans" at the Yamada coal mine. "They came in great numbers. There was a great need for coal, since warships were being built."[69] The first major influx of Koreans, however, was related to the boom in coal production during the First World War.[70] Because of their proximity to Korea, the Chikuho coalfields absorbed most of the immigrant labor. By 1928, the numbers of immigrants, however, were still relatively modest compared to the total number of people in the colliery workforce. In that year, there were 5,626 Koreans at 59 mines in Chikuho, in a total labor force of some 65,000 miners,[71] and 8,468 Korean men and 243 Korean women at major Kyushu mines (probably including Miike and perhaps mines in Yamaguchi Prefecture as well).[72] Although Korean males were first brought into Japan in "abortive experiments" by private companies and later were induced to come as sojourners by false promises of well-paid employment, in the 1920s, whole Korean families were brought in with government sanction. Up to 450 or 500 of the women were put to work at the coal mines, though relatively few underground.[73] Korean women were more apt to become sorters than to go into the pit and were more apt to work in factories than in mines, under blatantly discriminatory conditions.[74]

In 1928, the number of women in the mines dropped significantly as the larger Japanese companies began to implement exclusion orders supposedly aimed at "protecting women." From 1928 on, Korean men were inducted in greater numbers than previously in order to replace some of the excluded women, though not always at the bigger mines. There, companies such as Mitsubishi "created a more ethnically and sexually homogeneous and somewhat better paid workforce that managers saw as more compatible with the increasingly capital-intensive technology" that such mines were adopting.[75] But at other mines, Korean males were now often given the hauling work that young Japanese men, seeking promotion to the better paying job of hewing, had been eager to leave to women. It would be surprising if the greater respect accorded to *sakiyama* was not accompanied by lower respect for the Koreans who were assigned to what had probably become known as "women's work" (though some retired [male] miners denied that "they saw hauling coal as a job for women").[76]

Although there were very real barriers among Korean, commoner, and outcaste women, the accounts used here do not permit easy recognition of the differences in the working lives of women from different backgrounds. It has been assumed by many Japanese people that the discrimination and prejudice of the larger society was echoed in the coal mines. But the retired women do not evince such

24 Background

discrimination to the same degree. Although one woman felt that Koreans did not practice good hygiene and ate food unfit for human consumption, she applauded Korean women for learning the Japanese language quickly and for even sending their children to school. She seems to have sympathized with Koreans who suffered particularly harsh treatment at the hands of the overseers, exonerating one Korean who cut up a couple of drunken Japanese youths when they gratuitously insulted him.[77] Such expressions of empathy may be rare, but among the accounts, recollections of hard feelings and discriminatory action toward minority women are equally few and far between.

Morisaki seems to have felt that the differences in approaches to life between women of petit-bourgeois or peasant background and those who spent their lives in mining were more significant than these differences among miners of *buraku*, Korean, and other origins.[78] Whatever discrimination did occur among working class women had been fostered, according to Shindo Toyo, by a ruling class that wanted to "entrap coal-mine workers in mutually antagonistic relations," and to ensure that they remained "workers who would have no sense of themselves as members of a working class."[79]

This breakdown of the composition of coal miners should not be used to suggest that a preexisting uniformity and solidarity was somehow disintegrating as the industry was being "modernized." On the contrary, the accounts of the retired women support the thesis that their work brought them into close contact with other coal miners and, where induced competition did not pit them against each other, engendered an embryonic solidarity that threatened management's divide-and-rule policy. To understand this process, it will first be necessary to appreciate the nature of the women's work as a prelude to analyzing their attitudes to work and life in the coal-mining camps.

Notes

1 Morisaki, Makkura, p. 7.
2 For a map of the coal mines of Chikuho, see Nakamura Masanori, *Rōdōsha to Nōmin*, vol. 29 in the *Nihon no Rekishi* series, p. 134. See Smith, "Digging Through Layers of Class, Gender and Ethnicity," in Lahiri-Dutt and Macintyre, p. 113.
3 Sumiya Mikio, *Nihon Sekitan Sangyō Bunseki*, pp. 140–1.
4 Sumiya, pp. 26–7, 30–1, and 107–147, passim.
5 Tanaka Naoki, *Kindai Nihon Tankō Rōdōshi Kenkyū*, p. 82, Tables 1–6.
6 Sumiya, *Nihon Sekitan Sangyō Bunseki*, pp. 23, 139, 142–3, 215.
7 Sumiya, pp. 27, 30, 210–14.
8 Sumiya, pp. 27; Kobata Atsushi, *Nihon Kōzan Shi no Kenkyū*, pp. 56–61; Iida Kenichi and Kuroiwa Toshiro, eds., *Saikō Yakin Gijutsu*, vol. 20 of Nihon Kagaku-shi Gakkai, ed., *Nippon Kagaku-gizyutusi Taikei*, pp. 17–21, with the illustration of water extraction at the Sado gold mine on p. 18. See also the illustration in *Kodo Zuroku* by Futoda Nanse, in Saegusa Hiroto, ed., *Nihon Kagaku Koten Zensho*, vol. 9, no. 3 (*Saikō Yakin)*, p. 242.
9 Sakamoto Yuichi, "*Chikuhō Sekitan Kōgyō to Hisabetsu Buraku,*" in *Buraku Mondai Kenkyū*, no. 140 (Aug. 1997), pp. 92–3.
10 See a report by the foreign consultant, Potter, hired by Fukuoka Prefecture in the 1870s, in Sumiya, *Nihon Sekitan Sangyō Bunseki*, p. 212.

11 For Joban coal production in the latter half of the Meiji, see Tanaka, *Kindai Nihon Tankō Rōdōshi Kenkyū*, p. 82.
12 See Yoshida and Miyauchi, "Invisible Labor," pp. 138–41, where subordination to husbands is emphasized, but working systems are remarkably similar to those in Chikuho.
13 Ueno Eishin, ed., *Kindai Minshū no Kiroku*, vol. 2, *Kōfu* (Miners), pp. 131–47. For the experience of a married woman who did a stint underground in southern Hokkaido later in the period of this study but spent much of her time in coal transport and sorting on the surface, see "*Tankō no Seikatsu* (Life at the Coal Mines)," from *Hokkaidō Kōfu Chōshō* (Interviews with Hokkaido Miners) recorded by Yamazaki Shoji, in Ueno, pp. 131–4.
14 E. Patricia Tsurumi, *Factory Girls: Women in the Thread Mills of Meiji Japan*, particularly pp. 9–10.
15 Nishinarita Yutaka, "*Sekitan Kōgyō no Gijutsu Kakushin to Joshi Rōdō*," in Nakamura Masanori, ed., *Gijutsu Kakushin to Joshi Rōdō*, Table 5, p. 81. (The United Nations University Press has published an English translation of this book more recently [1994] under the title, *Technology Change and Female Labor in Japan*, but not having access to it in the early stages of my research, I have relied on the Japanese text for my interpretation of Nishinarita's article, translated in the newer publication [poorly, according to Donald Smith] as "The Coal Mining Industry.")
16 Tazaki Nobuyoshi, "*Josei Rōdō no Shoruikei*," in Nagahara Kazuko and Hirota Masaki, eds., *Nihon Josei Seikatsu Shi*, vol. 4 (Kindai), Tables 3, 4, and 5, pp. 167–9. From *Taisho 9 Nen Kokusei Chōsa Hokoku* (Report of the 1920 Census), vol. 2. This figure accords fairly well with, and may be from, the statistics for the same year published by the Mines Bureau of the Ministry of Agriculture and Commerce (Nōshōmushō Kōzankyoku) and taken by Donald Smith from the article by Nishinarita in Nakamura Masanori, ed., *Gijutsu Kakushin to Joshi Rōdō*. See W. Donald Smith, "Digging Through Layers of Class, Gender, and Ethnicity: Korean Women Miners in Prewar Japan," in Lahiri-Dutt and Macintyre, *Women Miners in Developing Countries: Pit Women and Others*, p. 112.
17 Yasukawa Junosuke, "*Hisabetsu Buraku to Josei*," in Josei-shi Sogo Kenkyu-kai, ed., *Nihon Josei-shi*, vol. 4 (Kindai), p. 207. Yasukawa gives the number of women employed in mining in 1919 as 112,000 out of a total mining workforce of 465,000.
18 Yasukawa, "*Hisabetsu Buraku to Josei*," pp. 208–9. Yasukawa notes that 73 per cent of the women worked underground in 1919.
19 Yasukawa Junosuke, "*Hisabetsu Buraku to Josei*," p. 198.
20 Mathias, "Female Labor in the Japanese Coal-Mining Industry," in Hunter, ed., *Japanese Women Working*, pp. 104–5.
21 Shindo Toyo, *Chikuhō no Jokōfu-tachi*, p. 13.
22 Nishinarita, "*Sekitan Kōgyō no Gijutsu Kakushin to Joshi Rōdō*," in Nakamura, ed., *Gijutsu Kakushin to Joshi Rōdō*, pp. 78–9, adapted from Ogino Yoshihiro, "*Nihon Shihon-shugi Kakuritsu-ki ni okeru Tankō Rōdō Kankei no 2 Ruikei*" (Two Types of Labor Relations at the Collieries in the Formative Stage of Japanese Capitalism), in *Enerugi Shi Kenkyū Nōto* (Research Notes on the History of Energy), no. 10, Kyushu Daigaku Sekitan Kenkyu Shiryo Senta, 1981.
23 Calculated from Table 1.1, also given in Nakamura, ed., *Technology Change and Female Labor in Japan*, pp. 66–7.
24 Kaneko Useki, *Chikuhō Tankō Kotoba*, p. 109.
25 Mashio, *Jizoko no Seishun*, p. 80. Nishinarita, "*Sekitan Kōgyō no Gijutsu Kakushin to Joshi Rōdō*," pp. 78–9.
26 Nishinarita's figures for aboveground workers also contain anomalies that obscure the roles of women in hauling and exaggerate the functions of men as "technicians" on the surface.

26 Background

27 Nishinarita, pp. 79–80, text and table.
28 Cf. Sumiya, *Nihon Sekitan Sangyō Bunseki*, p. 87.
29 Sumiya, p. 165.
30 "*Sekitan Kōgyō no Gijutsu Kakushin to Joshi Rōdō,*" p. 79.
31 Takematsu Teruo, *Kōnai Uma to Bafu to Jokōfu: Jizoko no Kiroku—Juso*, p. 120. See also Mashio, *Jizoku no Seishun*, p. 120.
32 Takematsu, p. 183. See also Sumiya Mikio, *Nihon Sekitan Sangyō Bunseki*, pp. 122–3.
33 Nishinarita, in "*Sekitan Kōgyō no Gijutsu Kakushin to Joshi Rōdō,*" pp. 78–80.
34 Idegawa, *Hi o Unda Haha-tachi*, p. 152.
35 *Nihon Sekitan Sangyō Bunseki*, p. 319.
36 Mathias, "Female Labor in the Japanese Coal-Mining Industry," in Hunter, ed., *Japanese Women Working*, p. 104.
37 Nishinarita, "*Sekitan Kōgyō no Gijutsu Kakushin to Joshi Rōdō,*" p. 80. For ages of women in the textile industry in the Meiji period, see Tsurumi, *Factory Girls*, pp. 87, 130, 178. Tsurumi's statistics are taken from the surveys of the Ministry of Agriculture and Commerce, compiled as *Shokkō Jijō* (Factory Workers' Conditions) in 1903.
38 Shindo Toyo, *Chikuhō no Jokōfu-tachi*, p. 19.
39 Nishinarita, "*Sekitan Kōgyō no Gijutsu Kakushin to Joshi Rōdō,*" p. 81.
40 Ibid.
41 Nishinarita, "*Sekitan Kōgyō no Gijutsu Kakushin to Joshi Rōdō,*" p. 74.
42 There were exceptions to the separation of bachelors and married miners, according to an extensive study of "The *Hamba* System at the Coal Mines" (*Tankō Kōzan ni okeru Hamba Seido*), in *Nihon Rōmu Kanri Nenshi*, vol. 1, 1962, p. 31. See also, Mashio, *Jizoko no Seishun*, pp. 53–5.
43 See Chapter 7 on surface life.
44 Sumiya, pp. 318–19.
45 Morisaki, p. 46.
46 Nishinarita, *Sekitan Kōgyō no Gijutsu Kakushin to Joshi Rōdō,*" pp. 76–7.
47 Sumiya, *Nihon Sekitan Sangyō Bunseki*, pp. 170–1.
48 It is interesting to note that wages in mining went down after 1881 in the first years of the Matsukata Deflation. Wages in the coal industry would continue to be based on output or productivity as late as the 1950s, with piecework rates negotiated for specific job categories. See John Price's dissertation, *Postwar Industrial Relations and the Origins of Lean Production in Japan (1945–1973)*, U.B.C., 1993, p. 236, citing *Shiryō Miike Sōgi* (Materials on the Miike Strike), p. 429.
49 Morisaki, *Makkura*, p. 183. See also Yasukawa, "*Hisabetsu Buraku to Josei*" in *Nihon Josei-shi*, vol. 4, re the economic dependence of women on their mining husbands after the 1928 revision of the Regulations for the Sustenance of Mining Labor.
50 Yasukawa, in *Nihon Josei-shi*, vol. 4, p. 210. See also Mikiso Hane's chapter on "The Outcaste in Japan," in *Peasants, Rebels, and Outcastes: The Underside of Modern Japan*, partic. pp. 139–47.
51 Matsumoto Kichinosuke, *Chikuhō ni Ikiru: Buraku Kaihō Undō to tomo ni Gojū-nen*, p. 31.
52 *Chikuhō no Jokōfu-tachi*, pp. 32–3.
53 See the novel, *Hakai* (The Broken Commandment), by Shimazaki Toson, for the climate of discrimination that made concealment of *buraku* origins the common means of assimilating into the mainstream.
54 *Chikuhō ni Ikiru*, p. 12.
55 Shimo-Mio (Lower Mio) was such a mining *buraku*, unlike Kami-Mio (Upper Mio), the location of the mine in which Yamamoto Sakubei (and his father before him) worked. Yamamoto, *Yama ni Ikiru*, pp. 24–30, 32–4.
56 Yasukawa, "*Hisabetsu Buraku to Josei,*" in *Nihon Josei-shi*, vol. 4, p. 192.
57 Quoted in Shindo, *Chikuhō no Jokōfu-tachi*, p. 38.
58 "*Hisabetsu Buraku to Josei,*" p. 208.

59 Shindo, p. 38.
60 See Sakamoto Yuichi's critique of Umahara's research, which (among others) prompts further questions about the numbers of *burakumin* participating in the industry. "*Chikuhō Sekitan Kōgyō to Hisabetsu Buraku,*" passim.
61 Shindo, p. 13. The percentages are omitted from Matsumoto's book, *Chikuhō ni Ikiru*, and the omission may be because he was not confident of their accuracy.
62 Shindo, p. 14.
63 Shindo, p. 166.
64 Shindo, p. 32.
65 *Chikuhō no Jokōfu-tachi*, pp. 58–64. It is surprising that Sachiko Sone, although using miners' songs in her dissertation to elucidate much information about the unique Chikuho culture, does not deal with this argument about the possibility of *burakumin* origins.
66 Yasukawa, "*Hisabetsu Buraku to Josei,*" pp. 209–10. Other data suggests that the ratio of wages for male Koreans to wages for Japanese miners was not quite as low as Yasukawa argues. See W. Donald Smith, "Digging Through, Layers of Class, Gender and Ethnicity", in Lahiri-Dutt and Macintyre, p. 124.
67 "*Chikuhō Sekitan Kōgyō to Hisabetsu Buraku,*" pp. 92, 95–106. Also, Smith, "Digging Through Layers of Class, Gender and Ethnicity" in Lahiri-Dutt and Macintyre, *Women Miners in Developing Countries*, p. 122.
68 Matthew Allen, *Undermining the Japanese Miracle*, p. 56.
69 Morisaki, *Makkura*, pp. 144–5. See also, p. 97.
70 Smith, in Lahiri-Dutt and Macintyre, p. 115.
71 Shindo Toyo, *Chikuhō no Jokōfu-tachi*, p. 34, and Nishinarita, "*Sekitan Kōgyō no Gijutsu Kakushin to Joshi Rōdō,*" Table 8, p. 83. Shindo takes the figures of numbers of mines and miners from a report of the Osaka Employment Office, but the original source is probably the same as Nishinarita's, the Fukuoka branch of the national system of *shokugyō shōkaijo* (employment offices).
72 Smith, "Digging Through Layers of Class, Gender and Ethnicity", in Lahiri-Dutt and Macintyre, p. 116.
73 Yasukawa, "*Hisabetsu Buraku to Josei,*" p. 208. Even larger numbers of Korean workers were brought to Japan under "Emergency Regulations" after 1939. Smith, in Lahiri-Dutt and Macintyre, pp. 112, 114.
74 Smith, in Lahiri-Dutt and Macintyre, pp. 121–2.
75 Smith, p. 116.
76 Smith, p. 124, including material from interviews conducted by Ichihara Hiroshi.
77 Morisaki, pp. 145–6.
78 Cf. *Makkura*, p. 23.
79 Shindo, p. 32.

2 Work and wages

Hotondo ningen waza to wa uketorarezu.
It's hardly a job fit for human beings.[1]

An examination of the nature of the production process in which female coal miners worked underground in synchronization with their male counterparts will help us to appreciate the significance of their contribution to industrialization in Japan in the late decades of the nineteenth century and in the early decades of the twentieth.

Hewing and hauling

In the first period of coal mining on the Hizen (Saga) and Chikuzen (Fukuoka) plains, Japanese miners usually followed the seam down from the surface. Most coal seams in northern Kyushu, however, were on mountain slopes or in valley bottoms,[2] where tilted seams made horizontal shafts or moderately sloping drifts uncommon and complicated the work of evacuating water. Small operations, initiated earlier by family groups working only in the agricultural off-season, began with the clearing away of flora and detritus, followed by removal of the coal from small open pits. As the surface coal was exhausted, the miners began to follow the seam into the earth, building cradles or framing tunnels where necessary to prevent in-fall of soil or rock. The narrow shafts tracing the route of the seams as they sloped into the earth were called *tanuki-bori*[3] because they resembled the holes that a badger burrowed into the earth.[4] Because these tunnel headings sloped downward, the more technically appropriate term for them was *oroshi* (descents). As the headings progressed downward, sometimes steeply, the miners found that they were increasingly difficult to work, both in hewing the coal and hauling it to the surface. Main shafts were therefore sunk down beside the seam, and galleries were driven into it laterally so that the miners could attack the coal from below. Cradling and timbering were used to support weak shaft roofs. With the removal of much greater volumes of waste rock (created by such auxiliary tunneling procedures), slag-heaps on the surface (*bota yama*) began to contend with high boiler chimneys and winding towers as symbols of the Kyushu coal mines. Eventually, these waste rock pyramids formed ubiquitous monuments throughout the Chikuho region.[5]

Expanded tunneling and waste removal operations required more labor power and resources than family enterprises could muster, and the bigger mines (a few of them already administered by feudal domains before 1868) were taken over by merchants or companies with financial backing. Horizontal or gently sloping main galleries (*kanekata*) made mining feasible in upward sloping *kata* or *nobori* (ascents), with many advantages in using the slope to get the coal out more easily. This did not eliminate the *oroshi*, however, for the mine operators still obliged their gangs to work downward as well as upward from the galleries and mezzanines.[6]

In the mountainous region of Chikuho, particularly in the upper reaches of the Onga River, seams rising from the pit entrance were rare, and outcroppings were usually higher up on the slopes, with the seams inclining downward into the mountain. The art of laying out vertical shafts, horizontal galleries, and *kata* and *oroshi* was therefore transferred from the mines of the plains by mining bosses or newly trained technicians. Simple gridworks of shafts and tunnels attempted to exploit seams thoroughly, but inevitably, deformations and faults as well as difficulties in supporting the roof prevented the seams from being exhausted by the unsophisticated techniques of the times. Pillaring and robbing methods were worked out slowly by experienced miners and engineers, with some knowledge of American and British practice. But much of Japanese coal mining continued to take place in small "rooms" worked by man-and-wife teams because of the availability of this type of labor. The skills and intuition of the miners were relied upon to a large extent by management, which rarely had technicians and engineers to oversee the actual mining operation.

In the Meiji period, it became common for a skilled miner in charge of an experienced gang to contract for the mining of a single small mine or a section of a larger mine.[7] Under this gang boss, male *sakiyama* and female *atoyama* or *atomuki* usually worked together in teams. (Males could be used as *atoyama* in special circumstances where women were not available.)[8] The team was called a *hitosaki*, suggesting the priority given to the digging work over the hauling and to the male hewer over the female haulier; the term also indicated that the team, although usually involving only one male hewer, might include more than one woman.[9] Sumiya Mikio, an astute historian of the coal industry, says that as early as the middle of the Meiji period, in deeper coal mines with longer hauling distances, often two hauliers were required to get out the coal dug by one hewer, giving rise to three-person teams.[10] Shindo Toyo, a scholar specializing in the role of women in the industry, speaks of teams consisting of two *sakiyama* and four *atoyama* being common at "large faces," probably in the bigger rooms (*harai*) of later room-and-pillar systems.[11] Innovations such as underground rail systems with coal trains pulled by ponies or winches were not incompatible with the one-man-one-woman teams in single headings. Daughters often helped their mothers with hauling, without receiving remuneration other than that included in the piece-rate family pay packet. Until the early Taisho period, when management

30 *Work and wages*

began to take over direction of underground operations from gang boss representatives in the name of greater "efficiency," the small team was usually assigned by the mining boss to work at a face (*kiriha*) in one heading.[12]

Because the tunnel headings followed the coal seams and as little rock as possible was taken out, the tunnels to the mining faces were usually narrow and cramped. Several women reported that the height of tunnels was equal to the length of a *tenugui* (hand towel, about 60 cm. or 2 ft.), which seems to have been a standard minimum.[13] Others described tunnels "so low that your head would pass under only if you lay down," or mentioned 3 and 5 *shaku* (one *shaku* = approx. 1 ft.) seams.[14] Even where relatively sophisticated layouts were being mined as early as the 1880s, Fukuoka Prefecture officials reported that "since the seam is not thick, it is impossible to stand up and they go in and out on hands and knees."[15] Thicker seams were found at greater depths in later years and were mined more expansively.[16]

By preserving the strata of rock enclosing the coal seam, miners limited the amount of preparatory timbering which had to be done in order to ensure that the roof did not collapse but left very little room to work in the narrower seams. In the low cave extending into the seam from the heading, the miner would crouch on his haunches or lie on his side as he hewed at the seam with his *tsurubashi*,[17] his sharp-pointed pick or mattock. Although it was easier—if not safer—to bring the coal down from higher up on the face, in order to limit the amount of *bota* initially scraped from the floor, the miners would often have to attack the lower part of the seam from a position level with it. The awkward posture of the miner lying on his side or crouching while prying the coal toward himself is featured in Yamamoto Sakubei's illustrations.[18]

The difficulty of hewing coal in this confined space was considerable. By the wavering light of a lamp, the miner would try to find fissures or weak spots in the surface of the seam where his pick could make an impression. One woman shows an intimate knowledge of the techniques required (Figure 2.1):

> Where the roof was low, you would lie on your side and go in hips first, drawing yourself forward while digging by hand. You would draw the coal down behind you with your feet. If you relied only on strength to dig, you would get nothing but pulverized coal. There are cracks in the coal, you see. If you could see the cracks well and struck them with the pick, the pressure from above would press down (with a sound like) *baritt, baritt* until it was ready to strip off and come down.[19]

When a shelf did break loose, there would often be a shower of smaller bits and dust, creating much discomfort for the miner. Then, still lying or crouching beside the fallen debris, he would have to draw the coal down behind him where the *atoyama* could get at and remove it. Creeping forward as he moved further along the seam, he might try to keep a small mat made of sailcloth or canvas under his hips to limit chafing and bruises. This *dongorosu* was used by women working in narrow entries as well.[20]

Work and wages 31

Figure 2.1 Hewing and hauling in cramped quarters (Yamamoto Sakubei, *Chikuhō Tankō Emaki*, 8th black and white illustration).

The *atoyama* would also strap worn-out straw sandals on her knees to prevent scrapes and bruises while crawling or climbing hunched over against the slopes.[21] Thus constricted and encumbered, she would first gather the coal lumps and the debris from behind the *sakiyama* with the *kaki-ita* (originally a "raking board," later a hoe) and scrape them into the *ebu*, a scoop-shaped wicker basket similar to a winnowing basket.

> When others were using the *kaki-ita*, they'd scrape back and forth any number of times. But if I made up my mind to do it in three strokes, I wouldn't be satisfied unless I got it in smartly in three.[22]

If working in the *oroshi*, the haulier might empty the *ebu* into two deeper baskets and sling them over her shoulder on a yoke. The whole carrying contrivance was called a *sena*. With her lamp hanging on the front basket, and a very short balancing crook (*shumoku*) in one hand,[23] she would scramble up the slope, keeping hunched over as close as possible to the incline to prevent her back from being scraped on the rough ceiling, and using her free hand to balance the load.

One woman recounted:

> If carried skillfully, the lamp swung rhythmically back and forth. It looked as if a ring (of light) swayed in the dark. If unskillfully, it was immediately apparent from the wobbling (light). ... If the positioning of the *shumoku* and the *kantera*, and of the forward and rear baskets, didn't allow a good rhythm, the lamp would go out or one would fall. Then one could only complete about five trips in the time usually allowed for eight. As to the size of the baskets, there were 100 and 80 *kin* baskets. When two or two-and-a-half scoops of coal in the *ebu* were put into the basket, it would be full. Women usually used an "eight basket" (80 *kin*) in front and a "hundred basket" (100 *kin*) behind. In about seven trips, a wagon could be filled.[24]

32 *Work and wages*

Figure 2.2 Hauling with the yoked *sena* (Yamamoto, *Emaki*, 23rd black and white illustration).

Yamamoto Sakubei, a retired miner, describes the baskets as about 45 cm in diameter and some 55 cm in depth, but the woman quoted here recalled two sizes of baskets, 80 *kin* and 100 *kin;* 100 *kin* was equal to about 60 kg or 130 lb. The common practice was to carry one basket of each size, the smaller one in front. Because carrying two baskets of 130 lb. each, or even two of 100 lb. each was obviously impossible, the total load must have been made up of half of each, or a burden of still well over 100 lb. Kaneko says that the basket size could be augmented with woven bamboo rings, and that the standard *sena* load was 100 *kin*.[25] Such a total load accords with this woman's recollection that in seven trips, the haulier would have filled a wagon. A wagonload of some 400 kg (about 880 lb.) was typical of early wagon capacity. In other words, the women's loads were extremely heavy.

A woman who claimed an exceptional degree of clumsiness in her early mining career recalled how she had struggled carrying the yoked baskets.

> The *sena* yoke rode from the shoulder over the back to the hips on a slant, and one carried up basket-loads of 100 *kin*. Since you climb the low [roofed]

Work and wages 33

slope, you can't stretch your hips and if you straighten your back, the yoke will slip and the load dump. ...

I was so bad when I began carrying the *sena* that, when I got up to the pit mouth, only about ten (*kin*) of coal were left in the front basket, and where others would take eleven loads to fill the measuring tub [*bara-kago*—1000 *kin* woven reed tubs without bases were common[26]], I would carry some twenty before it was filled.[27]

In early Meiji, the women would carry their loaded *sena* to the measuring tub at the pit mouth (Figure 2.3), if not further to a transport terminal.[28] The *sena* had been adapted from the load-carrying system of Japanese peasants and was a natural development of the needs of hauling in a *tanuki-bori* mine.[29] As mines sank deeper into the earth and auxiliary horizontal tunnels were driven into the seams, the *sena* would be off-loaded into wagons at an underground landing. These wagons were initially a form of cart adapted from those used in farm work.[30] Another female miner recounted:

At small coal mines, a cart called a *daibassha*, like the vehicle used in a horse cart, was pulled by human beings. On a big carriage, a box frame woven from bamboo was placed. As a child, I often saw loaded *daibassha*, pulled to the surface, coming out of the pit.[31]

Figure 2.3 Emptying *sena* at pit mouth (Yamamoto, *Emaki*, 73rd black and white illustration).

34 *Work and wages*

Figure 2.4 Sieving and hauling at pit mouth (Yamamoto, *Emaki*, 72nd black and white illustration.

Other women do not mention such "horse carts" pulled by people, and this could be because people-pulled carts were short-lived. Hand carts were soon replaced by deeper wagons mounted on four small, flanged, iron wheels running between rails in the manner of modern railcars. They could be let down the incline or shaft to galleries or landings by cable and pulled along the horizontal tunnels by horses. They were not commonly run up and down an incline in trains pulled by horses, as in the dangerous British practice.[32] Where wagon trains were used in more level haulage-ways, individual "tubs" would be separated from the train and run into the landings at the end of sloping headings, where they could be loaded.

Where the baskets could not be lowered into the wagons because of lack of clearance between the top of the wagons and the tunnel roof, they would be dumped on the ground, and the coal, sometimes after a preliminary selection process, would be loaded into the wagons with scoops or shovels. Shoveling coal into wagons, however, does not seem to have been as common a part of the work of hauliers in Japan as it was in England and America, where the wagons or trucks were more often taken all the way to the coal face.[33] In Japan, wagons would be taken to the face in bigger and more modern mines only at a later date, when the abundant and cheap labor of female *atoyama* might not be the decisive factor.

Another system of hauling coal from *oroshi*, the *tebo-karai*, was used later from the Taisho period (1912–26) on.[34] It was adopted in some of the larger mines where thicker seams and more headroom allowed the *atomuki* to stand upright. It was peculiarly suited to *oroshi*, where the tunnel followed the seam on a downward slope, because carrying the load up the slope would be less dangerous than trying to balance it on the way down a *kata*. The *tebo* (called a *tangara* in the Joban coalfields) was a deep basket slung over the shoulders like a rucksack in a manner of carrying called *karai*. Loaded, it weighed 50 or 60 kg (110–130 lbs.). It was usually made heavy by runoff water and condensed water vapor. It required six or seven loads to fill one wagon.[35] Cooperation might be required from *sakiyama* in shoveling the coal into the *tebo* while the *atomuki* braced themselves against a rung fastened between framing timbers. But the Tohoku practice of resting the basket on some form of cribbing was evidently used in Kyushu as well to relieve the *sakiyama* of loading responsibilities.[36] Yamamoto Sakubei suggests that usually men carried the *tebo*, but in the *Emaki* he also shows women carrying it, and other women remember carrying it themselves. Yamamoto calls the exceptions "heroic women" in his note, which also deals with the great weight of the *tebo*.[37] One of these heroic women asserted:

> I think that unless you are a woman, you can't do this kind of work. Men don't have the endurance (*shinbō*) for it. My husband carried the *tebo* only once. His body was covered in sweat and he asked why he should have to do such work and went out early.[38]

The *tebo* was unloaded at the landing from a one- or two-runged ladder placed against the side of the wagon. The *atoyama*, generally of shorter stature than North American women, had to master the knack of loosening one shoulder strap

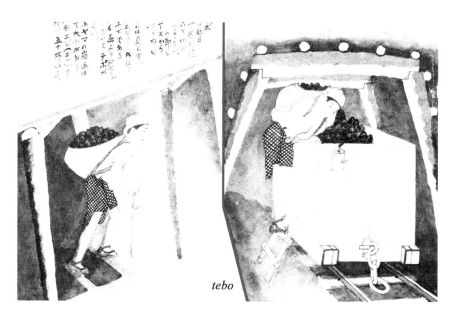

Figure 2.5 Hauling with the *tebo* (Yamamoto, *Emaki*, 18th black and white illustration).

of the basket while stepping onto the ladder and bending forward to dump the coal over the side of the wagon, without losing their balance or allowing the coal to spill over their head.[39]

The *sena* and *tebo* were largely replaced by the *sura* in north Kyushu in the late Meiji period, initially as a more efficient way of getting larger loads of coal out of descents.[40] At first, large bamboo baskets, called *battera* and similar to cartage baskets used by farmers, were mounted on wood or metal runners.[41] The early *sura* was pulled up the incline by a woman harnessed to the basket with ropes. She would use footholds cut into the incline or the bars of a ladder-like frame (*koro*) on the floor of the slope to get a footing on the usually wet and slippery surface. Yamamoto's illustration shows the basket sliding on wooden runners over the rungs of the ladder *between* the rails, in which case the frictional resistance to its progress up the incline must have been considerable.[42] Even with metal runners, it could not have been pulled or pushed up even gentle slopes without basket deformities making guidance difficult.

A partial solution to the deficiencies of the bamboo basket system was to use a more solid wooden box as the *sura* and either to mount it on solid wooden runners or to slide it *on top of* the wooden rails of the ladder.[43] The larger *sura* of later days would seem to have been mounted on the rails rather than sliding between them. Although the early wooden *sura* made of two "oil boxes" joined together held about 120 kg[44] of coal as opposed to the 150 kg of earlier *battera*, wooden boxes were less subject than bamboo baskets to deformities due to the weight of the load and to deterioration due to the effects of runoff water. With the

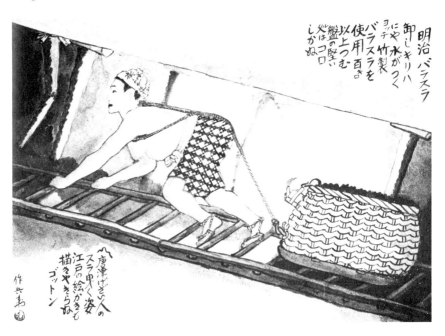

Figure 2.6 Hauling with the basket *sura* (Yamamoto, *Emaki*, 2nd black and white illustration).

Work and wages 37

larger wooden *sura*, moreover, water could become an aid by making the rails slippery and helping the *atomuki* push the box.

The loaded box *sura*, of course, would not slide up the slope of the *oroshi* as easily as it would slide down the slope of the *kata*, and this must have been immediately apparent to miners who were looking for ways to reduce their output of energy while increasing their output of coal. Yamamoto says that it was next to impossible to pull an "ordinary" *sura* up a slope of more than ten degrees.[45] It was much more efficient to let the *sura* slide down the rails and pull it back up empty than to do the reverse.[46] The widespread adoption of the wooden *sura* coincided with the shift to mining in ascents wherever possible at bigger mines as early as the Meiji period.[47]

One woman gives the dimensions of the *sura* as "from three to four *shaku* (approx. 3 to 4 ft.) on all sides," and adds that "metal was fixed to the bottom, so that it slid easily."[48] Yamamoto says the loaded capacity of a standard *sura* was "more than 200 kg."[49] This is probably an estimate of a later standard because in the earlier period, *sura* loads were not weighed to calculate wages. But weights may have been estimated by management in order to calculate productivity.

In the *kata*, sloping down from the face, the work was easier.[50] The miner pulled the coal down behind him using his pick or his feet. Working behind her mate, the haulier could gather it into the *ebu* basket using the incline to her advantage. The *ebu* could be dumped into the *sura* from the upper end or corner. Yamamoto shows the older type of basket *sura* tied to timber frames to prevent

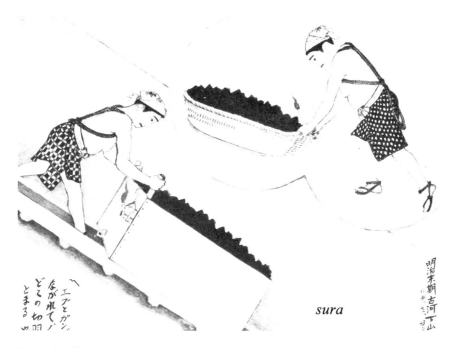

Figure 2.7 Two forms of *sura* (Yamamoto, *Emaki*, 22nd black and white illustration).

38 *Work and wages*

it sliding away down the slope.[51] The newer box type could be tied and/or wedged to prevent it from escaping. Even taking advantage of the incline, loading the *sura* was not easy because there was usually very little clearance between the roof of the heading and the top of the box.

> To load a *sura* about the size of an apple box, you had to get the *ebu* into the space between the roof and the *sura*, and dump the coal in. It was only about the width of a *tenugui*.[52]

The problem seems to have been partially overcome in some places by having removable boards at the top of the sides of the *sura*, as Yamamoto's illustrations show. One sketch depicts the boards removed for unloading. Another shows loading in a more spacious room where the boards were not needed because of space restrictions but for the convenience of the *atomuki* in that she was not required to lift the basket too high until the final stage of loading with the boards in place.[53] Nevertheless, it is clear that the original purpose of the removable boards was to facilitate loading the *sura* in low-ceilinged rooms. When the *atomuki* had filled the *sura*, she would lower it down the incline on the crude wooden rails of the *koro*, with the cross ties acting as rungs for her feet. Though on lesser inclines she might let it slide down in front of her, usually she would get behind and below it and ease it down with ropes around her waist and over her shoulder to make it "steady as she goes." On gentler slopes of about ten degrees, "where the surface was solid," *koro* were not laid,[54] and the woman would risk her life by using her legs to pull against the weight of the *sura*, which would have flattened her if it had started to move suddenly. The method was clearly dangerous and the ropes were said to have been in the configuration of a cross, a cross that the *atomuki* had to bear! On steeper slopes, the woman would "receive" the weight of the box on her head, in which case it was known as an *uke-zura*.[55]

The difficulty of managing one's own box was compounded at larger mines where a single heading led to more than one face or to a bigger room and several women would be letting their *sura* down the slope simultaneously. Each knew that to lose control would cause an accident, harming those below. Holding her lamp in her teeth, or later, hanging it on the box, the *atomuki* would guide the *sura* with her hands usually bracing the upper corners; groping for the rungs with her feet, she would step back down the ladder. The difficulties and dangers of the process are described by one woman who used the *uke-zura*.

> Crawling on all fours, grasping the rails tightly with the hands, and supporting the *sura* which one has fully loaded with coal on one's head so that it doesn't slide down and get away from you, one creeps gingerly backwards down an incline of more than 30 degrees. Carrying the *kantera* in your mouth, you see, since the wagons are parked below, you have to let it down to them from the face. ... With the toes of one's straw sandals, you feel for each foothold as you go down so that you won't slip and fall. Just slip once and see what happens! It's not a matter of danger only to yourself.

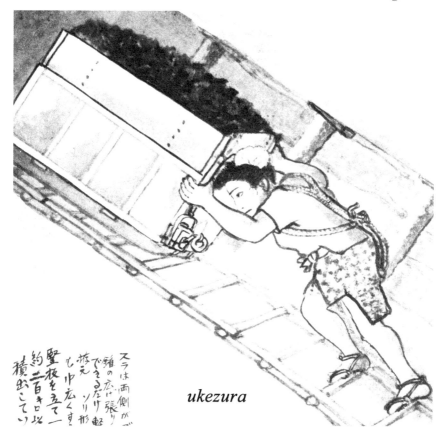

Figure 2.8 Ukezura (Yamamoto, *Emaki*, 24th black and white illustration).

Because everyone else is going carefully down the same way. There are even people carrying babies on their backs. And as water is sprayed to allow the heavy *sura* to run smoothly, it is always dripping *pota pota* and making the *koro* slippery. Every morning, at the pit mouth, we were always saying, "Today's okay, I'm not following," or "It's no good, not for me. I don't want to go in. I don't like following."[56]

Little light on the subject

Other women spoke of the difficulty of holding lamps in their mouths while letting the *sura* down the ramps or while pushing wagons out to the winding apparatus. The earliest miner's lamp was a wick soaking in a saucer of vegetable oil, the saucer tied with a loop to a pair of chopsticks held between the teeth to prevent the saucer from shaking about.[57] One retired female miner spoke of the evolution of miners' lamps in Japan.

40   *Work and wages*

> It seems that when my mother was a girl, they used a flaming saucer, but in my time it was the *kantera*. Vegetable oil was mixed with petroleum. Later it was carbide gas. Since lamps were expensive, we couldn't always buy them. Because we had to provide all our own tools, we had to make do. Until they became cheaper. Safety lamps didn't give much light. You see, they had steel bases. You couldn't see underneath.

She notes that improvements in the lamps had not always increased safety, let alone made it easier to work in the dark caverns.

> Because the handle of the safety lamp was made of steel, look! I have become buck-toothed like this and all my teeth are loose. Because I gripped the handle of the safety lamp tightly in my teeth while working. The weight of the safety lamp was almost one *kan* (3.75 kg). As the slope was as steep as this [she indicates], it really took a lot of strength in the teeth. Other people would wrap the handle of the lamp with straw and put the straw in their mouths, but for some reason, when I put the straw in my mouth I would suddenly feel like puking.[58]

Poor illumination must have made the next step in the hauling process difficult in the early days. The *sura* were dumped onto the ground at the landing and the coal sorted before being loaded into wagons.[59] Later, the *sura* were upended from a platform directly into the wagons and the sorting done on the surface.[60] The platform, of course, required more space in the tunnel and implied the removal of more of the ambient rock and more labor and supervision. One woman recalled that it usually took three loads of the *sura* to fill one standard wagon.[61] This must have been in the days when the wagon held less than the later standard of one and a half tons because that would have made the standard *sura* load half a ton (or more than 450 kg), much greater than could be handled by even the strongest and most skilled women. On the other hand, Yamamoto notes that, "Even the strongest men could not handle the (big) *sura* with strength alone. For this, women had the knack and were more skillful."[62]

The loading of wagons could be an art, especially when the *sura* or *sena* was dumped at the landing and some sorting done while putting the coal into the wagons. One woman described how Hei, a blind male haulier, demonstrated special skill at sorting and loading work.

> I admired the way he sorted the coal with his hands. He said that the temperature of the rock and coal were different, and as he quickly felt the large and small lumps, he could tell the difference in the warmth.[63]

She tells how Hei was exceptionally good at loading the wagons, "spreading" the larger lumps of coal and covering them with smaller ones to minimize the amount of coal in an apparently full wagon. Spreading would maximize the miners' output in terms of the number of wagons turned out in a day and thus increase their income.[64] Later, in big mines where the miners' output was calculated in actual weight of coal in the wagon, their talents would be devoted to just the opposite: getting as much coal into the wagons as possible.[65]

Obtaining and pushing out wagons

In smaller drift mines, a filled wagon might be pushed out to the pit mouth or pulled out by a windlass. Yamamoto depicts a horse-turned windlass that, he says, would pull out one "small" wagon of about 350 kilograms (around 770 lbs.).[66] In bigger mines, a steam-driven windlass might pull a train of wagons up the slope from the landing. But as the mines got deeper and more complex, the female *atomuki* were obliged to push their wagons to a central collection point from which trains would be pulled out by a pony or donkey engine or, more often, wagons would be lifted vertically to the surface by mechanical winding gear.[67]

In the Meiji period, horses had pulled the wagon trains in the galleries of some of the bigger mines, but even there the wagons would often have to be pushed out to the landings. Later, pit ponies were used in unmechanized mines to pull out smaller trains. Yamamoto says that "Pit ponies were chosen for their small stature and strength. They were used in small and medium-sized mines even in the early

Figure 2.9 The use of horses or "pit ponies" (Yamamoto, *Emaki*, 49th black and white illustration).

days of Showa (after 1926)."[68] His account reveals that the ponies shared some of the same deprivations as the mining women. In shallow mines, they might be brought out after work each day, but in deeper ones, they would be kept down for as much as a week at a time. He illustrates the exuberance of ponies breathing fresh air and seeing daylight after an underground stint of work. But in the bigger mines, ponies were housed underground, usually went blind, and never again saw the light of day.

The frequency with which the retired women mention the exertions of pushing loaded wagons, and the infrequency of their references to the use of horses, suggest that management would use human labor rather than horses when it was cheaper.[69] Not only was some effort required to overcome the inertia of loaded wagons and get them moving but many galleries were not level, and even more exertion was needed to keep wagons moving up a slight incline. On the other hand, some ingenuity was needed to keep empty wagons from getting away on the downhill return. In the northeast, a pointed pole inserted into the spokes of the wagon wheel was used to brake wagons on a steeper downward slope; a smaller stick, more like a drumstick, was used to brake wagon trains as well as to hold single wagons on a slope in Kyushu. The procedure, known as "putting in the boat" (*bōto utsu*), must have required considerable dexterity and could result in derailment if not done skillfully.[70]

Figure 2.10 Pushing wagons (Yamamoto, *Emaki*, 26th black and white illustration).

Work and wages   43

The women prided themselves on their strength, which they demonstrated in pushing heavy wagons.[71]

> Pushing wagons? You know that women are strong in the hips. In the tunnels if the wagons wouldn't budge any other way, we pushed them with our backs. Putting both hands against the roof, if the roof was low, gripping the *kantera* in our teeth, planting both feet on the rock floor, and pushing with our hips, we'd get it moving little by little. As there were places where, if you pushed it with your hands, the wagon and the roof were so close that your hands would get caught, we'd (have to) let go of the (top of the) wagon. … Later, as the wagons were of steel, we complained, and hook-shaped metal pieces were hung from the steel (sides) and we pushed holding these.

A leader in pushing wagons had similar responsibilities to those of women who followed others down the slope to the landing platform with the *sura*. The recollections continue:

> It was awful if you were at the front in pushing wagons. Rock (*bota*) would fall, coal would come down, and while pushing one's way through that stuff, if you missed the fact that there was a gap between rails at the "single cutter" (the points on the "truck" track switched by kicking with the foot), the wagon would derail. To cause a wagon to derail was a serious matter. But nary a one would help you. Even if they were working close by, they all pretended not to notice and stuck to their own work.[72]

Another retired female miner remembered:

> Coal wagons went from seven *go* (probably 7/10 of a ton) to a ton, and since the wood was green, the wagon was heavy. You couldn't push it easily, and the one behind only came on slowly. So when I was caught between two, only my toes were hurt, but in the worst case you could lose your life.
>
> I complained bitterly to the one behind who hadn't been watching while pushing. Even though she was an older woman, it was my life she was risking! This was my start as a bickering woman.[73]

Thus, the rivalry in getting out wagons led to conflict between the women, contending with concern for each other's welfare.[74]

The common urge to get one's wagons out promptly was the result of there being only a single track in the galleries at all but the biggest mines. Empty wagons had to be bumped off the track to let full wagons go by (except where a single full one met a train of empties), so the women competed to make sure that their wagon was not empty and in the way of full ones coming by their landing.[75]

> With the priority system of loading, there was a team which somehow always beat me. Hoping to find out why they were so fast, I paid close attention and

44   *Work and wages*

> found out that the two *atomuki* had four *sura* between them. So while others
> were loading their *sura*, they were taking out the *sura* which they had held
> in readiness after loading earlier. In such ways, everyone devised their own
> schemes.[76]

As she suggests, these schemes ensured that partially filled wagons did not have
to yield to competitors' full ones. Clever as her two competitors were, if empty
wagons were not available when the full ones were pushed out, they could not get
ahead in the race to load and count wagons as output for the day.

The competition for wagons

The problem of obtaining wagons was a bane of most women's lives in the coal
mines. Matsumoto Tsuya, a retired female miner, said that she often went in at
midnight in order to be assured of getting empty wagons for the ensuing workday.
Another woman echoes Tsuya:

> As it was that much less work, we started out early, hoping to get left-over
> wagons. But when you found wagons enroute and took them away, there would
> be bitter disputes. They'd get angry because they'd brought them that far....
> We'd look for empty wagons everywhere and pull them (to our landing).[77]

Shindo Toyo believes that the shortage of wagons was part of "labor management policy."[78] Spacing of delivery became a means of maximizing productivity
even later, when shortages were more easily overcome. Thus, systems devised
to cope with a shortage of wagons at an earlier time were retained later when the
shortage had been alleviated, because such systems were effective ways of
stimulating competition among miners for faster production.[79] Conversely,
management's failure to provide an adequate number of wagons could result in
some inefficiency because the wait for an empty wagon could be "up to an
hour-and-a-half or two hours."[80] Even at more productive mines, where nine or
ten wagonloads a day was the norm, a difference of one or two per day—caused
by unwanted waits—could be substantial. But the norm at the average North
Kyushu mine was only three or four wagonloads per day. One woman chose to
join the second shift working from mid-afternoon to past midnight because
wagons were difficult to obtain on the first shift in the morning.[81] Another says
she accompanied her stepfather at age 14, not so much to provide labor as to be
counted as an extra hand in securing an increased allocation of wagons. Couples
"received one wagon, but three people received two."[82] Although some young-
sters would crawl into an empty wagon and sleep[83] in order to prevent anyone
else from taking it, others began pushing wagons at an early age, sometimes with
disastrous results.

In many cases, a shortage of wagons led management to encourage a competition for them, which may have increased productivity but also ensured that
miners remained at odds with each other and, paradoxically, unlikely to mount

Work and wages   45

any concerted demands for an equitable distribution. The effects of competition are apparent from another retired woman's recollections that suggest quotas of wagons based on the number of miners at a face or wall.

> There were three wagons for five people. That fellow was monopolizing them. There were four people at our place. But (I said), "Hey! You can't do just as you please. We are five. So which are ours? One of us has gone to get the food. We want three wagons. You can't have them all. Do you think you can monopolize them?"[84]

Mashio's protagonist, Maki, confirmed the intensity of disputes over the acquisition of wagons in the northeast.[85]

The most infamous scheme of wagon distribution was labeled *hashiri-ban*, or "running priority." Under this system, the *atoyama* were obliged to gather at the pit mouth at the beginning of the day shift in the small hours of the morning. At a signal from the overseer, they would race into the mine to the landing where the empty wagons were stationed, hang their identifiable *tenugui*, lantern, or tally[86] on a wagon, and push it to their own heading in preparation for loading. Those who were too slow would have to wait for another set of wagons to be brought in to the landing, thus being delayed in the loading process. One woman recounts:

> As the pit entrance opened at 4 o'clock, everyone would run pell-mell down the rough incline of the shaft and receive wagons in the order in which they got there. We couldn't compete in this race with the young men.[87]

One wonders how a management could impose such indignities on their workers, even in the name of increased productivity.

Systems of allocation of wagons at other mines were less diabolical. The same woman described other systems:

> At the Miyoshi Mine there were what was called *oshidashi-ban* (pushing-out priority) and *tsumiage-ban* (loading priority). You'd load the coal which you'd brought in the *sura* into the wagon. The first one to finish loading would shout, *"Tsumiage-ban!"* And the fastest one would be the first to get the next empty wagon. ...
>
> Then the one who reached the winding-station first with a full wagon would cry, '*Oshidashi-ban!*' And according to loading and pushing priority, you would receive empty wagons. It was competition and more competition, nothing but competition. Someone who shilly-shallies even a little can't get along in the coal mines.[88]

But, she also remembers:

> At some mines there was an equal-allocation system (*wake-ban*). The wagons were allocated person by person. At such coal mines, there was no

46   *Work and wages*

question of who got out a full wagon first. After a person had passed, you could follow immediately.

This woman, who noted the value of rest breaks while waiting for wagons, also spoke of the need to ensure that wagons were properly identified so that the miners would be paid for the coal they brought out.

Putting our name tally in the loaded wagon, we sent the coal out. So sometimes there were those who switched name tallies after our coal had been dug out. But they would be found out quickly.[89]

Thus, there could be trouble over the proprietorship of loaded as well as empty wagons. Those who stooped to changing the marker tallies on others' wagons to claim them for themselves must have been quite desperate because a full load disguised as someone else's could usually be detected.[90]

Piecework wages and deductions

The reason for "spreading" coal in such a way as to take advantage of the spaces between lumps and make the wagon look full when it was relatively lightly loaded was, of course, that miners were paid by the wagonload of coal taken out of the mine. This was also the reason why the availability of wagons was crucial to the subsistence of the miners.

If we didn't go (down) early, we'd lose our chance to get a wagon. We'd pull the wagon which we had secured (as) close (as possible) to our own face. When we'd carried three loads of coal in the *sura*, the wagon would be full. That was one *kan*, and we'd push it several hundred *ken* (chains) to the winding head. Then it would be pulled out by the winding gear. Our name tallies would be hung on the wagons, and we'd receive wages according to our daily output of coal in terms of the number of wagons (we) sent out.[91]

Talking about mining in late Meiji, Yamamoto Sakubei says:

Around that time mining wages, called *kirichin*, were about 25 *sen* for each wagon-load of coal mined. ... Even a skilled *sakiyama* could only put out about 2 1/2 wagon-loads per day. That would be a weight of just one ton. An unskilled *sakiyama* would be lucky to get out two wagon-loads.[92]

Because only full wagons were counted in calculating wages, the two-and-one-half wagonloads of a skilled *sakiyama* must be an average. Part loads would not be left behind casually in mines where workers on other shifts might appropriate them.

For the standard daily output of three wagonloads claimed by some of the women in Meiji times, other records suggest the women received about 40 *sen* per day. That would be an income of up to 10 or 11 *yen* for 25 to 28 workdays a

Work and wages 47

month.[93] A woman who mined at the beginning of the Taisho period immediately following Meiji reported that they still earned between 30 and 40 *sen* a day.[94] Even in the relatively rich seams of the Hojo Mine, one wagon-load in three hours was considered a good rate of work, so that in a 12-hour shift, four wagons would be the average output.[95] At less well-endowed mines, extraordinary efforts and long hours were required in order to send out more than three wagons per day.

> As the tallies to put on the wagons and the safety lamps were given out at the pit mouth at three o'clock in the morning, we'd get up at one o'clock in order not to be late. ... [T]he evening whistle blew at nine o'clock. ... If we did four wagon-loads that would be a good day's work. If it was less than four, one wagon wouldn't be calculated in that day's work.[96]

Later on, however, at the better mines, some women would remember taking out six, seven, or even more wagon-loads per day.[97] Though Mathias concludes that "teams had to fulfill a certain quota in order to get any wages at all,"[98] the mining women do not confirm her statement, and only one reference to assigned quotas suggests that miners did not rely solely on themselves to decide how much output would allow them to survive.[99] At most mines, there were two shifts and no quotas at all.

In late Meiji and early Taisho, deductions were taken from the wages for deficiencies in wagon-loads. Wagons were subjected to an inspection process called *kentan*. Matsumoto says that one of the unpleasant jobs given to *burakumin* was to assist company officials in making these deductions.[100] But the power given to those who inspected the wagons could hardly be delegated to underlings, and it is also unlikely that *burakumin* were given the tasks of clerks and recorders of the deductions because their education was often deficient. Retired miner Yamamoto gives a detailed account of the effect of deductions on output and wages:

> Sometimes as much as three *gō* would be taken off. That would be like the confiscation of one wagon from an output of three wagon-loads.... At the end of Meiji, the daily wage of a miner would have been between 70 and 80 *sen*, and even if the face were particularly good, still less than one *yen*. But when 20 or 30 per cent was taken off that amount, the laboring miners could not endure it. Even overly honest people like myself, who would sort conscientiously so that even the smallest bit of rock was not mixed in, and would send out wagon-loads of coal piled high, when they came out of the pit and went to the reckoning office to collect their coal tallies, would invariably find them chalked all over with deductions averaging about 2 *gō*. In a word, we can assume that these deductions were planned from the outset to meet a norm of more than 20 per cent and were budgetted for accordingly.[101]

As a result of these deductions, Yamamoto continues, "the miners were increasingly embittered," and "looked for someone to vent their wrath on, and as well as resenting management, hated the *kanryō kakari* (wagon inspector) as a viper."

48 *Work and wages*

One woman recalls how in later days, at mines where they were paid according to weight, the *kanryō kakari* (now more appropriately translated as weighing supervisor) took his cut for giving full weight.

> Some among the *kanryō kakari* took liberties. In a wagon-load, the amount of stone mixed in was deducted. He was the one who decided that. If you greased his palm, he'd overlook it, but if you didn't have any small coins, he'd glare at you and make deductions.

During weighing, the miner might not always be there on the surface to be glared at by the weigher, but the latter's scorn for those who did not line his pocket would have been apparent at other times. She continues:

> He'd poke at the coal in your wagon and break it down to (find an excuse to) reduce the weight. It was called "pigeon-pecking," a nasty way of finding stone. On the way up to the surface it would be shaken about, so that it wouldn't be like the way you'd loaded it. But even if you loaded taking that into account, he'd take a slice out (of your wages).
>
> In the office, the *kanryō*'s coat would be hanging. If you put a little wad (of money) in the pocket with your name on it, you'd get away without the pigeon-pecking process. Sometimes that pocket would be swollen up as with a hand-ball.[102]

Figure 2.11 Tallying up the output (Yamamoto, *Emaki*, 61st black and white illustration).

Work and wages   49

In earlier times of economic downturn, the amount paid per wagon could be unilaterally reduced by management.

> Each wagon-load of coal was worth so much. If the *kirichin* per wagon were reduced, we'd say, "There's nought for it but to put out an extra wagon," and we worked knowing that this could happen. As minions of the capitalists, we still thought that whatever they gave us was our lot.[103]

Other types of deductions were made from the miners' wages. Repayments of loans incurred on taking employment at the mine, called *kataire-gin*, were almost universal. Along with repayment of those loans and earnest money, there would be the obligation to settle debts for starting up housekeeping, *shitaku-gin*, which would be deducted in installments from the wages.[104] Loans would also be incurred when a family member was ill. As we will see, inability to repay all of their obligations kept many miners in a recurring cycle of debt.[105]

The miners also had to pay for the very tools that allowed them to work and earn a living, as well as earning profits for the owners. Yamamoto says that tempering the pick point cost the miners 5 *rin* (half a *sen*); if a new blade was added, it was 2 *sen* 5 *rin*. Oil for the *kantera* lamp was 2 or 3 *sen*, and straw sandals cost 1 *sen* 5 *rin* or 2 *sen* per pair. "When these were all deducted, at best little more than 40 *sen* was left (of a day's wages)."[106] A female miner gives a similar list of deductions for basic means of production.

> *Kantera* oil cost 2 *sen* per day. Straw sandals were 2 *sen* per pair and as we (discarded) two pair (during the day), that was 6 *sen* (altogether). As well, there was the fee for tempering the pick which was 1 *sen*. This was the amount charged every day.[107]

Miners also were often expected to provide auxiliary tools such as mallets, chisels, and augers.[108] The injustice of charging miners fees for oil for lamps without which they could not work in the dark needs to be considered in conjunction with the fact that they had no right to bargain for better wages.

Because piece-rate wages were set according to such large "pieces" (i.e., full wagon-loads), manipulation of the rates was the equivalent of manipulation of the norms of production in industries such as textiles where smaller units were measurable. When a man-and-wife team was putting out an average of two-and-one-half wagonloads per day, they could, by working longer hours, ensure that they put out three full ones most days and thereby reduce the number of two-wagon days. But it was hardly realistic to think that if the rate per wagon went down they could produce a fourth or fifth wagonload when it took them three to four hours to fill one. Low piece-work rates of pay imposed heavy burdens on Japanese coal-mining women, and these rates were ameliorated only to a minor degree in better times, usually during a war. It could not have been much consolation to them that their wages were somewhat better than those of coal sorters on the surface or of female textile workers who were usually not supporting families on their meager pay.[109]

Framing and tunneling

As well as hauling, women were involved in the work of framing (timbering or propping) in the *oroshi* in the early days and later in the *kata* and main tunnels as well. Though early miners tried to keep the framing to a minimum by taking out only the coal of the seam, leaving the hard base rock to support itself, as they dug deeper and sought more room to allow for less arduous methods of hauling, they were obliged to take out some of the rock as well by drilling and blasting. Removal of the rock often weakened the roof and made timber framing a necessity.[110] The techniques of framing were further developed when main tunnels were driven into the seams to allow for upward sloping headings and horizontal or gently sloping inclines for wagon transport of the coal. Considerable skills were required to frame the more extensive tunnels of larger mines.[111]

To determine the necessity for framing, the miners would tap the roof and gauge its solidity by the reverberations. One woman suggested that it was usually the male *sakiyama* who did this kind of testing. She remembered a deaf mute ascertaining the characteristics of the roof by the nature of the vibrations on his hand when he rapped it with his pick.[112] But the women, too, were always alert to sounds of impending danger, and the acuteness of their auditory and tactile senses was attested to by their ability to do similar tests on the jerry-built wire-and-paper ceilings of their tenement houses. We know that miners in other countries used this kind of "sonar."[113]

Framing gradually fell to the lot of specialists, called *shikuri*. Although one retired woman miner recalls a "badger mine" where women did everything, including framing,[114] usually men led the work, setting the timbers in place and fastening the crossbeam to the stanchions, then wedging shims between the beam and the roof to stabilize the ceiling and the frame. An exceptionally skilled framer

Figure 2.12 Sounding out the roof and filling the *sura* (Yamamoto, *Emaki*, 37th black and white illustration).

Work and wages 51

might keep as many as three women busy providing him with timbers and shims, but often couples would work as a team, and two-couple framing gangs were not unusual.[115] The women carried the timbers to the men, sometimes cutting them to length as ordered, and whittled the shims or wedges to appropriate shapes and sizes. One woman boasted of the size of the logs she carried: "Because my husband was a *shikuri*, I went with him as an *atomuki*. I carried 12 *shaku* mine timbers (about 12 feet long) this big [she indicates their girth]."[116] Another woman earned the nickname "the Dumb Ox" (*dobiki ushi*) because of her prowess in hauling "10 or 12 *shaku*" framing timbers out of the mountain forests in a "Korean sling."[117] Timbers were provided by gang bosses or by mine management in later years. They were allocated to teams of framers, and sharing timbers could be a means of forming friendships among the women and the men as well.[118]

Mashio describes Maki's work carrying timbers for framing in the air shaft of a north-eastern coal mine:

> Maki San ... walked resolutely stooped over with protruding hips, carrying the long, heavy logs. That was usually men's work. Men could carry them easily on their shoulders, but it was difficult for women. The 15- and 17-year-old sisters carried the timbers as if carrying children on their backs.

The women interviewed by Morisaki and Idegawa give no indication that they thought carrying timbers was not "women's work."[119]

Among the tools miners (often the women) carried down into the pit was the framer's *yoki*, a sharp axe "honed till it glints like a razor blade," indicating that they were expected to provide the basic means of framing as well as hewing and hauling.[120] Later, in some of the bigger mines, framers left their *yoki* near their workplaces, either as a matter of convenience or as surety for their return to work, perhaps both. "It was said that the *yoki* was the framer's life, and it was sharpened until it could shave a beard."[121]

Speed and skill in framing were crucial for survival. When sufficient numbers of frames had not been inserted to stabilize the roof (whether due to parsimonious management or to the miners' eagerness to get on with the "real work"), it might begin to sag, making emergency operations necessary.

> When the ceiling threatened to come down, unless staves were put in to shore it up quickly, the frames wouldn't stand, so everyone worked flat out. When we *atomuki* went, we would immediately cut the staves and shave the wedges, but those who were new at it wouldn't have the knack of it and would shilly-shally. I would already be making wedges, hacking them into shape with the *yoki*, *tattattatt*. "Obasan, you're fast, aren't you?" a fellow who had been drafted for the purpose said with surprise.[122]

When more than a simple ceiling of staves driven in horizontally between augmented numbers of frames was required to hold up the severely weakened

52 *Work and wages*

Figure 2.13 Framing, or timbering, in the haulage ways (Yamamoto, *Emaki*, 31st black and white illustration).

roof of a large mining room, the framers might use a well-cradle in the style of the walls of a log house with the chinks open. One woman tells of the difficulties in getting the cradle up while the roof was in danger of coming down.

> After (an initial fall) the framing was very difficult. To hold up the roof, we used an "empty log-piling." The mine timbers were placed like a well-frame [in the shape of the Japanese word for well], but when we made too much haste, if one beam (timber) bent, the whole cradle would come down and someone might be badly hurt.[123]

One form of extra support in the tunnels was the "woman-and-man frame," giving the woman unusual priority in the naming of a timbering configuration that shored up an unusually wide passageway. Another similar form of support was the T-frame, probably called a *tonbo* (dragonfly) because a couple of frames seen in juxtaposition resembled the sedentary insect with its double wings. The miners could only hope that the cantilevered wings of the "dragonfly" would not flutter

Work and wages 53

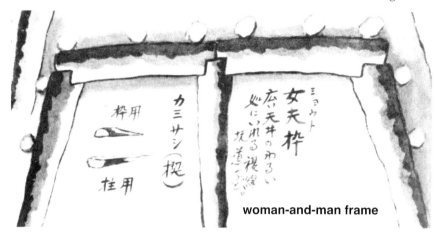

Figure 2.14 "Woman-and-man frame" (Yamamoto, *Emaki*, detail from 27th black and white illustration).

under the pressure of the roof! The *tonbo*, like the woman-and-man frame, could only be used in the mining room or where obstruction in the middle of the tunnel was not a problem for hauling or transport.

> The mine in Kasuya (District) from which we fled was a terrible place. Water dripped from the ceiling and the frames were far apart. *Tonbo* were placed here and there, but the roof sagged, so that there were many places where we closed our eyes and took a deep breath as we ran to get past.[124]

One woman was saved when many others were killed by a gas explosion because she was framing around a large boulder in preparation for its removal. This rock was in an air shaft, a concession to the miners' need to breathe less contaminated air. Such shafts took contaminated air out of the mine, and the cross entries between them and main shafts were accessed by swinging doors (*battari*) normally kept closed.[125] In this case, the protruding rock, while obstructing normal passage in the tunnel, also blocked the full force of the blast. She describes how the powerful "fire-wind" was deflected by the big rock, saving her but killing those on the other side of the boulder, including the *imin-tai* (the Korean team) "in the big room at the back."[126]

In some mines, framing in the main shafts became a specialized function in conjunction with tunneling.[127] Because those who did framing and tunneling and dug the slopes to the faces could not earn money for coal turned out in wagons, they had to be compensated in different ways. Mashio says that framing was paid at so much per *shaku* (roughly an English foot) in Joban,[128] but it is not clear whether this was based on the length of the tunnel newly timbered or on the existing frames kept in working order; perhaps it was for both but paid at different rates. In Chikuho, the work was done by a contract for length of tunnel or number

54 *Work and wages*

of frames; in larger mines, it was at a daily rate of pay. The wages were not divided in the same way as for mining work. "When tunnelling and framing, because the work of the *atomuki* was easi(er), the woman received four parts of the money (wages) to the man's six, but when mining, they received half each."[129] One woman recalled that after she lost her husband, her sister-in-law, and her child, she took her young brother-in-law down and received extra compensation in the form of coal taken from the tunnels or from newly driven headings.

> When I was *atomuki* on the tunnelling and we went together, they would say, "This is the widow's coal," or "This is the sister's and brother's coal," and set aside coal for us. In tunnelling, the cost of the tunnel is calculated at so much per *ken* [about 1.8 meters] of tunnel dug. ...Because our earnings didn't amount to much, they turned over what coal was found to us.[130]

The company, although not disallowing this generosity, was not, of course, responsible for it.

Miners would not commonly have had a choice between tunneling and mining coal. In smaller mines, it seems that *sakiyama* and *atomuki* were taken off regular mining work to do the necessary tunneling. When tunneling was complete, the team might go on to mine at the new face or return to one they had been working previously. In the early days, the allocation of tunneling and framing duties was done by the *kogashira*, the representative of the *naya-gashira* (gang boss); later it was done by the *kakari*, the foreman for the company.

Blasting

The introduction of dynamite into the tunneling work increased the hazards of mining, but because it was not simultaneously used to retrieve coal itself, it did not help the miners take greater volumes from the face. Higashisada notes that as early as 1885 and 1886, blasting powder and dynamite were bought for the Namazuta mine from "powder merchants" (*kayaku-sho*),[131] indicating that their use had become fairly common. But the operators of the smaller mines could not always afford to purchase it. Much later, the survey of Japanese mining published by the Mines Bureau of the Ministry of Agriculture and Commerce (1911) stated that at the Onoura Mine in the Miike complex, where several stopes in relatively thick seams were being mined in an advanced pillar-and-room system, "The mining is all done with picks (*tsuruhashi*), and machine cutters or rock drills are not used. Blasting powder is not used for winning the ore but only for tunnelling in the stone layers."[132]

Although the use of dynamite in the bigger mines of the Chikuho region had begun as early as the mid-1880s, its application to bring down the coal wall did not achieve general acceptance until the early Taisho period, some three decades later. And even then it was used sparingly. Apparently management saw the risk of gas explosions and did not immediately authorize the use of dynamite at the face in new short-wall or even bigger room-and-pillar type operations. Only when

Work and wages   55

long-wall operations began in the 1920s did the use of dynamite for bringing down the wall become common. But the introduction of cutting machines in the 1930s made that function obsolete in the large mines where such machines were used.[133]

Even when using dynamite for tunneling to new faces, up-to-date drilling methods were not employed. There were no steam drills used in the coal mines until well after the Meiji period, though steam power had been used to operate imported machinery in Kyushu since before the Restoration,[134] and steam was commonly used to operate pumps and lifting equipment at the mines after the 1890s. In the absence of power drills, arduous work by hand was necessary. One woman describes the use of dynamite in the tunneling work.

> It was our work to tunnel in to where the coal (*ishi*) was.… It was extremely hard (rock), so for every *shaku* (foot) we took out, (we had to use) dynamite. For every inch of progress, dynamite. It was all dynamite. We had brought the clay from above wrapped in a *tenugui*. There was no clay in the pit. So down there we made a kind of short stick called *gichi* by moulding the clay. Nowadays they have ready-made ones wrapped in vinyl. [She is describing "powder dummies" tamped into the hole behind the dynamite to prevent the force of the explosion from coming back into the room.] Then we opened holes in the rock wall with a chisel and put in as many as 20 *gichi*. And we set off the dynamite. Now they have drills, but in those days we dug with a chisel. … Putting the chisel against the rock, we would hit it with a hammer. With a rap, we would open a small hole. Then turn the left hand which was holding the chisel to the inside, *kuritto*. Hit it again, and turn it, *kuritto*. Hit it again, *kuritt, kuritt*, turn and hit. You'd have a hand full of blisters.[135]

Others used an auger, longer than this woman's chisel and held between the legs, to drill deeper holes, often in less accessible places.[136]

Several women boasted of being able to do all the work connected with the setting of dynamite by themselves. One said:

> I'd drill the dynamite holes, put in the dynamite, attach the fuse, and do anything no matter how dangerous. I'd almost go crazy from the smoke which couldn't get away; there was so much moisture that sometimes I'd have to wear a straw raincoat while drilling. The powder being wet, often you couldn't get it to burn.[137]

As we'll see in Chapter 3, the use of dynamite caused not only a great deal of discomfort and anxiety among the women but also many accidents.

In the early days, the miners themselves seem to have "fired the shots" for tunneling at many mines. When, later, they were allowed to use dynamite to bring down the coal itself, miners often clung to the right, if not to fire the shots themselves, at least to have skilled miners do it for them. Morisaki, in editorial comments in *Makkura*, says that the miners paid for their own dynamite;[138] although her interviews do not substantiate this claim, one of Idegawa's does.[139]

56 *Work and wages*

Figure 2.15 Preparation and use of dynamite (Yamamoto, *Emaki*, 11th black and white illustration).

Perhaps it was only later where they did their own blasting to loosen coal in the seam that they were required to provide their own dynamite. In the Taisho period, at the bigger mines, company foremen or overseers were obliged to take most of the responsibility for firing the shots.[140]

One woman recounted not only helping an unskilled *sakiyama* when he couldn't keep up with her hauling rate but also drilling and setting dynamite by herself. However, she acknowledged that often the *kogashira* would fire the dynamite for a woman working by herself.[141] (One can imagine this "favor" leading to the sexual abuse of a less formidable woman than this "Amazon.") Another woman makes it clear that the use of dynamite to loosen the coal made possible far greater output than previously,[142] arousing our surprise that it was not put to such use much earlier. Despite the women's claims to have been competent in the use of dynamite, the men usually took a larger share of the responsibility for its setting and firing, particularly when it involved bringing down the face coal, which had been the traditional male sphere of responsibility before the belated introduction of dynamite for this purpose.

Work and wages   57

Sorting and transporting

Atoyama were hard-pressed to keep up with their *sakiyama* if they had long hauls in small mines, so they had little time to sort as well as haul the coal. Before long, therefore, most of the output was brought to the surface for sorting by women who were employed for this work alone. Because the sorting was done by a work-force of different composition than the underground mining teams, and because the process was quite separate from the extraction of coal, the work of the sorting women will be left to separate studies.[143]

Though surface jobs were physically taxing, they were not done under such harsh conditions as jobs underground, and when they disappeared due to the advent of the railways or mechanization of surface hauling and coal washing, the women lamented the loss of jobs and the unemployment that resulted. Although conveyors may have come into use in Tagawa, a Kyushu center of coal mining, as early as the Meiji period, they were not common until late Taisho (after 1920).[144] And although surface work was being mechanized gradually, the hardest work for women, hauling underground, benefited from little innovation other than the provision of larger tunnels for access in the bigger mines and perhaps some improved ventilation and drainage in the smaller ones. Where smaller mining companies depended on maximum exploitation of human labor to maintain their "bottom line," the women's work remained arduous and unrewarding.

Notes

1   Konoe Kitaro, *Chikuhō Tankō Shi*, 1898, p. 76.
2   Sumiya, *Nihon Sekitan Sangyō Bunseki*, p. 50.
3   Kaneko, *Chikuhō Tankō Kotoba*, p. 66.
4   This Japanese type of mining has been characterized as "raccoon-digging" in English, mistakenly, I think, because raccoons were introduced into Japan later. Also, the usual configuration of Japanese coal mines before sloping and long-wall operations became common in bigger operations in the 1920s resembles the underground warrens or "setts" of badgers (otherwise called *anaguma*, rather than *tanuki*, in Japanese). Cf. Nimura, *The Ashio Riot of 1907*, p. 176ff.
5   Cf. Yamamoto Sakubei, *Yama ni Ikiru*, p. 76.
6   Cf. Orii Seigo, *Hōjō Daihijō*, illustration p. 13. Also Morisaki, p. 27.
7   The contract system, called *kinsaki-bori*, is described by one retired female miner in Idegawa, p. 144, and by Kaneko Useki in *Chikuhō Tankō Kotoba*, p. 80.
8   Sumiya, p. 49. Morisaki, p. 27. See also, Nishinarita Yutaka "*Sekitan Kōgyō no Gijutsu Kakushin to Joshi Rōdō*," particularly p. 82.
9   Cf. Idegawa, pp. 103, 222; Yamamoto, *Yama ni Ikiru*, p. 97.
10   Sumiya, *Nihon Sekitan Sangyō Bunseki*, p. 164.
11   Shindo Toyo, *Chikuhō no Jokōfu-tachi*, p. 16.
12   Morisaki, p. 27.
13   Morisaki, *Makkura*, pp. 21, 111.
14   Morisaki, pp. 94, 155. Also Idegawa, pp. 40, 99.
15   *Kōzan Shiryō Shirabe*, quoted in Sumiya, *Nihon Sekitan Sangyō Bunseki*, p. 164. See also Konoe Kitaro, *Chikuhō Tankō Shi*, 1898, quoted in Shindo Toyo, *Chikuhō no Jokōfu-tachi*, p. 20.
16   Cf. Idegawa, p. 17.

58 *Work and wages*

17 Cf. Kaneko Useki, *Chikuhō Tankō Kotoba*, p. 61, and Yamamoto, *Chikuhō Tankō Emaki*, 76th black and white illustration.

18 Cf. illustrations in *Chikuhō Tankō Emaki* and in Gardner and Flores, *Forgotten Frontier: A History of Wyoming Coal Mining*, p. 36.

19 Idegawa, pp. 146–7. Also, Mashio, *Jizoko no Seishun*, p. 133.

20 Morisaki, *Makkura*, p. 155. Kaneko, *Chikuhō Tankō Kotoba*, p. 152.

21 Idegawa, p. 14.

22 Morisaki, *Makkura*, p. 53.

23 *Chikuhō Tankō Emaki*, 23rd black and white illustration. Idegawa, pp. 41, 220.

24 Morisaki, *Makkura*, pp. 122–3.

25 *Chikuhō Tankō Kotoba*, p. 63. The weight of the *kin* varied in different regions and in different times even after standard weights were established in the twentieth century, so it is difficult to be precise about these loads.

26 Kaneko, *Chikuhō Tankō Kotoba*, p. 64.

27 Idegawa, pp. 123–4.

28 Morisaki, p. 27. Yamamoto illustrates how multiple loads of coal were measured in large, bottomless baskets in the Meiji period (*Chikuhō Tankō Emaki*, 73rd black and white illustration), and stationary wooden frames were used much later at *tanuki–bori* mines. (Mashio, *Jizoko no Seishun*, p. 135).

29 One woman claims that the *sena* rather than the *sura*, which replaced it at most larger mines, was used in the big and deep Takashima mines (Morisaki, p. 46). This, of course, may have been a temporary mode or one known by her husband and not used throughout the mines.

30 Yamamoto, *Chikuhō Tankō Emaki*, 72nd black and white illustration.

31 Morisaki, p. 37.

32 See Arthur Cronin's novel, *The Stars Look Down*.

33 Cf. Gardner and Flores, *Forgotten Frontier*, pp. 34–7; Schwieder, *Black Diamonds*, p. 35.

34 *Chikuhō Tankō Emaki*, 18th black and white illustration.

35 Mashio, *Jizoko no Seishun*, pp. 61–2, 79.

36 In the northeast, the women shoveled the coal into the *tangara* as it rested on a triangular platform of logs before hefting it onto their backs. Mashio, p. 79. Cf. Idegawa, p. 122.

37 *Chikuhō Tankō Emaki*, 13th black and white illustration.

38 Idegawa, p. 79. See also p. 14 and photograph (of a reenactment?) in Shindo, *Chikuhō no Jokōfu-tachi*, p. 11.

39 Yamamoto, *Chikuhō Tankō Emaki*, 18th black and white illustration. See also Mashio, *Jizoko no Seishun*, p. 79, where Maki describes the hazardous and embarrassing results of losing one's balance and falling into the wagon. When this happened, the appreciation of the difficulty involved apparently persuaded the unfortunate *atoyama*'s competitors to abandon their usually combative attitude and their own labors to help her right herself and climb out of the wagon.

40 See Morisaki, p. 27, for a description of the three main methods of hauling coal from the face.

41 *Chikuhō Tankō Emaki*, 20th black and white illustration. See Morisaki, *Makkura*, p. 37. Also, Sumiya, *Nihon Sekitan Sangyō Bunseki*, p. 49.

42 *Chikuhō Tankō Emaki*, 2nd black and white illustration.

43 *Chikuhō Tankō Emaki*, 22nd, 24th, and 25th black and white illustrations.

44 *Chikuhō Tankō Emaki*, 8th black and white illustration.

45 *Yama ni Ikiru*, p. 101.

46 Morisaki, p. 74.

47 *Chikuhō Tankō Emaki*, 22nd black and white illustration. The type with two wooden handles on the top end of the box had two guides under the box to prevent it from going off the rails, but it could not have been in general use.

48 *Makkura*, p. 19.

49 *Chikuhō Tankō Emaki*, 24th black and white illustration.

50 *Chikuhō Tankō Emaki*, first color illustration.

Work and wages 59

51 *Chikuhō Tankō Emaki*, 21st black and white illustration.
52 Idegawa, p. 40. The "apple box" must have been about the size of modern boxes used today for bulk transport of apples in the Pacific Northwest.
53 *Chikuhō Tankō Emaki*, 17th and 37th black and white illustrations.
54 *Chikuhō Tankō Emaki*, 25th black and white illustration.
55 *Chikuhō Tankō Emaki*, 24th black and white illustration; Idegawa, pp. 25–6, 41–2; Morisaki, p. 112.
56 Morisaki, *Makkura*, pp. 10–11. See Yamamoto Sakubei, *Yama ni Ikiru*, p. 99.
57 Morisaki, p. 30.
58 Morisaki, *Makkura*, p. 39. The 1970 film, *The Molly Maguires*, starring Richard Harris and Sean Connery, has a good depiction of the kind of oil lamps with open flames that Pennsylvania coal miners wore on their cloth caps and placed on ledges and timbers about 1876. See also Lynne Bowen, *Three Dollar Dreams*, p. 128, for fish oil lamps worn similarly by Vancouver Island coal miners on their caps in the 1860s and 1870s. There is an excellent exhibition of mining lamps from various eras and countries in the *lampisterie* of the Centre Historique Minier de Lewarde, south of Lille, France.
59 Yamamoto, *Chikuhō Tankō Emaki*, 14th, 15th, 16th, and 19th black and white illustrations.
60 *Chikuhō Tankō Emaki*, 17th black and white illustration. See also the illustration in Kaneko Useki, *Chikuhō Tankō Kotoba*, p. 65.
61 Morisaki, p. 11.
62 *Chikuhō Tankō Emaki*, 24th black and white illustration.
63 *Makkura*, p. 56.
64 Morisaki, pp. 55–6.
65 An American miner explained that he had learned from "foreigners," among them Japanese miners who had been brought to Wyoming mines, how to maximize the weight of a carload of coal. Gardner and Flores, pp. 83–6.
66 *Chikuhō Tankō Emaki*, 70th black and white illustration.
67 Morisaki, p. 27. *Chikuhō Tankō Emaki*, 45th–49th black and white illustrations.
68 *Emaki*, 49th b & w illustr. See also, *Yama ni Ikiru*, pp.130–1, 134, 172; Shindo, *Chikuhō no Jokō fu-tachi*, p. 88; Morisaki, p. 9. This was the experience of pit ponies in England, where people are often said to have been more humane than the Japanese in the treatment of animals. See Cronin, *The Stars Look Down*.
69 Cf. Takematsu Teruo, *Kōnai Uma to Bafu to Jokōfu*, pp. 20, 62–3, and the table (p. 246) where, however, the costs of feeding the horses may not have been included.
70 See Mashio, p. 81; Idegawa, pp. 34, 108; and Kaneko, *Chikuhō Tankō Kotoba*, p. 125.
71 One old-timer, on the basis of notes made at the time, says that at Miike around the turn of the century, wagons were "3 ft. 3 in. long, 2 ft. 8 in. deep, and 2 ft. 6 in. wide, weighed 450 lb. unloaded and carried (on average) 934 lbs of coal (0.42 T)." (Quoted in Tanaka, *Kindai Nihon Tankō Rōdōshi Kenkyū*, p. 318) He used English units of measure, presumably in line with the Japanese managerial practice at the time, and although the dimensions of the wagons seem standard, the weights given suggest that a loaded wagon weighed more than 600 kilograms, much more than was the standard at smaller Chikuho mines.
72 Morisaki, *Makkura*, pp. 46–7. See also *Chikuhō Tankō Emaki*, 44th black and white illustration.
73 Idegawa, p. 16.
74 See Maki's recollection, in Mashio, *Jizoko no Seishun*, p. 81.
75 *Makkura*, pp. 43–4, 89.
76 Morisaki, *Makkura*, p. 47.
77 Makkura, p. 185.
78 Shindo, *Chikuhō no Jokōfu-tachi*, p. 22.
79 I am indebted to Jerry P. White (then of the Faculty of Social Science of the University of Western Ontario) for suggesting, in response to my earlier paper, that such systems often persist for different reasons even after the initial reason for implementation has disappeared.
80 *Makkura*, pp. 43–4.

60 Work and wages

81 *Makkura*, p. 74.
82 Idegawa, *Hi o Unda Haha-tachi*, p. 107.
83 Idegawa, p. 196.
84 Makkura, p. 130.
85 Mashio, *Jizoko no Seishun*, p. 75.
86 Idegawa, p. 81. Mashio mentions both name tallies and "coal vouchers" (*tanken*) used to identify wagons. *Jizoko no Seishun*, p. 78.
87 Morisaki Kazue, *Makkura*, p. 47.
88 Ibid., pp. 43–4. Shindo Toyo gives the quotation in full, except for an unfortunate omission of the sentence concerning the shouting of *"Tsumiage-ban!"* Shindo, *Chikuhō no Jokōfu-tachi*, pp. 22–3. Cf. Idegawa, *Hi o Unda Haha-tachi*, p. 34.
89 Morisaki, *Makkura*, pp. 46–8.
90 See also Mashio, *Jizoko no Seishun*, p. 78. Mashio's cogent account of the "struggle" (*ubai-ai*) for wagons seems to rely to some extent on Morisaki's interviews.
91 Morisaki, p. 11.
92 *Yama ni Ikiru*, p. 102.
93 Shindo Toyo, *Chikuhō no Jokōfu-tachi*, p. 30.
94 Morisaki, *Makkura*, p. 12.
95 Orii Seigo, *Hōjō Daihijō*, p. 21.
96 *Makkura*, p. 87. See also Idegawa, p. 124, where the "Two-Wagoner" says that she was given that nickname because of her low productivity compared to that of others who took out four or five wagonloads.
97 Idegawa, pp. 41, 188; Makkura, pp. 47–8.
98 "Female Labor in the Japanese Coal Mining Industry," in Hunter, p. 107.
99 Idegawa, p. 93. For quotas in the textile factories, see Tsurumi, *Factory Girls*, pp. 148–53. In 1930, the Japan Coal Miners' Union was asking for six-hour shifts, no doubt for the male miners who did the digging, and this "demand" was linked with a request for a minimum wage and an end to the piece-rate system, which had made long hours obligatory for the women at least. Tanaka, *Kindai Nihon Tankō Rōdōshi Kenkyū*, p. 475.
100 Matsumoto Kichinosuke, *Chikuhō ni Ikiru*, p. 32.
101 *Yama ni Ikiru*, pp. 102–3. Deductions were dictated by an elaborate scale at bigger mines such as Miike. See the Coal Inspection Regulations (*Kentan Kisoku*) cited in Yamazu Naoko, *"Miike Tankō no Saitan Rōdō"* in *Mitsui Bunko Ronsō*, no. 8, 1974, pp. 121–2.
102 Idegawa, p. 136.
103 Morisaki, p. 13.
104 Morisaki, *Makkura*, pp. 27, 156, 175.
105 *Makkura*, p. 13.
106 *Yama ni Ikiru*, p. 103. Also, Morisaki, p. 14.
107 Morisaki, p. 14.
108 Morisaki, p. 39; Shindo, p. 70. See Idegawa, p. 178, for repayment of loans for tools bought by the miners.
109 See Smith, "Digging Through Layers of Class, Gender and Ethnicity," in Lahiri-Dutt and Macintyre, p. 115, footnote 7.
110 See Sumiya, *Nihon Sekitan Sangyō Bunseki*, p. 13, for added costs of timbering in Tokugawa times.
111 Cf. Idegawa, p. 78. Yamamoto Sakubei has illustrations of different types of frames and framing techniques in his *Chikuhō Tankō Emaki*; many of them are reproduced in a smaller format in *Yama ni Ikiru*. Mock-ups of mine shafts such as those at the Iwaki City Coal and Fossil Museum (see http://www.japan-guide.com/e/e7779.html) are another mode of illustration that gives a realistic, though partial, appreciation of the state of framing techniques at various times.
112 Morisaki, p. 56.

Work and wages 61

113 In John Sayles's 1987 film *Matewan*, the experienced black miner shows the novice white kid how to judge the soundness of the roof by tapping with the pick handle and feeling the vibrations with the other hand. This was in the early twentieth century in West Virginia. Cf. Gardner & Flores, *Forgotten Frontier*, p. 35, re the practice in Wyoming, and Schwieder, *Black Diamonds*, pp. 35, 37, for that in Iowa.
114 Morisaki, p. 173.
115 Cf. Idegawa, p. 90.
116 Morisaki, p. 114.
117 Idegawa, p. 157.
118 Morisaki, p. 75.
119 *Jizoko no Seishun*, pp. 63–4.
120 Makkura, pp. 11, 27, 39. Idegawa, p. 159.
121 Idegawa, p. 77.
122 Ibid., p. 78. Yamamoto, *Chikuhō Tankō Emaki*, 33rd black and white illustration. Also *Yama ni Ikiru*, p. 159. See also, Idegawa, p. 113.
123 Idegawa, p. 112. Cf. *Chikuhō Tankō Emaki*, 38th and 41st black and white illustrations; *Yama ni Ikiru*, pp. 157–8. Tunnel walls were held in place by rough lattices or by crude trellises running along the wall. See many *Chikuhō Tankō Emaki* illustrations.
124 Idegawa, p. 148.
125 See Schwieder, *Black Diamonds*, pp. 29, 49. Cross entries and air shafts served as alternative escape routes in case of fires or explosions.
126 Idegawa, pp. 166–7.
127 Cf. *Makkura*, p. 18; Idegawa, p. 68.
128 *Jizoko no Seishun*, p. 70.
129 Morisaki, *Makkura*, p. 177. Cf. Idegawa, pp. 42, 185.
130 Idegawa. pp. 112–3. See also, Mashio, *Jizoko no Seishun*, p. 80.
131 Higashisada Nobumasa, "*Chikuhō Sekitan Kōgyō ni okeru Kindai-ka Katei*," in Ogino Yoshihiro, *Senzen-ki Chikuhō Tankōgyō no Keiei to Rōdō*, p. 26 and footnote76, p. 36.
132 Quoted in Tanaka, *Kindai Nihon Tankō Rōdōshi Kenkyū*, p. 318.
133 For the (belated) introduction of various forms of blasting powders, drilling machines, and coal cutters, see Kozan Konwa Kai, ed., *Nippon Kōgyō Hattatsushi*, *chūkan* vol., pp. 261–76.
134 See Thomas C. Smith, *Political Change and Industrial Development in Japan*, p. 8.
135 *Makkura*, pp. 18–19. For illustrations of the drilling work and tamping dynamite, see Yamamoto, *Chikuhō Tankō Emaki*, first colored and 11th black and white illustrations; *Yama no Shigoto*, pp. 106–7.
136 Cf. Idegawa, p. 41.
137 Idegawa, p. 183.
138 Morisaki, p. 27.
139 *Hi o Unda Haha-tachi*, p. 165. "*Maito wa kōfu no jibun mochi yatta to yo*."
140 See Morisaki, *Makkura*, p. 177.
141 Idegawa, pp. 41, 47.
142 Idegawa, p. 79.
143 A fascinating account of the work of sorting or "picking" women in England, not very different from the methods used in Japan, can be found in Angela John, *By the Sweat of Their Brow*, pp. 82–5. See also John's *Coalmining Women*, particularly the picture on p. 28, and Yamamoto, *Chikuhō Tankō Emaki*, 71st black and white illustration.
144 Engineer-historian Nagatsumi Junjiro mentions the early use of conveyors in Tagawa but notes that the availability of cheap female labor precluded the widespread use of "such equipment." "*Ōshū Taisen-ji ni okeru Waga Kuni no Tankyō*" in Nihon Kagaku Shi Gakkai, ed., *Nippon Kagaku-gizyutusi Taikei*, vol. 20, p. 277.

3   Working conditions

Funa-nori wa issun no inochi
Gobu, gobu de owari.
Kofū wa ikkoku no inochi
Goto, goto de owari.[1]
   A seaman lives on the brink of disaster
   and his life ends as the water swallows him up.
   A miner subsists on one *koku*[2] of rice
   and his life ends as the cave-in engulfs him.

Darkness, wetness, heat, and grime

Those who "went down" as young women remembered their first impressions of the eerie nether-world into which they had descended. One recounted:

> Although I knew it would be dark, I was surprised how dark it was. I was afraid. If one's lamp went out, it wasn't just like a moonless night (above ground)! And in the mines, there were 15, or even 40 or 50 shafts branching out like the limbs of a tree in every direction. It was so dark that one felt you didn't know where the bounds were.[3]

Finding one's way in the dark was hazardous. In a Joban mine, Maki had been afraid of stumbling into a pool collecting the hot run-off water beside the main roadway.[4]

In the 1920s, electric lighting would be used in the shafts of the bigger mines, but the threat of sparks from defective or worn wiring and poor connections endangered the miners' lives. In illegal mining operations (*nusuto-bori*, literally robber mines), the darkness required to avoid surveillance was more dangerous than poor lighting.

> Since we were digging illegally in abandoned mines, why would there be any safety measures or anything like that? We did it only to earn money.[5]

Working conditions   63

In more common legal operations, undefined sounds and the scantiness of their clothing in the heat underground led some women to feel vulnerable and isolated. Some give vivid descriptions of the eerie quiet of the mine after the digging, framing, and blasting had ceased. Another woman remembered:

> To describe the mine, well, it was like a beehive. It was okay when everyone was there, but when you were left behind to load coal, it was silent and lonely all round. You'd look around to see if someone was standing behind you. It wasn't a good feeling.[6]

Accidents could happen between shift changes, leaving a woman without work-mates to assist her in time of need. One woman whose foot was caught under a boulder was not extricated until the second shift came to her rescue. Over a period of time, however, the women got used to the darkness as well as the uncanny silence.

> In the coal mines, although we worked in the dark through the whole year, the dark shafts weren't frightening. Well, of course it was terrible! But we got used to it. … When I was a girl, mould grew pure white on the timber frames, long strands of it waving about. When it shone white [probably in the light of the miners' lamps], it was frightening. As well, the silence underground was different from silence above ground. The soft thud, *pechan, pechan*, of one's "better-half" straw sandals would be absorbed in the ground water.[7]

Sandals deteriorated quickly in such conditions and were not adequate protection against coal fragments that could not be seen in the dark. In some mines, the best coal "was like glass, and when a piece of coal struck the foot, you'd remember it," another miner recalled.[8]

Other women described the invariably wet conditions, with the risk of floods at lower levels and the danger of slipping on watery walkways or on saturated ladders.

> In the first coal mine I went down, it was coming down in bucket-fulls. Water kept coming down like rain in the tunnels. Wearing rain-capes and hats, the men were up to their hips in water in the pitch dark.[9]

In many mines, heat and water combined to make conditions extremely uncomfortable.

> Carrying the *tebo* (basket) up from the bottom of the *oroshi* … the sweat poured off like an unscrolling bamboo blind. One's feet slipped in the torrent of water, and one's back dripped with drizzling water.[10]

Mashio says that in some coal mines in the northeast, the run-off water could be so hot that it stung the skin, and cooling-off tubs had to be provided for miners to dunk themselves between short campaigns at the face.[11] In Kyushu, pools were used for collecting the run-off water that flowed endlessly in many mines. Small

64   *Working conditions*

mines were often flooded out in the rainy season (mid-June into July), and some were soaked by normal precipitation and seepage in other seasons. This could halt mining for considerable periods of time or could sometimes close the mine. When water pressure broke through rock strata or dams in old workings, releasing accumulations of water, the resultant floods could drown miners.

As shafts went deeper into the ground, often below water tables, or under seabeds in regions other than Chikuho,[12] pumps were required to deal with excess water. In one mine,

> [a] pump continuously pumped out the water, but sometimes it broke down. The water built up in a twinkling. A voice would come down from above. "Hey! Come up! It's broken down!" and when the wagon came down, we'd jump in and go up.[13]

Mashio says that in two of the wettest mines of the Joban coalfield, as much as 30 tons of water at temperatures between 62 and 65 degrees Celsius had to be pumped out for every ton of coal taken.[14] Chikuho mines were similarly wet. As well as causing discomfort, water made the work difficult. Mining tools were difficult to grip and wield effectively, and the coal and waste grew heavier (adding nothing to the value of the wagon-loads and thus to the wages in the early days because the wagons were not weighed but merely counted). Water also made the scuttles and hauling equipment difficult to handle. But above all, the slopes up or down to the face became dangerous for the female hauliers. Heaving the *sura* up the wet rails was "like pulling a soaking wet wooden box up a ladder."[15] If, by chance, it was an exceptionally dry mine, the rails might be watered so that the heavy *sura* would slide more easily, but in that case "the dripping water would make the track very slippery."[16] Where miners were mining secretly in a relatively dry "badger mine," the need to make the *sura* slide was solved in a novel way. One miner recounted:

> We pulled the *sura* up distances of 100 *ken* (180 meters) or more, but on a steep slope with no ladder (*koro*), we were hard put to make the *sura* slide properly. We had to spread water and wet the ground, either spraying water from our flasks or, when that was used up, wetting the surface with piss.
> One after the other, we took turns pissing on it.[17]

Even in legal mining operations, where the slopes were slippery, the women did not like following others up or leading the way down the slope with the *sura*. A combination of the slippery steepness of the slopes and the awkward stooping positions in which the women worked resulted in stress, stumbles, and falls causing frequent miscarriages.

> Once, in a shaft where there was no track, water fell persistently. I was carrying the *sena* up the incline where notches had been cut in the ground. Slipping all the way. In a twinkling, I lost my footing and fell

Working conditions 65

into the wagon below. The light in my lamp went out. And I was covered with soot. The child in my belly was in its seventh month and I thought I would lose it.[18]

The presence of a lot of water may have ameliorated the discomfort from heat in some of the shallower mines. In new *tanuki-bori* mines near the surface, heat would not have been a problem except in the hot and humid Kyushu summers, and even then the cooler caverns may have provided some relief from the enervating climate. But as the shafts were sunk deeper in the Meiji period, the temperatures rose to virtually unbearable levels. The frequently cited report by Matsuoka Koichi in the newspaper *Nihonjin* in 1888 described conditions in the Takashima Mine off Nagasaki Harbor.

> The temperature got hotter the farther down in the mine one went. At the most extreme point it reached 120 to 130 degrees Fahrenheit [50-55°C] on the thermometer. The miners labor ceaselessly in this debilitating heat, their bodies seemingly bathed in pouring sweat. Air is lacking and breathing is painful. The stench of coal penetrates the nose and makes it almost unbearable.[19]

One retired woman recalled the excruciating heat:

> The Koyanose mines were certainly hot! If sweet potatoes were buried in the stones, they'd come out roasted. If new-cut frame timbers were put up, they'd become bone dry. If we couldn't push our wagons out to the winding frame and enjoy the cool breeze created by dumping the wagons, it was unbearable. Eventually, we'd plunge into puddles of collected water in our clothes just to cool off our bodies.[20]

Paradoxically, polluted water on the ground was not available for slaking the thirst of the miners. And in these conditions, the women needed to drink prodigious quantities of water to avoid dehydration.

> At this Nakama coal mine, most of the faces were hot. So hot that we'd drink up to five *shō* (9 liters) of water (a day). ... Just see what would happen if by accident your buttocks slumped onto the track! Sometimes the bare arses of men wearing only loin-cloths would be singed.[21]

Mashio described attempts by women in the Joban mines to deal with the heat.

> Even though they chewed 3 or 4 *umeboshi* (pickled plums) in a row, they consumed them without tasting any saltiness or sourness. Their thirst was extreme, and when they inadvertently drank too much water, their stomachs would be upset.[22]

66   *Working conditions*

Most coal miners wore very little clothing, not because of any lack of modesty but because of what another woman described as the "steam-bath" (*mushiburo*) underground.[23] At some mines, men left their living quarters clad only in a cloth or towel wrapped around their loins, and in the heat underground they often shed even these loincloths.[24] One woman noted that this lack of protective clothing subjected miners to all sorts of injuries.[25] The miners' apparent lack of inhibitions regarding nakedness was consistent with sharing by men and women of mine-operated and public baths above ground. In the deeper mines, women stripped to the waist.

Later, air shafts were dug and some ventilation equipment was installed at the larger mines, which also tended to be the deeper ones.[26] Still later, air pumps were installed in some of the smaller mines as well. But such facilities and equipment were rarely adequate.[27] The miners suffered heat rashes and other discomforts caused by sweating. Heat in the deeper coal mines made the heavy exertion required by mining methods of the time all the more enervating and often debilitating to both men and women.

Like the heat, the pervasive coal dust could not be avoided. It clogged the miners' nostrils and larynxes, making breathing difficult. One woman reported that even in a later period, "No matter how big a fan was deployed, there were times when the mine atmosphere made breathing impossible."[28] And after working in this atmosphere for some years, the lungs could become diseased and cause death. The unpleasant smell of the dust was added to worse smells in some recesses of the mines. Because of the absence of toilets, the miners sought out abandoned shafts and cross entries to defecate or urinate. They also sometimes went to these places to look for delinquent workmates.

> One's *sakiyama* sometimes went missing. Generally speaking, if he didn't dig coal for you, the *atoyama* couldn't work. What the Hell! What's he doing? one would wonder. If you went there (to the *bakku*) to look for him, it was so smelly that you'd have to hold your nose. Or you'd get sick to the stomach.[29]

Coal dust in the mines made work difficult and cleanliness impossible. Some women were allergic to it.

> My older sister was said to be a mining beauty. Because the coal dust irritated her skin, she powdered her neck and went down the pit with it as white as snow. In the dark, it looked quite beautiful.[30]

Although it was young women who were particularly conscious of their appearance, daily washing of hair was probably considered a necessity by women old and young. The coal dust would "stick like glue, even in the eyelids," one recalled.[31]

For nursing mothers who took their babies down into the pit with them when there was nobody to care for them above, the dust was particularly troublesome.

Coal soot would cling to us. When giving the breast to a baby, if one didn't moisten the nipples with saliva and wipe them, you couldn't feed it. Even the earholes and nostrils became completely black.[32]

At some of the bigger mines, babies were left in a hut near the pit mouth. Breast-feeding women who came out to nurse their babies also had to clean their breasts.

Resourceful miners were occasionally able to make use of the coal dust for their own purposes, however. When not allowed to collect carbon-laced rock or timber waste allocated to them as fuel by more enlightened managements, and when they could not steal it or pure coal, some would collect soot, mainly above-ground, and make briquettes from it.

We children would gather the coal soot which had been discarded, mix it with clay and make cakes out of it. As we weren't given much fuel, we'd make cakes of the soot, laying out hundreds of them on the floor. It was the children's job.[33]

But while on the surface the soot may have seemed a boon, underground coal dust combined with heat was a real menace.

As we were almost completely naked, we continuously suffered minor injuries, falling or being hit, and I have tattoos everywhere to show for it. With the soot just as it entered the wound, as we usually treated our own injuries, the coal (dust) remained black (under the skin).[34]

Disease

Surprisingly, the women interviewed by Morisaki and Idegawa did not show great concern about the effects of dust in the lungs, but some of the illnesses they reported were obviously due to breathing dust-laden air. One woman lost three husbands, one of silicosis—which is caused by prolonged inhalation of dust—and another of palsy.[35] Another lost her husband, her sister-in-law, and one of her children to typhus "within half a year."[36] From her experience mining in the Joban coalfields, however, Mashio's protagonist Maki argued that silicosis was not the main scourge of coal miners. Neuralgia and stomach trouble, caused by precautions that the miners took against dehydration, even occasionally drinking the polluted water that dripped from the mine roof, were much more common, she said. Another disease common in the northeast, called *akamari*, was similar to sun- or heat-stroke and required immediate therapy to stop the stiffening of muscles, swelling of arteries, and convulsions.[37] Regine Mathias asserts that digestive disorders were more pervasive among coal miners than respiratory illnesses, and that female miners were more susceptible than males to both kinds of ailment.[38]

Dr. Ishihara Osamu, in his pioneering study of working conditions in factories and mines between 1909 and 1913, confirms that the incidence of disease at the

68 *Working conditions*

coal mines was much higher among female miners than among males. This discrepancy was particularly pronounced among Chikuho miners, the largest group in his limited sample. In Japan as a whole, for every 1,000 male miners there were 963 incidents of disease on average, but among 1,000 females, 1359 incidents, indicating that some women suffered more than one illness per year; if some went unscathed, others must have reported two or more cases.[39] Although the reported incidence of tuberculosis (TB) at Japanese coal mines was surprisingly low (only 6.7 cases for men and 10 for women in every 1,000 cases of reported illness or injury), the ratio of deaths from those cases was high in the early years of the twentieth century.[40] As many as one-eighth of all female deaths in the coal mines, but only one-twentieth of all male deaths, were the result of TB. Thus, TB could be particularly lethal for women. Other respiratory diseases also reaped a high toll: one-fifth of all deaths among female coal miners were due to them. Ishihara found a higher death rate due to TB among women working at coal mines than among those working at metal mines, probably explained by the greater contamination of coal dust and the higher numbers working underground in the collieries[41] Female coal miners suffered similarly higher rates of mortality due to other respiratory diseases. In some Chikuho mines, the ever-dripping water may have washed some of the dust out of the air and decreased the hazards of air pollution, but such mines probably contributed to arthritic and rheumatic illnesses. As well, female coal miners had 55 cases of urinary and reproductive problems per 1,000 workers while male coal miners had only 23.[42]

Syphilis was not uncommon, and prognostications for the success of treatment varied.[43] If male miners were prone to venereal diseases, women in mining districts must have suffered from contact with them. One female miner contracted this "occupational disease" (*wazabyō*) during a youthful interlude when she was indentured to a "tea house" in the port of Hikojima;[44] such establishments in mining districts no doubt contributed to the significant incidence of sexually transmitted diseases among women as well as men. Ishihara reported an average of 23 cases of "social diseases" (*karyū-byō*) per 1,000 women working in Japanese coal mines, almost as high as that of men.[45]

Other diseases and physical problems plagued coal miners as well. Mashio, reflecting Maki's recollections, wrote:

> Athlete's foot on the toes was a trade-mark of those who worked under-ground. There was no one who was not covered with the eczema called *tanmake*. It was unbearably itchy. But if you once started to scratch it, you'd become so obsessed with it that you couldn't do your work. Even though boils formed and broke, the itchiness wouldn't go away.[46]

Fire and explosions

At some mines, coal dust represented an immediate hazard when gas was present. A gas emission, often igniting a fire, could initiate a chain reaction in which accumulations of dust would explode and spread fire throughout the mine. The recollections of several of the retired female miners suggest that the gas was usually methane, explosive when concentrated in dust-laden air. The accounts of the women remind us of stories about the dangers of "black damp" or fire-damp in the coal mines of England and Wales.[47] Before the introduction of safety lamps, Japanese miners followed their British counterparts in using live canaries to indicate the presence of dangerous accumulations of gas. "That was the deepest place, where there was a lot of gas," one miner recounted. "It was a place where you had to keep a canary constantly beside you to measure the gas."[48] Methane gas was lighter than air and, even when escaping in quantity, did not always fill the whole of a horizontal tunnel, as some accounts suggest.

> At the Fukuoka Mine of Nishijin, there was gas. It wasn't thick gas, but still there was gas. … At the time of the accident, my uncle, his younger sister and myself were down in the mine. We were wearing [ordinary?] clothes and my uncle was wearing his work-suit with a *tenugui* around his neck. It was a place near the mezzanine. When my uncle held up his lamp, flames jumped with a noise, *battsu*! It made a sound, well, like the sound of a big mine explosion. When you strike a match, so, it burns with a reddish or bluish flame, and that's the kind of a fire which breaks out. Gas doesn't burn lower down at first. "Ah! this is gas," I thought, holding my breath. "Everything will burn!" And while I was thinking so, it spread in all directions, *patto*! It wasn't burning down low. My uncle immediately dropped to his knees. (But) the fire was all over his suit. It was even burning the *tenugui* around his neck. Uncle attempted to crawl out. His face was badly burnt. … It was terrible![49]

Her uncle would be disfigured for life.

Another miner spoke of the speed with which a "fire-wind" (*hikaze*) spread and of the danger of ignition of the coal dust in a fiery explosion.

> In the mine, a gas fire broke out. Gas fires would run like the wind in mid-air through the tunnel. Since I was pushing wagons at the time, I hid under the wagon. *Dō-tsu*! The fire-wind flew with the sound and then came back again. That fire-wind was so terrible that a [heavy brattice] door which wouldn't move without four or five people pushing it was blown open by its force.
>
> That time, two people died. The woman was thrown down and her forehead split. The man was burnt right through his shirt. It was tragic!
>
> If coal dust caught on the gas fire, it was all over. If the coal dust had exploded that time, I would've died. So that the accumulated dust wouldn't catch fire, the mine labourers had been spreading rock dust and spraying water, but it wasn't easy to spread that rock dust. Carrying a lime bag on one's back, you had to scatter it until everything was white.[50]

70 *Working conditions*

This woman pointed out that where such fires could occur once, they could recur, and she and her husband were glad to put the Akaike Mine at their backs, even though it was a government-owned mine where conditions might be expected to have been better than in privately owned ones.

The standard advice to younger miners during a fire, as one man recounted, was "Don't stand up! And running is even worse. You escape in a crouch as low as if you are crawling with your belly on the ground."[51] Carbon monoxide (called *shibire-gasu*, or numbing gas, in Kyushu, and "white damp" in the United States), which resulted from explosions, was toxic at one part in 100,000 and lethal at one in 1,000. Most of the retired women, however, speak of the danger of initial methane explosions rather than of gas poisoning.

The Ogawa family, when obliged to leave the Rengeji Mine due to its closure, went to a small, shallow mine called Sugitani. The wife recalled a fiery explosion at the mine:

> There we worked by the light of naked flames. One morning...because we hadn't yet reached the coal (in a new heading), I was about to take a short rest and was squatting down behind my husband. My old man was digging with the naked flame down beside his haunches. I'd hung mine between the frames and was squatting behind him. At that moment, from the tunnel extending away on the left, came a sound, "*gusu, gusugusu, gusugusugusu*." It was just like water boiling.

Both husband and wife recognized the sound as one of an impending gas burst.

> The flame I had hung up went out all of a sudden. The gas beyond attracted the flame. When I yelled "Aagh!" he yelled "Don't panic!" but I wasn't panicking.

The Ogawas escaped, but not before warning their fellow workers of the danger. Some seem to have thought the warning was a false alarm, but the foreman was eager to preserve his own life.

> Then the foreman ... leaving his naked flame just as was, and all by himself, without saying anything, fled. So everyone, saying what a fool he was, went out after him. It all happened in such a short time, my heart was beating wildly. Escaping to a place where ventilation was good and looking back, everything was on fire. It burned bright red like the flames in a furnace. And made a sound like "*Gōtto!*"
>
> When we came out and reported it to the office, they said, "Can this really be? There's never been a gas leak here." So my husband took them (and showed them). The whole place was on fire. ...
>
> In the evening, thinking that it would be over, they borrowed safety lamps and attempted to enter, but it was no use. ... Where there's gas, the small flame of the safety lamp becomes longer. And the outside mesh burns bright red,

Working conditions 71

eventually bursting the glass cover. So even though they wanted to go in and see the condition of the shafts, it was too dangerous and they couldn't enter.[52]

There follows the tragic story of the entry of an inspection team the next day, when experimental digging at the location of the earlier gas leak caused an explosion that killed a miner who had taken her husband's place when he uncharacteristically became ill the night before. The victim's son, a 10-year-old, had just turned away to take his father's damaged pick point to be tempered when the explosion occurred, and only the hair on the back of the boy's head was singed. The supervisors were apparently saved by their protective clothing.

My husband was extremely sorry for the one who had taken his place, and said so over and over again. The unfortunate fellow died instantly. As if rags had been stripped from him, his skin peeled and hung down.[53]

Others attributed the Ogawas' salvation to their Buddhist faith.[54] Thinking of their own children, however, they were not willing to trust their faith at that mine any longer, despite the management's appeals to them not to leave.

"Don't say that! We're having everyone use safety lamps. We won't let them use naked flames. We've made sure that gas won't leak again, so don't quit. What will you do if you quit? How will you feed your children?"

Though Mrs. Ogawa felt these very concerns, she was not likely to be taken in by the fatuous promise to prevent further gas leaks. In the absence of any family funds or severance pay, they were forced to go to the notorious Miyoshi Mine nearby.[55] Among the bad working conditions at Miyoshi, there was the recurrent problem of gas.

In the far reaches, there was gas. So the safety lamp flame grew long. When it lengthened, we hid it carefully under our bodies. Only when we put it in the bosom of our clothing, the flame became small again. We worked with it like that.[56]

And now she thanked the gods and Buddhas that she had never been seriously injured, though she had seen her workmates killed and maimed.

The practice of hiding the safety lamps in their clothing, of course, obviated the warning function of the lamps and made working in the dark more difficult. Another woman describes a similarly dangerous practice:

There were faces [in the mine] where the flame in the *kantera* went out suddenly. Then we couldn't do our work. Removing the *kuchi* (bung), we'd cover it with an old cloth, so that the rag burned. And in places where gas was so common, we'd keep working while fanning it away with an *uchiwa* (round, non-folding fan) or spreading vinegar.[57]

72 *Working conditions*

Another miner spoke of similar simple precautions against gas:

> At a place where gas had been common recently, we'd do such things as spreading vinegar around. There was no ventilation at the *harai* (big mining room). We ate *natsu mikan* (summer oranges) so that we wouldn't be affected by gas.[58]

After the Hōjō mine explosion of December 15, 1914, when miners were still trapped underground, company officials cut up basketfuls of summer oranges and threw them down the main shaft, apparently hoping the oranges would help dissipate gas. When the rescue team went into the mine, "Each held a summer orange in their mouth and went down breathing only through their noses."[59] Even at the time it was known by some Japanese scientists that, "Such things as tangerines and summer oranges can have only restorative uses, and from the point of view of scientific functions there is no intelligible significance, so they are completely without value" for gas-suppression purposes.[60] Moreover, as Orii Seigo points out, the velocity of oranges (even if cut up) plummeting down a 280-meter shaft might have been enough to severely injure those who had gathered at the bottom to await rescue. The deficiencies of this type of accident response were typical of accident prevention systems as well in the coal mines of the Meiji period, when the danger of gas fires and explosions increased as the miners burrowed further into the depths of the earth.

Programs for responding to serious accidents revealed management's concern for the "bottom line." Among steps taken to curtail the spread of fires in the coal mines, the sealing of shafts was the most drastic—especially if there was a possibility that miners had miraculously survived the initial blast or fire-storm. Maki recalled the disaster at the Machida Mine in 1926 in which 134 people were killed:

> It was a Sunday. Those who worked hard, regardless of whether it was a holiday or a Sunday, were hit. Since the fire started at the bottom of the vertical shaft, if it wasn't dealt with quickly, it would spread. They must have thought that, even if some people's lives had to be sacrificed, the Company's damages had to be reduced, the mine saved. So, dare I say it, that was why the Company adopted the policy of putting a lid on the shaft to put out the fire. Since those who were working below had their exit blocked, there was nothing they could do.[61]

Maki's former boyfriend's father was among those "asphyxiated as if roasted." Based on Maki's recollections of the disposition of the corpses in some parts of the Machida mine, Mashio gives a gruesome account of the trapped miners' attempts to save themselves and their wives in their dying hours. By closing the shaft, escaped miners believed, the company prevented any survivors of the initial fire and/or blast from breathing and surviving longer. Company managers had already shown disregard for the lives and welfare of their

Working conditions 73

Table 3.1 Deaths in Various Sectors of the Hōjō Mine, December 1914

Sector	Deaths
Left Nogi Ascent	112
Right Mata Descent area	250
New Ōyama Fourth Descent area	60
Second New Kuroki Descent	88
Second New Mata, Right Slope	70
Ditto, Left No.3 Descent	50
Third New Mata Descent	50

(*Source*: Orii Seigo, *Hōjō Daihijō* [The Hōjō Disaster], pp. 61–2.)

workers in other ways, which fueled the miners' perceptions of their callousness after the disaster.

Like the casualties of the Machida fire, the victims of the Hōjō disaster of 1914 may have been denied any chance of escape by the closure of the shaft soon after the blast. The *Fukuoka Nichi-Nichi* newspaper reported a total of 680 deaths on December 22, 1914, one week after the Hōjō explosion.[62]

The Mitsubishi Mining Company history of 1976 (*Mitsubishi Kōgyō Shashi*) gives the total as 687 deaths, but Orii adumbrates considerable circumstantial evidence to suggest that the actual number was between 700 and 1,000 or more.[63] In the official count by Mitsubishi, 132 of the total deaths in the underground workforce were identifiable as female, though other bodies were so badly burnt that their gender could not be determined.[64] Although identifiable female deaths comprised about 19 per cent of the total deaths, only two of 19 people saved were female.[65] In such a widespread slaughter, the ratios of the small numbers of different genders saved may have little significance, but it is important to note that there was a large number of women working underground, and only a small number survived. Yet few males were probably widowed by the Hōjō disaster because most women worked with their husbands. It is difficult to comprehend the extent of such a tragedy—the number of lives lost, wives widowed, children orphaned, and friends obliterated.

The combination of coal dust in the air and leaking gas at the Hōjō mine had made for a highly combustible mixture. The gas was the common methane, not by itself easily combustible at the low concentrations claimed to have been present in most parts of the mine by scholarly advisers to the Mitsubishi management. Little could be done to prevent gas leaks because current geological expertise could not predict underground bodies of gas and map out ways of avoiding them.[66] But good ventilation could have removed both the gas and the coal dust in the air. Orii talked to Hōjō people who remembered that the company began to practice the approved methods of damping down coal dust *after* the explosion. Laying of the dust by spreading lava ash—done liberally when bigwigs were due to visit the mine, according to some miners—could lessen concentrations in the air. And sprinkling of water with hoses rather than random sprinkling "with dippers of water from an

74   *Working conditions*

Table 3.2 Major Japanese Coal Mine Disasters Before 1930

Mine Name	Date	Numbers Killed
Fushun Ōyama, Manchuria	January 11, 1917	917
Mitsubishi Hōjō Mine, Kyushu	December 15, 1914	671+
Ishikari Sekitan, Shin-Yūbari, Wakanabe Colliery, Hokkaido	November 28, 1914	423
Kaijima Ōnoura Mine, Kyushu	December 21, 1917	369
Toyokuni Colliery, Kyushu	July 20, 1907	365 (364 – Sumiya)
Mitsubishi Takashima, Kyushu	March 28, 1906	307
Yūbari, Second Incline, Hokkaido	April 29, 1912	267
Onoura, Kirino Mine	November 24, 1909	256
Toyokuni Colliery	June 15, 1899	210

(*Sources*: Disasters killing more than 300 from Orii Seigo, *Hōjō Daihijō*, p. 106. Sumiya relates the considerable number of disasters killing more than 50 people before 1913 to the spurt in growth of the collieries during and after the Russo-Japanese War [1904–05], when production was increased rapidly to enhance the military clout of the Japanese Empire. Sumiya Mikio, *Nihon Sekitan Sangyō Bunseki*, p. 342.)

oil can" could bring the moisture content of the remaining coal dust up to the 30 per cent at which it was noncombustible.[67] One miner remembered that these precautions were more rigorously carried out at the Onoura mines of the Kaijima Co.,[68] but such precautions may have been taken only after the lethal explosions of 1909 or 1917 at their Kirino shaft in Onoura. Soon after the 1914 Hōjō disaster, new regulations were instituted by the Fukuoka Mines Administration, and the spreading of nonflammable rock dust and the spraying of water—measures already taken in American and British coal mines—brought a modicum of safety to large Japanese mines. But until 1916, the reluctance of management to take such measures raised questions about their supposed concern for their workers and bred disdain among the mining women.[69] If such measures were instituted belatedly in large and deep coal mines, one can imagine the inadequacy of the precautions against explosive mixtures of gas and dust in the many smaller mines.

Table 3.3 Causes of Injuries in Japanese Coal Mines, 1924–26

Cause of Injuries	No. of Incidents
Cave-ins	1,557
Mechanical haulage or lifting	658
Coal wagons	549
Explosions (dynamite)	99
Electrical	52
Flooding	35
Combustibles (tobacco, matches, etc.)	5
Other	868

(*Source*: Orii Seigo, *Hōjō Daihijō*, pp. 166–7, citing *Nihon Kōgyō Hattatsu Shi*.)

Cave-ins and other nasty accidents

As serious as gas fires and explosions were, they were not as common as cave-ins and hauling accidents. Ishihara cites annual government statistics to show that about half of all injuries and deaths in Japanese mines were due to cave-ins.[70] This was consistent with the experience in Britain, where "about 50 per cent of the fatal accidents in coal-mines" as well as "40 per cent of the serious and non-fatal accidents" were due to "falls of ground," a situation that was not rectified until after 1945.[71] The *Nihon Kōgyō Hattatsu Shi*, a standard history of the Japanese mining industry published in 1932, shows that between 1924 and 1926, cave-ins and accidents with hauling equipment were the major causes of injuries in Japanese mines.[72] Further, many more casualties resulted from cave-ins in coal mines than in other types of mines.

One woman mixes her recollections of a particular cave-in with a description of the general conditions under which they occurred.

> There's always a warning when a cave-in is coming. Waiting for the (rest of the) roof to come down, the five of us kept only two lamps lit, and quickly tried to work our way out along the side of the roof, while others tried to get to us from the outside. While we were trying to make a way out and calling to each other from this side and the other, a girl who had become frightened was lamenting whether we'd be rescued, so I encouraged her, saying, "Don't be afraid! Since we'll surely get out, there's no need to cry. ..."
>
> If there was one fall, a second one might come *gadatt!* at any time, and the second one is worse. When my sister died, it was the second one that got her.
>
> By-and-by, we saw the light of the lamps on the other side. Thinking that we were safe, and that we should get out fast while the roof held, first the women, pushing aside the rock, crawled out on top, and, just after the men crawled out one after the other, another fall came, *daatt!* Really, it happened just like that![73]

Even if warning sounds were heeded, it was not always possible to escape before the cave-in occurred. Another woman remembered:

> When we were at Iwasaki, there were four of us, working just below the face. But fall-ins started to come down between us and the shaft mouth. It was a cave-in. While I was thinking, Oh oh! it all came down and the way out for the four of us was blocked. Water flowed. The evacuation pump was knocked out by the cave-in, so it couldn't help us where we were. Was it terrible? Well, that kind of accident happened countless times.[74]

"That kind of accident" happened so many times that she seems to have forgotten exactly how they were rescued and goes on to describe another incident, in which

76   *Working conditions*

her salvation was ascribed to her Nichiren faith. In confirming that faith, she forgets to account for her husband, but he was saved, perhaps after a less harrowing experience.

Being left behind to load after the *sakiyama* had gone out could endanger the lives of the *atoyama*. Kawashima Taka describes how she was caught in a cave-in and not released until the next shift came in. She had been raking up coal loosened from the roof that was shored up because a large section was unstable.[75] It came down anyway.

> I did my best to get out of there. But flee as I would, my feet slipped on the smooth rock. When I slipped and fell, my left foot was trapped under the edge of that rock and I couldn't move. ... When the second shift came in, they got me out, but the bone above my ankle was broken, and I took two months to recover. If I think that my life was spared, I can't complain, but that two months was certainly a long time. The pain in my foot was something that I alone had to bear. But my children had only worn-out clogs, and the family couldn't subsist on one man's income.
>
> I couldn't contain my eagerness to work. The doctor wanted to put me in a plaster cast so that I couldn't move, but if he'd done that, while my foot might have healed, starvation would have been the result.[76]

Without working, she couldn't sustain her family, so she had made straw sandals to sell during her attenuated convalescence.

Another woman suffered a nastier accident due to a cave-in:

> Her head was crushed. It had made a great noise and she had jumped away, but [she couldn't escape]. ... Her stomach was slashed open and bits of food which she had just eaten were spilled all over the place. It was covered with blood. It's painful, you know! The feeling of helplessness. People died many times like this.[77]

Other gruesome accidents were the result of wagons running out of control on the outslopes, another common cause of injuries.[78] Wagons were sometimes allowed to find their appropriate level by running with gravity down slopes designed for the purpose, their clattering in the dark scaring novices and their frequent ricochets causing many injuries.

> When the wagon came running with a roar, I was startled and cringed against the wall, making my body as small as possible. In that instant, my light went out and it was pitch black. Even now, I can see that wagon coming in front of my eyes, and as I couldn't move, my man came looking for me, calling my name. He shouted angrily, "What an idiot! If I hadn't come, would you stay all day stuck like a cicada to that post?!"[79]

Working conditions 77

Another female miner reported:

> My first husband was killed on the spot by a run-away wagon. I was on my way to the winding station pushing a wagon. We had gone in together, but I was the only one who came out walking. He had become a Buddha.[80]

The miners themselves might be thought responsible for another type of accident involving wagons. Some of the retired women speak of riding on the couplings of trains of full wagons in order to get out of the mine more quickly after finishing their work. This practice was forbidden by most management of collieries where trains were hauled out by mechanical means, but because the women worked long hours and were always in a hurry to get out to their families, they flouted the prohibition. Mashio described the practice in detail, along with its risks for the women, and her interlocutor, Maki, described how a young boy from Korea, though warned of the danger, kept raising his head above the wagons and was caught by a low section of the roof.

> When I stretched up to see after passing the lowest place, he wasn't there. I yelled to stop the wagons and got down to see, but the boy had been buried completely by the coal dust in the wagon.[81]

The boy's chin "had been caught by the low roof, and he had been dragged along as if being hung. With a trickle of blood running from his mouth, he was dead."

Though in metal mines about one-third of all casualties were due to cave-ins and runaway wagons, in coal mines 4,920 of 6,590 casualties were caused by such incidents, according to statistics compiled by Ishihara in 1910.[82] Moreover, the two causes could be combined in one disastrous event in a coal mine, as one woman relates:

> At the shaft mouth someone else's wagon had run amok. The coupling broke and it came down at full speed. It hit a frame, and starting at the shaft mouth, the frames were knocked down one after the other.[83]
>
> Logs and rock came tumbling down. As the lamps had naked flames, they instantly went out, and we could only hear the sound of the frames collapsing and a plaintive voice, "Dad! Dad!" calling in the pitch-black darkness. As I was walking behind, I could hear it coming from below. Where stones and frames had fallen, I couldn't get a foothold and was stopped. Rocks pelted down all around. Hearing the wailing voices of others, I felt I was a goner. I thought, "I've been buried alive!'[84]

After this woman and her husband transferred to the Meinohama Mine, one day he did not feel like working but went to work anyway because they needed the income. It was an unfortunate decision. He "met a cave-in," his wife recalled. "It was quite bad and he went into the hospital immediately. His hips were hurt so bad that he could hardly piss."[85] She was currently recovering slowly from postnatal problems and was obliged to travel about looking for medical assistance

78 *Working conditions*

Figure 3.1 A dangerous occupation (Yamamoto, *Emaki*, 99th black and white illustration).

for her sick child while her husband recuperated on his own. By this time, medicine and treatment could be obtained by employees at some big mines and there were a few rudimentary medical insurance schemes, but coverage was inadequate. When her husband recovered, they resumed mining, though she was not well and was more sensitive than ever to underground dangers. Entering the mine each day, she thought it could well be her last.[86]

Dynamite!

The dangers of using dynamite are generally associated with the women's experiences later in their working lives, at the same time that attempts at union organization were being made in the 1920s. In the earlier period, dynamite had been used to blast out rock to excavate shafts and to push drifts into the face but not "to bring down the coal." For excavation purposes, blasting could be done at times and in places where it did not interfere substantially with the mining itself. But when it became common to use dynamite to loosen coal at the face, it interrupted the mining process and posed a recurring danger. One woman recalled boldly grabbing lit dynamite that had not gone off and throwing it into the face.

> Even when we put in three sticks of dynamite, it didn't go off so, thinking that the detonator might be wet, with the fuse still attached, I lit a joss stick

Working conditions 79

to see, and found that it (the fuse) started burning, *jyu jyuts*. Throwing it, just as it was, into the face, I blew it, but the *kogashira* came running, yelling with disgust, "You dummy! What the Hell are you doing?!" He was mad that no coal was loosened. I, the one who, when I first went down, found the dynamite (explosion) terrible, and would run away as far as I could, was now grabbing dynamite that was lit.[87]

Needless to say, such practices endangered the miners' lives.

In most of the smaller mines, and even in some of the big ones, the miners were expected to provide their own dynamite, or they had its cost deducted from their wages, no doubt in an attempt by the mine owners to prevent wasteful use of this valuable commodity. Inferior blasting powders and kinds of dynamite were sometimes used. Poor quality and inadequate skills in "setting the shot" magnified the dangers of blasting. Another woman recounted a gruesome accident:

Not realizing that there was unspent dynamite left, the *sakiyama* at the next face put his pick into it and a disaster happened. Well, saying that we had to get him out of there fast, everyone was plowing through the rock on top of him, when he cried: "My eyeballs are gone!" and he emerged looking like a spectre all covered in blood. It had hit him directly in the face with great force and both eyes and both arms were blown away, so that he was pitiful to see. While he was being carried up to the wagon, he was completely unconscious. His 14- or 15-year-old daughter had been working as his *atomuki*, but since she'd gone out carrying the *tebo*, she wasn't hurt. When she got back to the face, seeing what had happened, she shrieked, "Dad has been killed!!" while clinging to a wagon. I couldn't console her.

I thought anyone would have died from it, but Fate was on his side and his life was saved. But without eyes or arms, he must've suffered the torments of Hell.[88]

There was no social security system to look after people permanently disabled in the mines, and unless their families cared for them, they would often end up as beggars.

When company officials fired the shots, they sometimes acted to show who was boss.

The superiors liked to throw their weight about, and if their feelings were upset, they might alter the amount of dynamite they fired. Where they should have used five sticks, they might fire seven or four.[89]

Excessively large explosions were of course quite dangerous but so was using too little dynamite because it could rupture the wall without bringing it down. Recklessness must also have caused difficulties for the women in removing the debris.

80 *Working conditions*

Among many references to the horrible results of accidents involving dynamite, one woman, who shared a working face with people from Hiroshima, makes it clear that the company tried to avoid taking responsibility for careless blasting.

> When my daughter and theirs were working as *atomuki* to her father, about 10 o'clock at night, (their) girl shouted, "Mother! Dad's been blasted by dynamite!" and came running out, stunned. She came to the shaft mouth and described it, but I couldn't stop myself from going down. ... It was already too late. There were holes all through his head. Our girl had been hit in the ears and eyes, and couldn't see. Someone from the office came to the place used as a pay shed and told us, "Don't say that he was blown up by dynamite. If the authorities come, don't say that. If they don't know, they'll think he died [in the regular course of duty]. If you keep it secret, they'll let it go as if he died." So we took the brunt of it. ... They collected 300 *yen* and went back to their country (Hiroshima).[90]

The Company thus paid compensation to the dead man's family but apparently not to that of the injured daughter, who, however, may not have been permanently blinded. And it avoided the onus of responsibility for improper use of dynamite. As early as the first years of Taisho (after 1912), mining companies were threatened with closure should big accidents kill too many workers. This might explain Mitsubishi's alleged underreporting of the number of victims of the Hōjō disaster.[91]

Nonpunitive damages

If compensation for injury or death suffered in the mines was inadequate even in the later period, in Meiji or in early Taisho there was next to nothing.[92] Later, when there were modest schemes for compensation, management would still question the cause of death or injury before they would "pay up." One woman recalls:

> The husband of someone I knew died as the result of gas poisoning. He worked as an underground technician, and when he was connecting an air intake pipe to a new face, he began to feel bad and came out. While thinking that he'd caught a cold and saying that his head hurt, his blood pressure was high. Then he became much worse, and staying in bed, he lost consciousness and died on the third day. His relatives said he was poisoned by gas, (but) his supervisor(s) said that he was (only) sick, and it seems that the hospital medical certificate said that it was softening of the brain (*nōnankashō*).[93]

Because encephalomalacia is a disease, the wife probably received no compensation, and to add insult to injury, she was obliged to remarry soon after in order to keep her accommodation at the mine.

Another woman recalls that at about the time of the Russo-Japanese War (1904–05), her family was given five *yen* when her father died. When her cousin died in an accident about 1921, the compensation was 50 *yen*.[94] Mitsubishi Mining established a standard compensation of 150 *yen* per victim in 1912,[95] but this was a maximum from which deductions would be made if the miner was considered to be at fault in any way. It can be imagined how much easier it was to pin responsibility on the miners for accidents at a small mine than at a big one such as Hōjō. There, although the managers tried to appease the bereaved families, they also coopted their colleagues from academia to blame miners for careless use of lamps and tobacco and for causing the 1914 disaster.[96] Yet Orii Seigo's statistics show that very few accidents could be attributed to the careless use of matches or tobacco in the coal mines of the late Meiji or Taisho periods.[97] He also notes that Hōjō officials found only the remains of playing cards and dice in the fragments of clothing on the victims. He is almost certainly correct when he says that the ability of the miners to smuggle in the means for gambling demonstrated their ability to hide the resources for a surreptitious smoke.[98]

The "goddess of the *sena*" notes that even as a young girl she was aware of the dangers of smoking in dust-filled tunnels.

> About the time I began my training, my father would say, "Go to the *sasabeya* (overseer's hut) and get (my) tobacco." To explain, the *hiban* [literally, "fire guard"] would ration out three plugs of tobacco at a time to the miners. … Receiving it, I'd smoke a bit of it myself and take the rest to my father. After the miners got their tobacco and while they were smoking, they'd take a rest in the *sasabeya*. … It was permitted to smoke like that only in the *sasabeya*. Not in other places because it was dangerous.[99]

Figure 3.2 Smoking at the *sasabeya* (Yamamoto, *Emaki*, adapted from 10th color illustration).

82   *Working conditions*

Other retirees confirm that smoking, by both men and women, was allowed only in the overseer's or fire guard's huts.[100] Nevertheless, the satisfaction of outwitting the bosses and a rather devil-may-care attitude resulting from the hardships of coal mining, as Mashio suggests, may have led some male miners to forget that they could be risking their lives for a soothing smoke. A similarly dangerous practice of Joban miners, according to Mashio, one proscribed by most management, was the "stripping" of the walls and roofs of rooms between framing timbers. Though the coal was easily obtained, the practice could bring down the roof, and as a precaution against it the *atoyama* climbed ladders to paint the roof with lime, making any flouting of the proscription obvious.[101]

Though management would reduce compensation if they could establish the miners' responsibility for accidents, when the Takashima Mine explosion of 1906 killed more than 300 miners, Mitsubishi, probably as a result of a blaze of publicity, accepted some responsibility by giving the dead miners' families 170 *yen* and the chief engineer's family the munificent sum of 6,500 *yen*. After the Hōjō disaster of 1914, which killed double or perhaps even triple the number of miners as the Takashima accident, the compensation was more generous than the standard. The vice president of Mitsubishi Shipbuilding stated that the Takashima precedent would not be followed and that the Iwasaki family, founders and owners of Mitsubishi, wanted the compensation to satisfy the bereaved families. The company promised to pay the families between 300 and 600 *yen*, depending on the length and nature of service and on the number of dependants of the dead miner. It also made some provision for the temporary care of orphans and paid some of the travel expenses of relatives who came to claim children or bodies.[102] Orii notes that the compensation was generous in terms of prices at the time, the average amount of 430 *yen* being the equivalent of 530–620 days' wages for miners. But an amount less than two years' pay for the loss of a breadwinner, or, as some of the women called themselves, the "rice basket" of the family, was probably not excessively generous in terms of the bereaved families' needs and certainly not when compared to the profits of the *zaibatsu*'s coal-producing branch. At least there seems to have been no gender discrimination in the matter of awards. Similar compensation for male and female victims may have recognized the fact that children relied as much on their mothers as their fathers for sustenance in coal-mining camps. On the other hand, there was discrimination against deceased workers; none of the common honorifics were applied to their names in company documents.[103]

The indomitable women who described some of the horrors of accidents in the coal mines also mention burials there. Because most miners had lost their fields and homes in their rural villages, they were buried at the mines, and the bigger companies seem to have taken some responsibility for these burials.[104] In cases where births and marriages were not registered, however, claims for compensation might be ignored by management acting to avoid "moral hazard." Even at the large Hōjō Mine, there were probably unregistered marriages that impeded the payment of compensation after the 1914 disaster. Anomalies in the records may also have interfered with the payment of funeral expenses by the company,

Working conditions 83

set at 15 *yen* for miners and 15, 20, or 30 *yen* for craftsmen, overseers, and staffers who died.[105]

In harm's way

One woman also spoke of the high incidence of smaller accidents. On the same day that her toes were crushed due to the alleged carelessness of the woman pushing the wagon behind her, her mother also suffered a foot injury.

> The one who carried me home on that day when I couldn't walk was Harano, who became my first husband. … When we reached my house, Mother didn't come out. She'd gone down on the first shift and should've come up earlier, but when I thought she wasn't going to come out and offer a word of thanks to Harano, and crawled in, Mother came out crawling as well. There had been a rock-fall, and the bones of her instep had somehow been hurt. Mother on the first shift, and daughter on the second, both had to have bandages wrapped similarly around their feet!
>
> Mother couldn't stand up for some time. I only took three days off, and dragging my hurt foot, went down the pit again. The money we got while not working was a pittance.[106]

This woman also details other misfortunes in her account of her working life after returning from six years of service in a "tea house" or brothel. Pulling or pushing the *sura* up and down the slippery slopes involved many risks, small and large.

> When we came to the *sura* (unloading) platform, if we didn't get out of the way, we'd be thrown into the wagon just like that! If we weren't sharp about it, we could be severely hurt. So at such times, if we didn't just let the *sura* go, we were in for it. The *sura* would be damaged, and the *sakiyama* would get mad. Because if it couldn't be used, coal couldn't be got out.

She goes on to tell of manipulating the *uke-zura*, always aware that "if your legs crumple, the *sura* will come down on top of you" and of being cognizant of other *atomuki* "whose inner thighs were gouged out by the blades of the *sura*."[107] Later, she mentions the dangers of empty wagons coming down the auxiliary shaft at full speed. One time, she was deliberately knocked down and pushed out of the way of a careening wagon by a workmate."The rope was lashing back and forth with the force of the descending wagon. If I'd been beheaded by that …" And she generalizes about the unsafe working conditions. In such circumstances, she remembers, some of the women prayed for divine protection.

> When we went down, we always prayed to the main frame at the pit mouth. When by chance we forgot, we'd come back and pray properly. If we went

84 *Working conditions*

in without asking the Mine Goddess for protection, we'd feel uncomfortable. Since we never knew when an accident would happen.[108]

As well as suffering accidents of all kinds, the women incurred injuries due to the extremely demanding conditions of their day-to-day work.

Bending one's back on the ascent, holding a *shumoku* stick shorter than a foot long, one pants, *haa haa, haa haa!* On the way, blisters formed on the place where the yoke rubbed. The skin would peel and it was like a burn, and coal dust would get caught in it. … How can one describe how it hurts? …

And you have to carry the yoke on that sore spot. If I said it hurt, my old man would show me scars from his own blisters and say, "How can you work as an *atomuki* if you're bothered by blisters? Take the load on your blister and ignore it!" …

Even now [some 30 years later], the scars of those blisters are still white. My shoulder is just one big wen (*kobu*).[109]

Another woman described how coal fragments penetrated large blisters incurred on a wet and steep ascent where she was carrying the *tebo*.

Since my feet were always in the water, the skin swelled up and red blisters appeared. Coal fragments pierced them like glass splinters. It was painful. … They looked like dried and cracked rice cakes. But just having some salve put on them at the works office, when dawn came I went down the pit as if nothing was unusual.[110]

What kind of treatment?

The ways in which the women dealt with accident and illness were little short of heroic. Although necessity forced them to bear injury and sickness with fortitude, their efforts to support their families, particularly their children, were extraordinary. Not being provided with adequate financial support when they were unable to work, they reduced recuperation time to a minimum, often going back to work before they had recovered. Kawashima Taka's doctor had recommended a plaster cast for her foot and two months' recuperation, but when family resources were exhausted, she went back into the pit.

The pain eventually went away naturally. Out of favour with the doctor, it became difficult for me to get into the hospital, but my foot is the foot of a poor person. It has its own character. … Crying Yow! Yow! (*Itai! itai!*), I got used to the pain. It wasn't the doctor who cured me. Poverty was my cure.[111]

One retired woman who had received a disfiguring injury while working in a large room remembered the difficulty in getting appropriate treatment and compensation following accidents.

Working conditions 85

Coal dust had got into the cut above the eye, and water from a kettle wasn't going to get it out. So it looked like a second eye had been added. The hospital doctor said, "A wound to a woman's face is a first degree wound, so you'll receive good compensation. Leave the coal dust there!" ... I'd heard many stories like this. When the wagon had crushed someone's finger(s), (the doctor) had said, "No matter how you dislike it, don't miss your chance to collect some money!" and amputated. ...

I appreciated the doctor's goodwill, but I refused, saying, "As a woman with children and a tattoo, no one will want me. If the *sakiyama* avoid me, I'll be in trouble, so please take out all the coal dust."

After that, the doctor said, "She's a woman without greed!" But rather than a woman without greed, I might have been one without attractions.[112]

Relief programs

Yamamoto Sakubei recalled that the first welfare systems for miners were established by miners themselves in the form of relief lotteries and informal mutual benefit clubs (*tanomoshi-kō*).[113] Early welfare schemes were usually operated in the names of the male heads of families, with benefits accruing to members of families only if the husbands did not squander them. Regulations accompanying the Japanese Mining Law of 1892 set standards for compensation to miners for serious injuries "if there was no obvious fault on the part of the person" claiming benefits.[114] Kaijima Tasuke and his managers (of the private company that was to become the nucleus of a regional *zaibatsu*) felt compelled to make some provisions for less serious emergencies as well. Mutual relief societies (*kyūsai kai*) were set up at some Kaijima mines in 1906 and 1907 to replace the "welfare" given to miners by the gang bosses under the old *naya seido*. However, the abolition of the old system was sought by managers in order to gain more direct control over miners and thereby increase production,[115] not to reduce risks in an industry where "the occurrence of injury and illness was conspicuously frequent."[116] The new system was far from an adequate way of providing for the welfare of miners and their families.

Indeed, the first Kaijima schemes provided only for staff—who were not likely to be major victims of injury or serious illnesses. Provisions for relief in the case of short-term layoffs were subsequently extended to miners at some Kaijima mines, relieving gang bosses of some responsibility. Other provisions, which were to become standard for miners as well as staff, awarded compensation for deaths due to injury or illness and for difficulties caused to families of employees who were called up by the army. Relief for those suffering from unexpected calamities could be used to favor compliant workers or their families in shows of Confucian-style benevolence. Provision for cash gifts from the relief society on the occasion of births or weddings, a direct replacement of traditional assistance from gang bosses on these occasions, was soon dropped from the Kaijima scheme.[117] Nor were the meager benefits provided solely at the expense of the company. Miners paid monthly subscription fees, collected by check-offs against

86 *Working conditions*

wages.[118] Although staff and gang bosses were required to contribute at fixed rates, the Kaijima Company made varying "donations" to the relief societies, at the discretion of the company directors of the societies. Only in the case of one society, at Mannoura, were the relief rates actually stipulated, and these were at meager levels. Bereaved families of Mannoura staff members were given significantly more condolence money than those of miners and artisans; the latter were offered less than at other major collieries, at least in the case of major disasters. Additional forms of assistance for soldiers' families and others in unforeseeable difficulties seem to have been distributed according to length of service at variable rates; they were not munificent.[119]

The varying relief schemes at different Kaijima mines were rationalized under one system in 1909, but the company was still trying to make relief pay for itself from the contributions of the miners. The subscription fees for various occupational groups were now fixed,[120] but there is one glaring omission from Ogino Yoshihiro's list of groups belonging to the new scheme. Although coal sorters, most of whom were women, are mentioned, female haulers are omitted, suggesting that they may have been uncovered except for loss of or injury to their husbands. In the early twentieth century, Japanese colliery companies were making women more, rather than less, dependent on their spouses for sustenance and relief from the vagaries of coal mining.

At the end of the Meiji period, the subscription societies were done away with and the Kaijima Company took over responsibility for relief as a recognition of the need to suppress worker dissidence or, as the managers euphemistically explained it, as part of the new policy of "cordiality between master and servant."[121] Workers were relieved of the burden of the subscription fees, but Ogino does not tell us whether the compensation rates were improved. We can only assume that the system was still inadequate in comparison with the workers' contributions to the industry and its profits. It was not until 1926 or 1927 that an "illness compensation" scheme came into effect at one of the smaller Chikuho mines, and one woman there said it was insufficient to feed her family.[122] Michael Lewis's conclusion that improvements in living conditions at some mines in the 1890s "did not immediately or substantially correct the many health and welfare problems" at most Kyushu coal mines is reflected in the situation much later.[123]

A dangerous occupation!

Although relief systems such as those of the Kaijima Company were slowly improving, the numbers of accidents were increasing with the expansion of coal mining in the Chikuho region during the second decade of the twentieth century. In 1914, in the jurisdiction of the Fukuoka District Mines Office, the number of casualties (deaths and injuries) was 96,766, while the number of miners was 170,220.[124] Thus, in a single year, there was more than one casualty for every two workers. Kato Shizue found that "the actual loss of miners per one million tons of coal mined in England is about ten persons, while in Japan thirty human lives

Table 3.4 Accidents and Rates of Injury in Coal Mines

Annual Averages (1917–1926)		Rates per 1,000 Miners
Deaths	757	2.74
Serious injuries	4,993	18.07
Other injuries	154,830	560.40
No. of miners	276,283	

(*Sources: Nihon Kōzan Kyōkai Shiryō*, First Collection, pp. 13–14, from Nihon Kagaku-shi Gakkai, ed., *Nippon Kagaku-gizyutusi Taikei*, vol. 20, *Saikō Yakin Gijutsu* [Mining and Metallurgical Technology], p. 289.)

are actually sacrificed for every million tons."[125] Hence Japanese miners suffered three times the death rate of miners in England in 1935. The ratio had not been any better in the years before 1930, though Britain's record had hardly been a good one in the nineteenth century.

Table 3.4 shows that there was an annual average of nearly three deaths and 18 serious injuries, as well as the almost incredible number of 560 lesser (but serious enough to be reported) injuries, per 1,000 miners working in the last decade of the Taisho period. Even if women made up a smaller number of the mortalities, their numbers among the casualties who survived must have been high because their work on the slopes and in the haulage-ways subjected them to risks comparable to those of the men.

Epitaph

Morisaki offers the following observation about the lives of *atoyama*:

> They lived, barely able to breathe, (working) at wages which squeezed the life's blood out of them. In such a place, there were those who had died many deaths. Their stories, from the time of earliest recollections, were interlaced with recurrences of emergencies and numbers of deaths. Almost all coal mine workers had chronologies which were loaded with death and there was even an elderly woman who let drop the phrase, "I am the Spirit of the Dead." But even such an old woman did not reflect on the experiences of her past with only the sinking feelings of a victim. "I still want to work," she said. ... Their work, no matter how inappropriate for human beings, had a way of linking them to a particular world. Many of the (former) *atoyama* feel that they are in an hiatus which has little meaning for them compared to that earlier time (when they were working).[126]

Most of the women seem to have accepted the inevitability of accidents and believed that fate was kind to them when accidents occurred all around them but not to them, or when they were buried alive but rescued, or when an explosion

88 *Working conditions*

did not blow them from Hell to Heaven. To be obliged to rely on fate, or faith, or luck, in situations so inconducive to well-being and survival—this was indeed the unfortunate lot of coal miners, women and men, in Japan before 1930.

Notes

1 Idegawa, p. 192.
2 Roughly five bushels, understood as an annual minimum for subsistence.
3 Morisaki, *Makkura*, pp. 103–4.
4 Mashio, *Jizoko no Seishun*, p. 62.
5 Idegawa, p. 49. See also, Morisaki, pp. 20–1.
6 Idegawa, p. 184.
7 Morisaki, p. 51.
8 Shindo Toyo, *Chikuhō no Jokōfu-tachi*, p. 23.
9 Morisaki, p. 18.
10 Idegawa, p. 14. Cf. *Jizoko no Seishun*, p. 62.
11 Mashio, *Jizoko no Seishun*, pp. 62–3, 82. These dunking tubs, called *bakku*, had to be cleaned of sludge if they were not to fill up and become useless, and one woman was given this job as a measure of relief from more onerous work. Idegawa, pp. 124–5.
12 Michael Lewis, "The Coalfield Riots," in *Rioters and Citizens*, pp. 194–5.
13 Morisaki, p. 19.
14 *Jizoko no Seishun*, p. 60.
15 Morisaki, p. 21. Also, p. 124.
16 Morisaki, p. 10.
17 Idegawa, p. 139.
18 Morisaki, p. 129. Also, p. 114.
19 From Matsuoka Koichi, "*Takashima Tankō no Sanjō*," (Dreadful Conditions at the Takashima Mine), in Ueno Eishin, ed., *Kindai Minshū no Kiroku*, vol. 2, *Kōfu*, p. 417. I have amended Mikiso Hane's translation in *Peasants, Rebels, and Outcastes*, p. 228, to conform more closely to the original. See also, Lewis, "The Coalfield Riots," p. 196.
20 Idegawa, p. 40. Cf. Mashio, *Jizoko no Seishun*, pp. 62–3, 82.
21 Idegawa, pp. 99–100.
22 Mashio, *Jizoko no Seishun*, p. 75.
23 Idegawa, p. 127.
24 Morisaki, pp. 20, 73.
25 Idegawa, p. 109.
26 Mashio describes the layout of air shafts and cross entries that facilitated "sending polluted underground air to the surface." *Jizoko no Seishun*, p. 63. The ventilation system's brattice doors in larger mines are depicted in Yamamoto Sakubei, *Chikuhō Tankō Emaki*, 52nd and 53rd black and white illustrations. No retired woman mentions minding more solid doors of the nature of those "manned" by boys (called *trappers*) in the shafts of British coal mines. See John Holland, *The History and Description of Fossil Fuel, The Collieries, and Coal Trade of Great Britain*, p. 193. Also Statham, *Coal-Mining*, p. 407.
27 Idegawa, p. 34.
28 Nomi interview in Tajima, *Tankō no Bijin*, p. 7.
29 Mashio, *Jizoko no Seishun*, pp. 91–2.
30 Idegawa, p. 109. The sister was killed in a cave-in at age 18.
31 Morisaki, p. 14.
32 Idegawa, p. 92.
33 Ibid., p. 187.
34 Idegawa, p. 109.

Working conditions 89

35 Idegawa, p. 32. The third husband died as the result of "involvement in a dispute"—!
36 Idegawa, p. 106. Though the typhus may not have been contracted from the mining work, certainly that work enervated adult miners and made them susceptible to such diseases.
37 Mashio, *Jizoko no Seishun*, pp. 82–3.
38 "Female labor in the Japanese coal-mining industry," in Janet Hunter, ed., *Japanese Women Working*, p. 113. Sachiko Sone adduces evidence to support this conclusion in her dissertation, *"Coalmining Women in Japan,"* pp. 149–50.
39 Ishihara, *"Kōfu no Eisei Jōtai Chōsa,"* in Sumiya, ed., *Shokkō Oyobi Kōfu Chōsa*, Table 8, p. 175. For the provenance of Ishihara's and related surveys, see Sumiya, *Nihon Chinrōdo no Shiteki Kenkyū*, pp. 280–1.
40 Ishihara, *"Kōfu no Eisei Jōtai Chōsa,"* in Sumiya, p. 178.
41 Ishihara, p. 187.
42 Ishihara, *"Kōfu no Eisei Jōtai Chōsa,"* in Sumiya, p. 178.
43 Sumiya, *Nihon Sekitan Sangyō Bunseki*, p. 82.
44 Idegawa, pp. 19–22.
45 Ishihara, p. 178.
46 Mashio, p. 77.
47 Cf. Cronyn, *The Stars Look Down*, pp. 184, 190.
48 Idegawa, p. 128.
49 Morisaki, pp. 40–1.
50 Idegawa, p. 38.
51 Orii Seigo, *Hōjō Daihijō*, p. 32.
52 Morisaki, pp. 91–2.
53 Morisaki, *Makkura*, p. 93. For another gruesome description of the burnt body of a woman's younger brother killed in a gas explosion at a different time, see Idegawa, p. 15.
54 In a climate of danger, where accidents were so frequent, there were of course many accounts of miraculous salvation and fortuitous victimization. Cf. Idegawa, pp. 35–8.
55 For the reputation of the Miyoshi Mine, formally known as Takamatsu No. 2 Shaft, see Morisaki, pp. 39, 187.
56 Morisaki, p. 94.
57 Idegawa, p. 42.
58 Idegawa, p. 15.
59 Orii Seigo, *Hōjō Daihijō*, p. 43.
60 Ibid. From the *Kyūshū Nichi-nichi* newspaper.
61 Mashio, p. 105.
62 Orii Seigo, *Hōjō Daihijō*, pp. 61–2.
63 Orii, pp. 132–164.
64 Orii, p. 96.
65 Orii, p. 146.
66 In the film, *The Molly Maguires*, a retired miner of long experience suggests that gas could be trapped and rendered harmless by "digging right," but his argument is probably anachronistic, more scientific expertise being required to determine the location of, and methods of effectively avoiding, gas accumulations.
67 Idegawa, p. 38; Orii, pp. 187–9. Japan would remain far behind the United States in passing legislation for mining safety such as that of Wyoming in 1925 and for adopting equipment such as the mobile water sprayer illustrated in Gardner and Flores, *Forgotten Frontier*, p. 153. It is noteworthy that after the 1925 legislation, there were no further major explosions in Wyoming mines, p. 156.
68 Orii, p. 185.
69 Cf. Idegawa, p. 38.
70 Ishihara, *"Kōfu no Eisei Jōtai Chōsa,"* in Sumiya, *Shokkō Oyobi Kōfu Chōsa*, pp. 198–9.

90　*Working conditions*

71　Statham, *Coal-Mining*, p. 513.
72　Cited in Orii, pp. 166–7.
73　Idegawa, pp. 111–12.
74　Morisaki, p. 52.
75　See Kaneko' note on the disposal of *tsuri-iwa*, in *Chikuhō Tankō Kotoba*, p. 75.
76　Idegawa, pp. 175–6.
77　Morisaki, pp. 111–12. Mashio records Maki's account of how a miner, pinned underneath a large fall of rock and fearing another cave-in, used his axe to chop off his foot and free himself, then dragged himself out of the tunnel, only to die of loss of blood when his workmates carried him to the surface. *Jizoku no Seishun*, pp. 66–7. The "axe" mentioned here is called a *tsuruhashi*, and such mattocks were not nearly as sharp as the framer's *yoki*.
78　Morisaki, p. 138. The description of how the young boy attempting to deliver a crucial message at the time of a disastrous flood in a northeastern England coal mine was run over and mangled by a "train of tubs" is remarkably similar, though the coincidence of accidents involving runaway wagons and flooding is not quite believable. Cronin, *The Stars Look Down*, p. 186.
79　Idegawa, p.123.
80　Morisaki, p. 173. See also, Kato Shizue, *Facing Two Ways*, p. 158, and Matsumoto Kichinosuke, *Chikuhō ni Ikiru*, pp. 30–1, where he says that occurrences of runaway wagons were invariably cursed with language that seemed to blame *burakumin* outcastes for such mishaps.
81　*Jizoko no Seishun*, p. 125. Harada Tsuma said that, whereas the men at her mine rode the couplings to get out in a hurry, the women were often timid and did not. She describes one awful accident when a man who had fallen for somebody else's wife, looking back to see if she was following the wagon train, did not notice a frame twisted by pressure from the roof and was "crushed to shreds" between the wagon and the frame. Tajima, *Tankō no Bijin*, p. 17.
82　From "*Kōfu no Eisei Jōtai Chōsa*," in Sumiya, *Shokkō Oyobi Kōfu Chōsa*, Tables, p. 198.
83　This description reminds one of the log chutes collapsing, domino-like, in Kazantzaki's *Zorba, the Greek*, so vividly portrayed in the movie with Anthony Quinn. But as comical as the collapse was in the film, it had serious consequences, as did the accident in the mine.
84　Morisaki, pp. 54–5.
85　Morisaki, pp. 59–60.
86　Morisaki, pp. 64–5.
87　Idegawa, pp. 156–7.
88　Idegawa, p. 165.
89　*Makkura*, p. 177. For the change from shot-firing by miners to responsibility by company men in Wyoming, see Gardner and Flores, p. 36.
90　*Makkura*, p. 176.
91　Orii, *Hōjō Daihijō*, pp. 132–64.
92　Morisaki, p. 58. See also Yamamoto Sakubei, *Yama no Kurashi*, p. 24.
93　Idegawa, p. 153.
94　Morisaki, p. 174. Although she says the standard was "50 *yen* per person," it is not clear that this standard applied to all five members of her cousin's family who died together in the accident mentioned on the previous page, and if so, to whom the compensation was paid.
95　Orii, *Hōjō Daihijō*, p. 117.
96　Orii, pp. 168–9, 174–7.
97　See Table 3.3, p. 74.
98　Orii, p. 166.

Working conditions 91

99 Morisaki, p. 124.
100 Morisaki, pp. 76, 162.
101 *Jizoko no Seishun,*, pp. 76–7, 81.
102 Orii, *Hōjō Daihijō*, pp. 117–8.
103 Orii, pp. 120–2.
104 Morisaki, p. 112.
105 Orii, p. 118.
106 Ibid., pp. 16–7.
107 Ibid., pp. 25–6.
108 Idegawa, p. 31. The pit-mouth frame was called a "cosmetic frame" (*kesho-waku*) because it was often made of big squared timbers, or even concrete or brick, often with the mine name overhead, in an ostentatious attempt to impress outsiders. See Kaneko, *Chikuhō Tankō Kotoba*, p. 97.
109 Idegawa, p. 124.
110 Idegawa, p. 162.
111 Idegawa, p. 177.
112 Idegawa, pp. 113–15.
113 *Yama no Kurashi*, pp. 24–7.
114 Ogino Yoshihiro, "*Taisen Zengo ni okeru Kaijima Tankō-gyō no Rōshi Kankei* (Labor-Management Relations in Kaijima's Coal Operations Around the Time of the First World War)" in Ogino, ed., *Senzen-ki Chikuhō Tankō-gyō no Keiei to Rōdō*, p. 91.
115 Ogino "*Taisen Zengo ni okeru Kaijima Tankō-gyō no Rōshi Kankei,*" p. 87. For conflicts surrounding the curtailment of the gang boss system and outlines of the early relief schemes at Ashio and other mines, see Nimura Kazuo, *Ashio Bōdō no Shiteki Bunseki* (Historical Analysis of the Rising at Ashio) and Nakatomi Hyoei, *Nagaoka Tsuruzō Den* (Biography of Nagaoka Tsuruzo), passim.
116 Ogino, p. 91.
117 Ogino, p. 93.
118 Ogino, p. 92. See also, Nimura, p. 25; Nakatomi, p. 101. Nimura notes that the Furukawa Company sponsored an official society, for which the fees were higher, as well as condoning, if not supporting, solely worker-supported mutual aid societies.
119 See Ogino, "*Taisen Zengo ni okeru Kaijima Tankō-gyō no Rōshi Kankei,*" footnote 13, p. 151.
120 Ogino, p. 92.
121 Ogino, pp. 85–6, 93–4.
122 Morisaki, p. 64.
123 "The Coalfield Riots," p. 197.
124 Orii, p. 129.
125 *Facing Two Ways*, p. 160. For further statistics on casualties in Japan's coal-mining industry in these years see Lewis, "The Coalfield Riots," p. 195.
126 Morisaki, p. 182.

4   Their life trajectory

Yome, yome to, iu ma wazuka yume no ma de
  Kaka no mijikasa, baba no nagasa yo.[1]

The time she is called Yome, the Bride, is as short as a dream;
She is "the wife" for a brief span, an old woman forever.

The lives of Japanese coal-mining women often had inauspicious beginnings. Pregnancy and childbirth were among their many mixed blessings. *Atoyama* had only a modest chance of bringing a pregnancy to term while working in the mines. One mother recalls:

In the mines, there were many who miscarried. Because we went up and down steep slopes carrying loads. I miscarried twice. … No one had cotton or *sarashi* [bleached cotton]. If a baby was born [in the mine], it would be wrapped in a ragged kimono, that's all. If there was a miscarriage, it was common to put it [the fetus] on some straw sandals or newspapers. Then to go back to work as if nothing had happened.[2]

If a woman became pregnant and suffered severe morning sickness, she might be coerced to work by piecework rates and the need to earn sustenance and by a husband conscious of this need. Company rules could compel women to go down even during the final stages of pregnancy. Regulations allocating wagons only to *hitosaki* or requiring a framer to work with an *atomuki* might lead a pregnant wife to accompany her husband, even if she was unable to provide real assistance, to ensure that the day's wages were not shared with a substitute.[3]

Even later, when working conditions had improved in some mines, babies would be born underground. As late as 1933, Mashio's protagonist, Maki, worked during her pregnancy, suffering her first labor pains underground 10 days earlier than expected. "Anyone who had difficulty working with a swollen belly couldn't hope to do work like that of an *atoyama*," Maki recalled.[4] One woman suggests that, in a period of labor shortage, some companies might send a nurse or doctor down to assist in an underground delivery.[5] But medical attention was unavailable in most mines, and Baroness Shidzue Ishimoto (Kato Shizue) does not refer to medical aid underground, even at Miike, which was large and profitable.

Their life trajectory 93

Some miners had a casual attitude to the advent of children and a low evaluation of their worth to the mining community. Maki said: "At the coal mines, ever so many are born underground. ... No one gave special treatment to *atoyama* who were pregnant. There were even *sakiyama* who urged: 'Somehow we must provide for the child in your belly by getting out an extra wagon load.'"[6]

Maki had helped one woman who gave birth in the mine. She had buried the afterbirth, not wanting the male miners to see any disagreeable evidence of the event. But, paradoxically, she deplored the men's inability to understand the difficulties of giving birth.

> [The woman she helped] was a first-class *atoyama*, a little older than 30. She was sweating profusely and seemed to use all her strength to stop crying out, really suffering. No one took over for her. No matter how normal the birth, the baby can't be born without seeming to rend one's hips asunder. My husband just thought it was like having a difficult crap [*katai unchi suru kurai*]. Really! And that the number of brats had increased, that's all.[7]

One woman recounts a particularly harrowing natal experience. Thinking that premature labor pains were just a stomach-ache, at the insistence of a woman working nearby, she was "put on mats spread in a cart for hauling framing timbers and winched out to the pit mouth."[8]

> Things were developing fast. Then I was brought back to my house on a stretcher, and before a bed could be made I gave birth, but it didn't cry even once. As the midwife didn't come in time, my mother-in-law and those who brought me out quickly boiled water and bustled about doing everything, but not one of them said anything to me about the infant. ... The child had been tangled in the placenta [*ena*—actually the umbilical cord?] and immediately after birth, without ever giving voice, died. With a blackish face. It's said that a seven month's baby will be reared but an eight month's child won't, but I felt as if I'd killed the child. I was unskilled in everything and had killed it while carrying it.[9]

And she indicates that she now understood why the child had aborted. "In mines which were like a steam-bath, bent over a heavy belly pulling the *sura* or carrying the *tebo*, it was likely that it would have an effect on the fetus. If I'd been a [staffer's] wife in a company residence, there would've been nothing like the death of my child!"[10]

Above ground, provisions for the birthing process were simple."When a baby was born, the middle half-mat [in a four-and-one-half-mat room] was taken up, and that became the child-bed."[11] The mother typically went back to work very soon. Matsumoto Tsuya went down about one month after the birth of her first baby. "At that time [1919], this was normal for coal-mining women," Shindo Toyo asserted.[12] Certain *buraku* women took as long as 50, 60, or even 70 days off after birth,[13] but these women worked at the large Miike Mine, where Mitsui's regulations may have

94 *Their life trajectory*

prevented them from going down sooner. At smaller mines, most women's need for income to feed their families necessitated a much hastier postnatal "recovery."

Some women gave birth to more babies than they could adequately care for. One woman whose husband was worse than useless in family matters recalls: "While thinking, 'I'll leave him, I'm going to leave him,' one child after another is conceived, and in those days if they were conceived you had to bring them to term. When they were born, you would have to put up with it and keep working."[14] Another woman speaks of surveillance by the authorities to ensure that abortion was not being used to keep families within manageable limits. "Unlike nowadays, you had to give birth to as many children as you could. It was a time in which, if you had a miscarriage, a policeman would come around to investigate whether you had deliberately aborted."[15]

Maki confirms that abortion was not an option in an era when the Japanese authorities were encouraging population growth.[16] Prohibitions of abortion, like large families, did not always favor the mining companies. Mitsui's ideal family for recruitment to its big Tagawa mines was "a couple with a 12- or 13-year-old child, all capable of working, and an elder to do the cooking."[17] Nevertheless, larger families had to be tolerated by the coal companies in the interests of national ethics.

At the same time, infant mortality among coal-miners' families was so high that often births were not registered until a child had lived to be two or three years old.[18] The feudal precedent of registration with a "family temple" was carried on unofficially by priests in some regions in the Meiji period, but the deficiencies of the new official registration process in coal-mining areas prevented high child mortality from becoming a national scandal.

When, despite high mortality rates, a coal-mining family had more children than they could sustain, adoption often became the only means of family survival. One woman told of the emotional consequences of giving up her child.

> This child turned out to be a girl. Not two months after she was born we were separated. I turned her over to someone else. ... As I was a daily wage earner, no matter how hard I worked, I didn't earn enough money, but if I didn't keep busy, I'd think of my child. To be told not to think about her was enough to start me worrying about her. ... After giving up the baby, my breasts would swell up. Forgive me! Bear with me, I would cry, and squeeze out the milk while wailing. ... [W]hen I felt that I wanted to put my breast into the child's mouth, I couldn't control myself. But I didn't know where she'd gone, and even if I'd tried, I probably couldn't have found her. I had to bear it. I thought this was my punishment.[19]

Oya no kao o miwasureru na yo (Don't forget your mother's face!)

As well as irrevocable separations, continual daily separations from infant children could cause suffering for mining women. The recollections of retired female miners in *Makkura* begin with those of a woman who remembers being concerned primarily about the possibility of an accident preventing her from raising her children and how important loving contact with them was to her.

> When we went down the pit, usually the sun hadn't risen. Not seeing the sun for a long spell gave one a strange feeling. But not being able to care for one's children, that was the greatest hardship. What gave one great pleasure, you know, was when work was done and we came up, to see in the distance, up above, the dot of a light at the pit mouth. To be able to see the children! I can meet my children, I thought.[20]

The pleasures of pit mouth meetings were often precluded, however, because the children were asleep long before their parents finished work. The daily ration of rice would often be delivered to the company store in the middle of the night,[21] too late for the children to fetch and cook it for themselves.

When she got the children ready for their day before going to work in the morning, the mother might have to get up very early.

> [A]lthough it was still dark, I'd wake up the sleeping children, roundly scolding the poor things who fretted, rubbing their eyes over and over. Putting up the lunches (*bento*) ... including one for each of the children, I'd take them to the crèche. The road was still dark, and the children would follow, crying.[22]

The provision of crèches came much later than the Meiji period and then at only the bigger mines. As late as 1919, managers of the large Kaijima mines were promoting the establishment of crèches to "induce women to work."[23]

One alternative to the crèche or local minder was reliance on an older sibling, usually a sister, to look after the young ones. One woman who remembered her earlier excitement at seeing her mother in the evening also recalled how, as the eldest daughter, she took the place of "housewife" from the time she was only ten years old, spending arduous and stressful days looking after her two younger brothers and the baby. The children were often asleep by the time her mother returned. When she did see them at other times, she would admonish them: "Don't forget your mother's face!"[24]

Retired grandparents and other elders might replace older siblings in performing child-minding duties. Although elderly women often took on the burden alone, this service could be shared by neighbors.[25] The philosophy that "better than distant relatives are nearby strangers" was no doubt implemented only in places where communal resources allowed. When no relatives, older sisters, or neighbors were close by, or when an older sibling rebelled against looking after younger ones, the mother had no alternative to taking a child down with her.[26] Some women seem to have taken their infants into the mines on their backs as a matter of routine.

> Pushing a full wagon, we'd shove it for several hundred *ken* with our infants on our backs. ... Putting the baby down on a board or something, we'd load coal into the *sura*. When the child got bigger, we'd put them in a basket and

96 *Their life trajectory*

hang it from the rafters. When we went to push wagons, we'd give (the basket) a little swing. … Sometimes we would give them the breast. When the child began to sit up, we'd put a cushion in a collecting basket and let them play at the face. But they'd begin to crawl around. And lick the coal in their play. As it was dangerous, we were always anxious.[27]

A single mother prototype?

Many women worked extra hours to sustain their families. At some mines, they left infants at the pit mouth in an unattended shelter. The mother would come up occasionally to breast-feed her baby, then go down again to continue her work. Mashio records that Maki, "after waiting with difficulty for three weeks of child-nurturing to end, went underground. She left her baby sleeping in a hammock slung between trees near the pit mouth. There were many other *atoyama* who had children, so those who came up to breast-feed [their babies] would look to hers, or children playing nearby would take care of it."[28] The young children sometimes played in "a hut full of cracks and chinks" near the pit mouth.

To earn enough money for sustenance, mothers of older children would take a second shift, starting in late afternoon or evening, after going out only long enough to eat and make *bento*, napping in the mines when they were too tired to work on.[29] In some circumstances, they would join with others to work extra shifts at illegal *tanuki-bori*. When such activities replaced their usual jobs, child-minding could become an even more serious problem. When her *sukabura* (idler) husband abandoned her temporarily, the "Japanese Cricket" recalls, she would spread straw mats near the pit mouth before going down:

> The children would crawl about there, putting mud pies in their mouths or following [me] crying. … "You mustn't come any farther than this!" I'd tell them severely, and hearing their plaintive voices behind me, "Mother! Mother!" I'd rush off down the dark shaft. When the children cried, I felt like crying too. One day, rain suddenly began to fall. When I went up to see, the five-year-old had put his younger brother beside him and pulled the ground mats over their heads carefully. … [L]ike a good elder brother, he had covered his young brother and was waiting patiently. … It was very touching![30]

But because it was impossible to continue looking after the children this way, she took work above ground. Labor on nearby construction or public works was the only alternative to work at the coal mines.[31] On a works project, the Cricket carried her youngest to the job in a mining basket and tied the child to a tree while she loaded earth into a cart and pushed it to the dumping place. While she was dumping her load, the child would wrap himself around the tree or get inextricably tangled in the rope or be stung or bitten by insects, and Mother would have to come to the rescue. "Whether snivelling or crying, it was unbearable to see how dirty [the boy] was!" she recalled.

Their life trajectory 97

As well as abandonment by a father, conflict between a husband and wife could, of course, have negative effects on the children. "What hurt me for as long as I can remember was the fact that father and mother never stopped quarrelling," Maki recounted. Her mother's sharp-featured face was usually "as expressionless as a Noh mask," and she couldn't remember receiving a hug from either parent.[32]

Schooling (or not)

Because older children were often required to look after younger ones, they rarely got consistent schooling. The ten-year-old "housewife" received only a little haphazard schooling:

> I'd take the points for the miner's pick to the blacksmith near the school and pick them up at the end of the day. Children who had that task would get a chance to go to school along with that duty, but they couldn't go unburdened. Carrying the baby on one's back, only days on which one had business with the blacksmith were school days.[33]

Some mines might have their own schools, which were similar to the temple schools, or *terakoya*, of feudal days. According to one woman, the education obtained there was rudimentary, involving reading "chapter books" in progression and doing sums in the pupils' heads.[34] This woman helped her sister in the mines during breaks between sporadic schooling. At one stage she was ready to go to the "main school" (*hon-gakkō*), but her father hadn't registered her when she was born, so she wasn't eligible. The woman's grandmother "said that if his daughter were registered, my father would sell me [into prostitution], and she wouldn't do it for us. She said, 'If you (are registered), your father will be free to do as he likes.'"[35] There were ample grounds for this suspicion regarding her father's plans for her, he having already disappeared once while taking his niece to introduce her into service away from the mines. The narrator makes no assumptions about what he did with her cousin, but it seems that he was willing to use his young female relatives in any way that suited himself. Other fathers were skeptical of the benefits of formal education. "What's the good of having miners' children able to write? Such was the way of thinking. There was no desire on the part of the parents to have them get ahead as the result of schooling. ..."[36]

Sometimes one child in a family received an education to the detriment of the others. One woman's sense of obligation to parents and family ensured that she would expend her youthful energy in the coal mines so that her brother could get a superior education.[37] Like her, most retired women thought of schooling as a pleasure and privilege, which they had been largely denied by the exigencies of their mining family lives.[38] Another woman spoke of the irregular nature of her education at the beginning of the Taisho period.

> As my parents moved from one small mine to another, I changed elementary schools more than ten times. Most of the time, I went while looking after my

98   *Their life trajectory*

little brothers. As a result, I couldn't go into the classroom but was in the "corridor class."[39]

She says that some children attended school in the mornings but often went home to help the family obtain sustenance in the afternoon.

Despite government statistics vaunting high rates of school attendance and literacy throughout Japan, many coal miners' children had very little schooling, if any.[40] Though elementary schooling was supposed to be compulsory, many children never went to school at all. Maki started school one year later than usual, attended irregularly, and only completed four years before being sent to Tokyo as an indentured spinning factory trainee at the age of 13. Only Maki's work made it possible for her younger sister to go to both primary and higher elementary school. Maki envied her sister's educational privileges, and this envy caused rivalry that added to the contention in her dysfunctional family.[41]

If education for miners' children was generally curtailed, for children of the *buraku* outcaste villages, schooling was even less adequate. Shindo Toyo describes how some *buraku* leaders made attempts to set up schools exclusively for *burakumin* children with their own teachers, but these attempts were not generally successful until the organization of the Suihei-sha, the national association of "levellers" in 1921. In the regular schools, which they were legally entitled to attend, *buraku* miners' children had to endure discrimination from teachers as well as from other children.

Child labor

If schooling for miners' children was not highly valued, economic incentives to put the children to work at an early age were compelling. In the compilations of Morisaki and Idegawa, retired female miners confess to putting their children to work at an early age and remember children of their own generation going into the pit very early. Without "borrowing the hands of their children," one woman recalls, mining couples "couldn't survive."[42]

When children between the ages of about five and thirteen were not caring for their infant brothers and sisters or going to school above ground, they might be given simple tasks below: removing stones and coal that had fallen off wagons; carrying tools, tea, and tobacco for their parents; or helping their mothers push *sura* or wagons.[43] The dangers of pushing these cumbersome conveyances were, of course, even greater for small children than for their sturdier mothers.

Nanatsu yatsu kara kantera sagete
Kōnai sagaru mo oya no batsu.

From age seven or eight, carrying the lamp,
Going down the pit is a punishment [inherited] from one's parents.[44]

Their life trajectory 99

Figure 4.1 Children underground (Yamamoto, *Emaki*, 5th black and white illustration).

Several of the women who went down the mine with their parents in the late Meiji period recall this epigrammatic song. In Idegawa's interview entitled "Nanatsu Yatsu Kara," the narrator remembers:

> Just as the song says, "carrying the *kantera*, from age seven or eight," I went down the pit with my parents from age seven. Was there any alternative? If an infant is strapped to one's back, it can't go its own way. If the parent is a miner, the child will be one too. ... My experience was nothing special.[45]

The age at which youths commonly began mining as full partners with their parents or other relatives was 14. Larger mining enterprises may have established company regulations concerning child labor when the Mining Law of 1905 or the Factory Law of 1911 were promulgated, and they certainly had such regulations on the books before the latter law came into force in 1916. But the regulations were honored mainly in the breach. In practice, youths working in the coal mines were commonly younger than the 16 years specified by these regulations.

100 *Their life trajectory*

Perhaps surprisingly, one woman told of her eagerness to go down.

> Standing at the pit mouth and watching the wagons come out of the shaft one after the other, one wanted to see what was inside. One wondered what made human beings work inside the earth, and assumed that there must be some attraction. With childish curiosity, I was in such a hurry to go in that I couldn't contain myself. ... It was 1913 or 1914 when I went in. When I was 15. The regulations said that you couldn't go in till you were 16, but I implored the recruiter. I was warned, "If you are asked and don't say that you are 16, there'll be trouble!"[46]

Another retired woman asserted that most daughters of miners went down at an early age, not always with their parents.[47] Later, at some of the bigger mines, young girls might be expected to work independent of their families and to do a full day's work though not yet fully grown. The woman who had been in the "corridor class" reported:

> After somehow finishing school, at age 13 I'd already gone down. ... As I was still small, when I came out from behind a wagon carrying the coal basket on my back with the lantern hanging down, the foreman laughed at me, exclaiming, "Oh! You startled me. I thought the *kantera* was walking!"[48]

"It was as if the *tebo* carrying-basket had sprouted arms and legs," miners told another child.[49] These girls were obliged to mature very quickly in the crucible of the mines.

Given the discrepancy between the old Japanese system of counting ages and modern reckoning, claims by some of the women that they went down at ages 13 or 14 may have meant that they actually went to work at 11 or 12.[50] Without completing an elementary curriculum in the allotted years, many performed other indentured labor for a year or two or went down the pits immediately. Starting work at this age was not unusual in the Meiji period. For instance, the women who trundled coal in carts from mine head to river barge, before rail transport became common, began work at an early age. "From about 12 or 13, under the direction of a gang boss, we worked as stevedores. We were mostly young women."[51]

Attitudes toward child labor

Though the life was undoubtedly hard, many girls seem to have found mine work preferable to other occupations. One woman remembered life as a servant to a better-off farm family (a common experience for young daughters of miners) as a particularly unpleasant episode in her life.

> When I reached 14, I went for a year's service as a child-minder. ... [I worked so hard that] my hands and legs became all chapped. The mistress kept all my [wage] money as payment against the loan. Then I learned that my

Their life trajectory 101

father, whose whereabouts had been unknown, was at the Namazuta Colliery. I said [to him], "I haven't been to Heaven or Hell so I don't know [what they are really like]. But I am in a Hell on Earth!" So he had me released from service to the farmer. And 14 days after I became 15, I went into the mine.[52]

The high incidence of accidents among mining youths would seem to have given many girls cause to be reticent to work in the mines. One woman recounted:

Young people, truly, often died. From my cousin's family, five people went out and all five died in the mines. They went out together, but not one of them came back to change their clothes! Five [sets of clothes] just hanging there!

My friend was a woman of great faith. She took her daughter and [other] young people down. A wagon came on the run, and all of a sudden came off the rails and hit the daughter. She died instantly. "I relied on God devoutly, but it didn't do any good! My daughter died anyway!" said my friend with great sorrow. I am not a believer. I don't intend to rely on God.[53]

Though the women may have developed skeptical attitudes over the course of their lives, some remembered feeling a certain awe at the mystery evoked by the darkness and silence when they first went down.[54] As they grew accustomed to the work, the young women often came to enjoy aspects of it, in spite of its difficulties and dangers. Many had fewer family responsibilities and, like the girl who implored the recruiter to let her go down at age 15, took pleasure in working with others of the same age. The normal way of working in two-, three-, or four-person teams with relatives in separated rooms, however, denied many the experience of interacting with their peers in larger groups. Underground work socialized the young women only to the extent that production methods would allow. Some forms of amusement were shared, perhaps on the way to and from work, but those of a younger generation could be different from those of their parents, such as the types of songs they sang. One recalled: "It seems that in my mother's time, they sang what we call mining songs. But in our time, we sang whatever songs were popular at the moment."[55]

Courting and marriage

Many parents who worked at the coal mines seem to have made efforts to keep their daughters away from single young men. The desire to keep the labor of young women available to the family contributed to this reluctance. The purpose, however, could be expressed in moral terms. "Since both men and women were virtually naked in the mines, to make sure that girls didn't get into trouble, usually a family formed a mining team," one former female miner recalled.[56] After this miner married, her husband continued to work as a team with his younger sister, while the woman went with an unrelated hewer to another face. In spite of such precautions, many young women had liaisons and affairs. Though girls who began to learn the skills of hauliers in their early teens were usually

102 *Their life trajectory*

trained by their mothers or older sisters and then worked with a male family member in a two-person team, there were times, because of the difficulty of pairing all family members, when young women worked with a *sakiyama* outside the family.[57] In later days, at some mines (particularly the bigger ones where surveillance was stricter and "hanky-panky" more difficult), voluntary pairing of unrelated girls and men seems to have been sanctioned by management. One woman recounted how, at one mine, "many girls of between 15 or 16 and 20" would "fly to the side of the [*sakiyama*] they liked" at the pit mouth and, "talking noisily, they would go in."[58] At most mines, however, the choice of the *sakiyama* with whom they worked was made much more discreetly or was made for the girls rather than by them.

At the smaller mines, where the cooperative nature of the early family-type enterprise did not disappear as quickly as at the big company mines, some congeniality fostered by sustained association at work brought young people together. Camaraderie could nurture relationships between the sexes. Sometimes larger work teams at the big mines also brought young people into contact. The easy association of people working in close proximity, if not in tandem, thus often led to love affairs—and marriage, if the relationships proved compatible. Many matches in coal-mining areas were based on love affairs without being arranged by families of the young couple. And love matches made outside coal-mining areas were usually accepted at the mines.[59]

Love affairs could lead to marriage or not, and status-conscious parents outside the strata of everyday coal miners were the ones to complain about "illicit" relations. The example of libertine and womanizing older miners induced some young males to experiment before marriage. Yamamoto Sakubei, in retrospect at least, took a personal stand against such premarital experimentation, though not out of morality.[60] He implies that a premarital affair would lead to deeper involvement and marriage, producing a family that would close career options for a miner. Because few such career options were available, however, many of the young men were not averse to taking such modest risks.

According to some observers, the scanty clothing worn in the heat of the mines encouraged promiscuous behavior on the part of the miners. Baroness Ishimoto reported that "[W]ives and daughters of miners went down in a half-naked condition, mingling with the naked men laborers. ... It was ridiculous to expect morality in such circumstances. Women who worked in the darkness had a pale complexion like the skin of a silkworm; they spoke and acted shamelessly, the last sign of feminine dignity sloughing off."[61] A pale complexion was generally considered attractive in Japan, a bias fostered by other classes against peasant women who worked in the sun. But the physiognomies of the young women were no doubt marred by the soot and grime that covered them while they worked.[62] Although other physical features must have been conspicuous in the women's minimal clothing, Maki remembered that even in the steam and vapor of hot and deep coal mines in the northeast, at least the women's "nether regions" were not visible.[63] But this was not always true in many of the mines and bared breasts, if not buttocks and groins, were common and visible in mines in all Japanese coalfields. In the deeper mines, however, extreme heat would probably have had a debilitating rather than a stimulating effect.

According to Maki, some young women were not flirtatious or brazen toward the young men in the mines. Even when Maki was not at work, she did not put cream on her face and did up her hair in the simple Awazu style, with a bun held by a pin. Long tresses of loose hair were considered signs of a dissolute woman. In accord with prevailing superstition, mining women did not comb their hair underground but "while waiting for empty wagons, re-arranged [disheveled] hair quickly by hand and covered it with a hand towel." And, lest female miners be accused of indiscreet displays, Maki says that it was considered "worse than death" for females to relieve themselves where a male suitor might see them.

Young people got their sex education in many different ways. One woman who showed a great interest in the sexual propensities of young people was a carpenter's daughter who eloped to the mines after an illicit affair. "Both men and women were naked because of the heat," she says, and tells of a "droll and witty" old storyteller.

> There was a man who was good at telling stories. In the cool of the evening, the children and young people would gather around his bench to listen to his amusing stories. This old fellow, imitating a ghost in the mine shafts, would frighten the young girls. To their 15- or 16-year-old brothers, he would tell erotic stories, and these could be said to take the place of today's sex education. This fellow was responsible for bringing many young couples together. He had a special talent for it.[64]

The miners related the eternal dynamic of sexual relations to many aspects of life in the mines. Mashio reports Maki's recollection that graffiti in a Joban mine dealt openly with sexual intercourse.[65]

The bathing facilities in mining camps did not segregate the sexes. "There was common bathing, and when the young men got into the baths, they didn't like to get out," one female miner remembers. "Because the young girls also came in. When we were young, we would put pepper on the edge of the bath or have fun doing other bad things."[66] Yet the baths were not particularly clean or pleasant places for rendezvous, and they probably fostered conviviality between miners of the same sex more than attraction between those of opposite sexes.

Young people found other ways of getting together. Maki mistook the intentions of a scantily clothed young man who came through the wooden screen door one night when her mother was working and her father was away gambling. She thought the intruder was a robber.

> The *futon* were not adequate and he got in between where we [children] were sleeping with them tugged over us. He was a *goro* from the *hamba* [an unmarried miner who boarded at the big dormitory] who had come after my older sister.

104   *Their life trajectory*

It may have been this "invader" who impregnated and later eloped with Maki's sister.

Younger women were not the only targets of such invasions, Mashio writes.

> Talk of men stealing into a house to see a woman at night was very common in the colliery tenements. Not only young women, but when men's wives were attacked, sometimes the victim herself would publicize the affair.
>
> "Last night, a young man came into my place. Although I pummeled him and kicked him in the nuts, he clung to my legs so I couldn't move!"
>
> It was a kind of woman's medal of honor.[67]

The carpenter's daughter claims that a vicious wound she received when attempting to stop a fight between her husband and another miner was ascribed by others to interference in lovemaking.

> Seeing this shoulder wound, they queried, "Were you struck asunder when you were on top of each other?" It was part of the fun to relate everything to that [sex]. As it was tedious [to explain] I just said, "Yes, that's it, quite true."[68]

The retired women indicate that carnal attractions and lustful liaisons were not uncommon in the Chikuho mines. The "Goddess of the *sena*" took some delight in describing the evidence of illicit rendezvous in the dark recesses of unworked shafts.

> [T]here were many stories. To the effect that someone's wife had been seduced. There were also young men and women. Love affairs [*renai*] were common. And it was warm where the pipes ran. "There are always people in the good places, and one is afraid of falling in places where people don't go," they'd say. You'd often see two people coming out together from places which weren't in everyday use.[69]

She and other Chikuho *atoyama* talked about how underground liaisons were often exposed by excrement on the backs of women coming out of the pit.[70] Maki confirmed that such goings-on, with the same kind of telltale evidence, happened in Joban coal mines as well.[71] She evidently had an unusually fastidious view of mineshaft liaisons.

> Intimacy was really smelly, you know. Even so, between men and women, that kind of thing isn't strange. No one said anything.[72]

The result of mine-shaft affairs between young people was often elopement and eventual formalization of the marriage. Mashio, echoing custom in Kyushu, declares that it was an unwritten rule at the coal mines that "if a man and woman succeeded in escaping to a place where the chimney of a vertical mine shaft could no longer be seen, they could be joined [in marriage]."[73] But Maki, speaking realistically, asserted that young people had to have somewhere to elope to, someone to rely on for employment and subsistence. Although her sister succeeded in eloping, the couple was informed upon, and they returned to their home base where they were allowed to set up house and, presumably, resume mining for their former boss. Mashio also told of a festival at a mining region temple that, in earlier days, had allowed young people to plight their troth without benefit of parental approval.

> There may have been young people who went up to the temple for the fun of it, but there must also have been couples who, unable to consummate their love, waited for the festival to realize the fruits of a thousand nights of dreams. … It was called the Temple of the Marriage Knot or the Temple of Love.[74]

Choice of partners

Physical attraction was, of course, a factor in drawing young people of opposite sexes together. But not all the young women realized their ability to captivate men. Maki told Mashio that as novices, she and her sister were envious of the older *atoyama*, who at a distance seemed attractive.

> But on closer inspection, they [must have] all appeared gruesome. They worked with eyes askew, coughing with tongues hanging out. But compared to themselves, carrying heavy logs with their hips sticking out, Maki thought they were quite heroic, quite beautiful, and was envious.[75]

Though physical strength was not considered a particularly attractive character-istic for Japanese girls in general, Japanese miners might not have subscribed to the nineteenth-century Scottish saying: "She is like the collier's daughter, better than she is bonny."[76]

Marriage arrangements were not always made in a careful or thoughtful way. Some youths might marry for love, while others accepted their parents' diktat. The "Goddess of the *sena*" chafed under an arrangement made by her gang boss father.[77] She thought her partner's lack of mining skills and work experience should have been considered in addition to her own feelings. Other parents might have been eager to choose someone with whom their daughter could hope to work easily and efficiently in the shafts or at the face. On the other hand, a need for compatibility at work may have led some parents to accept *renai* as a portent of a better future for their female offspring. The Goddess complained that a first, formal meeting with her prospective husband, a form of the *omiai* or arranged meetings between family-selected marriage partners in other strata of Japanese society, was dispensed with in her case.[78] In other cases, *omiai* was like a betrothal, with further meetings or formal courting considered unnecessary if the various parties accepted the arrangements.

There seems to have been less willingness to accept arranged marriages among the young people who sought their partners within coal communities. Though the

106 *Their life trajectory*

partners in love matches might suffer minor social sanctions, they do not seem to have felt superstitious forebodings about them, nor did they ascribe unfortunate incidents to their failure to satisfy their parents' wishes.[79] And in mining communities, where the good name and assets of the prospective suitor's or bride's family were minimal or nonexistent, these were unlikely to be given the same importance as in the outside society.[80]

Some young male miners who had been recruited or who had come on their own from other areas had marriages arranged for them in their home villages and took brides back to the mines.[81] On the other hand, women in special positions, such as the "Offspring of a Wandering Mother" (another daughter of a *naya* boss), had husbands brought in for them from outside their own mines and not necessarily from their home villages. The Offspring's husband came from a rural background in Hiroshima Prefecture, and she felt some sympathy for his plight at the notorious Takashima Island mine outside Nagasaki Bay. Desperate to get away from the concentration camp-like mine, where an all-male work force was obliged to use outdated mining methods, he fled with two other miners and a policeman in a small boat.[82] Whether this harsh experience endeared him to the Offspring and contributed to her acceptance of a marriage proposal is not clear, but in later life, she seems to have tolerated some ineptitude and laxity in his efforts in the mines, a toleration not granted by many other wives.[83]

One arranged marriage that was certainly not "made in Heaven" was that of the "Japanese Cricket [*higurashi*]," as she was later labeled by her husband. Her situation was typical of coal-mining women who went into marriage without knowing much about their prospective husbands. The Cricket's marriage was arranged by the gang boss. It got off to an ominous start when she was obliged to cross a mountain pass on foot, arriving at her husband's mine after "sweating and panting" up the steep slope. She had gone down to work in a mine with her parents at age 13 and had not suffered too much from the work, but now her true suffering began.[84]

Her wedding to "the No. 1 Idler in all the World," consisted of the traditional exchange of cups of *saké*, perhaps presided over by a Shinto priest.

> [Then,] being full of booze, even after we went to the row house which was to be our new home, the drinking continued noisily through the night, so that it was nearly dawn when the men went home.

At this stage in the nuptials, the new husband, completely drunk, fell asleep "like a sandal-worm." No matter what she did to try and wake him, he wouldn't budge. At sunrise, when she was ready to flee in desperation,

> his eyes fluttered, and what do you think my husband said?
> "Where did you come from?"
> "I'm your wife. Don't you remember?" …
> "What's your name?"

Their life trajectory 107

"Chiyo."

"Chiyo, is it? A nice name."

It's not a joke! That's how the conversation went. Well, all because the arrangements were made without us knowing each other's faces. ...

His words, "Hurry up and feed me!" were the unforgettable opening sally in our [lifelong] struggle.

Before half a year had passed, my husband revealed his lazy nature, and after a year, from "the bride with a cute name," I had become "the shrew whose name alone is cute" in the scornful words of my husband.[85]

It was not unusual for arranged marriages to take place without the couple getting to know each other beforehand.[86] Snatched by her father from the pit mouth as she came up from the shaft on a cold winter's day, Maki met with her prospective husband in an *ōmiai* that was casual in the extreme. Her feelings were seemingly irrelevant to her father. On the way home after the meeting, Mashio wrote, "Her father said, 'He's really a good man. And he seems to have taken a fancy to you,' and he hummed a tune as he walked." And that was that. The marriage seems to have been remarkably similar to Chiyo's. Mashio tells how Maki walked to her wedding with her "slightly drunk" father carrying her belongings in a small portmanteau. Part of the dowry money of 20 yen, paid by the future husband's family who were obtaining the valuable labor of a daughter-in-law, had been consumed by Maki's father in the form of *saké*. This wedding, too, seems to have been blessed with little formal ceremony, and the bride was certainly not the object of much attention.

Not having even a borrowed gown and being taken to the shrine, I was embarrassed. You couldn't tell which was the bride, with the go-between in a patterned dress and I in a plain cotton one.[87]

No mention is made of the presence of Maki's mother at her wedding, or of any sadness at parting from her. But perhaps her mother's alleged "spinelessness" partly accounts for Maki's indifference. Her mother had agreed to Maki's engagement with no hint of serious concern for her daughter's feelings or future.

Maki's wedding reception was a modest party at her husband's family home with few guests. It was here that she first became aware that her new husband had two nonworking parents and two younger sisters who brought little income home from their jobs as maids to local farm families. At the wedding party, some coal-mining songs were sung by her husband's uncle and her father, the only recorded entertainment. After the party, the bridegroom took his bride to a corner of the family room where a makeshift bed was set up behind a screen, and the marriage was consummated in an area so restricted that "one couldn't move feet or head without careful deliberation." The real significance of the wedding for Maki was her escape from an oppressive father. "She had no expectations or enthusiasm for her marriage, but only felt relief at being liberated from a cruel parent."[88]

108 *Their life trajectory*

The loose bonds of marriage

Many marital pacts, some of them no doubt happier than that of the Cricket, would prove less durable. The vagaries of life at the mines could terminate marital relationships at an early stage, when the bonds were not very strong. One woman remembered that three or four days after a newly married couple arrived at her mine, the wife died. Her husband then departed, leaving behind his wife's spirit in the form of a Buddhist altar tablet,[89] morally unforgivable behavior. In the Buddhist scheme of things, the young wife's spirit was doomed to wander the mine where she and her husband had worked together, searching for the mate who had abandoned her. Other wives imagined that her spirit was responsible for the clanging of ventilator shaft doors, eerie reflections of safety lamps, and unheeded warnings of wagons coming. They dressed her spirit in "splendid *kasuri*," fitting for someone at least one step removed from the grime and soot of mining work, thus offering partial compensation for her husband's fickle behavior. But her workmates did not have the metaphysical power to release her from the Buddhist purgatory and send her to heaven.

Another woman spoke of a similarly weak marital bond in its early stages. She was married at 19 to a man whom she had never met. She moved with him from one of the larger mines to the small Fukasaka Mine.

> While there, suddenly he died in a flooding accident. We had only had two years together. So I wasn't deeply attached to him. ... And a man was little more than a nuisance.[90]

What might be called the elasticity of marital bonds at the coal mines is suggested by the story of a wife-and-husband swap that occurred in the process of a mass escape from a mine—one where the previously mentioned escapee from Takashima had become *nayagashira*. He was not too concerned with preventing the escape.

> There was one time when four couples fled at once. ... When they ran off, since there were woods on all sides, if they melted away quickly into these woods, they wouldn't be found out. ... It seems that the members of the four couples all took off in different directions. According to what I heard later, although they seem to have agreed on a place to meet, as the result of fear or other factors, they didn't reassemble as planned, and in the process, the eight people formed different couples.[91]

Even though the realignment of the partners is hearsay and we cannot assume that the marital bonds were loose among all four couples, the lack of disapproval on the part of the woman telling the story suggests that such "rearranged" marriages were not uncommon.

Laxity in registering marriages, as well as newborn children, facilitated marital rearrangements and common-law marriages. Maki had heard of one woman who

Their life trajectory 109

bore three illegitimate children by three different fathers as the result of underground rendezvous.[92] One of Morisaki's interviewees remembered:

> (C)hildren weren't registered. Wives neither. So there were many, many common-law wives (*naien no tsuma*). But when the kids grew bigger and it became necessary to register them, their wives were registered at the same time.[93]

Yasukawa claims that before the 1928 revision of the Regulations for the Sustenance of Mining Labour (*Kōfu Rōeki Fujo Kisoku*), which were intended to remove women from underground work, "female miners, on the basis of their economic independence, had the ability to enjoy their own true love and sexuality free from the bonds of registration and so on." He quotes a miner: "No matter how many times I was asked, I kept on saying that I wouldn't be registered as living together with my husband. Since I could feed myself and my children by my own efforts, and could get away at any time, I absolutely refused to register with him. ... By the grace of God, somehow or other I have lived with him until age 65."[94]

Most women, however, accepted the necessity of registering their marriage in order to have some recourse should the male member of the mining team abscond without his wife and children. Though Yasukawa sees a model for the liberation of women in the supposed independence of female Japanese miners before 1928, given the difficulties of providing sustenance for their families in the absence of a working husband, we might argue that the economic and social bonds in that era were not so easily loosened.

The "Old Woman of the Mountain" recalled that there were many "elopements (*kakeochi*)" at the mines. Yet although some women talked of husbands disappearing, perhaps temporarily, the Old Woman asserts that although women left children behind to run off with another man, she had never heard of a father running off and leaving his children.[95] However, the somewhat greater mobility of male miners brought them into frequent contact with women other than their spouses, and thus provided them with greater opportunities for dalliances and alternative relationships. And many earnest statements of concern for the sustenance of their children belie the supposed willingness of mothers to leave their children behind with a poor provider. The Old Woman is almost certainly wrong about the greater incidence of female infidelity.[96]

The necessity for an attachment to a male working partner nevertheless created incompatible relationships. Most widows, if they were not living and working with their deceased husband's family, found it necessary to reattach themselves to a man (and thus to a gang) in order to be allowed to stay at the mines.

> They wouldn't let out a row house to a household led by a woman. It was unfortunate if there was no man. You would be evicted. Widows had to raise their children, and no matter how much they disliked it, most of them would remarry to secure a place to live.[97]

110 *Their life trajectory*

Despite what Morisaki calls "the coincidental nature" of many youthful liaisons at the coal mines,[98] it seems clear that married women with families were more concerned with feeding and raising their children than with securing more compatible partners.

How wives dealt with the "big change"

It was common for prospective bridegrooms to have sterling reputations—at least in the accounts of go-betweens—as hard workers and abstemious men who would make good husbands. But among the women whose recollections we are citing, several brides had to deal with revelations of their husband's rather different characters after they were married. Chiyo became aware of her husband's alcoholism on their wedding night, but others did not make similar discoveries until later. The wife of the carpenter-cum-collier seems not to have discovered her husband's gambling habit until the third year after their elopement. She ascribed his hot temperament to his *shokunin kishitsu* (artisan's disposition) and in doing so was acknowledging a tradition of tolerance for unruly behavior arising from a desire for respect and independence on the part of artisans who would brook no challenges from mortals of a different status, either higher or lower.[99] But even among "ordinary" miners, drinking, gambling and brawling were common. Such behavior caused their young wives much distress.

The ex-carpenter's wife tells of her dilemma in disliking her husband's wayward behavior while lacking confidence that she could survive at the mines without him. Hearing of his involvement in a set-to over gambling, and

> Flying into the thick of the sword fight, I grabbed my husband without thinking, and his opponent's sword sliced my shoulder, *basatto*. Going to the extent of eloping to become his wife, it would've been simply appalling to have become a widow as the result of a silly quarrel. I didn't want to be left a widow, a single woman, at such a mine. It would be better to die along with him.[100]

Although typically only a man won fame from being wounded in the macho world of the mines, she gained notoriety as one who had taken on her husband's opponent by supposedly grabbing his sword. While her husband agreed to give up his gambling following the sword fight,[101] such agreements were destined to be broken, and jealousy on the part of the husband apparently led him back into his bad habit.

> [B]efore long I got the nickname of "the Slashed Auntie." ... I had really become someone who couldn't go back to her parents! And so I made up my mind to remake myself into a mine woman. Before long, I became well known and made money because the wagon distributor (*nori-mawashi*) sent wagons my way. ... "It's not your skill but your wound that made me fall for

you, *obasan*," he'd say. While this went on for some time, my husband grew more and more disgruntled. He was one who'd make a mountain out of a molehill. And so, little by little he took to gambling once again.[102]

For many women, there was no escape. In the absence of alternative partners, they were obliged to stick with men who were bad-tempered, unhelpful, and unfaithful. Working teams in the mine needed a certain amount of cooperation to get the coal out and to earn enough to feed their children, and it was the wives who had to compensate when their partners lacked devotion to work and family. The women often made strenuous efforts to secure some degree of cooperation from their mates.

The marital struggle

According to the interviews recorded by Morisaki and Idegawa, "*matsuba meoto*" (felicitous couples)[103] were a rare phenomenon. Only one of Idegawa's nine interviewees, a woman who sought a "home for the heart,"[104] did not express serious dissatisfaction with her husband. The very real resentment most of these women showed toward husbands, whom they labeled as gamblers and wastrels, is striking.

The Japanese Cricket's early married life, starting on the morning after the nuptials and drinking orgy, was, to say the least, a discouraging start for the young Chiyo. She realized, however, that she could not have safely withdrawn from a marriage that had started so badly. She believed that if she had run off to her parents' home, the gang boss who had arranged her marriage would have retaliated against both her family and herself. With a husband such as hers, she was doomed to a life not only of penury but also of contention and strife.

After this unsatisfactory start to the marriage, things became steadily worse. She objected to her husband's boast that he could get by on ten days' work in a month while she worked every day to earn subsistence for them. He took up gambling and spent money recklessly. His wife tried to indulge him, to no avail. It was inevitable that her resentment would grow.

> [B]ecause the money won in gambling is often spent recklessly in an outpouring of generosity, it gathers people to one. It seems that made him very happy. He put much more weight on having good relations with men than on pleasing his wife and children. To treat women well is a man's disgrace; such thinking was common among men at mines in the old days.[105]

He would frequently absent himself from his job and family, leaving her in the lurch. It was not unusual for women to resign themselves to their husbands' absences, feeling more independent but no doubt hoping that the miscreant would continue to contribute some support for their family.[106] There were times when the Japanese Cricket needed her husband, such as when she was about to give birth, and at such times, it seems, he could usually be counted on to be missing.

112 *Their life trajectory*

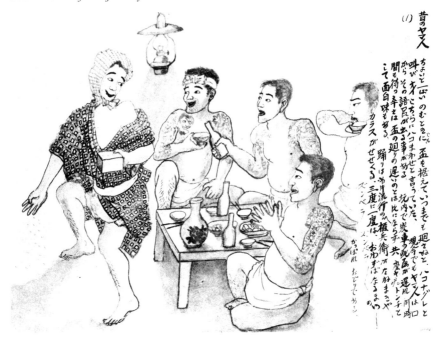

Figure 4.2 The men partying (Yamamoto, *Emaki*, 86th black and white illustration).

The Cricket also found it difficult at other times to get her husband to share the work in order to feed their family.

> [T]he idler is subject to whims, and an ordinary mortal can't understand the way he thinks. Just when I thought he was going to take another day off, shedding the fox's bad habits, he'd take up the pick and go off [to work]. Treating him to a bottle of evening *saké*, and feeling good myself, when morning came I couldn't have moved him with a crowbar. "Last night you gave me one *gō* too many of *saké*. Even though I didn't ask for it! Look what happens when you give me something I don't need. I'm hung over and my head won't work this morning." What nonsense, "hung over"! It's the excuse of an idler. I never questioned, "Oh! Is that so?" When it got too much, I would tell the *kogashira* and have him dragged into the pit. Even then, he'd find some excuse to goof off early.

The male propensity to look for excuses to quit early (*noson*) seems to have earned frequent resentment among wives. At times, the Cricket's husband worked hard, but not consistently.

> When on occasion he did work, he was a tyrant. If I rested just a few minutes while waiting for coal to take out and started to drift off for a short

Their life trajectory   113

nap, he'd yell, "What are you doing, falling asleep? Hurry up and get that *sura* out! Don't you intend to work?" Just as if he were a great worker!

Chiyo's story continues with a generalization about male quarrelsomeness that is corroborated by the stories of other women compiled by Idegawa.

> There were sometimes *sakiyama* who'd say angrily after a marital quarrel, "Today the old lady's out of control (*kaka-baré*)," and leave the pit.

Kaka-baré was a derogatory term, referring to the collapse (*baré*) of the walls or roof of a mine shaft,[107] and by implication the crumbling of the sanity of one's wife (*kaka*). It was customary to blame the wife when things went wrong, and blame was usually accompanied by verbal, if not always physical, abuse. Chiyo's claim that she and her husband never brought their quarrels in the pit home with them[108] seems to have been part of the folklore of the coal mines. The "Amazon" said that she could be a tiger in the mine but became a pussycat when she left the pit.[109]

The Cricket attempted to control her husband's spending and gambling by giving him drink at home.

> [Then,] pretending to be drunk, he'd fall into a sham sleep (*tanuki neiri*) in order to fool me. Feeling relief and taking my eyes off him, I'd go to do the wash or bathe in the public baths, and when I came back, he'd be gone. I got pretty angry at that sham sleep, you know. … Going out like that after he'd drunk his fill of *saké* was just as if he'd struck me callously. … How did he feel, pretending to snore? Like a real man? … When I think of it I almost go crazy.

Though she recognized the skills of her husband at framing, his quick temper and contempt for the abilities of female workers were less than admirable. "He was the kind of person who wouldn't let a woman like me cut even one wedge. He would say, 'Can the likes of a mere woman do work that requires savvy?!'"[110]

Coal-mining men typically treated women as inferiors. The "Two-Wagoner" remembered being made to feel incompetent by her husband early in her working life underground. Although she claimed that his disapproval had obliged her to become more efficient at her work,[111] few women felt such criticism was warranted. According to several, women did not have to do what the men wanted underground. But where safety and efficiency required a certain degree of cooperation, others admitted that "women couldn't do just as they liked."[112] Indeed, the exigencies of mining and caring for their families gave the women little scope for challenging their husbands on any score. Competition for greater output often made the men irascible and abusive. Mashio recounts an episode where Maki was training a young woman to work with her and an unrelated *sakiyama*. Being in a bad mood, he commanded the trainee to "Bring a *yagi*!" and she, being a farmer's daughter, mistook his need for a reinforcing stave for a demand for a goat, which,

114　*Their life trajectory*

of course, she could not find in the mine. Her failure incited further abuse from the *sakiyama*.

> If I tried to help [the young woman], it'd be said that she relied on me too much. In such a case, he'd try to have the last word, saying, "If it's only something like that, let her do it herself!" And he would knock me with his pick. I thought, "What an ass!" Not to be outdone, I'd shout, "You could use the time taken to complain about the *atoyama* to dig more coal!"[113]

Maki, clearly, was not one to take abuse, whether from her husband or an unrelated *sakiyama*.

A revelation

At one point the husband of the Japanese Cricket contracted for tunneling work in "the lowest *oroshi*" in a deep, hot, and wet mine. Hauling coal from this miserable place was so arduous that she herself withdrew in a state of semi-illness.

> In the same way, my husband eventually took to his bed. He had an ongoing temperature, contracted pneumonia, and was at death's door. While caring for him, I reflected on it. He was an idler, but on the rare occasion when he put forth an effort, this was what happened. If this was the result, it seemed that it would have been better to avoid work permanently, and I was wrong to nag him to work all the time. Had he been born to be an idler? It was just a strategy (*waza*).[114]

Similarly, Chiyo realized that her husband's gambling addiction was not simply a function of an inherently "bad character" but symptomatic of a pathological weakness. "Since he would go as far as to use the contents of the Buddhist altar as security for his betting, one could only think that my husband's gambling was an illness."[115] But though she was attentive and solicitous when he lay in bed on the verge of death with pneumonia, she was poorly rewarded. Unexpectedly recovering, he took up drinking and gambling once more, forgetting commitments he had made to reform. Chiyo characterized her husband as one who would "piss in the face of a frog." When he cashed in all his chips to remove himself from their mine, she was left with two boys, an infant son, and no money.

> I had to work on, ignoring the crying child. I felt resentment against my husband. Causing his little children such suffering, there was not one word from him as to where he might be wandering.

Mining women, she rather bitterly suggests, had to put as much energy into their work as mining men put into their recreational pursuits.[116]

Chiyo had further difficulty in dealing with an eventual communication from her husband saying that he was "in the care of the police." Although she often

Figure 4.3 Incessant conflict (Yamamoto, *Emaki*, 112th black and white illustration).

wanted to separate from him, both before and after his absence, she could not create the conditions under which she could raise her children without some normative attachment to a man. This was the dilemma of many mining wives.

Her husband had other deficiencies that contributed to their unhappy marriage. He raised cocks for prizefighting and gambling, thereby finding another way to squander money that should have gone for sustenance for their children. A gambling-related quarrel resulted in a nasty wound that he chose to regard as a symbol of valor. When she questioned his braggadocio, he grew angry and called her a fool. "Don't women understand anything? A wound is a man's medal of honour. You don't have any regard for my reputation!" But she had a good appreciation of the relative value of such symbols. "If such a wound is a *man's* distinction, being hit by rocks, crushed by wagons and so on, I have wounds all over my arms and legs," she pointed out. "And what distinction do these give *me*?"[117]

Her husband was more concerned with obtaining goodwill from his neighbors and acquaintances than with satisfying the needs of his family. He "would be the first to climb someone else's roof to repair it when ours was leaking badly," and "would involve himself in the marital quarrels of neighbours whom he hardly knew." But a not uncommon consequence of such intervention was rejection of the mediator by both combatants. Then he would have to buy placatory *saké*. When he went to festivals, this cavalier father would not take his children with him, and he objected to his wife going out to entertainments of any kind. "For

116 *Their life trajectory*

women to spend money to see that kind of thing is a waste," he would say about her desire to see just one movie during her lifetime.[118]

The head of the family was undoubtedly the man, but the burden of family responsibilities was dumped onto the woman. Husbands often used their authority to lead their wives and families into the darkness of night, fleeing to supposedly better but usually unpredictable situations at other mines. The Cricket's husband did this more than once. If he fled separately, she would be surprised when he summoned her to join him at the new mine, if in fact he did. It became such a habit that even when she realized that he was going, she wouldn't bother to ask where. "If it's so bad, get lost and go where you like on your own!" she told him angrily.[119]

Chiyo admits that there were good times when she and her family had enough to eat and drink. But at such times her husband would gamble away any leftover cash. Once retired, he continued to make her life as difficult as ever, deriding her efforts to make money by cultivating vegetables and selling flowers in the town. He continued to call her a *higurashi*, a Japanese cricket that makes an incessant rasping sound. It was somewhat ironic that retirement, bringing with it a lack of income for drinking and gambling, put a severe crimp in her husband's lifestyle, making him even more difficult to deal with. Other women described the difficulties of handling idle and frustrated mates when they lost their jobs at the mines due to age, disability, or redundancy. The Cricket could tolerate some of her husband's bad habits as long as he was working, but she was not going to let him monopolize her time when he was retired and she was still trying to earn an income. She could not be very sympathetic when high blood pressure brought on serious illness; he was still unpredictable and difficult.

> If he got a little better ... he'd say he was going to work. Why would he say such a thing now when he was ill? How I could rebuke him for saying what I'd wanted to hear him say in the past! "Am I hearing right? Does a person who has been an idler all his life want to work? It's enough to make one laugh! I'm so surprised to hear such a thing from you that it's likely to give me a stroke. Why don't you shut up?" I said, laughing bitterly.[120]

Only on his deathbed did he finally admit that he had caused her to suffer, and then only grudgingly: "I've caused you some difficulties."[121]

> Just hearing those few words, there was nothing more I could say. How much grief had my husband's pleasures caused me? My resentment was beyond words. Four days later my husband died.

This long-suffering wife put gambling cards in his coffin, "intending that he would not lead a dreary existence in the other world." But she wondered who would put what emblems of her own life in her coffin.[122]

Funerals at the mines were simple affairs, highlighted by a procession such as the "jangles" at the Ashio Copper Mine described in fiction by Natsume Soseki.[123]

They were simple affairs de-emphasizing the corporeal existence of the deceased. A woman who described her younger brother's badly burnt corpse also remembered:

> At the funeral in continuously falling rain, the mourning came from our hearts. The couple from Tosa who lived up the street also died, and in the rain, their eight-year-old daughter, leading the three- and four-year-olds by either hand, followed her parents' coffins with a dazed look. Even now when I recall it, I am overwhelmed and the tears flow.[124]

Getten

For many coal-mining women, then, the frustrations and stresses of their work and daily lives were transmuted into animosity toward their husbands. Yet redirecting frustration was the very thing they accused their husbands of doing. Both the men and women, of course, had ample justification for their frustrations, but they did not always realize that its root cause was the nature of their work and the pressures imposed by company management and gang bosses.

Several uncommon expressions for the turning of bad tempers against others are found in the accounts of retired female coal miners. *Nejire getten, kuso getten*, and *mawashi getten* all indicate bad temper directed at others. Kaneko's dictionary of *The Language of the Chikuho Coal Mines (Chikuhō Tankō Kotoba)* says that "the hard base rock or stone without cracks appearing in a coal seam was called *getten*. A person who stubbornly refused to listen to what others say was also called *getten*, but it is not clear which was the original meaning."[125] The women interviewed by Idegawa, however, use the word to signify frustration and bad temper, something more than mere unreceptiveness.

The ways in which frustration due to the nature of the mining work and to subjection to severe exploitation could be taken out on a mate is illustrated by the Amazon. She saw marital conflict in the context of the difficulties of the work underground. When she was as "late" as 5:00 a.m. in getting to work at the face, having been delayed by morning chores, her husband (who had gone down at 2:00 a.m.) would get cross.

> Dashing down, when I got to the face I'd find a pile of coal already there. If I couldn't get a *sura* out immediately, my husband would roar in a fit of anger (*getten mawashite donaru*): "What have you been fooling around at till now?"[126]

And there was conflict over the always difficult task of pushing wagons, at which she had earned her nickname, "the Amazon" (*dairiki onnago*). Her husband, envious of her strength and ability at pushing two empty wagons in tandem, once told her to let him bring in the pair. When she had filled a wagon and the empties did not come, she went to find him leaning against them,

118 *Their life trajectory*

exhausted. Swearing at the "shitty" wagons, he turned his *getten* on her, saying that her strength was wasted on a woman and threatening to go out.

> Having someone with such a bad temper (*kuso getten*) is troublesome. If you confront him, he gets mad. If you don't confront him, he gets mad anyway. Since there's always something to make him upset (*getten no tane*), you never know when he's going to explode. Leaving him alone is the best way.[127]

The Amazon criticized the male chauvinism that spread like a plague among coal miners after the early days of family operation of small mines had passed.

> Why is it so bad for a woman to be stronger than a man? It shouldn't be wasted, this strength that enables us to eat. Wasn't it strength that saved me, one who couldn't read or write? I'd be punished if I wasn't grateful for it.[128]

But she regrets the waste of energy involved in dealing with her husband's frustration when they were both in their prime.[129]

Great stamina was necessary for mining women who were burdened with household chores as well as the work in the mines. One woman says:

> Men have no endurance (*shinbō*). When a woman's young, if she can't push wagons, for instance, she'll be embarrassed if they say, "That woman doesn't like to push wagons," and so she'll work at it. When she's older, she works for her family. Men don't think of such things at all, but only do what they want.[130]

Some women recognized the need for their husbands to get rid of the frustrations associated with their work, though they deplored the standard ways of doing so. The man could let off steam, but the woman was expected to endure the many hardships of life at the mines. There is no denying the toll of the coal-mining work in misdirected energy and psychological damage.

Reproduction and conflict

Many women, though at odds with their husbands for most of their working lives, gave birth to children, often (according to Morisaki) out of an initial desire to create a real bond with their mate.[131] When that proved difficult or impossible, at least they could find a diversion from bickering and substitute maternal for conjugal love. Maki perceived that her mother felt fulfilled only in the process of producing children. "Even if a woman is with a man whom she hates enough to want to kill, as long as they are together, children will be born, won't they?" she comments.[132] Other women spoke of the desire to be rid of their husbands and how it was thwarted by the arrival of children.

> I was just a working tool. When I thought that a couple shouldn't be like that, I shed silent tears. When I couldn't stand it any longer, I made up my mind

to leave, but while I was wondering whether this or that would be the day when I took off, morning sickness began. Now I had to somehow be patient.[133]

In the narrow confines of the tenement housing, there was little chance of intimacy in private once children were part of the family. Conditions at Kyushu coal mines were similar to those in the northeast described by Maki.

> The colliery houses were all single rooms. Even after grandfather died, the five of us all slept together. In such circumstances, a man and wife couldn't do it (*aré*) as they liked. Wasn't that the main reason why, when [my father] was drinking, he picked on my mother? It wasn't only our family. The fact that quarrels took over in the colliery tenements must have been due to that.[134]

Her father's dissatisfaction with life at the mines disposed him to gambling and drinking, which in turn added fuel to her parents' quarrels. Maki's mother, apparently having witnessed a gruesome accident in the mines that persuaded her never to go down again, worked at various odd jobs above ground for which she was not well suited and that did not bring in a comparable income. As a result, her self-esteem was low, and having a weak heart as well, she seems to have been an ineffectual mother, neither a good provider nor a role model for her children. Maki admired her mother hardly more than her wastrel father, wishing that she would go down to bring in more money and better support the family.[135]

The quarrels of a mining man and wife often ended in a beating for the wife. Mashio recounts the typical development of a confrontation between Maki's parents, starting with the drunken demands of her late-returning father for more *saké*. When her mother tried to ignore his clamor, he would get angry and "open fire," throwing rice bowls and sewing scissors at her and wielding the kettle, "still with hot water in it," as a weapon. Maki would physically intercede, and

> the commotion could be heard throughout the tenement, but there was no sign of anyone getting up [to stop it].
>
> "Even when we have nothing to eat!" mother would say in a low voice. And father would roar like thunder. "What the hell! The hell you say!" and it would become an all-out exchange of blows. Yes, mother would raise her eyes and hit back.

Her mother, usually meek and taciturn, could become confrontational and even belligerent in the face of her husband's anger.

> But she couldn't do anything against such a strong man. She would collapse with a "*Hi i i!*" in a dying voice. Since I was brought up seeing such goings on, I had little chance of becoming a sweet young thing.

Such wild mêlées and beatings would not be cause for a woman to leave her man in the mining camps, given the standard dilemma women faced: If they went

Figure 4.4 Domestic violence (Yamamoto, *Emaki*, 98th black and white illustration).

out on their own, they would probably be unable to earn a living and might even have to give up their children. "A woman who didn't work [in the mines], even if she lived with the Devil himself, could only survive by staying and bearing it," Maki recalled.[136]

When Maki herself had been married for some time, she found it impossible to satisfy her husband's sexual urges. After the postnatal death of her second child, Maki "must have been enervated," Mashio writes, "but though little time had passed since the birth, as a means of satisfying his immediate carnal desires, he demanded she yield to him. Maki San felt repulsion even for the body odor of her husband. And in order to produce and raise the next child which her husband did not want, she would have to work underground."[137] Later, when Maki heard that her husband was enamored of a woman at the brothel, she felt both anger and resignation. Her exhaustion after work left her incapable of challenging him, but on the nights when he stayed home, she resented his advances. "When she thought of how these arms had embraced a prostitute, she felt murderous thoughts towards him. But her severe exhaustion and somnolence incapacitated her." Maki recounted:

> I'd push him away without thinking. And when I did this, he'd say, "You're not the only woman in the world, you know." That was probably why he'd gone to the other woman earlier and why he went to the brothel. You can understand my feelings when he said that. My body just wouldn't respond. I didn't feel any eroticism or desire. ... The old man was hewing and had

days when he goofed off, so he had extra energy. But when I was made to work up to my eyeballs, after I had taken care of the children I couldn't even follow my own inclinations as I liked.[138]

As in the agrarian society from which they or their forbears came, the women were inured to "doing their duty" for men without whom they were unable to survive, even though they did so much of the work both above and below ground. Their marital lives, even if they began with some hope of connubial congeniality, soon deteriorated into lives of servitude, conflict, and tedium.

Debt: another source of marital friction

Although miners were tied to the mines by their indebtedness to the bosses and the company, their propensity to blame spouses for incurring debts, even though the conditions of their life and work were actually responsible, exacerbated marital friction and helped make families dysfunctional. The men were loath to give up recreational pursuits that put them into further debt and resulted in family sacrifices. And when it came to placating their bosses in order to acquire and retain employment, the men were often ready to offer the sweat and tears of their wives before they would work harder themselves.[139]

Sometimes, in the face of great burdens and stress, the wife would be strong-willed enough to take charge of family finances and even family welfare in general. One recounted:

> Somehow we had built up a debt of more than 5 yen and had to pay it back. I worked out ways of getting by. Not only in matters of money, but even looking for [new] mines. Since my old man was one who didn't bother with such matters.[140]

More often, in cases of indebtedness incurred by the husband's drinking, gambling, and whoring, the debts could cause open marital friction and disaffection. The account of Strong-as-an-Ox, who had been obliged to send her daughter into service because of debt, shows how this friction could reach calamitous proportions. Before her husband could terminate the service arrangement in order to send the daughter to an even more dubious employer in a more distant place, for which he might gain a bigger prepayment—ostensibly to pay off his debts but more likely to indulge himself still further—the mother demeaned herself by appealing to the current employer for further financial assistance. Her resentment of her husband's gambling habits and his callous attitude toward her daughter's alienation from her is apparent in her account of her visit to the "master" and his indentured maid.

> He was the master of a house with a dubious reputation in the village. ... "Did you come as a parent? Or as a pimp (*zegen*)?" There was no way to answer. My daughter was holding back tears and staring at me. Fearing her

122   *Their life trajectory*

master, she didn't even try to come to me. Seeing my daughter's tears, instead of listening to what he said, my pain was unbounded. Throughout my life and even now, I can't forget it.

She managed to borrow five yen from the employer, but her sorrow and shame were such that she took a roundabout way of returning home so that no one would recognize her, see her tears, and realize the disgrace that her husband had wrought upon her. And although she initially told him that she would work to pay off his debts over and above the five yen, her anger simmered until she was ready to do away with him.

My daughter hadn't said anything to me. Nor did she come close. But he didn't ask how she was, and not thinking of her, said only, "Could you only borrow five yen?"

It was always the way while he was alive. So for three nights, I agonized over it. How many times did my hands go for the framer's axe? It's the truth!

I wanted to kill him for the [four other] children's sake, but then I thought that, for their sake, I couldn't do it, and in that way the nights passed. As long as I was around, I made up my mind that there was nothing for it but to work and endure it, thinking only of nourishing the children. I was the family rice-winner. Until the children grew up, there was no time to complain. I was the loach (*dojō*) in the cooking pot.[141]

The *dojō* was a coarse fish found in the muddy ponds and marshes of Japanese farmland and eaten as a last resort by peasants as a protein supplement. The analogy means, of course, that there was no escape for this woman from her Fate as a miner and a miner's wife.

Notes

1 Idegawa, p. 105.
2 Morisaki, pp. 114–5. This woman birthed and raised a son (if not other children as well) after her miscarriages.
3 Idegawa, p. 96.
4 *Jizoko no Seishun*, p. 119.
5 Morisaki, p. 132.
6 *Jizoko no Seishun*, pp. 119.
7 *Jizoko no Seishun*, pp. 119–20.
8 Mashio says that mothers exhausted from childbirth in the mine were put on coal wagons and lifted out by the winding apparatus. *Jizoko no Seishun*, p. 120.
9 Idegawa, pp. 126–7.
10 Idegawa, p. 127.
11 Idegawa, p. 178. This woman goes on to say that similar arrangements were made for washing the body in the center of the room after a death in the family.
12 Shindo Toyo, *Chikuhō no Jokōfu-tachi*, p. 24.
13 Shindo, pp. 258, 260, 265.
14 Idegawa, p. 73.

Their life trajectory 123

15 Idegawa, p. 164.
16 Mashio, *Jizoko no Seishun*, p. 88.
17 Nishinarita, *"Sekitan Kōgyō no Gijutsu Kakushin to Joshi Rōdō,"* p. 74.
18 Idegawa, p. 171.
19 Idegawa, pp. 149–50.
20 Morisaki, p. 9.
21 Morisaki, p. 187.
22 Morizaki, pp. 9–10.
23 Ogino, *"Taisen Zengo ni okeru Kaijima Tankō-gyō no Rōshi Kankei,"* p. 139.
24 Idegawa, pp. 59–60.
25 Idegawa, p. 134.
26 Morisaki, pp. 53–4.
27 Morisaki, pp. 185–6.
28 *Jizoko no Seishun*, p. 116.
29 Cf. Morisaki, p. 186.
30 Idegawa, pp. 70–1.
31 Cf. Morisaki, p. 33.
32 Cf. *Jizoko no Seishun*, pp. 13, 20, 23, 69.
33 Idegawa, p. 60.
34 Morisaki, pp. 34–5. See Sone, *"Exploitation or Expectation?"* p. 44, for this woman's description of her elementary education.
35 Ibid., pp. 35–6. Cf. Sone, p. 45.
36 Idegawa, p. 107.
37 Idegawa, pp. 109–10,
38 Cf. *Tankō Bijin*, p. 155.
39 Idegawa, p. 33.
40 See Sone, *"Exploitation or Expectation,"* pp. 38–40.
41 Mashio, *Jizoko no Seishun*, pp. 14–15, 71–2.
42 Idegawa, p. 60.
43 Morisaki, pp. 104, 124.
44 This song, common in northern Kyushu, is quoted with slight variations in most manuscripts concerning the colliery workers. Other sayings emphasized the continuity of the miners' inheritance (e.g., "If you carry the *sena* for three days, you'll know your obligation to your parents.") Idegawa, p. 123.
45 Idegawa, pp. 195–6.
46 Morisaki, p. 103. See also, Nomi interview in Tajima Masami, p. 6.
47 Morisaki, p. 173.
48 Idegawa, pp. 33–4.
49 Idegawa, p. 61.
50 A child was aged one when it was born and two on the New Year's Day following. Thus it was possible to be aged two, or in the second year of life, several months (or even weeks) after being born.
51 Morisaki, p. 167.
52 Morisaki, p. 121. This girl would seem to have gone down after the customary two-week holiday at the old lunar calendar New Year, suggesting that her age was counted in the old Japanese way and indicating a persistence of the custom in some "backward" coal-mining areas.
53 Morisaki, p. 173.
54 Morisaki, p. 51.
55 Morisaki, p. 48.
56 Idegawa, *Hi o Unda Haha-tachi*, p. 110.
57 Cf. Mashio Etsuko, *Jizoko no Seishun*, pp. 72–4.
58 Morisaki, pp. 75–6.

124　*Their life trajectory*

59　Cf. Morisaki, *Makkura*, p. 114.

60　*Yama ni Ikiru*, p. 97.

61　Kato, *Facing Two Ways: The Story of My Life*, p. 161. (For issues of "morality" involving British mining women, cf. John, *By the Sweat of Their Brow*, pp. 30–1, 40, 45, 50.)

62　In his book, *Tankō Bijin: Yami o Terasu* (Coal Mine Beauties: Dispelling the Darkness), Tajima Masami associated the self-confident, dignified, and often droll but withered faces of 46 retired female coal miner interviewees with a kind of beauty that he admired in their characters (passim).

63　Mashio, *Jizoko no Seishun*, p. 89.

64　Idegawa, p. 101.

65　*Jizoko no Seishun*, p. 61.

66　Morisaki, p. 14.

67　Mashio, pp. 70–1.

68　Idegawa, pp. 101–2.

69　Morisaki, p. 127.

70　Cf. Morisaki, pp. 194–5.

71　Mashio, *Jizoko no Seishun*, p. 92.

72　*Jizoko no Seishun*, p. 92.

73　*Jizoko no Seishun*, p. 86.

74　*Jizoko no Seishun*, pp. 94–5.

75　Mashio, pp. 74–5.

76　John, *By the Sweat of Their Brow*, p. 40.

77　Ibid., p. 128.

78　Morisaki, p. 128.

79　Cf. George DeVos, "The Relation of Guilt toward Parents to Achievement and Arranged Marriage among the Japanese," in Sugiyama Lebra and Lebra, *Japanese Culture and Behaviour*, pp. 91–9. The remorse suffered by the ex-carpenter's wife, quoted here, can probably be ascribed to her earlier status outside coal-mining society.

80　Eg. Morisaki, p. 140.

81　Cf. Sone, *"Exploitation or Expectation?"* p. 41.

82　Morisaki, pp. 45–6. Cf. *"Takashima Tankō Kōfu Taigu Kinkyō"* (Recent Conditions and Treatment of Miners at Takashima Coal Mines), *Saga Shimbun*, August 17–19, 1888, in Hidemura Senzo et al., eds., *Hizen Sekitan Kōgyō Shiryō-shu* (Compendium of Documents on the Coal-Mining Industry of Hizen), Bunken Shuppan, 1977, p. 414.

83　Morisaki, pp. 58–9, 63, 65. For the many inadequacies of male partners, see Idegawa, *Hi o Unda Haha-tachi*, passim.

84　Idegawa, pp. 61–2.

85　Idegawa, pp. 62–3.

86　Morisaki, p. 112.

87　Mashio, *Jizoko no Seishun*, p. 110.

88　Mashio, p. 111.

89　Morisaki, p. 88.

90　Morisaki, p. 112. See also, Idegawa, p. 111.

91　Morisaki, p. 45.

92　Mashio, pp. 87–8.

93　Morisaki, p. 159.

94　"Hisabetsu Buraku to Josei," in *Nihon Josei-shi*, vol. 4 (*Kindai*), pp. 221–2.

95　*Makkura*, p. 144. On p. 68, Morisaki seems to agree that "many women left husbands and children to run off with men with whom they could work effectively," but although younger women may have done so, there is a notable paucity of such cases in the records I have seen.

96　It may be an extreme case, but one retired miner tells how her husband brought his girlfriend home to sleep with them, and apparently stayed behind with the woman when the narrator went to work the next day. Tajima, *Tankō Bijin*, p. 40.

Their life trajectory   125

97 Idegawa, p. 152.
98 Morisaki, p. 68.
99 One story of how an artisan builder of a reverberatory furnace in the Mito domain insulted officials at the completion ceremonies in 1856, was then exiled in disgrace, but was reinstated to build a second furnace, is documented in my dissertation, "The Origins of the Modern Japanese Iron and Steel Industry" at page 106.
100 Idegawa, p. 91.
101 Idegawa, p. 92. The words *"inochi morau bai"* probably meant that he would devote the rest of his life to her wishes because committing suicide would not serve her interests.
102 Idegawa, p. 93.
103 See p. 186 for Idegawa's description of *matsuba meoto*.
104 See Idegawa, pp. 171–93, particularly p. 174.
105 Idegawa, p. 64.
106 See Idegawa, p. 46.
107 Idegawa, Glossary, p. 221.
108 Idegawa, p. 67.
109 Idegawa, p. 48.
110 Idegawa, pp. 67–8.
111 Idegawa, p. 130.
112 Morisaki, pp. 127, 195; Shindo, p. 17.
113 Mashio, p. 76.
114 Idegawa, p. 69.
115 Idegawa, p. 74.
116 Ibid., pp. 71–2.
117 Idegawa, pp. 74–5.
118 Idegawa, p. 75–6. On the other hand, Yamamoto's illustrations suggest that a variety of entertainers came to the mining camps, and women as well as children would see their open-air shows. *Chikuhō Tankō Emaki*, passim. But I believe Sone exaggerates the variety of entertainments available in mining areas away from the towns, particularly in the early days of Chikuho mining. "Coalmining Women," pp. 216–18.
119 Idegawa, p. 76–7.
120 Idegawa, pp. 83–4.
121 Ibid., p. 84. Adding to the nice coherency of her narrative, she repeats what she had said by way of introduction to her story on p. 58.
122 Ibid., p. 59.
123 Soseki, *The Miner*, pp. 90–3. Jay Rubin, translator of *Kōfu*, uses this particularly felicitous word for funeral because funerals in the northeast were called *janpon*, suggesting the clamor of bells in the funeral procession. See Mashio, *Jizoko no Seishun*, p. 66. It may be noted that after the Hōjō disaster, bodies of those registered in locales other than Hōjō and whose relatives did not come forward to claim them were cremated at special crematoria set up in the town, while Hōjō victims were all buried. Orii, pp. 102–3. Orii describes the splendid treatment of the bodies of technical and staff members of the company at pp. 104–6.
124 Idegawa. p. 15.
125 Kaneko, p. 75.
126 Idegawa, p. 38–9.
127 Idegawa, pp. 42–4.
128 Ibid., p. 44.
129 Ibid., p. 50.
130 Morisaki, *Makkura*, p. 44.
131 Morisaki, p. 68.
132 Mashio, p. 23.

126 *Their life trajectory*

133 Idegawa, p. 125.
134 Mashio, p13.
135 Ibid., p. 22.
136 Mashio, pp. 46–7.
137 *Jizoko no Seishun*, p. 118.
138 Ibid., p. 124.
139 In the play "The Female Miner (*Onna Kōfu*)," based on the experiences of coal miners in Kumamoto Prefecture around the end of the Meiji period, a miner who cannot repay the *maegashi-kin* (loan money) advanced by the gang boss, insists that his wife take in a new recruit as a boarder in order to relieve a shortage of housing. The wife argues that the 30 *sen* paid for room and board will hardly cover the cost, but her husband chastises his wife for confronting the boss with the truth of their situation. Losing his temper, he throws a rice bowl at her during the confrontation. The veterans of the coal wars who advised the scriptwriters apparently felt that such trouble between man and wife over debts and obligations was so pervasive that the scene was not improbable. Shindo Toyo, *Chikuhō no Jokōfu-tachi*, pp. 66–9.
140 Morisaki, p. 59.
141 Idegawa, pp. 159–61.

5 The daily routine

Tankō no onago wa, futari yaku mo sannin yaku mo shiyotta desubai.
Women at the coal mines did two or even three people's work.[1]

Early in the morning

In the daily routines of families living at the mine-head, the women took the leading roles. In the early years, before mining camps sprang up at viable mines, miners walked to work.[2] Although their accommodations might vary in their home villages, their routines and the roles of women were similar at their villages and in the mining camps.

In the Meiji and Taisho periods, the morning began very early—before dawn—at most mines. In order to eke out an existence from the coal seams, the women worked as many as 12 to 16 hours underground.[3] These long working days left few hours for caring for their families and for doing household chores. Thus *atoyama* had even less time than their sisters in the textile industry (who were more often unmarried) to bathe, do up their hair, and get adequate rest.[4] In the absence of assistance from all but the most dedicated of husbands and fathers, of whom there seem to have been few,[5] this heavy burden was one that the women bore with fortitude, though they often complained to interviewers later.

The little hovel

Families at the mine site woke up in the "little *naya*," a single room in a long tenement with between five and 13 similar units.[6] These tenements were better than the shanties built by the miners themselves at the first small coal mines in the mountains.[7] But although their original name, *nagaya*, emphasized their length, the standard corruption of the term, *naya*, was written with Chinese characters that suggest a warehouse for bodies. Mashio Etsuko describes the arrangement of the tenements at a mine-head village in the northeast, an arrangement typical of Kyushu coal camps.

128   *The daily routine*

> At right angles to the narrow river as many as ten buildings were lined up, with black paper roofs. ... One building had five units; each unit had one room of 6 *jo* (six *tatami* mats). If a lamp were lit in the neighbouring unit, this one also became bright.[8]

Some of the camps must have been rather dreary, especially where the eaves of the rows came so close to each other that sunlight did not reach the ground between them.[9] On the other hand, indoor light from adjacent units might be troublesome for miners trying to sleep off an underground shift.

Light, smoke, and noise were shared because miners were divided from their neighbors only by a rough plaster wall to ceiling height.[10] In the cruder tenements of the early Meiji period, the earthen floor was leveled from the hillside of mine sites in the mountain valleys and covered only with straw or other rough matting. Another straw mat (*mushiro*) would be hung from the entranceway lintel to act as a door and to provide limited protection from the outside climate.[11]

Although the long roofs of the early tenements imitated the straw or reed thatch of large farmhouses, over time the supporting beams and posts bent and the "roof (lines) rolled like waves."[12] Later, thatched roofs would be replaced by wooden shingles or tar paper—and even by baked clay tiles or tin roofing at some of the bigger mines. Shingles would warp to the shape of curved *sembei* (rice crackers) in the north Kyushu summer heat and would blow off in the wind, leaving the *futon* and *tatami* to be ruined by monsoon rains.[13] Mashio says that in the northeast, tarred paper roofing had to be retarred every three or four years by the miners themselves to prevent serious shrinkage and cracking in temperature changes from winter to summer. The tarring had to be done in late autumn or in the spring because in summer heat the coal tar would run off and in winter it would not spread properly. More modern roofing made the tenements look less like farmhouses and more like barracks,[14] or, where they were replicated in rows, "like harmonicas lined up."[15]

Where colliery companies were obliged to provide somewhat better accommodations for scarce labor, the floor of the main room might be raised on a wooden frame with a bamboo lattice covered with *tatami* mats. But even these floors were far from adequate. One woman remembered:

> The floor was woven of bamboo, and the *tatami* mats laid on it, so that when the men got to drinking and carrying on, they might plunge through it. The tables would be overturned. And they would fall on their bums. All Hell would break loose![16]

Yamamoto Sakubei says that where this construction was used, the *tatami* were so poor ("the worst in Japan") and the bamboo lattice so undependable that "When people in the old days were offended, they would retaliate: 'May you die by having your balls caught in the bamboo flooring!'"[17]

In the center of the older tenement rooms, an *irori*, or cooking hearth, was surrounded by a wooden frame, and a wooden or metal hanger was suspended from the rafters for the cooking pot.[18] In most later tenement units, the cooking was done on a brick platform on the dirt floor of the area that served as the entranceway, storage space, and kitchen. But the cooking pot would be hung over the *irori* when meals were being served. A *gangan* heater might be placed in the center of the floor to provide warmth if the tenants had inadequate *futon* quilts. Many retired Chikuho miners remembered the smoke from the coal fires and the cooking odors wafting through the whole length of the building, though some families later developed ingenious systems of plastering newspapers onto wires to make ceilings that, in winter, would keep in some of the heat of the fire.[19] In the more severe cold of the northeast, Maki criticized her mother for failing to paper the ceiling properly. "What with the glue and dust, and accumulation of detritus, the paper peeled off and fell."[20] Some miners also tried to improve the units in other ways by "putting rough plaster on the walls and building shelves to make it somehow liveable."[21]

Most of the women complained about inadequate space in the cramped quarters. Yamamoto described the typical housing unit:

> The housing of miners with families, in part of a tenement, was about 9 by 12 ft., and where there were *tatami*, one room of four-and-a-half *tatami* only, with no closet. There was a dirt floor area of about 3 ft. in depth and 9 ft. (long), with a single rain shutter (*amado*) at the entrance. For light, there was one lattice window or a push-up window. Things were so bad that where the family was large, they couldn't get into the four-and-a-half mat room, so at night they spread rough matting on the dirt floor and slept on it.[22]

About 1930, when Maki was first married and living with her in-laws, Maki and her husband slept on a makeshift wooden floor over part of the dirt area. But the rough divider between the two sleeping quarters was an insufficient barrier to keep her father-in-law from trying to molest Maki in her "room" when his son was away at work and the mother and sisters-in-law were sleeping.[23] Where a single family slept "cheek-by-jowl," there could be little privacy, but large families kept each other warm on winter nights. One retired woman asserted that the fire was placed in the center of the room "because ... three families out of ten had no quilts."[24] In later days, miners would be provided with sets of quilting by the *nayagashira* (gang boss) when they were recruited. But where the turnover of miners was high, newly borrowed bedclothes were likely to be as worn and stained, if not as dirty, as those slept in for long periods by old hands who were never able to cleanse themselves of coal soot.

Some improvements?

An adulatory description of the efforts of large collieries to "clean up their act" in the provision of housing was penned by Konoe Kitaro in 1898. The tenements were praised for adequate construction, generous spatial arrangements, and for being clean and orderly. They were "infinitely better" than the housing "of a

130 *The daily routine*

remote mountain village,"[25] not itself a very high standard. Similarly, the officially sponsored 1908 *Kōfu Taigū Jirei* (Regulations for the Treatment of Miners) reported six- and eight-mat rooms with *oshiire* closets, and even detached houses for larger families.[26] The retired women, on the other hand, remember no such grandeur and confirm that the housing at most mines continued to be cramped, poorly built, and far from weather-proof.

After the turn of the century, the Mitsui Company boasted that it provided a closet for bedding and storage in dwellings at its new mines but also had to admit that "There was no ceiling ... no fittings for a closet door ... no kitchen facilities."[27] Although these units had single three-*tatami* rooms with a dirt floor entranceway and working space, the rooms seem to have been about the same size as the four-and-a-half-mat units that most retired women reported as typical.[28] Mitsui later proclaimed itself ready to offer one mat per member of a miner's family, the same norm that the company offered in its crowded textile mill dormitories.[29] But variations in standard mat sizes among regions (and even among different types of accommodations) made this an offer of dubious value. Yamamoto describes a shingle-roofed unit of six mats in size with "a cooking area of one *tsubo* (about one square meter) covered by a projecting roof of galvanized iron (or tin)" as the kind of unit that might have been offered at "a small mine in the Meiji period."[30]

It was only in the Taisho period that large families sometimes sought employment at mines that regularly offered six-mat units,[31] (i.e., ones with about 100 square feet of finished floor space). In the Joban region of the northeast, a somewhat higher standard of housing is reported; each unit was made up of six or eight *tatami* with a dirt-floored area as well.[32] There were instances where large families were allowed two of the typical four-and-a-half-mat units, which they might combine by taking down part or all of the intervening partitions. One of Morisaki's interlocutors notes, however, that at her mine they paid rent for the housing at so much per mat,[33] and the cost probably discouraged most miners from indulging in more than one unit. Yamamoto says that by 1920, miners at bigger mines were housed in units of two rooms of four-and-a-half and three mats in area, with a closet divided between two units.[34]

No matter how generous the mining companies claimed to be in attempting to attract workers to the mines, inadequate housing continued to be a major factor in high labor turnover. One woman remembers that there were no sliding screen doors as dividers between the entranceway and main room (as there were in most farmhouses), no sliding shutters to the outside, and only one window for light.[35] Another woman remembers that in her childhood the door to the communal toilet was a hanging straw mat similar to the primitive entrance door.[36] At Joban mines, Mashio reported, there was only one *benjo* (primitive toilet) and washing place for two or three tenement units.[37] Ablution facilities were no more generous in Chikuho. One retired miner recalls that when she went to the Shinnyu Mines (a substantial operation) in 1918, "We lived by the light of the miners' lamp since there was no electricity" in the married quarters.[38] Without any electric light or

The daily routine   131

any real protection from cold weather, waking up in such a poor hovel would have been particularly unpleasant in winter.

Furnishings for these living quarters were less than adequate because the miners were usually expected to provide for themselves. The "few eating facilities"[39] might include a food box, short-legged table, and crockery. A dynamite box might accompany a toolbox at mines where the miners were expected to provide their own tools (and were not required to keep them all underground). And quilts were lacking at parsimonious mines, as were mosquito nets. The "comforts of home" were few indeed. In fact, for most of the period and at most mines, the housing can best be described as rude and miserable.

> *While people are dreaming,*
> *I'm in front of the stove;*
> *How hateful the 3 o'clock whistle!*[40]

Until the 1920s at least, many of the larger coal mines in North Kyushu began the first shift at 3:00 a.m., well before first light.[41] However, Morisaki Kazue reported that starting and quitting times were not fixed at the smaller mines, but were determined by the miners according to how much they needed to earn. At others, "There were two shifts, and it was common to start at 4 o'clock in the morning and evening."[42] But where hours were not fixed and wagons scarce, they went down earlier, "about two o'clock," in order to get leftover wagons from the second shift.[43]

To prepare for the day, the women would usually get up earlier than the men, after inadequate rest. Mothers worked quietly in order to avoid waking sleeping infants and husbands. They would start a fire for cooking in the *gangan*, the rudimentary stove fashioned from half of a small oil barrel and used at both Kyushu and Joban coal mines.[44] At the Joban mines in the 1910s, the fire in the *gangan* was apparently started outside, even in the coldest weather. The fact that coal, once ignited, "would not go out even in the rain" was a big advantage. Yamamoto remembered that in Kyushu they cooked on the *gangan* outside only in good weather.[45] Chikuho women were sometimes given allocations of coal for cooking as well as heating the main room of their houses,[46] but these allocations were rarely adequate. Only managers could be said to have enjoyed a "comfortable" standard of living with heated houses.

According to Mashio, in Joban it was the children's responsibility to start the morning fire in the *gangan*, not only in families like Maki's where her mother was not strong of body or spirit.

> Exhausted by heavy labour, the parents would wake the children and go back for a short nap. Roused from their sleep and rubbing their eyes, (the children) would burn paper waste and small branches and gradually add coal. When whiffs of acrid smoke began to rise, the coal had caught fire. Even the 3- and 4-year-olds, when they woke up, would quietly surround the fire.

132   *The daily routine*

Maki recounted:

> When the coal glowed red and the smoke stopped rising, it would be time to take the *gangan* in to the hearth in the house. It was so hot that children couldn't hold the handle, but we'd look for someone in the neighbourhood and, one way or another, get them to help us. Even if our parents were fast asleep, somehow we'd manage it.[47]

When the rice was cooked, the children could wake their parents and infants who might be still sleeping. At some Chikuho mines, and probably at many Joban mines as well, the children would wake to find their parents already gone to work. In this case, the children were left to fend for themselves, older ones caring for the infants and sometimes falling asleep in the evening before their mothers returned.[48] They would be extremely lucky to get a good breakfast, let alone "three square meals" a day.

In the few instances where child-minding facilities were provided at larger mines in later times, the women might start work after taking the children with their lunches to the kindergarten or crèche. But the older children would still have no one to care for them after school.[49] In the Joban region in the 1930s, the women could go down later than the men. "It was acceptable for the *atoyama* to begin work after a certain amount of coal had been dug out," Mashio says.[50] But in the earlier period, and later at smaller mines where the women carried some of the tools, water, and food for the men, they had no such flexibility, and the couple would have to go down together.[51]

Water!

A common morning task was to fetch water because in early days at most mines, and even later at smaller ones, it was not piped into the lodgings. The water might come from an on-site well, though Morisaki says that "There were not many places (mines) where wells had been dug."[52] Where there was no well, the water might be carried some distance from a creek, pool, or spring. A woman who emphasized the scattered nature of early coal mines in "wooded hills" said about one mine: "From the *naya*, passing wax trees and then fields and meadows, below that there was one well. The women could not get water easily."[53] Upon going to a mine where she had heard that there was a crèche, another woman found that "there was no water available."[54]

Yamamoto Sakubei recounted:

> At all the coal mines, the most serious problem was fresh water. Even if there was rice, if you didn't have water you couldn't live.
>
> Since under the surface everything was disturbed by mining, underground water disappeared, and no matter how many wells were dug, water didn't appear. The sole source of water at Kami-Mio was a spring on the low ground below the level of the *naya*. This, too, tended to dry up in summer,

and the line of people with buckets waiting their turn wound about almost endlessly. When your turn finally came, the water you carried was used as if every drop counted. Even the water for washing the rice wasn't thrown away, but used for dish-washing. It was so precious that we children were even concerned about drinking tea.[55]

Yamamoto noted that "When the dry season came, only as much water as a horse pissing came out, so it was used as if it were as important as eye medicine," and was rationed. And "in the summer, the (wooden) buckets would tend to dry out, and it was unfortunate to have to use water to moisten them." Other than the brick-lined well, there was only one well "at the village border in a cryptomeria wood," but it "was as much as one kilometre away and its water had such a metallic taste that you couldn't drink it."[56] Water was so important that in 1918, according to one woman, when some miners were so poor that they had few other belongings, their families were described as "(one) bucket households."[57]

Many women had to fetch water at a distance, often in the early morning or late at night. Wells were unreliable, and water from pools and streams was sometimes brackish and only usable as "grey water."[58] Even where water was piped in, at many *nagaya* there was only one standpipe at a central wash place for a building of between five and ten dwelling units.[59] And "since the washstand was outside, when the weather was bad, it was always difficult to wash the dishes."[60] Cleansing the body in the morning may not have been an important part of the routine for

Figure 5.1 At the well (Yamamoto, *Emaki*, 91st black and white illustration).

134 *The daily routine*

people who expected to get dirty in the grime and filth of underground shafts. But the needs of cooking, laundry, and child care were not well served by such limited supplies of water. And miners needed substantial quantities of drinking water in the heat underground. In the northeast, Mashio says, the *atoyama* was responsible for taking a two-*shō* flask (the equivalent of two large bottles of *saké*) of water into the mine each day for the *sakiyama* and herself.[61]

A single communal toilet for each building must have been severely taxed in catering to the needs of several families.[62] Baroness Shidzue Ishimoto (Kato Shizue) reported from personal observation that, at the supposedly modern Miike mines in 1915, "There was only one lavatory for a whole row of barracks. There was neither gas nor water service."[63] No wonder that pissing against a wall became a habit accepted by all but the most fastidious of mine dwellers! But indiscriminate excretion could have unfortunate consequences. The Old Woman of the Mountain recalled:

> Until that time (probably the Taisho period), water was taken from the Yamada River. Typhoid got worse and worse and nothing could be done about it. It happened because piss water from the area flowed into the river. So Mitsubishi made a deal and water was brought in from the Okuma River. All because piss had gotten into the water which they'd been drinking.[64]

If matters of sanitation were not well understood, neither were modern Japanese habits of dental hygiene, if the women's failure to mention them is a guide. On the other hand, sanitation and personal hygiene were said to be matters in which outcaste people were seriously deficient. But the "*eta* housing" provided for the many *burakumin* who worked at the coal mines was reported to "discriminate against them down to the very design of the toilets,"[65] and we cannot suppose that these arrangements encouraged high standards.

Preparation for yet another day

In preparing for breakfast, the cooking pot would be filled with enough rice for breakfast and lunches, if enough were available. In their recollections, the Chikuho women make no mention of the necessity to use cruder grains such as *awa* and *hie* (millet and sorghum) to take the place of rice in times of dearth, which was a common complaint of peasants in the Tokugawa period and even of farmers in the northeast in the 1950s and 1960s. The women, however, did complain of being short of rice in hard times and of being required to work long hours to earn enough for the family rice pot even in good times. Bachelors in the big dormitories might be relatively well fed in most periods, but Matsumoto Kichinosuke recalled that all *buraku* miners who commuted to the mines, like families in the tenements, had to feed themselves even at a time when "12 or 13 hours of continuous work brought in only about 30 *sen*."[66]

The daily routine   135

Condiments would be added to the rice if, for instance, the children had been able to find seasonal herbs on the nearby mountainsides. Maki said that her mother's philosophy concerning subsistence was based on her knowledge of the availability of nature's "abundance" (more often in the form of grasses and weeds than edible herbs).[67] *Okazu*, dishes to supplement rice at a proper Japanese meal, and even soups, were notably lacking from the breakfast menu, though they are more often mentioned in connection with the evening meal. One woman, whose husband was ill and unable to work, could only afford potatoes and squash as *okazu*, very poor supplements from a Japanese point of view. And, in typical maternal fashion, she ensured that the children and her husband were fed before she partook of the leftovers, though this left her weakened for the underground work.[68]

Claims by others that coal miners ate well relative to poor farmers or townsmen[69] seem to have referred mainly to the quantity of rice that they consumed rather than to variety and nutrients in their diet. Dr. Ishihara reported a significant incidence of beriberi among miners, an indication of an unbalanced diet.[70] We might be dubious about Mashio's claim that coal miners invariably ate well,[71] though her rationale for their desire to do so certainly seems valid.

> Miners who worked hard ate meals which were substantial and even sumptuous. This was at least partly because it was heavy labour and they used up a great deal of energy. ... It was human nature to think that if they could just reach the surface without injury that day, even if they had to borrow money, they would like to fill their stomachs with something tasty.

But Mashio also reports Maki's recollections of a horrible stew with potatoes and greens chopped into the rice. And

> Maki San could not recall ever having eaten a meal with pure rice. ... Her father was extremely lazy and a quarrelsome drinker. If her mother washed rice for the evening meal and left it sitting in the pot, it might be surreptitiously converted into *saké*. At such times, there was nothing for it but to dash off to the pawn shop.[72]

The families of other men who were addicted to *saké* and gambling resorted to various stratagems to get enough to eat. Not remembering any nourishing meals, Maki would have liked to eat hot rice and fresh *miso* (bean paste) and longed for some of the treats of New Year's.[73]

Along with making breakfast, the preparation of lunches was a crucial part of most morning routines. One woman says that if they were short of supplements for the lunch box rice, a neighbor would share hers with them.

> If you said, "There's no *okazu* for our lunches," someone would say, "At our place we have such-and-such pickles; shall I cut you some?" and everyone in the neighbourhood would live by sharing what they had.[74]

136 *The daily routine*

The practice of sharing food, even rice, was common.[75]

Another retired woman describes the lunch boxes:

> The *bentō* (box) was called a *kuragae*, and even now if you go to a wood-cutter's place you can see them. They are made from bamboo with two layers in the shape of a *koban* (big elliptical piece of Tokugawa period cash). The top and bottom are covered with cryptomeria wood. (The food) put up in this, in the case of a bachelor, it is tied up with crossed cords and carried on the shoulders hanging from the (miner's) pick. Among us women, there were those who wrapped it in a *furoshiki*. I did it that way for each of the children as well.[76]

Yamamoto Sakubei says that aluminum *bentō* boxes came into use as early as the end of Meiji (1910–12), adding that the *kuragai* (his pronunciation) "was deep enough to put rice in both top and bottom, up to four or five *gō*, and there was also a small compartment for vegetables." The single vegetable, however, was usually only "one *sen* worth of pickled radish (*takuan*). ... The container for hot tea was made of tinplate and was called a *gamé*."[77] Hence the miners' term for seeking a new job, *gamé-tsuki ni iku* (to seek a job providing a teapot).[78]

Going down

When the breakfast and lunches were ready, Kyushu colliery mothers woke their husbands and children. If, for some reason, the miners slept in, the gang boss ensured that they would get to work by having his dispatcher rouse them.

> Beside the sink, there was a small window with a wooden lattice shutter. Opening the window from the outside, the *kurikomi* came around waking up (the miners for) the first shift. Since many of the miners didn't have clocks, the *kurikomi* came round and (shouted), Go down! Go down! at three o'clock in the morning to let them know it was time.[79]

The tenements were built with such a hatch window for the express purpose of waking the miners. Sometimes beatings gave emphasis to the commands.

> Guys under the gang boss would wander about with cudgels. They'd go round to the houses of their underlings every morning. "What! Your head hurts? Fool! You've drunk too much *shōchū* (low-grade distilled spirits). Come out! You won't come out?" and they'd be beaten.[80]

Another woman told the story of how the husband of a woman she knew pleaded that he was not well enough to work but was dragged from his bed, beaten until he sustained serious injury, and then made to work. The result—he died.[81]

Early morning rousing combined with the need to fill a certain number of wagons in order to obtain the day's sustenance compelled the miners' wives to prepare the food and get the men to work. One woman who was not successful in this endeavor had her "lazy" husband dragged to work by the *kogashira* when he was delinquent in supporting his family. Another preferred to do the dragging herself.[82] After the beginning of the twentieth century, at big mines, when flexibility in working hours was gradually attenuated with the assignment of jobs by functionaries of corporate management rather than by the agents of gang bosses, the women felt oppressed by the stricter regimen. One recalled:

> [The government-run Akaike Mine] was different from the small mine at Koyanose where I was together with my parents, and they (at Akaike) were serious about times for going in and out. It was very difficult until I got used to it.[83]

Some parents also had to get used to delivering children, often crying or complaining, to the crèche or a minder in the early hours before dawn.[84] The provision of such facilities as crèches at bigger mines came later, but in earlier days, the problem of getting the young ones to a child minder when there was no one available in the family was much the same. One woman says she paid 8 *sen* (in the early 1910s) to have the children cared for from morning to night when her daily wage was 30–40 *sen*.[85]

When the man-and-wife team went into the mine together, the woman often carried a major share of the day's needs, as described by two women.

> Three or four short picks, clamps, saw, metal tags, food and a water flask. … Just try to walk carrying a load like the seven essentials of Benkei. It's almost more than one can do.[86]
>
> (We carried) saw, framer's axe, a hand towel full of the mud for dynamite tamping sticks. And a tea pot this big round [she gestures]. Also carrying three or four picks, although it was still dark, we would clatter along. And the *sakiyama* … carrying that *sakiyama*'s *bentō* and one's own, all those things together, we would have to go down quickly so as not to be late.[87]

The women might be required to carry these loads for considerable distances, not only to the pit mouth but then down to substantial depths in the mine.

> We didn't ride in any wagon. We went down along the side of the haulageway, walking where people and carts shared the passage. It was a mine with *kantera* lamps, and we reached the face after walking for up to 30 minutes.[88]

Inadequate clothing

At some of the coal mines, the miners went to the pit in what are described as work clothes.[89] But there is no indication in the recollections of the retired women that smaller companies allocated clothes as part of the recompense, as employers of farm labor and indentured weaving apprentices had customarily done in late Tokugawa and the early days of Meiji.[90] Some of the larger mines would have

138   *The daily routine*

standard work uniforms in the 1930s and 1940s.[91] But in the late nineteenth and early twentieth centuries, miners usually wore clothing inadequate for the weather above ground and their work below. At some mines, the men went to work in very scanty clothing, amazing a woman who was new to such a custom.

> [We came] from a small mine to Kyushu Saitan. … Kyusai wasn't a particularly big mine but compared to Kojaku, it was much deeper and because there were many more miners, the first thing that surprised me on coming over was their clothing in the shafts. The men left their houses naked. In a single loin cloth. No wonder I was surprised! And you know, even the women were naked. Because it was deep and hot. They wore only a short underskirt. Both embarrassed and alarmed, I said to my younger brother's wife, "Oh! they're like robbers, aren't they? Can we work with them? Shouldn't we be frightened of such people?" and felt very small.[92]

In mines where it was not extremely wet, men and women stripped to the waist for work. One woman who went to work in a new mine (Shinnyu) in more substantial clothing soon learned to adjust her attire to the heat.

> The men were stark naked, and the women were working in much the same state. Not knowing anything, I outfitted myself in a long skirt … but it was hot, very hot. … If I didn't take it off, I couldn't endure it. Even when I wrapped just a single hand towel around my hips, it was too hot.[93]

Baroness Ishimoto says that women lived half-naked above as well as below ground in the summer heat of North Kyushu.[94]

Though some women, working with their husbands, "threw caution to the wind" (or heat), most worked in a specially made miner's skirt after taking off their shirt or smock. Matsumoto Kichinosuke, probably referring to the skirts of *buraku* women in particular, notes that they were "all hand-made,"[95] mostly, no doubt, by the miners themselves. One woman described the standard mining skirt (*mabu-beko*)[96] with dimensions not more substantial than a modern miniskirt and just as revealing.

> It is fastened with a cord, tied in front like a garment wrapped around the hips. But since it is short, things can be seen when you bend over.
> After some time, (Western-style) drawers became available. Even though they were called drawers, they were really only short pants (*sarumata*). They may have been better than modern panties. But now things could be seen from the front.[97]

In extreme heat, the women might remove even the drawers.[98] Yamamoto's illustrations show that the common female miner's skirt opened at the front to allow ease of movement in cramped quarters and in awkward loading and dumping operations and, sometimes, even hewing. But just as it facilitated the work, it also left the women open to prurient curiosity and ribald comments from the men.

The woman who described the skirt in detail described the female miner's shirt and the waistband (often worn only on the way to and from work) as "eight *shaku* (feet) of bleached cotton ... wrapped around (the waist) tightly and tied at the side. When it was tied at the side, it was known as a Daté."[99] Although the style of waistband worn by peasant women of the Daté feudal domain in the northeast was apparently copied by Kyushu mining women, the sleeves of the *mabu-jiban* were more like narrow Western sleeves than the loose, slit sleeves of traditional Japanese clothing, which farm women had to tie up when working in the fields.

> The head towel was known as *kōnai kaburi* (underground head-covering), as it had just one end hanging down loosely behind. In front, it came down low over the forehead so that it wouldn't come off, and that (style) was called *tsuya*.[100]

If the head-covering actually "came down low over the forehead," it also would have served to keep the soot off the forehead and, with luck, out of the eyes. Yamamoto does not illustrate this style of covering, but keeps the forehead and forelocks uncovered, a style attested to by at least one retired woman.[101] The torso was usually bared for work, leaving younger women feeling vulnerable.

Straw sandals

Another element of the standard accoutrement of the miners was their sandals. The male miners wore straw sandals that consisted of a tightly woven sole and twisted straw braids between the big and second toes and looping around the foot and ankle. But there were mine tunnels too constricted to accommodate even the thickness of this footwear, in which case the sandals were temporarily discarded.[102] The women used straw sandals (*waraji*) in the early days, though not invariably those of the same design as their male partners.

> *Pechan, pechan* was the sound of one's *tsuma-waraji* (wife's sandals) drenched in the water underground. We worked in sandals which covered only half of the foot, called *tsuma-waraji*.[103]

These "better-half" sandals, covering only the toed half of the foot, and also called *ashi-naka*, or "part-feet," were insufficient to protect the feet from falling or loose rock or from coal or the swinging pick of the *sakiyama*.[104]

Straw sandals wore out quickly as the women strained against the rough floors of the hot and humid headings. Several women testify that they always took down extra pairs, often hanging from their waistband, and usually wore out two pairs in a day. This provision of extra sandals became a custom connected with superstition in the minds of some women where the need was not palpable.[105] One woman recalls a "mountain" of worn and rejected sandals in front of the public baths.[106]

140 *The daily routine*

Figure 5.2 Woman hewing in *mabu-beko* (Yamamoto, *Emaki*, 4th black and white illustration).

One woman whose foot was mangled beneath a boulder from a cave-in took up the weaving of sandals during her recuperation.

> Since I wore them myself, with that in mind, I pulled the straw close and wove them tightly, so that they were made really well. Usually, we went down with a change of sandals, but there were people who said, "If Taka San made the *waraji*, one pair is enough," and bought them for 3 *sen*.[107]

Because there was a demand for sandals, other female miners made them at night to supplement their mining income, though most did not have spare time to weave sandals when they worked long shifts. It may have been mainly *burakumin*, given the less remunerative jobs underground, who were obliged to add this extra load to their working day in order to supplement their incomes.[108]

At some mines, somewhat later, straw sandals were proscribed in favor of more adequate *tabi*, the canvas foot covering worn by Japanese workmen until recently. But the cost to the women was often prohibitive. One woman tried to evade the proscription but was stopped and lent a pair of "boots" by her foreman who was impressed by her diligence.

> Having come to the pit mouth with my *bentō* early in the morning on my way to work, there was no way I could buy underground *tabi*, and thinking that I'd have to go home and "grind tea,"[109] I felt like crying with vexation. ... Even though I worked that hard, there was no way I could afford even one pair of miner's *tabi*.[110]

Hygiene and sanitation

The women lacked adequate provision for daily or even monthly hygiene. It was customary at the coal mines to forbid women who were menstruating from entering the pit.[111] According to traditional Japanese beliefs, menstruation was considered a form of pollution. Menstruating women continued to be excluded from underground work throughout the Meiji period and at larger mines even after that. Referring to a later time period (probably the 1930s), one Chikuho woman commented: "If you said, 'Today I'm bleeding,' that was the only thing about which the *rōmu* (foreman) wouldn't make trouble."[112] But, of course, the time off would mean loss of income to support the family. Thus, many women at the smaller Joban mines worked through their monthly periods; women in Chikuho often did the same before 1930. Management turned a blind eye to breaches of custom when it benefited "the bottom line."

Chikuho women who could not afford to take time off probably dealt with their monthly periods in much the same way as did women in the Joban region of northeastern Japan. Mashio's protagonist, Maki, says:

> There are some things which a woman has difficulty preparing for. Unlike the present, there were no convenient aids, and we used cotton rags and so on.

"In the cross-tunnels, they dug a trough and buried them like a dog," Mashio records. But although this must have been degrading and embarrassing, Maki "never said anything about the great discomfort of working during her period." Without toilet facilities underground, the younger women learned ways of dealing with menstruation from their elders.

> (Maki) said that a middle-aged veteran *atoyama* taught her. After throwing water over oneself at the *bakku* (cooling trough), you just douched yourself roughly with your hand. Even if you changed sanitary cotton, it would soon get wet with sweat, so you wrung it out with water and used it over and over again. Since you were not out in the sun but in the dim tunnels, surely it would all be washed away without the colour or anything else being seen.

142 *The daily routine*

But as a young woman Maki did not find that solution satisfactory, Mashio says.

> People were always going to and coming from the cooling trough. And Maki San was not brave enough to do so. Looking for an abandoned shaft or hiding in the cross-tunnel, she did her business.[113]

This "business" included all forms of purgations. If this was the situation at such a major coal mine, Mashio argues, it could not be expected that toilets would be provided at the smaller ones.

Adornment

There were differences in approach to personal adornment among the women, such as hairdos and make-up that were regional, local, or personal in provenance. Although one woman suggested that female miners had no time to think of such things,[114] others reported considerable effort to make themselves, if not attractive, at least presentable on their way to work. Apparently sorting-station women made efforts to titivate, at least before and after work, but underground workers had little opportunity to compete with their sisters on the surface.

One woman reported (and this may have been in the 1930s after our main period) that in a mine that was apparently modern enough to provide for scheduled time off for its workers, the women not only wore the conventional head covering but also enjoyed special and frequent hairdos. However, "in the old days, either everyone did their own hair or skilled people among the miners might act as hair-dressers." She suggests that the women's preference for "the Japanese style" of hairdo was quite impractical. "It was showing off, but since we got filthy, I now think it was a great waste of time."[115]

Another woman expressed some contempt for the excessive make-up of modern women—"they use pancake make-up (*beni-keshō*) and refuse to be bested only in expressions of vanity"[116] —but recalled attempts at self-enhancement by members of her own generation.

> The young women tried to look smart when they went in, wearing make-up and towels on their heads. They paraded in so vivaciously that the local farm women used to say, "They dress up like that just to make a show on their way to the pit." They wore ornamental hairpins in hair done up tightly. There were also some with combs in their bobs. The hairpins had red knobs or blue ones.[117]

These adornments, however, were not common before 1930. This woman also describes fine splashed pattern (*kasuri*) shirts and bleached cotton (*sarashi*) waistbands that were only for show and were cast off along with any fashion pretensions while the women worked. In deference to the Mining Goddess, who was said to have "frizzled hair" (*chijire-gami*) and to be jealous of anyone who tried to maintain a nicer coiffure,[118] they left their hair unattended to and covered. Of course, the women got filthy in the shafts and had probably lost any semblance of respectability as they carried their clothes out with them after their shifts.

Eating underground

The mining work proceeded with very few breaks. Lunches were often eaten while waiting for wagons or during other unscheduled rest breaks needed to stave off hunger or exhaustion. One woman's recollections of working conditions around 1930 suggest that lunch breaks, now scheduled at a better mine, were highly valued. But, "if we got hungry while waiting for wagons, we would get the bread and rice-balls which we had brought in (and eat them)."[119] The pleasure of sharing meals with friends may have been rare at more strictly regulated mines. Nevertheless, one woman suggests that although they were not dependant on the men, they liked to eat their *bentō* in a mixed group, and Yamamoto Sakubei paints a gang having an apparently pleasant lunch break at the haulage-way.[120] This was not possible, however, when isolated man-and-wife teams were working to maximize output and could take breaks only when a lack of wagons or disjunctions in their work routines required them to put in "dead time."

In a particularly hot and humid mine, Mashio reported a typical loss of appetite.

> In the mine, not only was ventilation bad, but the unique stink of coal hung about. They ate their *bentō* at the winding station ... but when the smell of

Figure 5.3 Lunch break underground (Yamamoto, *Emaki*, from the 8th color illustration).

144 *The daily routine*

coal entered their nostrils, their appetite failed. They were even repelled by the smell of their garlic. But if they left *bentō* uneaten, they would have no strength.[121]

Although Maki took up smoking in a nugatory attempt to dispel nausea and to restore her appetite, another *atoyama* hinted that queasy stomachs could be overcome with the passage of time.[122]

Another struggle was to keep awake during the brief respite at lunch.

Since we worked without (regular) breaks, we'd be so tired that while we were eating our food, we'd drop our bowl, *poton!* Just like that, without realizing it, we'd fall asleep while eating.[123]

Long shifts

According to a woman who helped prepare food in her uncle's dormitory kitchen, the male *sakiyama* would often quit work when they had hewed what they considered a sufficient amount of coal or when their bodies could no longer endure the physical punishment or their minds, the tedium.

Since the first shift came up when they liked, we could never get things cleaned up. *Noson*—that is, quitting early. There'd always be some who practised *noson* and came back early, and they would eat. So this random order continued forever.[124]

But although male miners worked only as long as necessary to hew what they thought was a reasonable amount of coal, the *atoyama* usually came up in late afternoon or early evening, having worked 12- to 16-hour shifts.[125]

One woman spoke of being able to belt out her loud prayers at home only when she worked the first shift at Iwasaki because when she worked the second or third shifts elsewhere, she had to restrain herself so as not to bother the sleeping neighbors.[126] Her mention of three shifts probably refers to the late 1920s when ten- and even eight-hour shifts were instituted at a few of the larger, mechanizing mines.[127] Other women say that they came up after dark, rarely seeing daylight, and sometimes working double shifts to earn enough to survive.

After working all day, we often came up to the pit mouth about the time the nine o'clock whistle blew. ... When we were going to be too late coming out, I'd come up alone, prepare some new food, and go down again.[128]

Because they had begun work at 3:00 a.m., this working stint implied an 18-hour day. Another woman recalls that double shifts were worked often in order to support families.

We'd go in again at 12 o'clock at night (after starting about 2 a.m. the previous morning). Coming out briefly, we'd eat a meal, prepare food and go in again for the second shift. We might do a little sleeping in the shaft. When we needed money, we had to carry on like that. Time was meaningless. When we came out, it would be dark again. There were many times when I didn't know how long I'd been in.[129]

In her time at the mines, she implies, the women got no regular days off.

That the men did not often work such long shifts probably did not make them any easier for the women.[130] In cases where they shared the work "fifty-fifty" or where the *sakiyama* and *atoyama* were fond of each other, the man might stay behind and assist with loading. It was only where the husband was particularly considerate that "the woman would go out first."[131] Some fortunate women, as already noted, were also allowed to go in later than their husbands in the morning. More often, however, the women went in with the men and were left behind to finish loading at the shift's end.

One woman talked about how difficult it was not only to leave her children early in the morning but to stay down to finish the loading in the evening.[132] There were also those who stayed behind not only to load but to dig their own coal and make up for the shortfall of incapacitated or wastrel husbands.

> I often got it out by myself. When I worked with an unrelated *sakiyama*, I'd load out the coal that he had dug, and after that was done, left on my own, I'd dig, load, and get out another two wagon-loads before coming home. Putting on my own metal tallies, I'd report faithfully to the office and come out.[133]

Even if waiting for wagons provided the women with a rest or food break, such breaks would lengthen their working day, keeping them away from their infants and household chores.

> When the wagons didn't come round, impatient *sakiyama* would shoulder their picks and go out quickly, but the women would wait for the wagons to come. … Waiting patiently, after loading and going out, (you found that) you had spent 12 hours or more. The infants put out to care would be waiting with eyes swollen with tears.[134]

But if days of work were long, days without work could be disastrous for coal miners. One woman spoke of half pay, perhaps for "busy work," when coal could not be gotten from the face.[135]

Late in the evening

One woman described their evening's activities and duties.

146 *The daily routine*

> We'd come up covered in soot, you know. Quickly washing off the dirt from our hands and faces, we'd immediately plunk the coal which we'd brought back into the one-*tō gangan*, and put it into the middle of the 4½ mat room. … When the fire was going, we'd run to the office taking our seal and a bucket. Receiving the money for that day, next we'd have to go to the distribution center to buy rice.[136]

Many female miners recall that wages could be paid daily, every three days, once a week, or twice a month.[137] Earlier in Meiji, wages were paid three times a month at one Kyushu mine in Matsuura, which Sumiya Mikio calls typical; according to the lunar calendar, that was once every nine days. But other mines settled accounts (wages and the cost of provisions) six times a month or twice a month.[138]

Among the various wage systems, daily payment in the Taisho period was the one that caused the women the most difficulty and about which they complained most often because it forced them to purchase rice one day at a time.

> When we received that day's wages in that way, we'd hurry around to the shop and buy our one *shō* of rice—we'd buy that day's rice one *shō* at a time—and prepare the evening meal.[139]

They might also buy some *miso*, also just enough for one day.[140] In some cases, delivery of the daily rations might come late at night, which was more than a casual inconvenience.

> The day's rice would come about twelve o'clock at night. So you'd have to go to buy rice in the middle of the night every time. Only one day's rice at a time. Since extra never came, you couldn't buy enough for several days. And there wasn't enough money, anyway.[141]

Another woman spoke of buying three or four days' worth of rice at a time to save money and make ends meet. This was the woman who ate as little as possible to ensure that the rest of her family got enough to eat when "a person could earn from 30 to 40 *sen* a day."

> If you worked from 12 to 16 hours it was about that much. It was probably about the time when rice was 13 *sen* per *shō*. There were times when we didn't receive money but only rice vouchers or cash chits.[142]

This was the invidious system whereby management ensured that "their" miners bought supplies at company-managed commissariats or independently managed stores that were contracted to accept company vouchers or chits. One woman reported that, at the Iwasaki Mine, they were paid half in cash and half in vouchers redeemable at designated shops in the nearby towns of Katsuki and Nakama.[143] The miners sometimes sacrificed lamp oil vouchers to treat the children to candy.

The children often begged us, "Give us the oil voucher!" The oil voucher was the one for buying the oil for the lamps we used underground, and in the mining camps they were used like money. If we handed them over, saying, "Here you are!" they'd run happily to buy candy. "Don't chew it all up! Suck it properly!" we would say.[144]

Because miners could not have worked without oil for their lamps, it would seem that the vouchers were issued in sufficient quantities to allow for a small surplus. Management may have encouraged productivity by pegging vouchers to the number of shifts worked, or miners may have acquired more vouchers than they actually needed for lamp oil. In either case, the inability of mining women to buy candy for their children from their regular wages suggests the inadequacy of their incomes. Our earlier narrator spoke of being given rice for *omochi* cakes at New Year's and two batches of vermicelli (*sōmen*) at the Obon festival in midsummer in the absence of any other bonuses.[145] Other women spoke of candy received as bonuses on special occasions as one of the few pleasures they had enjoyed as girls working underground.

In the aftermath of the Rice Riots (i.e., in the 1920s), wives were often obliged to serve "Chinese rice" (*karamai*) to their families. Such imported rice was said to be smelly and stale-tasting and often had impurities such as imperceptibly small stones mixed with it. The term "foreign rice" (*gaimai*) came to exemplify inadequate and unpalatable food. At the large Miike mines, Mitsui provided "contract rice" at substantially cheaper prices to induce miners to stay and work hard.[146] But this rice was the notorious "*Nankin-mai*," coarse and smelly. Soaking the imported rice in water and polishing it further themselves, the women could remove some of its odor and improve its texture, but its only merit was its inexpensiveness. This allowed Chikuho miners to eat rice regularly, however, and perhaps save money for the occasional purchase of good Japanese rice. At some mines, they sang:

> *Rice goes up and wages go down*
> *We can't even smoke five sen (Golden) Bats!*
> *Crunch! Crunch! (Bari-bari)*
> *Is this crunch time? Now*
> *We can't even eat black third class (and stinky) rice!*
> *Crunch! crunch!*[147]

Bari-bari indicates a harsh crunching sound, perhaps a gnashing of teeth at the inability to buy and smoke even the low-grade Golden Bat cigarettes, and definitely a sound that should not accompany the chewing of rice.

What food there was could not have been as fresh as that in farming and fishing villages, as one woman reported with some chagrin. "When we first came to Chikuzen, I found that the fish wasn't fresh, and thought that to have to eat such rotten stuff was terrible. The vegetables weren't fresh either."[148] Although Yamamoto argued that no one starved at the mines, talk of white rice and fresh fish was just talk, used by outsiders to describe what they saw as a relatively good

148   *The daily routine*

food situation at the mines. "Talk of pigging out (*abare-kui*) on pure white rice was just that," he said. "If one could do that, one wouldn't give a fart for a little repression. But in fact, the repression was limitless, and they didn't give us much rice to eat."[149]

One woman told how wages at Miike were paid in equivalents of rice rather than cash, and how in addition to an apparent maximum of one *shō* of rice per day, bonuses of only one- or two-tenths of one per cent of average wages were paid for extra work.[150] The woman who spoke of buying the day's rice before preparing the evening meal, went on to explain that the family budget left little for supplements to the daily diet.

> One *shō* was about 13 *sen*. When it got up to 30 *sen* there was a strike at Yawata (Iron and Steel Works). Then we could only buy 7 *sen* worth of *shōchū* in a *bobura tokkuri* (a small jug in the shape of a gourd) for the evening meal.
>> When rice is 10 sen, *yakkora sa no sa*
>> We can't eat peanuts, *yakkora sa no sa.*[151]

The song is from an earlier era when people were concerned that if rice went up to 10 *sen* per *shō*, they would (literally) have to live on peanuts, which was impossible, as the English saying goes.

The evening bath

Bathing was an important part of the daily routine of most miners because work in the mine invariably made them dirty. Even so, one woman remembers, "There were people who only went to the baths a couple of times a month."[152] It was commonly perceived that *burakumin* had such "unclean" habits. Another retired miner recalls the routine:

> When we had finished eating, we would take the children [to the baths]. We were covered with soot, even between our eyelashes. The women were absorbed in washing their hair.[153]

If they had not been able to use company baths on coming out of the pit, it must have been trying for most mothers to prepare the evening meal and feed their husbands and children before they were able to go to the public baths to get rid of the day's covering of soot and grime. But such a postponement would have been consistent with the custom whereby Japanese males bathed first and benefited from cleaner water, even where provision for washing outside the tub before immersing themselves in the hot water was common. Yamamoto Sakubei writes:

> Since the coal mines had this deficiency of water, the baths were not fit for human beings. ... The water came out of the mine, and looked as murky as well-boiled *miso* soup.[154]

The daily routine 149

Figure 5.4 The common bath (Yamamoto, *Emaki*, from the 9th color illustration).

Yamamoto says that the water was pumped up from the underground shafts and heated by steam from the pump "so that there was no waste."[155] This careful use of mine effluent and failure to change the bath water frequently, he suggests, was because coal mining had disturbed the water table in mining districts and had resulted in severe shortages of subsurface as well as surface water.

Unpleasant bathing conditions, of course, did not encourage fastidiousness among miners.

> Since, in the water raised from the mine, cylinder oil from the steam pump was mixed and metallic deposits were substantial, they would stick to you and you couldn't get it off. *Sakiyama* who were dirty black from head to foot, without washing off first or even getting their bums wet, would jump into the water. Since they would even use soap in the tub, the filth was like that of an indigo pot.

As for the bath accessories, they were also inadequate, Yamamoto points out.

> One lump of soap was 3 *sen*, later 5 *sen*, and was a combination of lime and soda. If it got in your eyes, they would sting and become red. The towels were Japanese-style *tenugui* and became blackish. Since they were used for cleaning out the nostrils, they took on the pattern of a splotched blackboard cloth. Towels also cost 3 *sen* and went up to 5 *sen*.[156]

The baths for *burakumin* were even worse than those for "regular miners." Using a pejorative word for *burakumin*, they were called "*eta-buro*." Not only

150   *The daily routine*

were they smaller, but they seem to have been even dirtier than the regular baths. Shindo Toyo reports:

> It was common for the (*buraku*) miners who came up from the mine all covered in soot to take a bath at the pit mouth and, after getting rid of the soot from their heads, faces, ears and the rest of their bodies, to hurry home. This bath, which they could not do without, was much smaller than that for the ordinary miners and very dirty.[157]

Burakumin may not have been required to wash in the same bath as the pit ponies at many mines, but ex-miner Matsumoto Kichinosuke is reported to have said that at Mitsubishi's Namazuta Mine, "The *eta-buro* was the horse bath (*uma-buro*). We bathed with the horses. In the corners of this bath, horse dung floated about."[158] If *burakumin* had to bathe in water even dirtier than the mine effluent used for the regular baths, this could not have improved their image among the general population.

A woman's work is never done

After immersing herself in the company baths at larger mines (or even before going to the public baths where there were none at smaller ones), the woman's first task of the evening was usually to prepare the "coming-up *saké* (*agari-zaké*)" to begin her husband's evening relaxation.

> Even if you'd been beaten with the handle of the pick by your husband, when you came up the first thing you'd do was to warm the *agari-zaké*.[159]

More rarely, a spirit of cooperation might take hold in the evening, even from a husband who would berate and quarrel with his wife underground.

> We couples would come out together, and my man would make the fire while I went shopping. Though it was called the distribution center (*haikyū-shō*), it had few things to sell. Sometimes there were *buen* (unsalted things and fresh fish—Morisaki), like sardines or whale meat. And salt, *miso, takuan*.[160]

The "distribution center" might have fulfilled some of the social functions of a village well-head if the women had had time to stop and chat in the evening. This center was the result of devolution of the distribution function of the *kanba*, or pay office, which in simpler operations handled provisions for the miners and took their costs from the miners' pay. At bigger mines, the distribution center evolved into a company store that had the exploitive function of its counterpart in North American company towns. Perhaps because of the miners' dislike of that function, but certainly because of the women's lack of spare time, the distribution center-cum-company store could not become a social center for coal-mining women in Japan.

The daily routine   151

The women did find other ways of getting together in the evening. A certain measure of communal living was implied by cooperation in preparing the evening meal among neighboring families.

> If the neighbours were late in coming out of the mine, when we lit our *gangan* we'd light theirs too. If fish was being sold we'd buy some for them and cook it.[161]

In hard times, sharing of food for supper as well as lunches seems to have been common. This woman says that the diversity of geographical backgrounds of the miners did not undermine their sense of a common background of poverty. They shared their food as well as their fate, unlike during the postwar years of her retirement, when if someone went fishing they would try to sell the catch to a neighbor.[162]

With supplements (*okazu*) such as fish and pickles to go with the staple food (rice) in short supply, sojourners from other parts of Japan—called *kane-nokoshi* because they made efforts to save money—ate very poorly.[163]

> There were people who came from Hiroshima living next to us, and they were saving money. They put *sōmen* (fine noodles) in boiling water, and no salt or anything with it, and without rinsing it in water, ate it just as is. They said that the juice from the boiled *sōmen* was salty. They all ate together, the *sōmen* just as it was with the stems of the taro boiled and mixed in. If one said, "There can't be much taste in that," they answered, "Well, it's not so bad; you probably haven't tried it." I couldn't get it past my lips.[164]

Preparing and supervising the evening meal was only part of the evening routine for coal-mining women.

> Then we'd have to prepare for the next morning. And cuddle the children to sleep. When the children wheezed in their sleep, I'd carefully take one sleeve of their kimono off, then gently take off the other, and cover them with my kimono which was warm. Then make do with my mining clothes. Doing the mending and the preparation for the school-age children, finally I'd sleep.[165]

Many of the women spoke of doing such mending in the evening. It was crucial to repair clothing that could not be replaced because of lack of money to buy either new clothes or material to make them. Still others did sewing in order to earn extra money.

> After coming out, I would deliver charcoal and briquettes in a rear car (bicycle-drawn cart). Deep into the night, I sewed a *yotsumi* kimono. If you sewed one kimono, you'd get 10 or 15 *sen*.[166]

152 *The daily routine*

Another mining woman's recollections of mending her children's clothes that "looked like dishrags" come from the time of the Second World War, when her husband was away, but her family responsibilities were similar to those of coal-mining women in earlier times. The mending, which risked the women's eyesight in poor lighting after an arduous day, was a matter of necessity, not of trying "to conserve things and work for the benefit of the country."[167]

Working long hours meant that finding time to do the laundry was a major problem for the women. It too was typically done after a tiring shift.[168] The long and narrow panels of quilts and full kimonos were traditionally separated for washing, then sewn together again after drying. One woman wished for just one or two days off per month to do the washing, but invariably, if she planned a day off, the labor boss would ask her to replace someone who could not work.[169] In the 1920s, Maki claimed to have washed the tieband of her skirt, "the only elegant (*oshare*) part" of her costume, every day.[170] As a youth who did not have responsibility for a family, she was aware of the effect of her appearance on the young men in the mine. Later, at the bigger mines in Joban, the women and men were given "bonuses" for working more than 20 or 25 days per month. But there were penalties as well for girls such as Maki who attempted to escape from the mines; Maki not only lost her bonus but was made to work regular holidays.[171] Because the women came to rely on the bonuses for basic sustenance, they were in no position to take time off and forfeit them.

> We received wages which were so low that if we didn't work, we couldn't eat. That was why, after I got together with my old man, we worked a month straight through. There was no such thing as a fixed day off. Everyone chose their own days to take off.[172]

Another woman spoke of the evening routine and the need to deal with infant children, to do the daily shopping, and to feed the family, all while trying to maintain her husband's willingness to work. The care and feeding of unmotivated husbands could be no less demanding than the care of children. This woman plied her husband with *saké* in the evening, saying that if she could get him to work steadily, "two or three *gō* of *saké* would be a small price to pay."[173] Other women confirmed that the preparation of the evening's ration of *saké* or *shōchū* was a priority among their duties, though they chafed at or reluctantly condoned this indulgence.

Not even a song at twilight

As well as pleasant images of her surroundings in the twilight, Maki remembered babies and young children crying for their mothers' attention, quarrels between her mother and *saké*-drinking father, and a general hubbub among the tenements at the Joban mines. The recollection suggests a preponderance of dysfunctional families.[174]

The daily routine 153

As a first-grader, Maki was often sent to the coal depot after dark to steal coal for her family's cooking and heating fires. The company's allowance of coal for these purposes was meager and could be cut off when Maki's father was punished for gambling. Maki was always afraid of being caught and once was restrained by the husband of her school teacher and let off with a warning. She thought other parents would not be so unkind as to require their children to steal coal. But gathering coal from the waste heaps was an often unrewarding and dangerous alternative, the "mountain" being subject to spontaneous combustion and avalanches. Under more lax management, though, some women might collect enough from the waste to sell on the black market or to exchange for farm products.[175]

Like women in Joban, women in northern Kyushu spoke of meager allowances of fuel for cooking and heating. At some mines in Chikuho, miners were given small rations of good coal, but references to picking coal from waste heaps are common.[176] Such activity must have felt demeaning for the women, reducing them to the state of beggars. And the need to garner what combustible material they could no doubt persuaded other parents to tell their children to steal coal from the storage depots, hoping that company men would be compassionate if they caught mere kids. Some miners had the opportunity to fulfill their needs for cooking and heating coal by working clandestinely at a "badger mine"

Figure 5.5 Evening routine (Yamamoto, *Emaki*, 97th black and white illustration).

154 *The daily routine*

(*tanuki-bori*), although their main output was for sale. In these circumstances, the normal daily routine might be compromised in order to keep the operation secret.[177]

The usual routine might also be compromised on the day after payday. According to one retired woman, attendance, at least of the men, at pit mouth roster calls was very poor on that day. The miners often spent the evening of payday carousing and thus were unable to work the next day. And when they did show up for work, they were inspired to ask for small loans to make up for the wages they had spent. The bosses' responses to such requests could be full of scorn for the miners' profligacy, accompanied with exhortations to work harder. Although some gang bosses and foremen took a more casual approach in good times,[178] even then the need for money to support their families and/or their spending habits obliged the men to do the very thing that the bosses prescribed, that is, to work harder after their post-payday binges. If, however, delinquent mates could not be made to work, the women no doubt went down without them if they could attach themselves to a *sakiyama* who was more diligent.[179]

Marxists talk of the workers' need to restore their reproductive power, not only by eating and sleeping but by enjoying relaxation, whether in the form of recreation, study, or entertainment.[180] But the daily work routines of Japanese coal-mining women left them with little, if any, surplus time or energy to devote to these pursuits. On the contrary, those routines were guaranteed to enervate and, sooner or later, destroy their bodies. The few of them who lived to ripe old ages, in telling their stories, recalled how their working lives were lacking in healthy recreation and personal fulfillment and were destined to make most of them "old before their time." That some survived into their seventies and eighties is a tribute to their hardiness and to the endurance of the women who carried the *sena* and *tebo* and pulled the *sura*, all while accepting their family burdens, at the coal mines of Chikuho, Ube, and Joban.

Notes

1 The "Amazon," in Idegawa Yasuko, Hi o Unda Haha-tachi, p. 39.
2 Shindo, *Chikuhō no Jokōfu-tachi*, pp. 36–9.
3 Morisaki Kazue, *Makkura*, p. 12; Yamamoto Sakubei, *Yama ni Ikiru*, p. 39; Shindo Toyo, *Chikuhō no Jokōfu-tachi*, p. 30; Idegawa Yasuko, *Hi o Unda Haha-tachi*, p. 80.
4 Cf. the report by Dr. Ishihara Osamu, "*Jokō no Genkyō*," in Kagoyama Takashi, ed., *Jokō to Kekkaku*, p. 178.
5 For the worst cases of paternal negligence, see Morisaki, *Makkura*, pp. 33–4 and Idegawa Yasuko, *Hi o Unda Haha-tachi*, pp. 70–2; also Idegawa, pp. 39–40, 76, 154, 164.
6 Tanaka Naoki, *Kindai Nihon Tankō Rōdō shi Kenkyū*, p. 90. From Konoe Kitaro, *Chikuhō Tankō Shi*, pp. 83–4.
7 Sumiya Mikiyo, *Nihon Sekitan Sangyō Bunseki*, footnote 11 p. 172. See also, Nakamura Masanori, *Rōdō sha to Nōmin*, Nihon no Rekishi series, vol. 29, p. 120. From *"Chikuhō Kōgyō Tōryō Den"* (Lives of Chikuho Mining Bosses) also in Ueno Eishin, ed., *Kindai Minshū no Kiroku*, vol. 2, *Kōfu*, pp. 31–130; particularly, p. 39.
8 *Jizoku no Seishun*, p. 59.

The daily routine 155

9 Morisaki, p. 26.
10 Yamamoto Sakubei, *Yama ni Ikiru*, p. 24; Morisaki, pp. 12, 140.
11 Morisaki, p. 12; Idegawa, p. 48.
12 Morisaki, p. 26.
13 Yamamoto, *Yama ni Ikiru*, p. 24; Idegawa, p. 200.
14 Yamamoto, *Yama ni Ikiru*, p. 39.
15 Mashio, p. 35. Some women spoke of seven or ten units back-to-back in single buildings, facing onto different "streets" between the rows. Cf. Tajima, *Tankō Bijin*, p. 167.
16 Idegawa, p. 178.
17 *Yama ni Ikiru*, p. 24.
18 Morisaki, *Makkura*, p. 32.
19 Cf. Morisaki, pp. 9–12.
20 Mashio, p. 60. Cf. Ueno, *Kōfu*, p. 134.
21 Morisaki, p. 179.
22 *Yama ni Ikiru*, p. 24. See also, Saraumi Toshiko interview in *Tankō Bijin*, p. 167.
23 *Jizoko no Seishun*, pp. 111, 113.
24 Morisaki, p. 11.
25 *Chikuhō Tankō Shi*, pp. 83–4, in Tanaka, *Kindai Nihon Tankō Rōdō Shi Kenkyū*, p. 90.
26 Ibid., footnote 34, p. 119.
27 Tanaka, *Kindai Nihon Tankō Rōdō Shi Kenkyū*, p. 91. From *Yamano Kōgyō-sho Enkaku Shi* (History of the Yamano Mines), vol. 15.
28 Cf. Idegawa, p. 178.
29 Tanaka, ibid., p. 91, from *Mitsui Kōzan Gojū-nen-shi Kō*, (Draft of the Fifty Year History of Mitsui Mines), vol. 16, p. 191. Also, Tsurumi, *Factory Girls*, p. 133; Ikeda Yoshimasa and Sasaki Ryuji, *Kyōyōjin no Nihon-shi*, vol. 4, pp. 216–7.
30 *Yama ni Ikiru*, p. 39.
31 Cf. Morisaki, p. 143.
32 Mashio, *Jizoko no Seishun*, p. 35.
33 Morisaki, p. 140.
34 *Yama ni Ikiru*, p. 39. See also, Takagi Hisae interview in *Tankō Bijin*, pp. 126–7.
35 Morisaki, pp. 11–12.
36 Morisaki, p. 32.
37 *Jizoko no Seishun*, p. 35.
38 Idegawa, p. 175.
39 Idegawa, p. 178.
40 Song transcribed by Morisaki Kazue, *Makkura*, p. 26.
41 Morisaki, pp. 9, 87.
42 Ibid., p. 27.
43 Ibid., p. 185.
44 Mashio Etsuko, *Jizoko no Seishun*, p. 36.
45 *Yama ni Ikiru*, p. 25.
46 Morisaki, p. 9. Ide Kozue interview in *Tankō Bijin*, p. 36.
47 Ibid., pp. 36–7. One woman spoke of the smoke from the "*gangan shichirin*" pervading the tenements. Idegawa, p. 102. The *shichirin*, or *konro*, was a more modern, manufactured form of the portable stove, burning briquettes without smoke but with some noxious fumes.
48 Idegawa, *Hi o Unda Haha-tachi*, p. 59.
49 Morisaki, pp. 76–7.
50 *Jizoko no Seishun*, p. 117.
51 See Morisaki, p. 11.
52 Morisaki, p. 26.
53 Morisaki, pp. 187–8.

156 The daily routine

54 Idegawa, p. 200.
55 *Yama ni Ikiru*, p. 25.
56 *Chikuhō Tankō Emaki*, 91st black and white illustration.
57 Idegawa, p. 89.
58 Morisaki, pp. 87, 178–9.
59 Cf. Mashio, p. 35.
60 Yamamoto, *Yama ni Ikiru*, p. 25.
61 *Jizoko no Seishun*, p. 78. A Chikuho *atoyama* says up to 5 *shō* a day. Idegawa, p. 99.
62 Cf. Idegawa, p. 89.
63 *Facing Two Ways*, p. 162.
64 Morisaki, p. 139. Standard contracts proposed for the Takashima mines in the Meiji period required that care be taken in matters of sanitation. Oyama, *Kōgyō Rōdō to Oyakata Seido*, p. 52. But such stipulations resulted in little more than cosmetic improvements. See the 1888 "Report on the Sanitary, Hygienic, and Physical Condition of the miners at Takasima and Nakanosima," by C. Arthur Arnold, made "At the Request of the Mitsu Bishi Sha," in Tanaka, *Tankō Rōdō shi Kenkyū*, pp. 215–7. Concerning future Prime Minister Inukai Tsuyoshi's whitewash of conditions at Takashima, the Tōun (Shinonome) Shimbun editorialized in September 1888: "The Choya Newspaper reporter does not say on what standard his reports idealizing the dormitories are based, and in saying that there are no deficiencies in sanitation and no deficiencies generally, has left us ample room for doubts as to his veracity." Quoted in Tanaka, p. 226.
65 Shindo, *Chikuhō no Jokōfu-tachi*, p. 61.
66 *Chikuhō ni Ikiru: Buraku Kaihō Undō to tomo ni Gojū-nen*, p. 24.
67 Cf. Mashio, pp. 189, 199.
68 Morisaki, p. 64.
69 Morisaki, pp. 141, 158.
70 "*Kōfu no Eisei Jōtai Chōsa*," in Sumiya, ed., *Shokkō oyobi Kōfu Chōsa*, Kosei-kan, 1970, p. 178.
71 Sachiko Sone repeats this generalization at several places in her dissertation, *Coalmining Women in Japan* and claims that coal miners ate better meals than peasants and the urban poor.
72 *Jizoko no Seishun*, p. 44.
73 Ibid., p. 84.
74 Idegawa, p. 102.
75 Idegawa, p. 135. Morisaki, pp. 74, 143.
76 Morisaki, pp. 9–10.
77 *Chikuhō Tankō Emaki*, notes to the 123rd and 125th black and white illustrations.
78 Idegawa, glossary, p. 218.
79 Idegawa, p. 178. See also, Morisaki, p. 174.
80 Morisaki, p. 15. Also, Yamamoto, *Yama ni Ikiru*, pp. 97–8.
81 Ibid., p. 51.
82 Idegawa, pp. 66, 158.
83 Idegawa, p. 35. Mathias outlines a later change in the degree of flexibility in the women's schedules in her perceptive article in Hunter, *Japanese Women Working*, p. 107. There seems to be, however, a serious misprint in Mathias's statement about the loss of flexibility under stricter regimes in later periods (manipulating routines became *impossible* for miners).
84 Morisaki, pp. 9–10.
85 Ibid., p. 12.
86 Idegawa, p. 13.
87 Morisaki, p. 11.

The daily routine   157

88 Idegawa, p. 35. Up to an hour at one mine, according to Takagi Hisae. Tajima, *Tankō bijin*, p. 129. George Orwell described the rigors of the long walk into the coal mines of northern England in *The Road to Wigan Pier*.
89 Morisaki, p. 72. Work clothes are sometimes referred to as *kōnai-chaku* (p. 122) and may have been standardized at some of the bigger mines.
90 Cf. Tsurumi, *Factory Girls*, contract cited on p. 176.
91 Yamamoto, *Chikuhō Tankō Emaki*, black and white illustrations 12, 28, 64–8, and *Yama ni Ikiru*, passim.
92 Morisaki, p. 73.
93 Idegawa, p. 175. Cf. Morisaki, p. 160.
94 *Facing Two Ways*, pp. 156, 161.
95 *Chikuhō ni Ikiru*, p. 17.
96 *Mabu* was the old North Kyushu word for coal face or mining room.
97 Morisaki, p. 20.
98 Morisaki, p. 140.
99 Cf. *Makkura*, p. 160.
100 Morisaki, p. 20. Cf. Yamamoto, *Yama ni Ikiru*, p. 100.
101 Morisaki, p. 48.
102 Yamamoto Sakubei, *Yama ni Ikiru*, p. 101.
103 Morisaki, p. 51.
104 Idegawa, p. 203.
105 Morisaki, p. 79. Other superstitions held by mining people are mentioned here.
106 Morisaki, p. 14.
107 Idegawa, pp. 176–7.
108 Matsumoto, *Chikuhō ni Ikiru*, p. 16.
109 One Japanese character used in this phrase is a homonym for one in the common expression for "killing time," a derivation from the custom of having red lantern district courtesans ("tea-house maids"), while waiting for customers, grind tea leaves in feudal times. *Kōjien*, p. 1386.
110 Idegawa, pp. 183–4.
111 Nishinarita Yutaka, *"Gijutsu Kakushin to Joshi Rōdō,"* p. 77.
112 Idegawa, p. 134.
113 Mashio, *Jizoko no Seishun*, pp. 90–1.
114 Morisaki, pp. 84–5.
115 Morisaki, p. 48.
116 Morisaki, p. 155.
117 Morisaki, pp. 159–60. One is reminded of the priest buying a *kanzashi* (hairpin) for his lover in the popular Tosa song.
118 Morisaki, p. 79.
119 Morisaki, pp. 75–6.
120 Morisaki, p. 125; Yamamoto, *Chikuhō Tankō Emaki*, 8th color plate.
121 *Jizoko no Seishun*, p. 76.
122 Morisaki, pp. 137–8.
123 Ibid., p. 191.
124 Morisaki, p. 159. Also, p. 11.
125 Morisaki, pp. 12, 189. See also Mashio, p. 81, and Shindo, *Chikuhō no Jokōfu-tachi*, p. 30.
126 Morisaki, p. 53.
127 Yoshimura Sakuo, *Nihon Tankō-shi Shichū*, (A Japanese Coal-Mining History Memoir), p. 75.
128 Morisaki, p. 87.
129 Morisaki, p. 186.
130 Morisaki, p. 11. See also Yamamoto Sakubei, *Yama ni Ikiru*, p. 96.

158 *The daily routine*

131 Morisaki, p. 76.
132 Morisaki, p. 11.
133 Idegawa, p. 161.
134 Idegawa, pp. 79–80.
135 Idegawa, p. 116.
136 Morisaki, p. 12.
137 Morisaki, p. 28. See also p. 77, and Idegawa, passim.
138 *Nihon Sekitan Sangyō Bunseki*, pp. 165, 166.
139 Morisaki, p. 13.
140 Idegawa, p. 89.
141 Morisaki, p. 187.
142 Morisaki, pp. 12–13.
143 Morisaki, p. 77.
144 Morisaki, p. 14.
145 Morisaki, pp. 16–17.
146 Takematsu, *Kōnai Uma to Bafu to Jokōfu*, pp. 122–3.
147 Shindo, *Chikuhō no Jokōfu-tachi*, pp. 72–3. The parenthetical censure may be a variation in the song or an explanatory addition by Shindo.
148 Morisaki, p. 85.
149 *Yama ni Ikiru*, pp. 76–7. Cf. Shindo Toyo, *Chikuhō no Jokōfu-tachi*, p. 14.
150 Morisaki, pp. 190–1. Cf. Yamamoto, *Yama ni Ikiru*, p. 79.
151 Morisaki, pp. 12–13.
152 Ibid., p. 144.
153 Morisaki, p. 14.
154 *Yama ni Ikiru*, pp. 25–6.
155 *Yama ni Ikiru*, p. 59.
156 *Yama ni Ikiru*, p. 58. See also *Chikuhō no Emaki*, 9th color illustration.
157 *Chikuhō no Jokōfu-tachi*, p. 30. See also, Yamamoto, *Yama no Shigoto*, p. 25.
158 Quoted in Shindo Toyo, *Chikuhō no Jokōfu-tachi*, p. 31, and Yasukawa Junosuke, "*Hisabetsu Buraku to Josei*" in *Nihon Josei Shi* (4), pp. 209–210. In Japanese coal mines, as in British, the pit ponies were often kept underground and brought up only for the occasional bath. See Takematsu Teruo, *Kōnai Uma to Bafu to Jokōfu*.
159 Idegawa, p. 48. Cf. p. 97.
160 Morisaki, p. 186.
161 Morisaki, p. 152.
162 Ibid., p. 153.
163 Yamamoto affirms that some 30 Hiroshima miners brought to Kami-mio Mine about 1899 worked "harder than Ninomiya Kinjiro (Sontoku)" to put aside some savings so that they could return to their homes in style and live comfortably thereafter. They lived frugally and asserted that they did not even need vegetables with their rice. Only about half of them accumulated savings and returned home; the others piled up debts due to illness, injury, or other misfortune, according to Yamamoto. *Yama ni Ikiru*, pp. 76–7.
164 Morisaki, pp. 175–6.
165 Morisaki, p. 14.
166 Idegawa, pp. 115. She also "did up" hair for local women.
167 Idegawa., pp. 137–8.
168 Idegawa, p. 184.
169 Morisaki, p. 87.
170 Mashio, p. 89.
171 Mashio, *Jizoko no Seishun*, p. 98. See also Ogino Yoshihiro, "*Daiichi-ji Taisen…*," in Ogino, *Senzen-ki Chikuhō Tankō-gyō no Keiei to Rōdō*, p. 116.
172 Morisaki, p. 58. See also, p. 64.

173 Idegawa, p. 65.
174 Mashio, pp. 38–9. See also, Idegawa, p. 202.
175 Mashio, pp. 40–41.
176 Cf. Makkura, p. 191.
177 Idegawa, p. 49.
178 Morisaki, p. 160.
179 Morisaki, p. 180.
180 See Karl Marx, *Capital*, vol. 1, chapter 6, "The Buying and Selling of Labour-Power," Moscow, Foreign Languages Publishing House, 1961, p. 173. I assume that a certain amount of relaxation and sleep would be indispensable in the renewal of the "vital energy" of the worker, female as well as male, and that some evaluation of these "commodities" should be included in any comprehensive calculation of the cost of labor in modern societies. That most of the vital energy of the female coal miners was consumed in their work underground and not renewed except through the reproduction of children, who in turn would become coal miners, was a feature of the inhumanity of the capitalist system that Marx so trenchantly criticized.

6 Solidarity, divisions, bondage, and resistance

Monku nukasu to sena-bō de dotama
Sarashi tenugui chi de someru!
 Let out one complaint and your thick head will be cudgelled
 Till your bleached cotton hand towel is stained with your blood![1]

Although the women may not have been frequent victims of the physical reprisals administered to recalcitrant miners by callous overseers and gang bosses, and though the "Company" was a remote and amorphous entity, the women were cognizant of the power that its agents wielded over them.[2] Matthew Allen writes of an "institutionalised political powerlessness" of Chikuho miners and a "culture of violence" that "dominated relationships between mine management and miners."[3] The stories of the retired women suggest, however, that they were sometimes able to mitigate the harshness of the regime. They occasionally ignored the regulations and operating systems prescribed by the company. Sometimes they let the bosses understand that they knew how to accomplish mining tasks more efficiently without interference. (Miners were free of the intensive supervision that accompanied "modernization" in the textile industries as long as piecework rates of pay could ensure serious application to the work.) In emphasizing the "isolation, powerlessness, and dependence" of the coal miners with regard to their employers, Allen perhaps undervalues evidence of solidarity and resistance born of camaraderie among miners, male or female.[4] A shared fate brought them together in an embryonic common struggle to improve their lives, at least where imposed competition did not irrevocably divide them and render them incapable of perceiving the common good.

A shared fate

It would seem natural that miners developed feelings of solidarity as a result of being dragooned into working together under harsh conditions in the coal mines. Awareness of common work and life experiences and consciousness of a common fate could be expected to permeate the colliery ethos. So also could

Solidarity, divisions, bondage, and resistance   161

recognition, perhaps later rather than sooner and only subconsciously, that they were all being exploited by colliery managements. But although there is considerable evidence of such feelings among Japanese coal miners, solidarity was weakened by the divisions among ethnic and social groups as well as between individual workers and work gangs thrust into competition with each other. On the other hand, the women rarely considered themselves a separate group because of their gender.

Several retired women attested to a natural solidarity among coal miners as the result of suffering a common fate in their daily lives, regardless of disparate social and regional origins. Morisaki Kazue entitles one of the female miners' narratives "*Kyōyū*", or "Sharing", and the cooperative spirit of the miners, though perhaps idealized in retrospect, shines through this testimony. Indeed, the retired miner challenges the interviewer, Morisaki, to find a similar cooperative spirit elsewhere, contrasting the warm-heartedness (*aijō*) of miners with an alleged lack of concern for the needs of others, a desire for privacy, and a tendency to mind one's own business on the part of townspeople. She then refers to a change in attitudes among different generations of miners themselves, emphasizing the need for cooperation in days when resources were scarce.

> When we got married, well, about 1927, about that time at the coal mines all the miners used to help each other. They showed their affection for one another. … People living near us were closer than our parents or brothers and sisters. There were no (distinctions between) males and females. … Everything was everyone's business, and there was no difference between what was yours and what was mine.[5]

At another point in her story, she emphasizes this same lack of possessiveness, applying even to the borrowing of each other's footwear.[6] And common life experiences brought miners together.

> Since we lived together, other people's troubles were just like our own. Look what happened when someone got sick! People would be coming and going, in and out. It didn't matter who was ill, others would be as concerned as if they were one of their own. Being poor or worse than poor, everyone had given up their miserable three *tan* of land and took refuge (at the mines). None of us were coal miners to begin with. To get here, all of us trod paths too painful to talk about. We're all from different prefectures. I still wonder why we got along so well and felt so strongly for one another.[7]

Although they had little schooling and many had been vagrants or ne'er-do-wells, she says, miners never trampled on others to get ahead. And although other women spoke of fellow-feeling for those from their own prefectures, such affinities did not preclude positive feelings toward miners in general.

Although competition did bring the miners into conflict, they expressed a belief in harmony and cooperation. It seems that they had a strong sense of "being

162 *Solidarity, divisions, bondage, and resistance*

in the same boat" and realized that they depended on each other for survival. Another woman recounted:

> We were able to work [very hard] because everyone helped each other. People at the mines are not concerned only for their own welfare. ... Everyone was in it together, and they didn't treat each other in an unfeeling manner like today.[8]

There were, of course, differing degrees of generosity of spirit among the women. One was proud of her own generosity as well as of her belief in the rightness of sharing and was critical of another for being willful and greedy.

> She'd snatch wagons, and bully newcomers. I didn't like that. Even though I was strong, I was soft–hearted. If someone said they had nothing to eat, I'd give them rice. If they were suffering from a lack of money, I'd find a way of helping them. When I couldn't [give them money], I'd take the smock off my back and send them off to the pawn shop [with it].

Even when there was friction between these two women of different temperaments, there was a sense of a common destiny and a tendency to forgive.

> I was always saying, "Just try to put your hands on someone else's wagon! I'll bust both your arms and your legs!" But even though we would glare at each other, before the quarrel could come to anything, it would be gone, just like that![9]

And this woman had a grudging admiration for the other miner's "splendid physique."

The "Old Woman of the Mountain" recalls that the women saw reciprocity as a desirable norm in their relations, even though they might not demand it from people of lesser means. Scrupulous about returning borrowed goods or money, they deplored cheating on one another.

> We wouldn't do anyone out of a five-*rin* piece.[10] No one cheated. I've been here for forty and more years but I've never been cheated once. Those who've suffered watch out for each other. They'd never cause us any trouble. [But] they'd run away, bilking the *ōnaya* [i.e., the gang boss] out of their loans. I don't look down on anyone. I'm willing to share almost everything. There are some who go to the baths only twice a month. Everyone can't be the same. You have to help poor people.[11]

Such tolerance and compassion may not have been universal in the hard days of late nineteenth- and early twentieth-century coal mining in Japan, but other accounts suggest that common hardship and poverty led to a substantial degree of cooperation and embryonic solidarity among the women.

Mutual aid

Chiyo, the "Japanese Cricket," tells of her husband's exaggerated efforts on behalf of his fellow miners, despite his avoidance of familial duty.

> He played the happy-go-lucky big-spending husband, but he was very good to other people. He would do anything for them. Even though our roof was leaking like a sieve, he would be the first to climb up to help repair someone else's roof—it was always like that. How such a husband could think so highly of himself as one who helped others, pretending to be serious, I just don't know![12]

As we have seen, he would even try to mediate neighbors' marital quarrels, turning both parties against him. This was hardly an effective expression of solidarity, but his wife was describing norms of cooperation that were not, apparently, atypical.

Another woman told how one wagon distributor would not only ensure that miners were aware of dangers from overhead electric wires when riding empty wagons but also warn them in time to get out on the last wagons of the shift.[13] Such solicitude would seem to have been extraordinary for a male in a dominant position, but this wagon dispatcher apparently considered himself one of the commonality of miners rather than a superior. The woman also remembered the unselfishness of experienced miners who helped her and her husband "learn the ropes" upon their arrival at a bigger mine than they were accustomed to, comparing it to grudging resentfulness among farmers.

> People at the mines are better than rural people [*chihō no hito*]. Rural people are nasty [*kitanai*, literally dirty, but probably mean-spirited here]. They become mean. They're always griping, "What's wrong there? What's the matter with that?" At the coal mines, people ask to borrow rice or even money and they lend and borrow without charging any interest.[14]

But she recognized that farmers and miners were put at odds by the single-minded or careless planning of coal workings under arable land.

> We hardly ever went to town. [She probably includes villages in differentiating stable population centers from the mining camps.] Because their fields subsided and water collected due to mining disturbances, the farmers were upset. But if they tried to go to the mines to ask for compensation, they'd be set upon and slain [by company goons?], so they bore it in silence.[15]

Yet, as she was aware, most coal miners had rural origins. There is no reason, of course, why proletarian coal miners should have assumed responsibility for the subsidence that ruined farmers' fields. Negative feelings toward the people from whom they had come could only serve the interests of the managers and the owners of the coal mines, who tried to keep miners isolated from the outside world in order to exploit them without interference. Lacking communication

164 *Solidarity, divisions, bondage, and resistance*

between miners and their rural counterparts, there could be no solidarity among the working class as a whole.

Some miners were conscious of their distinctiveness and reputation among other social groups, and some realized limits to their unselfish attitudes toward each other. The woman quoted earlier tells how she went to ask some people named Kobayashi if she could "borrow" their extra mine props and found that they, like her, were from Oita Prefecture.

> And we became good friends. Our temperaments matched. And we were able to talk about our debts, our sorrows, and everything. Our husbands also became good friends. ... And while working away, we'd sing.[16]

Other women mention being forbidden to sing, however, because supervisors thought it would prevent them from hearing sounds in the roof that portended cave-ins.[17] This prohibition meant the curtailment of an activity that invariably promotes feelings of solidarity. Nonetheless, the woman says,

> Our working days were our best times. In the mines there's nothing like the country ways where everyone is cold-heartedly concerned whether everything is mine or yours. And they'd get angry with you if you didn't respond when the talk got lively. It's not easy for anyone to understand the pleasures of work in the mines.[18]

This reference to "lively" talk suggests a form of the *idobata kaigi* to which Matthew Allen refers—"women's informal gatherings at the local wells, a common means of disseminating gossip."[19] But although the coal-mining women no doubt exchanged gossip while going to and fro or while waiting their turn at the well, such opportunities for this kind of exchange, with its associated enhancement of solidarity, were limited at the mines.

The Indomitables

Solidarity among the women could be developed early in the larger mines, where young women worked in closer proximity to each other than in the dispersed rooms of the smaller ones. The story of how a group of indomitable young women strove to thwart the regulations that forbade riding out on the couplings of the loaded coal wagon trains illustrates the kind of resistance to company authority that could arise from such solidarity. These young women, though not always working in the same large "room" (*harai*), were near enough to each other to come out together and conspire against a foreman who tried to prevent them from riding out on the couplings. Punishing them required identification of the culprits because feudal methods of making whole groups responsible for the actions of individual members of the group seem to have been abandoned in at least some of the coal mines.[20] To catch the transgressors, the foreman hid in the recesses along the haulage-way, throwing chalk dust on them as they rode past in the dark. Such methods of identifying the insubordinate young women aroused further resentment, however, and a determination to resist the indignity.[21] Some women conspired to thwart the foreman, washing the chalk dust off themselves and turning their kimonos inside out, thereby avoiding the "severe scolding" borne by others who were caught. These others, it can be assumed, would either have to desist and make the long trek out on foot henceforth or face much more severe punishment if caught again. Their esprit de corps encouraged the recalcitrants among the young women to further evade detection by covering their heads and by wearing their clothes inside out regularly to deal with the chalk on illicit rides. Collective evasion of the regulations made persistence possible.

Success, as well as popular backing from her workmates, no doubt persuaded Toshie, the narrator of this story, to face the challenge of the foreman, Yamashita, with a great deal of bravado. She feigned innocence and lied blatantly. The confidence of the group led them to walk away from work in an action that nowadays would be called a wildcat strike, although it was mainly aimed at Yamashita and punishing him for his arrogance. Subsequently, they beat him into submission and tied him to the rails, obliging him to plead for his life and make concessions of changes in the future. Although the young women expressed some differences over the extent to which they should go in beating him up, these tactical differences did not divide them and make them individually susceptible to retribution from management. Their solidarity contributed to the feeling that, as women, they should not be mistreated by men like Yamashita. In facing down another, seemingly well-intentioned supervisor, they proclaimed that they were women, not girls, and should be treated accordingly. And they wrested concessions from the supervisor who would normally have meted out punishments rather than mediate their dispute. Toshie told her workmates that it was not timidity that made her argue against beating Yamashita up again for "squealing" but a belief that he would now behave himself. The solidarity of the young women contributed to a remarkable degree of audacity toward the representatives of the company and seems to have ensured a notable measure of success in challenging the customary order of personnel relations and control within this mine.[22]

Rivalry and conflict

At first glance, such testimony about solidarity among the women seems to be inconsistent with the testimony of other women regarding an intense spirit of competition among miners underground. Among male miners, the rivalries and animosities produced by gambling, drinking, and quarreling above ground were reflected in the underground milieu. Most women, however, distanced themselves from the quarrels of their husbands, even if they could not distance themselves from the quarrelsome husbands themselves. Still, one woman indicates that the atmosphere underground was far from one of cooperation and goodwill.

> Mining work requires really close attention to the job. As miners have bad tempers, they let their tongues run away with them. At work, they often yell, "I'll kill you!"[23]

166 *Solidarity, divisions, bondage, and resistance*

Other retired women, however, suggest that bad tempers and sharp tongues were not always given free reign. One admits that there was competition underground but does not remember it affecting the generally good relations among the miners.[24] Nevertheless, competition among female hauliers often led to bad feelings and even sometimes to physical conflict.

Mashio tells the story of Maki's rivalry with her sisters early in her working life. Though normal sibling rivalry was a major element in their struggle, the nature of the framing work imposed on Maki and her older sister by a negligent father exacerbated it. The two girls, aged 15 and 17, were doing heavy work, clearing rock and carrying timber props in the air shaft that their father had contracted to keep open for proper ventilation.

> Although only the two of them were working in the air shaft, her sister often got angry. She found fault with everything Maki did. While quarreling, they were handing logs of more than two meters in length from one to the other and, getting out of sync, they would drop them. This became another cause for bickering. …
>
> One time, Maki was wrestled to the ground. Her lamp went out. The cross-entry was pitch black. In the air shaft behind, her sister watched her, shoulders heaving with panting breath. (Maki) felt her way along the wall and came out into the main entry.[25]

Maki was humiliated and wept bitterly. Just into puberty, she was sensitive about her appearance and did not want to be seen in a state of disarray by the young men in the mine. Humiliation at the hands of her sister seems to have dissipated any sense of solidarity on Maki's part that might have arisen from their common fate, forced to do their father's work while he drank or gambled away the proceeds of his contract with the company. Later, when her younger sister attended higher elementary school with the money Maki had earned in the mine, Maki's sense of deprivation of some of the pleasures of book learning and craft work mounted.[26]

Because of the nature of her work in the mine, young Maki found herself at odds with her older and younger sisters. Although some of the retired miners had happier memories of working with siblings underground, one can imagine resentments aroused by differences in the way they were treated by their parents exacerbating conflict over the demanding work of hauling and framing.

Feisty termagants or subdued proletarians?

Some of the women were used to putting up spirited resistance to perceived affronts, resulting in confrontations and, at the least, verbal conflict with fellow workers. They did not spurn reputations as feisty termagants. One boasted that she would stand her ground against any man, though the incident she relates concerns only the right to pass with her load along a narrow tunnel.

> There was a guy who liked to show off his tattoo. I met him in a narrow corridor. I was pulling the *sura*. Why should I yield to him just because he

Solidarity, divisions, bondage, and resistance 167

had a good physique! When I gave him the evil eye, he said, "What are you looking at my face for?" … trying to pick a quarrel.

"What indeed! Because your face is in the way, I'm staring at it. If it's such a bad face to look at, wrap it in a *furoshiki* when you're walking!"

That fellow came to call me *neesan* [a respectful term for older sister].[27]

She was challenging the Japanese taboo against looking others in the eye and was suggesting that mining women did not accept it as readily as "more refined" women. This woman also offered to help her unusually meek husband in any quarrels that others might pick with him. "The men would say, 'That woman is a brassy one!' and they'd respect me," she remembered. Most of the women had a sense of what constituted their basic rights, a sense of natural justice. And the constant struggle for subsistence made them short-tempered and quick to take offense at perceived violations of customary practices, often at the same time that they flaunted those practices themselves.

Many of the women also showed an uncompromising attitude (*maken ki*), which did not allow them to make concessions easily at work. "Ready to quarrel," they were determined "not to lose out," one said. "We worked so hard it would surprise you."[28] Their determination not to "lose out" applied mainly to their perseverance at arduous and dangerous work, but it also colored relations with their fellow workers. Another retired woman recollects that tenacity in the competition for sustenance and survival was common in female coal miners. "We were always full of the spirit, 'You'll not catch me going under!'"[29]

Though these women found many causes of frustration in the work system imposed on them by the bosses, they were generally good-natured and unselfish in their relations with their fellow workers above ground. Their generosity of spirit persisted even when they were exhausted from long hours of hard labor. But when they were working and striving to earn a living under harsh conditions, the frustration and enervation that they suffered almost continuously made them edgy and combative, quick to take offense and to express it in negative and even anti-social ways. The cry "I'll kill you!" was often heard underground, though it was a relatively meaningless threat. However, it did represent an attitude that divided the women at times and that prevented the consistent building of a spirit of solidarity and cooperation.

Recruitment by subterfuge

Matthew Allen summarizes the main obstacles to resistance among Japanese coal miners as "isolation, powerlessness, and dependence."[30] Given the competitive and extremely frustrating and tiring nature of their work, the development of resistance to managerial impositions, in the smaller mines at least, was likely to be sporadic and ephemeral. The mining companies used carrot-and-stick methods to prevent worker solidarity. The carrots were usually monetary inducements to come to the coal mines, the sticks actual clubs or cudgels commonly wielded to keep workers compliant.

168 *Solidarity, divisions, bondage, and resistance*

The retired women interviewed by Morisaki and Idegawa describe recruitment methods used by coal-mining companies similar to those that occurred at the Ashio copper mine as related by Natsume Soseki in his fictional work *The Miner*,[31] a story very close to one recorded by Emi Suiin, perhaps a pseudonym for a writer who interviewed an escapee from Ashio near the end of the nineteenth century. The recruiter's promises to male itinerants and ne'er-do-wells included the possibility of building up a substantial nest egg from earnings at the mine, money for travel expenses "up front," easy work, and a pay scale with generous increments for increasing experience. These promises and a supposedly free meal given to the recruits on the way to Ashio, along with the removal of all their worldly belongings, amounted to entrapment, and families were recruited to the less remote coal mines of northern Kyushu with much the same false promises though perhaps less vigorous strong-arm methods.[32]

One woman described the deceptions used by recruiters:

> About that time [of the Rice Riots and the worldwide flu epidemic after World War I], if a young man and woman passed along a road near a mine, someone would come up to them and accost them. "Say, you there! Don't you want to work?" It would be a recruiter for the mine. If they said they'd work, they'd be taken to a nearby fixed-meal restaurant [*ichizen meshiya*] and given food and drink. The recruiter would eat and drink with them and then lead them away. They'd be given setting-up money and be settled at the mine, but sometimes there were miners who'd take the money and disappear. The cost of the food and drink for the recruiter would be laid on the miners and would be deducted from wages. There was no getting away from that.[33]

Recruiters enticed down-on-their-luck farmers with promises that they could "eat all you want," including plenty of "white rice and fresh fish," at the coal mines, promises that usually proved to be half-truths. And once they had started work at the mine, force was often used to prevent miners from running off without repaying their loans. This widespread use of extra-economic coercion invalidates any claim that a free labor market existed in Chikuho.

Despite their best efforts, colliery management was hard pressed to prevent miners from being pirated away to other mines. Recruiters and agents were used to try to induce miners, often heads of families, to come to coal mines where working and living conditions were claimed to be better than those under which they presently labored. The methods used in early attempts to prevent labor piracy were brutal and hardly lawful (though usually winked at by the Law). Seeking new workers, recruiters would visit competitors' mines surreptitiously and make offers to their miners of working conditions that could not be verified until the miners actually made the transfer. The women, of course, were expected to go along with the offer and with the man to whom it had been made.

One daughter of a *nayagashira* tells the story of how one such clandestine operation was uncovered, with serious consequences for the infiltrating recruiter.

Solidarity, divisions, bondage, and resistance 169

He had made the mistake of trying to entice the neighbor of one of his targets, who was so unenthusiastic that he reported the inveiglement to the boss. The boss immediately took retaliatory action against the recruiter.

> With his arms tied around behind his back, he was strung up.[34] His feet were off the ground. When he was beaten, *whap! whap!* his arms were wrenched up above his head. It's a wonder they didn't break. ... When he lost consciousness, muddy water from the paddies was thrown over him. The miner who had intended to move to the other mine was also beaten. My father who went to recover the two couldn't stand it. He appealed, "The guy who wanted to go can't sit down, so why don't you stop?" But the overseer shouted, "Do they think they can make fools of us?" and went on beating.[35]

Enterprising recruiters, of course, would hire agents for such work in order to avoid the consequences of being caught. Such methods of recruiting could not continue for many years, however, before miners themselves became more cautious. The raiding contributed to the establishment of a grapevine of spies and informers, the effective operation of which might preclude success for all but the most wily and unscrupulous recruiters.

Figure 6.1 "That will teach him a lesson!" (Yamamoto, *Emaki*, 103rd black and white illustration).

170 *Solidarity, divisions, bondage, and resistance*

They owed their souls to the company and the boss

The all-male workforce at the Ashio copper mine was housed in dormitories as if in a prison, with barred windows and locked doors to prevent miners from escaping.[36] Convict labor at the Miike coal mines, also all male, was similarly kept in confinement, with the added restraint of steel fetters for the serious offenders, the bulk of the early felons there.[37] On his appointment as the first general manager after Mitsui's takeover of Miike in 1889, the eminent Dan Takuma was said to have been surprised at the oppressive conditions under which the convicts were held, with armed guards supervising their work.[38] By the late Meiji period, however, convicts were not the only workers who were kept at the coal mines under duress. With the shortage of labor in boom times, families were kept at small mines as well as large by a combination of indebtedness and brute force. Under these conditions, overt resistance was next to impossible.[39]

It was common for miners to be unable to repay the *maegashi-kin* (loan money) advanced against wages by the boss of the labor gang when they were first recruited.[40] Straitened circumstances could be connected with extra expenses such as those related to pregnancy and the death of a premature baby or with the birth of children and the advent of more mouths to feed. But they were usually simply the result of a general inability to match basic living expenses to incomes. Repayment of recruitment loans would usually be deducted from the miner's wages by the boss who received the contract fee or wage fund from the representatives of the mine owners; he then passed on any monies remaining, after deductions, to the family head. This created a situation in which new debts were invariably incurred before the next payday. The gang boss might temporarily forgo repayment in order to keep the miner solvent and working for him. The advance loan thus became a form of indenture to the gang boss.[41]

Maegashi loans might be offered as removal expenses, an inducement to come to Chikuho from other regions. Various forms of recruiting money would be dangled in front of indigent peasants or itinerant miners. Although the miners did not always make a clear distinction between *maegashi-kin* and *kataire-gin*, the latter seems to have been a recruiting bonus, given to the miner for himself and his wife (and for other working-age relatives employed with the head of the family). This money would allow the miner's family to live until the first pay was collected. Presented as a bonus, one can imagine the dismay of the miner when he found that it, like other forms of *maegashi-kin*, had to be repaid and was deducted in regular increments from the wages.

> Married couples would be given *kataire-gin* and assigned to a tenement unit. *Kataire-gin* was money for signing on, and with it they'd buy household needs, food and so on. If three people worked, they would be lent 50 *yen*; and if two people, about 30 *yen* [in the era after the First World War]. We collected our wages every two weeks from the *ōnaya* [gang boss], and then the *kataire-gin* would be deducted from them, a little at a time.[42]

Solidarity, divisions, bondage, and resistance   171

Another woman admitted that she and her husband moved from mine to mine "looking to collect *kataire-gin.*"

> Before we came here, we moved to new coal mines, from Chikuho [District] to Onga, Ebizu and Kasuya districts. Looking to collect recruitment money, while feeling terrified, as if every strand of our hair was standing on end, sometimes we hid in the bamboo groves, walking all night in the dark to get away.[43]

But dangerous conditions in a Kasuya mine persuaded them to save their lives by fleeing, leaving as much as 50 *yen* in unpaid debts behind. This was in the early Showa (after 1926) when miners' earnings were two or three *yen* per day. She recalls mine employers who were generous in recruiting but stingy when it came to sustaining their employees.[44]

At some of the larger mines, on the other hand, there were provisions for those who could not earn enough money to sustain themselves in their first days getting used to the mining work.[45] These provisions were for basic subsistence, nothing more, and the supplement would be discontinued when the miner reached the stage of competence that would give him or her more than the "minimum wage." And all of these "benefits" were loans that had to be repaid. Their real purpose was not the enhancement of the welfare of the miners but the induction and retention of them in the workforce.

Shitaku-gin, or setting-up loans, had a purpose similar to that of *kataire-gin* and were common, particularly in later years. Some gang bosses provided household essentials in lieu of cash.

> Even to people who'd run away from other mines, bringing nothing with them, the boss of the *ōnaya* would provide things like pots and pans and *futon*, so those who came as they were could go right to work. But on pay-day, they'd have to repay the cost of the equipment.[46]

And though the women do not complain about the state of the second-hand, or perhaps ninth-hand, wares, the gang boss had discretion in establishing their rental value, which might not recognize the extent of previous "wear and tear." Nevertheless, such "loans" of household goods made it possible for miners to subsist until their first payday, and cash loans made it possible for the miners to buy other necessities. Another woman recalled:

> Even if [absconding miners] made good their escape and got to another mine, there were those who, if they found it not to their liking, came back to their original tenement. When they did so, they'd be told, "Well, every crow has black feet [everyone has a skeleton in their closet], so get back to work." They wouldn't be scolded or anything. And they'd be lent *shitaku-gin*. Because it'd be no use if they couldn't buy daily necessities.[47]

172   *Solidarity, divisions, bondage, and resistance*

The term *shitaku-gin* came to be used for the cash sum offered by the boss or company to the family so that they could provide the household goods for themselves. "When you entered a coal mine, they lent you *shitaku-gin*,"[48] another woman says simply, speaking of the late 1920s, by which point *shitaku-gin* had apparently become a generic term for all advances against wages.[49]

Although families could budget for repayment of money given to them in order to make their own purchases, if the value of goods given to them by the gang boss was not specified upon recruitment, deductions from wages could be arbitrary and punitive. Moreover,

> Even if [the main rice-winner] died, the loans of *kataire-gin* and so on had to be repaid. And the gang bosses wouldn't lend to households headed by women [*onna shotai*].[50]

Indebtedness was not only a matter of loans at recruiting time. When miners got into financial difficulty, they would borrow from the gang boss.

> If someone got ill, they had to borrow [money]. If they borrowed, since it'd be deducted from the wages, they'd have to borrow again. As a result, most of us never saw any money of our own.[51]

Another woman recounts:

> Since we'd borrow enough to balance the budget, on real paydays we saw little money and we'd have to borrow the difference [between expenses and pay] again. So we did it over and over. … From month to month, it was usual for us to live without seeing any real money.[52]

Although some miners may have had the illusion that they were making ends meet, in fact the mines could be said to be keeping them alive so that they could work.[53]

Should the miners occasionally earn wages that gave them even a small cushion for saving, the larger colliery companies managed to impose savings schemes on them that acted to bond them further to their work.[54] These forced savings schemes, or "term deposits," yielded little benefit to the miners but gave the company leverage over their lives. The women were not well informed about them. Asked by Morisaki about forced savings, one woman replied:

> Deposits required by the Company? Well, we were told that certain amounts were deducted from our wage packet every time, and that was because we'd received *kataire-gin* originally. It was supposed to be used to pay off that.[55]

This woman's family had moved to a bigger mine on the advice of neighbors, where they received better wages and were able to save money. But although they

Solidarity, divisions, bondage, and resistance   173

may have escaped from indebtedness by leaving the small mine, if their savings were held by the company at the bigger one, this financial "service" could be used to bind them just as surely as debts at smaller mines.[56]

And to the company store

The company store was another institution that ensured that miners were kept in thrall to the colliery management. Its operation devolved from the distribution function of the *kanba*, or pay office, which in simpler operations handled provisions for the miners and took their costs from the miners' pay. The *kanba* "is set up to handle daily provisions, everything from perquisite grain, to salt, *miso*, oil and firewood, and reckoning days are set three times a month, miners' pay being calculated on those days, and expenses (for provisions, etc.) being deducted to settle the accounts," the *Examination of Mining History* recorded.[57] As in coal mining communities in other countries,[58] the store, managed by preferred employees or by contractors of the company, usually had a monopoly on the provision of staples to the miners. This monopoly was so obvious at some mines that the store was called the "ration shop (*haikyū-sho*)."

> [The wages] might not be in money, but in rice vouchers or cash coupons. They could be used only at the ration shop for that mine. Even in that scrip, if you received what you earned in full, you were lucky.[59]

Later at the bigger mines, other shops were set up to cater to the miners, but the management of these shops colluded with mine management, if not to keep miners in poverty and thralldom at least to ensure the profitability of the shops. The vehicle of this collusion was company scrip. In more prosperous times, the overseers might express their contempt for the alleged profligacy of the miners while using their desire for cash to indenture them ever more tightly.[60] Although the miners might be able to take a day off without losing their jobs in such relatively good times, this was the extent of their resistance to company fiat, and they risked further indebtedness and reduced levels of subsistence to do so. The coal-mining women were the victims of a "credit" system that dominated their lives just as pervasively as the credit systems of modern society bind consumers today.

Subservience to the gang boss

There was another purpose served by the indebtedness: subservience to the gang boss. When coal miners owed substantial sums to the boss, they were not likely to challenge his authority and risk more onerous burdens of repayment. And most of the retired women make reference to the difficulties of paying off loans. Because the terms of the loans were rarely specified in advance and terms of repayment were apparently hidden from the borrowers, they had little ability to challenge those terms. To secure further loans, moreover, miners had to demon-

174 *Solidarity, divisions, bondage, and resistance*

strate "proper" subservience, perhaps grumbling among themselves but showing at least a grudging respect for the bosses in their presence.

Mining men showed some admiration for men of various backgrounds who had achieved the status of gang boss. Although some bosses were the successors of the skilled miners who contracted work at smaller mines, others, through strength of arm if not strength of character, and often through cunning and manipulation, rose to the position through favor with the employers. There was little reason for the female partners of less "successful" miners to have respected such men. These bosses, after all, "exploited their whole beings."[61] Yet the female miners were not quick at the time to condemn either the gang boss system or those who managed it. One step removed from obligation to the bosses because the loans were not made to them (wives were customarily kept waiting outside while their husbands appealed for indulgence),[62] they only occasionally showed their dissatisfaction with the system. Insofar as they "owed their souls" to the bosses through their husbands, most coal-mining women were unable to resist the exploitation of their "superiors."

The women had differing degrees of attachment to their gangs.[63] Mashio, the modern scholar, notes, "Though it was not sanctioned, in that region (Joban) if you could get away from the sphere of influence of your gang, you would be struck off their register." And her protagonist, Maki, recalls that during the almost continuous expansion of the industry up to and during World War I, "even if you didn't have a single *sen* [penny], if you joined a new gang the next day, you could get work. ... The gangs were all recruiting miners all year round."[64] In such circumstances, loyalty to the gang and the gang boss was certainly not as strong as the bosses would have liked.

The miners were at the mercy of the gang bosses as long as the bosses collected the wage packet from the company office and took their cut before distributing the remainder among their gang members.[65] The women did not know the size of the rake-off.[66] Maki, working in the Joban coalfields, understood her dependence on the boss, a dependence that did not allow for insubordination.

> If you weren't a member of a gang [*hamba*[67]], you couldn't work in the coal mines, and this was well understood so we never talked about it. The specialty of the gang boss [*hamba-gashira*] was collecting his rake-off. ...We feared the boss. Since there were some who wore wire-rimmed glasses and business suits, they stood out. We contented ourselves with bowing our heads [to him], but saw him as an important person. ...
>
> You may think we were fools to [allow ourselves to] be ripped off and lorded over, but when people have empty stomachs, they're weak in front of the one who gives them food. It was a case of calling oneself an idiot and gritting one's teeth. But we never let it show on our faces.[68]

The dependence of the miners, male and female, on the gang bosses, combined with the company's sanction of the bosses' use *in extremis* of brute force against the miners, prevented colliery workers from building on their solidarity, organizing, and from striking back.

Ketsuwari—indirect resistance

Although they usually did not dare to show insubordination to the gang bosses, the miners did plot secretly to abscond and remove themselves from the worst places of abuse in an abusive system. All of the recollections of the retired female miners refer to *ketsuwari*, or "withdrawing one's arse."[69] One woman illustrated the frequency of absconding by noting that all of her seven children were born in different places.[70] Another gave a remarkable list of major large mines at which she and her husband worked before they tried smaller ones, ending up back at Koyanose where they had started. "When you come to the face, they are all the same,"[71] she said, suggesting the similarity of working conditions and the difficulty of finding better situations. Some of the women recalled moving from mine to mine in hopes of obtaining higher wages and new loans for housekeeping; others sought to get out from under the burden of debt by disappearing in the night. Many miners absconded so often that they sometimes referred to their own ilk as "itinerant miners" (*watari kōfu*).[72] And high turnover rates caused by frequent movement from one mine to another continued long after 1930.[73] The use of blacklists of runaways by colliery employers, however, was not as widespread as it was among textile mill managers after the 1890s.[74]

Some miners were said to have made a game out of running. The women as well as the men took delight in the supposed success of slick operators in deceiving the bosses. The story of the "Turtle" (*suppon*), who came with a horse cart full of luggage actually empty of all but waste and who took full advantage of setting-up money and a wild welcoming party, only to disappear the next morning,[75] is obviously apocryphal, but the narrator took great delight in telling it. She says that the boss made futile efforts to find the absconding rascal, but all that remained of the ruse was the empty luggage.

Mine management got around the fickle nature of male bachelors by favoring family labor, reasoning that those with children would not run off as easily.[76] However, although debt may have been considered by management to be effective in keeping families from running, escaping from old loans and searching for new ones instead became a major aim for many family heads. The difficulty of extricating their families along with them persuaded some men to run off to other mines and leave their wives "in a real pickle." Some women tried to make up for the resulting shortage of income by working in "badger-hole" or illegal mines while continuing their shifts at their usual places of employment,[77] but this option was not open to most abandoned women. Other men worked out elaborate stratagems for the escape of the whole family.

Like most major decisions, that of when to leave one mine for another was usually made by the husband and father. One woman recounted her husband's decision with some sarcasm.

> "I don't like this mine, so get ready to leave." But he was not the man to talk things over with me. Women were very crusty, and you couldn't understand what they were saying. He said it was better if they didn't know anything.[78]

176   *Solidarity, divisions, bondage, and resistance*

Maki, in retrospect at least, deplored the fact that her father had made all the decisions about her working life until she married, but excused her mother for rather spinelessly accepting one decision to move because her mother did not share in the underground work. Mashio declared:

> The fact that Maki's father had passed through nearly every mine in the Joban coal fields was largely due to quarrels with gang bosses or his inability to hold his head above the deep waters of debt.[79]

Maki's father was a temperamental and quarrelsome man, and he exhibited an uncommon degree of recalcitrance against the bosses.

Leaving a mine was made simpler by the ordinary miner's lack of worldly possessions. The lack of ownership by the miners of any but the simplest means of production released them from close attachment to any particular worksite. And a dearth of even the most basic of household conveniences relieved them of perceived obligations to the company. Maki remembered:

> Since we had nothing, there was no problem. We had no such thing as a *tansu* [bureau with drawers]—nothing like that. Putting just a few clean underclothes in one of those old bamboo hampers, after that there was only the toolbox. With just the chisels used in the mine and a few other things in it. Then the rice pot and the pickle pot, just enough bowls for the family, one small washpan, and if you had a couple of pairs of worn-out quilts, you were well off.[80]

A Chikuho woman recalled:

> There wouldn't be a day when you didn't hear, "They've gone [*ketsuwatta*]! Today so-and-so left." No one had any household goods. But at the same time the bottom of the [cooking] pot of every household was always polished so it shone brightly. … Putting the pot in the *futon* and tying it up tightly, father would shoulder it, and for the rest there were a few changes of clothing only. Wrapping them in a *furoshiki*, mother would take it up and that would be all.

However, the bosses might be aware that something was up and try to stop a family from taking off.

> Throughout the year [miners] would be hard up all the time and wouldn't know where to turn. So they'd run away secretly. By the time it'd come to that, even the boss would have an inkling of it, and the foreman would hang about the house saying, "You think you can run away [*ketsuwaru*], don't you, you devil!" Even so, somehow they'd get away.[81]

Although their workmates were often forewarned, secrecy was necessary to avoid forestallment or capture.

> Finally came the time when we took off. Grasping the hands of our three children, we had to run through the bush. It was already getting dark. Then

Solidarity, divisions, bondage, and resistance 177

Figure 6.2 Ketsuwari. (Yamamoto, *Emaki*, 102nd black and white illustration).

we ran pell-mell down a back road. If we were caught, the beating would be terrible. It got dark. The children couldn't run any further. Since we thought that they wouldn't come after us this far, we went to a farm-house nearby and asked, "Since anything will do, please put us up for one night."[82]

But the farmer would not even allow the family to flop in one corner of the dirt floor entryway and turned them out into the cold. "[So] that night, since there was no other way, we hunkered down under the eaves wrapped in straw mats." This farmer was afraid of retribution from the mining companies and gang bosses for harboring miners who were considered criminals for withdrawing their labor in such a manner.

On the other hand, there were farmers who were sympathetic toward absconders. More than one apparently assisted a runaway after he had first been hidden "in the waste-coal box at the front" of a fellow miner's house, sequestering him in a nearby village and helping him escape in a horse cart along the Onga River.[83] In this case, the miners involved took pains not to reveal any names, preempting retaliation against their allies. Familiarity with such experiences persuaded most female miners, if not their husbands, that absconding was a desperate measure that should be attempted only in dire circumstances. Such circumstances, however, recurred frequently.

178 *Solidarity, divisions, bondage, and resistance*

To facilitate another surreptitious escape, one woman, who had initially failed to realize the import of her fellow miner's request, hid the miner's framing axe in a sling for carrying babies. She desisted from asking questions about the prospective escapee's destination. "If I knew, it would continue to bother me, and my mouth dried right up," she remembered.[84] It was better not to know, as the information might be extracted from her by force or subterfuge. Management at this mine obliged the miners to keep their tools in the mine, probably attempting to prevent them from running away.

Maki heard that guards were ensconced in the dormitories at her mine to ensure that potential escapees among the bachelors there were discovered before they absconded.[85] It could not have taken the bosses long to realize that toadies among the workers could also fulfill a function as spies and informers. In addition, at most Chikuho coal mines, if the living areas were not surrounded by forested mountains, brick walls were put up and the normal routes of egress guarded by company goons who, if not always armed, were at least strong enough to catch and hold escapers. The Slashed Auntie managed to talk her way out of a mining camp on the way to another job, but the difficulties are apparent from her story.

> This mine had a very strict regime. Only in a very few cases would they let miners go. If you said anything they didn't like, you'd be half killed [by beating]. Near the pit mouth a guard-house had been built. Those coming from outside and those going out were looked over carefully. Anyone who tried to escape or even run past was half killed. …
>
> Thinking that if one showed weakness, you'd be told off, I spoke to [the personnel managers] boldly. "I'm finished with this mine, and am leaving."
>
> If a man said this, it would be considered belligerent, but since I was only a woman, they wouldn't gang up and overpower me. … They said, "If you say you're leaving, there's nothing we can do. We'll have to let you go." … It was the first time a woman had ever come to challenge them to let someone go. … I was the notorious 'slashed woman' who had no fear for her life; my sword wound gave me immunity.[86]

This was the woman who had intervened in her husband's sword fight with another man. But the bullies had the power to stop anyone and punish them for trying to evade their purported obligations to the company.

Another woman admitted the possibility of being allowed to leave the notorious Miyoshi Mine but only under the most adverse conditions.

> When miners quit, they wouldn't be let go easily. On one excuse or another, they'd be made to [continue working], and on a day when the rain and wind was awful, they'd be told to get out suddenly and would be driven away.[87]

This woman's husband had a rather lenient attitude toward the escape of his gang members when he was gang boss. His experience being recruited to work at the infamous Takashima coal mines through entrapment and his surreptitious escape

Figure 6.3 More exemplary punishment (Yamamoto, *Emaki*, 104th black and white illustration).

from the island apparently gave him some sympathy for their plight. He winked at the evidence of their preparations to abscond and allowed it to happen. He and his wife, after apparently being removed as "gang parents [*oyakata*]" and falling on hard times, absconded later themselves.[88]

Because negotiated withdrawals and sympathetic bosses were all too rare, most miners resorted to elaborate stratagems in order to flee in the darkness of night. The derring-do of many miners led them not only to risk getting caught but even to disseminate stories that romanticized their escapades (hence the earlier story about the four couples who absconded into the woods, only to emerge later with different pairings).[89]

Maki's story of how her mother either left behind or lost en route her grandfather's funerary urn during one of her family's "removals" shows the intensity of the fears involved in absconding, and the dangers, while adding a comical touch. It also indicates that readying the cooking pot for transport was as important in the Joban region as it was in Chikuho. Preparation for the escape involved a subterfuge to deceive any snooping company officials or bullies of the gang boss.

> If we spread the quilts and plumped them up with pillows, it looked like someone was there. When neighbours slid open the wooden doors to see what was up that day, thinking that we had slept very late and asking, "What's wrong? Don't you feel well?" they'd pull back the quilts and find the bed empty. That happened any number of times.[90]

180 *Solidarity, divisions, bondage, and resistance*

It happened this time when Maki was 10, her younger sister 6. Until they got out of Fujiwara, where Maki's father had worked in a mine for only three months,

> [t]hey hurried as if escaping from a fire. If their feet dragged even a little, they were scolded and pulled along by the hand. This girl in her third year of elementary school, hunched over under a *furoshiki* containing her school supplies, a change of straw sandals, and a sooty Toyama medicine bag. From a tear [in the *furoshiki*], the blackened handle of a wooden serving spatula stuck out.[91]

This escape was different from others in that it took the route of a horse-powered, coal-moving railway, increasing the risk of detection but providing a clear-cut path for the fleeing family. Maki's father typified a certain reckless spirit among male miners, used to risking their lives underground and treating life lightly in their carousals and gambling above. Maki was alarmed to find him defecating on the railroad, narrowly missing being caught with his pants down by an oncoming "train" and making obscene gestures at the rear of the horse as it passed.[92] But she also recognized a certain indomitable spirit on the part of her father and other miners who put an optimistic gloss on their escapes, even if they rarely found the better conditions they sought at other mines. The grass, of course, always looks greener on the other side of the hill, particularly if it is covered with coal soot and withering on this side.

Repercussions

The kind of solidarity that kept impending flights from the knowledge of the bosses was essential in light of the severe measures taken by management to punish offenders who were apprehended. The miners were well aware that "if you were caught trying to escape after borrowing so much money, you'd be beaten half to death," in Maki's words. Such beatings were known as "lynchings" (*rinchi*), a term borrowed from the American South after the Meiji period.[93] Though the victims were not usually put to death, they were commonly strung up before being beaten.

> If it was found out early and you were caught in the act, you were tied up and brought back. Then you were cudgelled without mercy. You'd lose consciousness. Water would be dashed over you and when you regained consciousness you'd be beaten again. The dirt from the floor would turn your body yellow, and that punishment was called "making soybean flour" [*kinako ni suru*] or "making one bite the dust" [*doma wo neburaseru*].[94]

The water thrown over the "criminals," as well as bringing them back to consciousness, dilated the ropes so that "the binding cords tightened and cut into the flesh, causing unendurable suffering."[95]

Solidarity, divisions, bondage, and resistance   181

Just as an occasional sympathetic gang boss winked at the escape of his minions, others are said to have refrained from taking serious action against those who were caught. The miner daughter of a gang boss claimed:

> Miners were always running off [*ketsuwattoru*]. ... There were so many of them that I couldn't remember. ... No matter who it was, I always asked that they not be beaten, since there was no profit to be made by beating them, and they all lived a miserable life. There were hardly ever any beatings at our *ōnaya*.

In her mother's time, however, defaulters had been beaten severely at the Kaijima mines.

> When they were whipped, their big toes and their thumbs were tied tightly and they were strung up. Then they were beaten badly with a green bamboo [rod]. Apparently they would swing back and forth. Just to hear about it was to suffer. Oh! those who became idiots or went crazy were the lucky ones.[96]

This may have been some variation of the *chōchin-mage* (lantern-bending) torture that Yamamoto says was not used at the Chikuho mines in his day (the Taisho period).[97] The threat of such punishments was probably thought to be a sufficient deterrent to absconding or to insubordination by hidebound management, which let miners know that such a lynching or beating was always an option.

Children who were made to watch their parents being beaten for attempting to abscond also suffered a kind of torture.

> They would be sat down at the dirt floor entrance of the office beside their parents and would howl pitifully. If they tried to cling to their mother, they'd be kicked. And their fathers and mothers would be beaten with a cane to the verge of unconsciousness. The fact that they had run off and were being made an example of would be written in big phonetic letters and hung from their necks. ... And sitting beside them and bawling or looking vacant, their children would seem so pitiful that one couldn't stand to look at them. Those who were caught would have no choice but to go back to work. ... Even though they'd been brought close to death, they'd run away again. And this time they'd do it so they wouldn't be found out.[98]

The punishment for absconding seems to have been particularly harsh if a miner was caught running off with someone else's mate.

> [If they were caught] both the man and the woman were stripped and their hands tied behind their backs, and they were strung up on the loading platform. "Such people as you bring punishment on yourselves!" And the man would be beaten with a green bamboo (cane) and the woman stabbed until they lost consciousness. But if the woman's husband forgave her, only the man would

182　*Solidarity, divisions, bondage, and resistance*

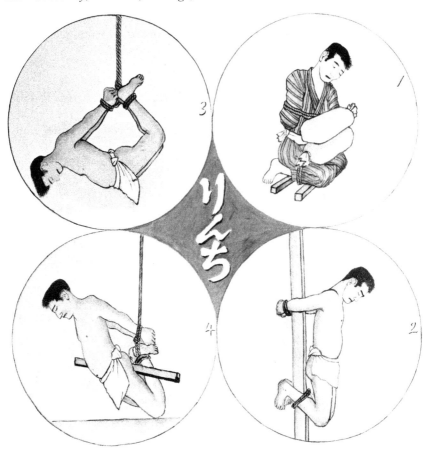

Figure 6.4 Rinchi—lynching. Forms of punishment (Yamamoto, *Emaki*, 107th black and white illustration).

    be beaten and expelled from the mine. The woman sometimes went with him and sometimes stayed behind. I didn't like watching such lynchings.[99]

It seems that the women were "stabbed" by being poked or pierced in the vagina, one of the most brutal tortures still used in some countries nowadays.[100]

    Although only organized forms of absconding can be described as "a primitive form of political protest,"[101] the willingness to risk corporal punishment in order to flee from loads of debt and harsh working conditions would seem to be as much a form of resistance to exploitation as a modern strike. *Ketsuwari* may not have been organized in the sense that more than one family often cooperated in the enterprise, but certainly the logistics had to be well organized within the family in order to ensure any chance of success. It would seem that only an improvement in living and working conditions could have effectively countered

Solidarity, divisions, bondage, and resistance 183

Figure 6.5 "Moral correction" (Yamamoto, *Emaki*, 106th black and white illustration).

the high rates of absconding, or, in business management terms, high labor turnover rates. But although there is some evidence of a gradual decline of these rates over the half century between the 1880s and the 1930s, the women's testimony gives little evidence of any deliberate and coherent policy on the part of management to attempt to retain workers by improving living and working conditions at the coal mines.[102]

Brutality as a management strategy

Matthew Allen has found a pattern of brutality and violence in colliery management's treatment of miners in a period later than ours. Most of the recollections of the retired female miners dealing with the period before 1930 similarly refer to the brutality of the bosses in forcing people to work and in trying to deter absconding. Some women spoke of a pattern of brutality extending throughout "repressive mines" (*assei-yama*). One retiree mentioned that at the "government-run" Igisu Mine "the regulations were stiff," but "it was not a repressive place like other mines."[103] The Miyoshi Mine at Takamatsu, on the other hand, seems to have had the reputation as the second worst *assei-yama* after the notorious Takashima Mine in Nagasaki Bay.[104] One of Idegawa's interviewees reported that several different shafts of the Nishikawa Mines were "all so-called

184 *Solidarity, divisions, bondage, and resistance*

assei-yama."[105] She seems to list them in order of the severity of repression, and miners may have ranked other mines roughly in the same way.

There is some evidence that the brutality was worse in earlier years. Yamamoto Sakubei's description of the "hanging-spider (*sagari-gumo*)" punishment is a prelude to his mention of some reforms following the Russo-Japanese War (i.e., after 1905), which, however, did not fundamentally alter the risks and penury of the coal miners' lives. He tells how children, of which he was one, took a morbid interest in watching cruel beatings (at least when the victims were not their parents) and suggests that the miners became inured to harsh treatment by company and *nayagashira* representatives. Parents followed their own admonitions to their children to "mind their own business," he says, although adults who showed an interest in the beatings were considered peculiar.[106] He also claims that

> [i]nsolent or insubordinate [*furachi*] miners were beaten without resisting and were probably resigned to the idea that it was [appropriate] retribution for the crimes they had committed.[107]

One wonders whether Kyushu women so readily accepted punishments that seem to have been quite arbitrary and out of proportion to misdemeanors. Tsurumi's conclusion that "physical punishment was an accepted part of supervision,"[108] however, was certainly as applicable to the coal mining industry as to the "modern" textile industry.

The power of the boss

> *The miserable dispatcher, the cruel overseer,*
> *and the unfeeling gang boss … Gotton, gotton.*[109]

This mining song, "which was full of satire," Yamamoto remembers, was not sung very openly at the Kami-mio mine where he worked. If it was heard by the bosses, "they would have your hide (*abura o torareru*)." Most of the bosses were not ones to let even implied criticism pass without a rather vicious response, so the miners usually kept any scorn and resentment to themselves.

Yamamoto also recalls that strong gang bosses and respected company officials could have an immediate impact on the quarrels that arose among the miners themselves, even when they arose outside their field of direct supervision. This suggests that their writ ran large through the mining communities.[110] However, his evidence echoes that of the retired female coal miners who say that the gambling quarrels and drunken brawls went on without systematic intervention at most of the mines during the Meiji and Taisho periods.

> Since there were those who went from one place where they could gamble to another, fights were frequent. They were all con men [*ikasama bakari*]. Though the repression was severe, the strong survived. Since they used bamboo spears in fights at the gambling places, one or two of the supervisors

alone couldn't interfere. It was always, today someone was slashed, today someone was stabbed, they died, etc.[111]

The endemic violence seems to have diminished only with the establishment of strong unions and the improvement of working and living conditions after the Asia-Pacific War. But Matthew Allen suggests that the violence associated with a dysfunctional society recurred with the closure of most Chikuho coal mines in the 1960s and 1970s.[112]

"Behavior modification"

In a climate of incessant conflict between male miners, it is not surprising that the women were preoccupied with keeping their men at work and away from the fighting associated with gambling, drinking, and womanizing. They had little time and energy to devote to broader struggles for the emancipation of miners from the exploitation that was the root cause of their frustration and immiseration. One woman interfered in her husband's gambling, a common form of recreation at the mines, at least for the men, despite its general prohibition.

> In my prime, I was very strong, and if I found out that my husband was secretly gambling, he wouldn't get off lightly. I had his solemn promise [that he wouldn't gamble]. So when I found out where he was, I immediately took up the butcher knife and ran there. There was a great to-do at the gambling den.
> "Your wife's coming to make trouble!"
> "Quick! Quick! Get away on the roof from upstairs!"
> [Hearing] shouts like this, my old man tumbled out of a window and ran.
> If someone caused havoc in the gambling house, usually they wouldn't get off so easily. They might be wrapped in a straw mat and dumped into the Onga River. But in my case, the master of the gambling den [*zamoto*] just said, "Today's gambling is now postponed," and the matter was over.[113]

The earlier narrative about the wife who intervened in the fights of her gang boss husband to quell the wrath of his antagonists and blunt his reputation as a trouble maker illustrates well the women's role in trying to stop dissension among male miners. Their daughter could admire her father's willingness to negotiate with other gangs, but she almost certainly felt that quarrels among gangs were not conducive to peace at the mines where her family worked. Nevertheless, the gang relied on her father for work and survival, and she was aware that he had the ability to improve the members' lives by moving the whole gang from one mine to another when working conditions proved unacceptable.[114]

The "Old Woman of the Mines" recalled conflict at the Yamada mines about the time of the First World War:

> When we came, the overseers [*yakunin*] were bad in every way. They were haughty. They would pummel us. The people [other miners] were bad too.

186 *Solidarity, divisions, bondage, and resistance*

Figure 6.6 The officious staffer (Yamamoto, *Emaki*, 131st black and white illustration).

> They'd been convicted of first or second degree offenses, had tattoos, and were always shouting, "To hell with you!" Even the women.[115]

The women of nearby Tagawa, like those of other parts of Chikuho, made use of the "vulgarities" of the local dialect, and colorful language seems to have added to their reputation for audacity.[116]

"Subtle" and not-so-subtle forms of resistance

The Old Woman seems to accept the characterization of miners as "bad" people but also notes the unfortunate background of many of them and justifies their dislike of the oppression by mine management. Rough ex-convict miners often refused to "take shit" from anyone, she says. Subtle forms of resistance were used against a haughty "official" from the company who came to her house asking for information about her family.

> He couldn't read the character for my elder brother's name and asked, "How do you call the oldest boy?"

Solidarity, divisions, bondage, and resistance 187

It was Takumi. "It's the character for a _hagama-tori_."

The word _hagama-tori_ came from a handle made of wood which was used for taking the cooked rice (pot) away from the fire. Since it was in the shape of the [cursive?] character for _takumi_, I explained it that way.

"You say, _hagama-tori_, but is there such a name?"

"If I say so, there is. It must be written there."

"You may read it that way, but you're probably having me on."

"You don't need to pretend that you don't know (how to read it)! Aren't you an official? We may be illiterate, but is there any reason why you shouldn't know it? You don't deserve more pay, do you? Don't try to make fun of us."

The neighbours were gathering round, saying, "What a hoot! You telling him off!", and laughing.[117]

Although such teasing, and the enthusiastic support that it could attract, might infuriate a hapless staffer, it of course had little functional efficacy as a means of resistance. The satisfaction of bringing the intelligence or ability of representatives of the company into disrepute may have provided some psychological benefit, but any real challenge to these representatives would require a much higher degree of confidence in the miners' ability to resist company fiat. And in the Meiji and Taisho periods, although providing some relief against the importunities of mine managements, such recourse to mockery or ridicule could also antagonize the overseers and contribute to one's reputation as a troublemaker.[118]

Among the mining women who were not cowed by company authority above ground was the mother of Yamamoto Sakubei. She embodied the spirit of the women who lived in the mining district up the Onga River (the _kawasuji kishitsu_), he recalls. Though of mining stock, she would not only fail to cringe before the mining bosses, or anyone else, but would even challenge them if she thought her rights were being trampled on. He relates an incident that must have occurred in late Taisho or early Showa, a time when miners had begun organizing and were becoming more conscious of their rights.

It was when I was still a child. Taken by my mother, I found myself in the bath for company staff. She was reproved by a staff member. But while it might have been cause for her to apologize, she instead turned on the staffer and shouted him down.

"What the hell, you bastard! Are you a human being or a god? … [I]f you're a human being, who are you to say whether we can go into that bath! If you don't stop your blather, I'll throw you in the miners' bath and see how you like it!"[119]

Such spirit helped women survive in the mines, Yamamoto argues, particularly in the earlier Meiji period.

Although some women mounted limited challenges to authority, attempts to counter the directives of bosses could redound against the offenders. Underground,

188 *Solidarity, divisions, bondage, and resistance*

the miners were at the mercy of the overseers. The arbitrariness of their power is suggested by the case of one unfortunate young woman.

> Although we worked in such a [terrible] place, there were some who were killed underground. A 17-year-old woman was accused of not listening [to orders] and was beaten to death with a pickaxe. And thrown into the old mine workings.[120]

No doubt confrontations on the surface also contributed to a miner's reputation and worked against him or her underground.

Regulatory and discriminatory regimes

The coal mines seem to have had a less explicit and comprehensive regulatory framework than the textile mills in the Meiji and Taisho periods.[121] Each mine had its own rules. However, the similarity of the operating systems meant that often these rules were not recorded but were simply expected to be "understood" by workers. The regime may not have been as arbitrary as that of feudal stipulations in the Tokugawa period, where the victims were sometimes informed of the regulations that they had broken only after they were arraigned,[122] but it did make similar assumptions about the duty of the miners to know the rules and to obey them. Some rules were a matter of what overseers would have seen as common sense. For instance, there was to be no questioning of authority; no retorts to men in command. One woman reported:

> At every mine, the men in charge of workers would beat us with cudgels. "Do you dare to talk back, you vermin!" they would shout haughtily. You weren't allowed to answer back at all.[123]

Igisu was exceptional, she remembers, in that "if you obeyed the rules, you would not be beaten or kicked."[124] Her statement implies that elsewhere there was a regime similar to that in the cotton mills of Japan, where "management and supervisory personnel had a great deal of discretionary power with which to enforce regulations—improper behavior could be the way a girl looked at her boss."[125]

One woman emphasized the role of haughty and callous "officials" at the Mitsubishi mines.[126] When she felt like running away after an accident that killed another miner, the dispatcher chastised her: "If you think it's so bad for someone to be killed, get the hell out of the mines!"[127] Other women told of beatings for minor infringements of the regulations, and one said that they commonly "just worked on without seeing, hearing, or saying anything."[128]

Yamamoto rationalizes the harsh treatment in terms of punishment for infractions against the social order that would also have been punished by the authorities in the less tumultuous society outside the mining camps. In Yamamoto's list of violations subject to beatings, however, he loses the distinction between what

Solidarity, divisions, bondage, and resistance   189

would seem to have been infractions of company rules and what were inscribed in public statutes as crimes.[129] Mine overseers winked at such distinctions as well as at "modern" norms of humane behavior in the prosecution of their duties. Their arbitrariness in the doling out of punishments was indicated by another retired woman:

> At the coal mines … if you so much as spoke to the daughter of the gang boss, you were beaten, and if you said you were short of food, you were beaten. So you might say that miners' wounds [from such beatings] were an emblem.[130]

The punishments for similar infractions of rules were not always the same at different mines. One woman noted that at the repressive Miyoshi Mine the management practiced "cruel exemplary punishment" (*mugena miseshime*) but that at the Sugitani Mine "they were not so strict."[131]

There seems to have been a lack of rules for the behavior of the greater numbers of male workers toward female miners. Because of the necessary comingling of the sexes underground, there were no "company regulations" such as those in cotton mills, which "might stress strict separation of female and male workers."[132] In the mining milieu, the regulation of such behavior was by custom rather than statute. Many other rules of customary behavior originated in the prescribed relationship between gang bosses and gang members. The Goddess of the *Sena* outlines the customary response to accidents, probably at a large mine.

> When a person was hurt, the boss had to give a cup of *saké* to each person who had provided aid. Not only to his own gang members, but often people from other gangs who had given help as well. You didn't know when you might need help again, and if you were the slightest bit careless, you could lose your life. So you couldn't treat members of other gangs who gave aid as if they didn't count.[133]

And although miners who absconded often left behind debts to gang bosses, custom, ironically, dictated that they also leave behind household goods "lent" to them by those erstwhile masters.

Another tradition required miners to stay with one gang boss as long as they stayed at the same mine. "I've never heard of someone becoming a member of a different gang at the same mine," one woman said. "It wasn't forbidden, but there was an obligation there. Everyone kept it in mind."[134] In the recruiting process, more than one boss might bid for them, but once they had been chosen by or assigned to a boss, they could not change to another gang without risking severe reprobation or ostracism by fellow workers. The effect would be the same as *mura-hachibu*, the feudal form of ostracism whereby a peasant and his family were prevented from receiving most (eight-tenths) of the usual benefits of communal living.[135] Indenture with one gang boss benefitted the company by ensuring a measure of stability in the assignment of work sites and duties.

190 *Solidarity, divisions, bondage, and resistance*

The suppression of Korean miners

There were many workers, of course, who did nothing overt to gain reputations as difficult employees. Koreans, whether impressed for labor under the colonial system or lured by promises of "good jobs" in Japanese mines, were victims of the frustrations of overseers who could not extract the desired degree of productivity from them. Language problems, limited training and education, lack of work experience, as well as resentment at the situations in which they found themselves, could all make Koreans less efficient workers than their Japanese counterparts. But they had few means of resisting the consequent abuse. Nevertheless, when Korean workers were beaten and mistreated, sympathy could be aroused among some of their Japanese workmates, particularly among some of the female miners. One woman recalls:

> They were whipped, by the dispatcher [*hitokuri*]. Japanese were also beaten, but Koreans were struck even harder. It was something terrible! Beaten with a cane. The blood spouted out. They were doused with cold water. Although their food was not good, if they staggered while walking, they would be yelled at—*Kora!*—and beaten. They were [treated] like non-people [*hinin*] or outcastes [*eta*].[136]

One Korean who had achieved the unusual distinction of becoming a dispatcher—and who was apparently treated with some circumspection because of his intimidating mode of speech (*kuchi ga kowai*)—offered to pay the bar bill for two young punks who were short of cash. When their response was scornful abuse, he took a butcher knife, killed one, and wounded the other. "Yotchan" was given hard labor. Korean women, of course, were also subject to discrimination and abuse at the mines (where they rarely worked underground) but did not react as fiercely as Yotchan.

Although some women spoke of conflict, including mêlées, between Korean and Japanese miners, others recalled getting along well with Koreans underground.[137] One woman spoke of "singing together with the people from the Peninsula" while riding the coal wagons at the Kojaku mine.[138] Another, like her, felt that the Koreans "were all good people. Until that time it had been said that Koreans were stupid or prone to quarrel, but that was a lie."[139] Yet another woman remembered Koreans as kind: "They would take on the hardest work. And we would form mining teams with them, where there was no distinction between Japanese and Koreans, and work hard to get out the coal."[140]

The retired female miners did provide a few stories about Koreans living at the mines that portrayed them in an unfavorable light. One Korean woman is said to have shown another miner bedbugs kept in a bottle but expressed little inclination to get rid of them. The Korean women, this retired miner said, also had the unfortunate habits of washing diapers in the water barrel or washbowl and of eating animal flesh with the hair still on it.[141] But this same woman also extolled the Korean women for learning Japanese quickly and noted that the

Solidarity, divisions, bondage, and resistance   191

treatment of Koreans at the mines was abominable. The rarity of discriminatory remarks about Koreans and the relative frequency of sympathy expressed for them among the retired women, though perhaps partially the result of postwar re-education, convinces me that prejudice against the "People from the Peninsula" was not as widespread at the coal mines as in other social milieu. My evidence, admittedly fragmentary, suggests that what prejudice there was could be diminished by the shared experience of exploitation and mistreatment of workers of all stripes.

Whatever real empathy was felt between Korean and Japanese miners probably led to few overt actions on the part of their Japanese fellows to change the situation of Korean workers before the 1930s.[142] But where management did not succeed in getting Japanese workers to sublimate their resentments against management into antipathy toward Koreans, some feelings of solidarity were aroused. Though normally forced to remain latent in the prewar coal mines, such feelings could eventually support a wider movement of worker solidarity, even an international one in the postwar period.

Divisions and solidarity

It may be argued that the mistreatment of Koreans was merely part of a pattern of inhumane treatment of all miners. And that this pattern was not the peculiar responsibility of management contending with a social stratum made up substantially of misfits and outcastes from mainstream society who were prone to gambling, drinking, and fighting among themselves. It is true that convicts were used in large numbers at some of the bigger mines, and that some of them, in the absence of wage-earning alternatives, stayed on at the mines after their terms had been served. It is also true that there were large numbers of *burakumin*, outcaste people, working at some of the mines, and that their imported reputation as mean and dirty—remarkably similar to the reputation of Korean workers outside the mines—was likely to affect the attitudes of many who worked with them. There also were people who had sought sanctuary at mountain mines where the law could not catch up with them. But the greatest number of those working at coal mines had come from bankrupted small holdings and were "failed farmers" (*tsubure-byakusho*).[143]

Despite the anxieties of ex-farmers about associating with convicts, toughs, and *burakumin*, they were not always ready to involve themselves in a dog-eat-dog struggle to pick the bones flung to them by mine management. When they were fully entrenched in mining life, they could adopt discriminatory attitudes toward the very rural society from which they had come. The woman who earlier said that rural people were "dirty" (*kitanai*) probably meant grasping and grudging rather than unclean. (Despite their frequent bathing, often in less-than-clean water, miners would not likely have claimed to be clean relative to their rural cousins.) Such discriminatory attitudes from and about outside groups, though harmful in many ways, nevertheless helped to cement feelings of solidarity among miners as a distinctive social group.

192 *Solidarity, divisions, bondage, and resistance*

The retired women, no doubt affected by the postwar re-education in attitudes toward *burakumin* and disadvantaged people, usually expressed some sympathy for the outcastes and ne'er-do-wells, as well as for the Koreans, with whom they worked. Some female miners noted the common separation of *burakumin* women at coal-sorting stations and in special living accommodations but also mentioned attempts to overcome such divisions.[144] One woman even tried to counter the common Japanese belief that *burakumin* could be distinguished from "ordinary" Japanese by their unattractive appearance.

> Young women in the old days were beautiful at work. Forty or fifty came to work at sorting. Young girls. From the vicinity of Okuma. They were all outcastes (from the unliberated villages—*mikaiho-burakumin*). The "all-fours."[145] They all came wearing make-up.

She describes how their peculiar way of dressing made them look quite beautiful.

> As well as these, three or four ordinary girls came. And they [*ano hito-tachi*—referring to the *burakumin*] made friends with the others. At least, that was the way it seemed. But they were talking to each other, and didn't make an appearance even when it became late. If they didn't come out, they wouldn't get any work done. So the others went and got them. When it was time to go home, in the washroom they all took out little mirrors and did their make-up. Before and after, they were always making up.[146]

The "ordinary" girls and the outcaste newcomers had something in common in striving to make themselves presentable, and their washroom exchanges seem to have brought them together as a work team.

A notable lack of mention by the retired women of distinctions between *burakumin* and other workers underground, and occasional mention of cooperation between them, suggests that discrimination on the basis of caste among miners was, if not absent, at least muted. It might be argued that the *burakumin* could keep their origins hidden at the coal mines, but in fact most did live separately, either in specially designated housing (*tokushu naya*) or in their own villages.[147] Only if they kept their origins from recruiters in the same way as ex-convicts or escapees from the law often did, and mingled among other miners, could they avoid the risks of discrimination and unfavorable treatment by overseers.[148] And living and working in close quarters with them, other women were likely to discern evidence of *burakumin* origins and be unable to refrain from revealing the secret. In the accounts of the women, however, most of the conflicts among miners seem to have resulted from quarrels over gambling debts, drunken brawls among males of similar status, and rivalries between gangs (usually from different mines) rather than from blatant caste or ethnic discrimination.

The lack of intervention by mine management in intramural struggles suggests a willingness to let divisions operate for the benefit of the company. Although many mines had policemen assigned to support the company diktat, they, like company officials, were noticeably reluctant to keep the peace when it involved only fights among miners. Police timidity in the face of intra-miner hostility, and antagonism between miners and representatives of the state, were both typical of collieries. Although deploring the failure of the police to stop the rowdyism in the coal camps, the female miners, like their menfolk, resented police interference in labor disputes.

The Rice Riots and attempts at organized resistance

Ordinarily aloof, the forces of the state in times of crisis could be effectively aligned against coal miners. Some big mine owners used the equivalent of private police forces to control their workers, although most other owners were ready to call on local police forces as if they were adjuncts of management. One woman recalled:

> Those private cops at the coal mines only did what was good for the Company. At repressive mines, all the personnel bosses [*rōmu*] and the police swaggered about. If someone died as the result of sword wounds, they would tell us to put [the body] in the mine, and deal with it by saying [the miner] had died in a rock fall or some such.[149]

Some issues could not be disposed of as conveniently as miners' bodies. The Rice Riots of 1918 were started by wives of fishermen and female stevedores in Toyama Prefecture who were concerned about the escalating price of rice.[150] Wives of miners in northern Kyushu were similarly concerned.

> It was a time when rice was expensive, more than 50 *sen* [per *shō*].
>   At the time there were insurrections all over the place. … My friend was at Omine in Tagawa [district] and said there was a rising there about August of 1918. Troops were apparently dispatched there from Kokura. There were people killed by gunfire, too—killed by mistake. It was said that, when [people] went running to see, [shouting] "What's up? What's up?" they were mistaken for rioters and shot. It was terrible.

The coincidence of this disturbance at the Omine coal mines with the first occurrence of the riots in Toyama suggests that miners were responding to an inflationary rice market throughout the western half of Japan.

> There was trouble at Wakamatsu as well, and at the rice shop[s] it was said that the *saké* barrels were uncorked in front of the store and ladles provided. Those who were running around making trouble are said to have gulped it down and rushed off again to destroy buildings [*uchi-kowashi*]. The police marked the backs of the miners with ink, so that when the disturbance was put down they could catch them. At Wakamatsu the offshore longshoremen called *gonzō* were supposed to have been the most numerous. They thrashed about with roof tiles and such. Those were harsh times.[151]

194 *Solidarity, divisions, bondage, and resistance*

Figure 6.7 Uchi-kowashi—house wrecking (Yamamoto, *Emaki*, 154th black and white illustration).

Shindo Toyo, on the evidence of others who had worked as miners at the time, speaks of the riots "spreading like wildfire" in mining districts.[152]

In his account of disturbances at some Chikuho region coal mines in 1918, Ogino Yoshihiro shows that they were primarily concerned with the relationship between rice prices and wages and hence with standards of living at the end of World War I. Profiteering resulting from collusion between merchants and coal companies angered miners, as did the role of the state in backing the companies with police and military force. Some companies made concessions on food prices and wages that temporarily ameliorated the difficulties of mining families, but arrest, incarceration, and dismissal of leading dissidents certainly caused greater hardship for many others.[153]

The women's role in these "strikes," as in most of the labor struggles of the 1920s, was that of support and backup for the men.[154] Mathias writes:

> After 1918, women who worked underground participated in the labour movement, but they did not obtain leading positions. Their participation in strikes was limited to providing food for the men and encouraging them by singing labour songs.[155]

Solidarity, divisions, bondage, and resistance 195

Figure 6.8 The state intervenes (Yamamoto, *Emaki*, 156th black and white illustration).

As well as providing food and moral support during strikes, women helped men who were trying to organize, hiding their presence from authorities and refusing to identify "trouble-makers." Asahara Kenzo, a leader in these attempts to organize, recorded the presence of women at one "demonstration" to protest the mauling of leaflet distributors by company goons at Otsuji Mine; the women backed up an initially orderly protest by male activists.[156] Although relatively passive, the women and children supported the activists and allowed them to escape through their phalanx when management marshalled more bullies and the "fire brigade" to drive them off. Mining women may have been unruly at times, but usually they were subjected to intimidation, both by managers and male miners, that kept them "in line" and playing subordinate roles in disputes.

The women certainly understood the reasons for the struggles and strikes of the post–World War I period. One who was at the Taisho Mine in 1925 recounted:

> The dwellings about that time were roofed with wood shingles. They were in very bad shape. So as well as [concern over] the fall of roof rock [in the tunnels], a dispute erupted with the demand, "Repair the dwellings! Raise the wages per wagon-load of coal!"

196 *Solidarity, divisions, bondage, and resistance*

At a lumber storage yard,

> [t]he men all gathered there for a sit-in. The women took food to them. For about ten days, nobody went down the pit. And even Asahara Kenzo, who had shut down the blast furnaces at Yawata, came to give support. He seems to have been No.1 on the Company's hit list. At that time there were small disputes everywhere at mines throughout Chikuho, and everyone was worried. After a ten-day struggle, it ended in defeat, but nobody had said we should give up. But the dwellings stayed the same. Everyone was given two *yen*.[157]

During a strike in 1918, the miners had carried their lamps—normally returned to the company lampisterie after their shifts—to a rally on the Onga River dike that the overseers and cops could not prevent.

The larger companies responded to strikes, riots, complaints, and public censure by offering new services such as modest medical facilities,[158] reducing the powers of the *nayagashira*, and attempting to institute management–worker "harmonization" programs. But smaller mining companies had less leverage in such matters, and when the postwar depression of 1919 hit, many of them were obliged to lay off workers or even close their mines. The multifarious effects of the depression hampered workers' efforts to organize unions that might have ameliorated the consequences of layoffs and the deterioration of working and living conditions. In 1927, when the worldwide depression began to affect the Japanese coal industry, further statutory impediments were put in the way of worker organization. And, as usual, the women were victims, unable to see their way out of a situation in which the cards and the rules were stacked against them

Epilogue—the potential for change

One eventual outcome of the cooperative spirit and embryonic solidarity among coal miners was the growth of labor unions. But at least for one woman, better living conditions, access to consumer goods, and the freedom to speak her mind were mixed benefits of union organization. Unselfishness was lacking, she believed. In the post-1945 era, she declared:

> There's ample opportunity for the women to give their opinions. Well, of course, I think that's a good thing, but even though it may be better that they can loaf about in their houses and speak easily, isn't democracy different from that? … It seems that modern people think that happiness means not working. … We were always full of the spirit, "I won't give up!" Modern women don't have that. They only refuse to admit defeat in matters of vanity and cosmetics.[159]

In her view, better conditions do not make a better life for women, hard work being good for the soul. Such approval of the character building function of hard work and suffering is not uncommon in other times and places among people with this type of work experience. Although it breeds acceptance of working conditions that otherwise would be deemed unacceptable, it may, at the same time, have been one of the few means of establishing some self-esteem in a system seemingly designed to wipe out the modest strains of pride and decency fostered among the mining women by their work, their families, and their coworkers.

Notes

1 Morisaki, *Makkura*, p.108. The *sena-bō* was the wooden pole with which coal baskets were carried over the shoulders, mainly by women, and that could be used to "cudgel" recalcitrant miners. The song may derive from the early period when men also carried the *sena* and were the main victims of overseers' abuse.
2 I have used a proper noun for the women's abstraction referring to colliery companies in infrequent mentions because the women did not refer to them by name and undoubtedly thought of "the Company" as a powerful, overweening organization.
3 Matthew Allen, *Undermining the Japanese Miracle: Work and Conflict in a Coalmining Community*, p.2.
4 *Undermining the Japanese Miracle*, p. 4 and passim.
5 Morisaki, pp. 151–2. Cf. *Undermining the Japanese Miracle*, p. 29.
6 Morisaki, p. 160.
7 Morisaki, p. 152.
8 Idegawa, p. 205.
9 Idegawa, pp. 27–8.
10 A very small sum, similar to a ha'penny in England at the time.
11 Morisaki, pp. 142–4.
12 Idegawa, p.75.
13 Morisaki, p.72.
14 Ibid., pp. 74–5.
15 Ibid., p.78.
16 See the 8th color illustration in Yamamoto, *Chikuhō Tankō Emaki*, reproduced in black and white in Yamamoto, *Yama ni Ikiru*, pp. 146–7.
17 See, for example, Morisaki, p. 49.
18 Morisaki, p. 75.
19 *Undermining the Japanese Miracle*, p. xiii.
20 The *gonin-gumi* system was revived at some mining camps about the turn of the century to improve sanitation and to "rationalize" relationships among mining households. Yamamoto Sakubei, *Yama no Kurashi*, pp. 25–6. It is not certain how widely this collective responsibility system was used or how much interference there was from the company in its administration. It is not apparent from the recollections of the female retirees that any such system was used to punish groups for offenses by their individual members. See Ogino, "*Taisen Zengo ni okeru Kaijima Tankō-gyō no Rōshi Kankei,*" pp. 115–6 and footnote 48, p. 155. Also Tsurumi, *Factory Girls*, pp. 136–7.
21 In more recent times, we have examples of the spraying of indelible color onto "rioters" (in South Korea, for instance) and the photographing of demonstrators by agents of the police in "advanced" countries to identify opponents of "properly constituted authority" and deter them from further "unlawful activities." The result is probably counterproductive in many cases.
22 Morisaki, pp. 105–110.
23 Morisaki, p.48.
24 Morisaki, p.76.
25 Mashio Etsuko, *Jizoko no Seishun*, pp. 64–5.
26 Ibid., p. 72.

198 *Solidarity, divisions, bondage, and resistance*

27 Idegawa, pp. 26–7.
28 Idegawa, p. 81.
29 Morisaki, pp. 154–5.
30 *Undermining the Japanese Miracle*, p. 4.
31 Translated into English by Jay Rubin and published by Stanford University Press, 1988. In his Afterword, Rubin overlooks the similarities of parts of the book with the article by Emi (see following note), one possible reason (there are others adduced by Rubin) why Japanese and other critics give this particular Soseki work such short shrift.
32 Emi Suiin, *"Ashio Dōzan Kōfu no Hanashi,"* in *Taiyō*, vol. 4 no. 25 (Dec. 20, 1898), pp. 79–80.
33 Morisaki, pp. 116–7.
34 This torture is illustrated in Yamamoto, *Chikuhō Tankō Emaki*, 107th black and white illustration, and reproduced in *Yama ni Ikiru*, p. 70.
35 Morisaki, *Makkura*, pp. 126–7.
36 Tragic accidents as the result of such imprisonment of factories' workforces in industrializing countries today remind us that cruel exploitation continues in the name of "development."
37 Miike Tanko Rodo Kumiai, ed., *Miike Nijūnen*, main text, p. 7.
38 *Miike Nijūnen*, p. 7, from *Dan Takuma Den* (The Story of Dan Takuma). This latter work is a sample of Japanese hagiography that attempts to give a humane character to one of Japan's corporate elite.
39 Cf. Matthew Allen, *Undermining the Japanese Miracle*, particularly pp. 210 to 215.
40 Cf. Shindo, *Chikuhō no Jokōfu-tachi*, pp. 66–9 and Oyama Shikitaro, *Kōgyō Rōdō to Oyakata Seido*, pp. 51 and 55 for employment contracts at the Takashima coal mines.
41 Cf. Oyama, pp. 24–5, as cited in note 63 below.
42 Morisaki, p. 156.
43 Idegawa, p. 147.
44 Idegawa, p. 162.
45 Shindo, *Chikuhō no Jokōfu-tachi*, p. 70. These stipulations probably come from Mitsui's mine operating regulations in the Taisho period. Shindo emphasizes the low level of wages and their inadequacy, but I would reiterate that the indebtedness incurred in such initial loans and further borrowing to meet expenses could easily become a form of bondage for the miners.
46 Idegawa, p. 178.
47 Morisaki, p. 16.
48 Morisaki, p. 64.
49 Morisaki, pp. 116–7.
50 Idegawa, pp. 199–200.
51 Morisaki, p. 13.
52 Idegawa, p. 168.
53 See also, Morisaki, p. 59.
54 For systems of holding back wages under the euphemism of "savings" in the textile mills, see Tsurumi, *Factory Girls*, pp. 113, 118, 153.
55 Morisaki, p. 73.
56 The recommended form of contract at the Takashima mines in the Meiji period dictated that such-and-such amounts "are to be taken from the wages and deposited to provide for necessary expenses for returning to one's native village and so on." Oyama, *Kōgyō Rōdō to Oyakata Seido*, p. 52. See also the list of household expenses claimed as average for a family of five at Miike at the time of a 1924 strike, including "contingency fund (deposited with the Co.): 3 *yen*." Shindo, p. 73. For changes in the savings and loan policy of the Kaijima coal enterprise in Kyushu in the years between 1907 and 1924, see Ogino Yoshihiro, *"Taisen Zengo ni okeru Kaijima Tankō-gyō no Rōshi Kankei,"* particularly p. 95, concerning the *chokin seido* of the Kaijima Company.

Solidarity, divisions, bondage, and resistance 199

57 Sumiya, *Nihon Sekitan Sangyō Bunseki*, p. 165. There are minor abbreviations and errors in this quotation from the "*Kōzan Enkaku Shirabe*" that I have attempted to rectify in the translation.
58 See Schwieder, *Black Diamonds*, pp. 21–2, 97–100, 137, and Gardner and Flores, *Forgotten Frontier*, pp. 44, 103–5, for the company store in the United States, and the 1995 film, *Margaret's Museum*, concerning the role of the company store in a coal-mining community in Cape Breton, Canada. The latter is based on the writings of Sheldon Currie. Note the well-known miner's song:

> *Ya load 16 tons, and whaddya get?*
> *Another day older and deeper in debt!*
> *St. Peter, don't you call me, 'cause I can't go.*
> *I owe my soul to the Company Store!*

59 Morisaki, pp. 12–13.
60 Morisaki, p. 160.
61 Yamamoto, *Yama no Kurashi*, p. 43.
62 Morisaki, p. 126.
63 Oyama analyzes the relationship between a boss and his gang members in terms of their dependence on his ability to find work for them and the norm that dictated that he should provide subsistence for them in the (relatively rare) circumstances when work was not available. Although he notes that this dependence created bonds of loyalty, "cordiality," and a sense of mutual obligation between boss and [male] minion, he also emphasizes that this was not a case of workers selling their labor to an employer as a bargain between equals in an open labor market. *Kōgyō Rōdō to Oyakata Seido*, pp. 24–5.
64 Mashio, *Jizoko no Seishun*, p. 52.
65 See Sumiya, *Nihon Sekitan Sangyō Bunseki*, pp. 316–22.
66 Morisaki, p. 161.
67 The boss of the big dormitory, known originally as the *hamba* or eating place, took his name from it in regions other than Chikuho, becoming known as the *hamba-gashira*; attachment to a *hamba* in those regions signified membership in the gang. Kaneko, *Chikuhō Tankō Kotoba*, p. 169; Oyama, *Kōgyō Rōdō to Oyakata Seido*, pp. 32–3.
68 Mashio, pp. 130–1.
69 Kaneko defines *ketsuwari* as "fleeing without notice (*mudan de tōsō suru*)." *Chikuhō Tankō Kotoba*, p. 177. Sone translates the word more literally as "dividing the hips" and suggests sexual connotations for the act of "getting out from underneath" the bosses. "Coalmining Women in Japan," p. 207.
70 Idegawa, p. 58.
71 Idegawa, p. 35.
72 Cf. Idegawa, p. 149.
73 Turnover continued at high levels right into the 1960s, when even during the downsizing of the industry as a whole, the Labour Ministry reported 300,000 hirings during a nine-year period when 500,000 were laid off. John Price, "Postwar Industrial Relations and the Origins of Lean Production in Japan (1945–1973)," U.B.C. dissertation, 1993, pp. 392–3.
74 See Tsurumi, *Factory Girls*, passim. A revisionist view, which is econometrically persuasive but historically untenable, can be found in Gary Saxonhouse, "Country Girls and Communication among Competitors in the Japanese Cotton-Spinning Industry," in Hugh Patrick, ed., *Japanese Industrialization and its Social Consequences*, particularly pp. 120–3.
75 Idegawa, pp. 179–80.
76 Cf. *Miike Nijūnen*, p. 17).
77 Cf. Idegawa, p. 70.
78 Idegawa, p. 76.
79 Mashio, *Jizoko no Seishun*, p. 14.
80 Mashio, p. 21.

200 *Solidarity, divisions, bondage, and resistance*

81 Morisaki, p. 15.
82 Morisaki, pp. 63–4.
83 Idegawa, p. 205.
84 Idegawa, p. 77.
85 *Jizoko no Seishun*, p. 131. Concerning similar repression at *assei-yama* (repressive mines), see also Orii Seigo, *Hōjō Daihijō*, pp. 92–4.
86 Idegawa, pp. 94–5.
87 Morisaki, p. 41.
88 Morisaki, p. 63.
89 Morisaki, p. 45.
90 Mashio, p. 53–5.
91 Mashio, pp. 48–9.
92 Mashio, p. 52.
93 Cf. *Yama no Kurashi*, p. 61.
94 Morisaki, pp. 15–16.
95 Yamamoto, *Yama no Kurashi*, p. 67. *Chikuhō Tankō Emaki*, black and white illustration no. 104.
96 Morisaki, pp. 50–1.
97 *Yama no Kurashi*, pp. 66–7; Emaki, black and white illustration no. 107.
98 Morisaki, p. 115.
99 Morisaki, pp. 127–8.
100 Yamamoto, *Chikuhō Tankō Emaki*, black and white illustration no. 106. See Amnesty International annual reports.
101 Allinson, *Japanese Urbanism: Industry and Politics in Kariya, 1872–1972*, p. 49.
102 Under wartime conditions of surveillance and regimentation, it became virtually impossible for miners to escape, according to Yamamoto (*Yama ni Ikiru*, p. 115). He says that he witnessed two suicides of miners who blew themselves up in the 1940s.
103 Morisaki, p. 19.
104 Morisaki, pp. 39–40.
105 Idegawa, p. 156.
106 *Yama no Kurashi*, p. 56.
107 *Chikuhō Tankō Emaki*, black and white illustration no. 104.
108 *Factory Girls*, p. 165, citing Hazama Hiroshi, *Nihon Rōmu Kanri Shi Kenkyū*, (A History of Japanese Labour Relations), p. 274.
109 *Yama no Kurashi*, p. 45.
110 *Yama no Kurashi*, pp. 83–4.
111 Morisaki, p. 174.
112 Allen, *Undermining the Japanese Miracle*, passim.
113 Idegawa, p. 96.
114 Morisaki, p. 41.
115 Morisaki, p. 136. Mort Rasten, the director of the modern film, *Margaret's Museum*, seems to accept the evaluation of Sheldon Currie, the writer of the story from which it is taken, of the coal miners of Cape Breton as somewhat loose in morals, but he was also keen to insist, in a television interview at the time of the 1995 Vancouver International Film Festival, on the heroic characteristics of Margaret, who "refused to be a victim" of the coal-mining system.
116 Allen, *Undermining the Japanese Miracle*, p. 26.
117 Morisaki, pp. 136–7.
118 Japanese miners could hardly contemplate the kind of action of a hardy "trammer" who was said to have picked up the mine superintendent and threatened to drop him down the shaft if he complained again about an alleged lack of productivity in a British Columbia gold mine in the 1930s. Irene Howard, "Home Brew," *Highgrader Magazine*, vol. 5 no. 3, May/June, 1999, pp. 34–5.
119 *Yama ni Ikiru*, p. 41.

Solidarity, divisions, bondage, and resistance 201

120 Morisaki, p. 139.
121 Cf. Tsurumi, *Factory Girls*, pp. 52–6, 127–8, 131, 147.
122 Burton, "Peasant Struggle in Japan, 1590–1760," *The Journal of Peasant Studies*, vol. 5 no. 2 (Jan. 1978), pp. 157–9.
123 Morisaki, p. 19.
124 Yamamoto says that private collieries supplying the Japan Iron Works "retained some of the character of the period when they were run by the Government," and "as a result, the regulations were strict, and not only anyone who was absent from work without reporting for more than five days, but also anyone who broke such proscriptions as those against gambling, fighting, or adultery, would be summarily dismissed. It was possible to carry this (dismissal) out easily because they didn't lend setting-up money like private mines. Those who worked at (other) private mines, because they had loans from the Company or gang bosses, could not be let go for minor causes." *Yama ni Ikiru*, p. 40.
125 Tsurumi, *Factory Girls*, p. 152.
126 Matthew Allen discusses the role of the *rōmu* and how it evolved into control of unemployed miners in conjunction with *yakuza* gangs. *Undermining the Japanese Miracle*, pp. 106–184 (particularly 109–10), 148, 168–9, 182–4.
127 Morisaki, p. 139.
128 Idegawa, p. 136.
129 *Yama no kurashi*, p. 63.
130 Idegawa, p. 31.
131 Morisaki, p. 91.
132 Tsurumi, *Factory Girls*, p. 166.
133 Morisaki, p. 125.
134 Morisaki, p. 16.
135 In my article in *The Journal of Peasant Studies*, vol. 5 no. 2 (Jan. 1978), I have emphasized the solidarity that this power of ostracism promoted among the peasantry; there is reason to suppose that it created feelings of solidarity in miners' gangs while promoting rivalry among gangs from different mines and disaffection among aggrieved members of one gang.
136 Morisaki, p. 145.
137 Cf. Morisaki, pp. 115–6, 145–6.
138 Morisaki, pp. 71–2.
139 Morisaki, p. 97.
140 Idegawa, p. 135.
141 Morisaki, p. 145.
142 W. Donald Smith, in an article lent to me and entitled, "Korean Workers in Japan's Chikuhō Coal Field, 1917–1945," the basis for his article in *Korean Studies* (no. 20, 1996) and later incorporated into his PhD dissertation for Washington University as Chapter 4, "The Asō Strike: Obstacles to Labor Solidarity," discusses the failure of Japanese miners to join their Korean workmates in the strike of 1932.
143 Cf. Lewis, "The Coalfield Riots: Riots as Labor Dispute," in *Rioters and Citizens*, pp. 199–201.
144 Morisaki, pp. 146–7, 167.
145 *Yotsu* seems to have been a term used commonly to demean the *burakumin*, suggesting that they were like four-legged animals, but the narrator is obviously using it here merely to explain to whom she was referring.
146 Morisaki, p. 147.
147 See Shindo, *Chikuhō no Jokōfu-tachi*, pp. 34, 36–7.
148 In the Meiji period, coal miners along the Onga River were referred to by local people as *gezainin*, meaning ex-convict, outlaw, or vagrant, but essentially signifying an outcast or an exile from normal society. See Kaneko Useki, *Chikuhō Tankō Kotoba*, p. 177.
149 Idegawa, p. 30.

202 *Solidarity, divisions, bondage, and resistance*

150 Cf. Lewis, *Rioters and Citizens*, p. 45ff.
151 Morisaki, p. 116.
152 Shindo Toyo, *Chikuhō no Jokōfu-tachi*, p. 21.
153 Ogino *"Taisen Zengo ni okeru Kaijima Tankō-gyō no Rōshi Kankei,"* pp. 132–4. Michael Lewis has a detailed analysis of the "The Coalfield Riots," and their significance in labor struggles, in *Rioters and Citizens*, pp. 192–240.
154 See Sone, "Japanese Coal Mining: Women Discovered," and Smith, "Digging Through Layers …" in Lahiri-Dutt and Macintyre, pp. 69, 126. Smith's article about the 1932 Aso strike includes references to the role of Korean women in that strike. "The 1932 Asō Coal Strike: Korean-Japanese Solidarity and Conflict," in *Korean Studies*, no. 20 (1996).
155 Mathias, "Female Labour in the Japanese Coal-Mining Industry," in Janet Hunter, ed., *Japanese Women Working*, pp. 114–5.
156 "*Ōtsuji Tankō Jiken Kiroku* (Records of the Incident at Otsuji Mine)," in Ueno, *Kōfu*, pp. 249–65, 271–2.
157 Morisaki, pp. 17–18.
158 Ogino Yoshihiro tells of the creation of medical clinics at the big Kaijima Company mines as early as 1911, but further evidence of the company's desire to reduce medical costs during and after World War I suggests that concessions to the medical needs of their employees were not high on the list of management priorities. Ogino, "*Taisen Zengo ni okeru Kaijima Tankō-gyō no Rōshi Kankei,"* pp. 93, 115, 134. The way in which new welfare facilities were used as "carrots" to appease miners at the same time their dependence on the company was being intensified (and independent thinking being wiped out by threat of the "stick") is described in *Miike Nijūnen*, edited by Miike Tankō Rōdō Kumiai, the Miike union, on pp. 26–8. See also, Lewis, p. 199.
159 Morisaki, pp. 154–5.

7 Common seams, common attitudes

Sogena tokoro de hataraki yoru kōfu no kurashi cha,
doko mo onaji yō na mon.
  The lives of miners who work at such places
  [were] the same everywhere.[1]

When talking in general terms, the retired mining women spoke as if developments in coal mining affected men and women in similar ways, which might lead us to believe they had little consciousness of having a distinctive voice or even any desire to seek one. But neither is the case. One of Morisaki's interviewees was relatively taciturn in the presence of her husband but quite effusive when talking in his absence, leading Morisaki to decide not to plumb "the silent caverns" when her husband was there.[2] Apparently this woman liked to express herself in ways that her husband would not necessarily approve and was inhibited in his presence. Other women also clearly had their own voices, at least when comfortable expressing them. Although they often spoke with bitterness of the harshness of their mining experience, they also exhibited a "brightness" (*akarusa*) or optimism that their menfolk could not suppress.[3]

There were some differences in working methods and conditions at large mines operated by *zaibatsu* (national or regional) and smaller mines operated singly or in local groups of two or three. One woman recounted:

> Of course there are many different kinds of mines. There are [everything from] small ones where the load is carried up from the face to the pit mouth in yoked baskets [*sena*], to mines where electricity [incandescent light] shines brightly everywhere and there are fine underground offices [*sasabeya*] as in the centre of a city. ... But when you come to the coal face, they are all the same.[4]

Other women also spoke of the similarity of the mining experience. The "Slashed Auntie" ruminated on the unpredictability of life, but she was referring mainly to her unexpected turn of fortune when she left her role as daughter of a shrine carpenter for the less secure life of a miner's wife. Unfortunately,

204   *Common seams, common attitudes*

the life of most miners was all too predictable, with little chance to escape penury and hardship.

Although management and operating systems made some difference to their lives, the common work experiences of miners as well as their daily lives in the mining camps gave the women many attitudes in common. Those attitudes derived from their struggle for survival under conditions of harsh exploitation and oppressive poverty. One woman noted how their common experience did a great deal to bring the women together in spirit. "'We've all gone without. At least feed your children,' they would say, while lending or borrowing. And this was not the well-to-do who had something to spare doing the lending."[5] That their fate was shared helped the women get through their ordeals. "If there were ten of us, all ten had similar stories. I felt that I was not alone in suffering."[6] Their shared experiences of harsh toil and raising their families in poverty brought them together in spirit even if the competition underground sometimes divided them.

Lacking a "Nobler" cause

The women did not evince a great deal of pride in their collective contribution to any cause beyond a pragmatic devotion to the sustenance of their families and their own survival. There is little evidence of coal miners being exhorted by management to produce for the glory, or even the prosperity, of the Empire, in the way that textile factory management exhorted *jokō* to spin and reel "for the country."[7] It could be that appeals to patriotism were made but that the women found them so fatuous that they consigned them to insignificance. If few such appeals were made by management in the period before 1930, that was probably because the bosses could not expect a positive response from miners who were already being exploited to the limits of their endurance.[8] Only the "Two-Wagoner" makes reference to demands for greater production to serve the needs of the "Great Empire of Japan," and she relates them to the later period of mobilization before World War II and during the war itself.[9] Among miners' songs, there is a notable lack of mention of coal stoking the furnaces that cast the metal for the guns that would spread Japan's dominion over Asia and no reference to miners being "the Army of the Deep."[10]

If the women were not encouraged to think of themselves as making a valuable contribution to their country, neither were they given credit for making significant improvements to hauling methods in the underground shafts. They were proud of specific innovations that they had initiated in their work but did not see these improvements as affecting the production methods in the industry as a whole. Rather than giving miners praise and rewards, bosses and management treated them roughly and callously, seemingly as part of a campaign to keep them from having any sense of self-worth.

One reason why management did not encourage miners to have a sense of pride in their work was, of course, that they did not want them to seek rewards commensurate with mining's dangers and difficulties. If miners had little reason to be grateful to their country, having fallen to their low estate as the result of economic and other conditions either created or condoned by government, they could not easily be encouraged to devote themselves to patriotic service in uncomfortable, demanding, and risky conditions. Had they believed in the importance of their work, they might have demanded better remuneration and some amelioration of those conditions (as some of the men eventually did in the 1920s). Though the conditions of work and pay were better in the bigger mines than in the smaller ones and they did improve in times of prosperity for the industry as a whole, the basic parameters of work underground and life on the surface did not change before the 1930s. And such improvements as did occur were not sufficient to encourage either men or women to believe that their work was recognized as valuable and worthy.

> Exhausted or ill, even if you wanted to take one day off, they wouldn't allow it. The managers or dispatchers would come round from house to house with a big wooden sword in one hand, and "persuade" you to go to work. The dormitory bachelor miners, in particular, were just like slaves. They were [treated like] shit [*jinken mo kuso mo arimasen*].[11]

Spiritual strength, self-confidence, and survival

Although the women do not talk much about their contribution to the nation and the industry, they do evince a sense of pride in their accomplishments, despite the lack of encouragement from management. They also intimate of a self-esteem and inner fiber that helped them survive and endure their harsh circumstances. One woman who was known for her strength and versatility prided herself on her ability to get around without getting lost in the rabbit warrens of the mines.[12] Another woman, who had the blacksmith forge a hoe of her own design so that she could work more efficiently, said that her spiritual faith sustained her and allowed her to work effectively.[13] Another made a similar claim to strength and resourcefulness.

> I had this kind of a body, and when I was young, I had strength. And because I had a hard time of it and suffered, my spirit was strong. I wasn't afraid of anyone. ... If a foreman complained one whit, I was ready to say, "If you feel like hitting me, go ahead and try! I'm not the kind of a woman to be hit twice by someone like you!" and the fellow would back down.[14]

Because of their reliance on themselves for survival, several of the interviewees were skeptical about the efficacy of faith and religion. They saw little transcendent value in their own lives.

> I'm nearly ready to pass on into the other world. Looking at those who died in the mines, I came to believe that there were no gods or buddhas. ... Whether we died suddenly or led a long life, our lives were like the waste rock, worthless![15]

206 *Common seams, common attitudes*

But the dangers of the work, paradoxically, gave many of the women a keen sense of the existential value of life, including their own and their mate's. One woman's life was saved by luck and the diligence of her fellow miners, leading another to comment:

> When someone's life is saved, no matter what, it pleases you. Though someone might stand on the suicide rock at Hikojima one day and then the next, thinking that life had no meaning, when you go deep into the earth and work like this, suddenly life becomes valuable.[16]

Their fear of being widowed persuaded some women to be vigilant in protecting the very husbands whom they were eager to be rid of in less rational moments. One verse of a collier's song lamented:

> *Bereaved of my mate*
> *Surviving myself*
> *I moan under the burden*
> *Of the label of widow.*[17]

Yet mining widows were sometimes seen as desirable partners, if they were available for underground work and did not come burdened with many mouths to feed.[18]

Self-esteem and indignities

The women, then, did develop some pride in their accomplishments and palpable self-esteem, along with satisfaction in raising their children successfully. Though some stated that appearance was not a true measure of worth, young women born to mining also demonstrated concern for their appearance despite the dark and dirty atmosphere of the underground tunnels. The lack of natural light in those tunnels might contribute to a luminous pallidity of their skin, creating a "*kōnai bijin*" (underground beauty) that satisfied the traditional standard for a beautiful complexion among Japanese women of the samurai and merchant classes. Those women who had come from rural areas after years of working in the fields were likely to retain the sunburned, dark complexion that the Japanese elite stigmatized as peasant homeliness. Those who, in the Meiji period, combined work in the fields with off-seasonal mining work would also have been of dark complexion. But there were women among the interviewees who claimed to have been good looking when they were younger. The woman who had spent six miserable years as a teahouse prostitute recalled, with no shame and not a little pride, that after she came back to mining, "Since I didn't see the light of day, at least my complexion was pale (*shirokatta*). I was even called a *kōnai bijin*."[19] Another woman spoke approvingly of her sister's youthful beauty. "My sister was said to be a *kōnai bijin*. Since coal dust hurt the skin, she went down after powdering herself white with neck powder. It was very dark, and she did look beautiful."[20] Young women were self-conscious about appearances, and novices were often dismayed when seeing older miners at work, given their grimy and wizened features.[21]

As we have seen, the women wore scanty work clothing, and as a result, they were conscious of being the occasional objects of humor, scorn, and prurient interest. Baring breasts at work was not uncommon for older farming women, but young Japanese women were conscious of *chichi* as organs of erotic interest to men, and young women working underground did their best to avoid unwanted attention. The high temperatures in most coal mines, however, persuaded even younger women to follow the custom of their older sisters and strip down to the minimal working skirt, the *mabu-beko*. But they did not feel comfortable in skirts that often revealed more of their private parts than they wished. Some young women apparently took delight in countering the lewd remarks of the men with similarly ribald and vulgar rejoinders, but it can be assumed that most were, like Maki as a young girl, intent on avoiding attention and embarrassment.

When the young women went to the "backs," water tubs or pools, they would "sometimes bump into a man," Mashio wrote. Maki, recalling a time when she had become more inured to the mining milieu, said:

> You would be showing everything. Well, since [everyone] could see it all anytime, [we] didn't care. … Mind you, the men wouldn't touch or fondle our breasts there. They'd only give you a little poke with a finger sometimes. And even then, a girl would tell him off with gusto. … The man would say, "Oh! I didn't mean anything," and keep his hands to himself.[22]

Most of the women seem to have become used to the indignities of underground work in middle age and less concerned with avoiding humiliation. When older, these women might lose what little sensitivity they had had to the judgments of others. Morisaki saw one of the retired women whom she had interviewed earlier in the day urinating on the railway tracks as she went along collecting bits of discarded wood.[23] Although this may have been a simple case of incontinence, it is not difficult to see that an absence of dignity and self-respect could result from the life of female miners.

It is possible that the lack of toilet facilities in the mines had inured women to self-consciousness about bodily functions. But Maki's reminiscences suggest otherwise.

> Thinking about it now, for the *atoyama*, the most difficult thing wasn't the work. It was the lack of toilets in the mines. To do it, we would go into the shafts of old workings where there was no more coal. All the time holding our breath lest someone else should come. So we couldn't take our time about it. Turning down the light of our lamps. If Mitsuru [her boyfriend] had seen me there, I'd rather have died![24]

208 *Common seams, common attitudes*

Such indignities might be thought to have dulled the spirits of the mining women and replaced self-confidence with self-effacement or even self-deprecation, but there is ample evidence that this was not the case.

The women offer recollections that counter any image of beaten-down, defeated humanity. In particular, most of the women expressed some pride in their ability to do any job in the coal mines, no matter how demanding. Maki stated:

> Whether it was [working] as *atoyama* or putting in supports, or after the War, hauling up the slopes at a badger mine, there was no task which I didn't do.[25]

In order to eat, there was no other way. Nonetheless, they were proud of how hard they worked.[26]

Reactions to bondage

Japanese women, of course, did not have freedom of choice as to where they would work or live.[27] Wives had obligations to their husbands, and the daughters of coal miners were often treated as chattels by their fathers as well as by mining companies. Many, if not most, girls were put out to child-minding when their fathers felt they were old enough to make a contribution to the family income, usually at the age of 12 or 13. If they were sent to a better-off family in a nearby rural village or town, the father would collect *maegashi-kin*, a loan against their wages accompanied by a contract that turned the youth into an indentured servant. Child-minding might become a small part of onerous household tasks that left these girls no time for personal development or innocent recreation. Contracts were usually for one or two years, imposed on the father and the guarantor for the loan, and were unbreakable by the girl herself except with the direst of penalties. The labor of these young *komori* was used to pay down the loans to their fathers, bringing little benefit to the girls themselves. And the position of debtor was often extended beyond the initial contract period as the result of appeals to the employer for further aid.[28] Many miners' daughters, therefore, began their working lives under a system of financial obligation imposed on their families.

After stints as child-minders or maids to better-off farming families, many young single women became part of the family mining team, and at the smaller mines, the family income was collected and spent by the father. He would pay bills at the company store and cover whatever other household expenses he could while keeping aside money for his own pleasures or addictions. In her later teens, Maki was indentured to a mining gang boss for a loan to her father to pay his fish-poaching fine. This kind of bondage continued during her "prime of life underground." Later, like many other daughters working for their families, she was obliged to marry a man chosen by her father because of his connections in the "*kōsai kōfu*" (affiliate miner) system.[29]

Common seams, common attitudes 209

Young women sold into the sex trades by their fathers suffered servitude no less onerous than Maki's. The retired miner whom Idegawa calls "The Transient" says of the transaction that plummeted her into prostitution: "Fathers sell their daughters, and husbands, their wives and daughters-in-law (*yomejo*). A thing that one heard about often was now happening to me."[30] Yet she did not think of it at the time as being sold by her father because she had come to her own conclusion that she should "go into service" (*hōkō ni deru*) to help her parents get away from a miserable life at the coal mines. Although such arrangements were not thought of at the time as the marketing of human bodies, by the time of her recollections they were understood for what they were. Although not wanting to cause her parents embarrassment while they were alive, she admitted now that she had gone into prostitution of her own accord, wanting to assist them financially.

> It was not as if I had done something wrong, and I am resigned to the fact that rather than make someone else suffer, suffering oneself allows one to sleep better. I feel it's nothing to be ashamed of.

One senses that she is chagrined at the recollections of her miserable life as a virtual sex slave in a brothel in Hikojima but not about the fact that she went into it by choice. She did not foresee that the alternative could be as bad as coal mining.

> Thinking of the lifeless face of my younger brother who had been burnt [to death in the mine], I resolved that, "If one can die that way, three years of service can't be all that bad," and I told my parents: "Make use of me to borrow as much as you can. I'll do my best."[31]

Though she says that she was the only girl from the coalfields among 18 prostitutes at the "teahouse" where she worked, there were many coal miners who either felt that their daughters might be safer in a brothel than in the coal mines or who succumbed to the inducements of substantial "loans" against their daughters' services in the sex trade. The Transient's account of her absence from her true love and her experiences during six (not three) years in the brothel lead one to believe that no amount of money could properly compensate for her father's decision.[32] And although their fathers' main consideration was usually the need for the loans, one can imagine how the mothers of girls sold into prostitution must have felt about using their daughters as collateral.

The limits of endurance

Most of the women seem to have accepted long hours and poor working conditions as inevitable (*atari-mae*). At most mines, they could not rest or recover from illness or injury by taking days off. Maki remembers how she was penalized by the piece-rate system and scolded by her father for not making enough money:

210 *Common seams, common attitudes*

> [He] would say, if my wages were even a little less [than usual], that I'd been loafing [*asonde*] underground. But human beings can't work for 365 days at the same pace. There were times when you'd give up on a wagon you'd secured with your coal tally and come out of the mine. You'd been given the wagon on the understanding that you'd fill it. But even though it was awful to give up a wagon, it was no good mourning over it.[33]

With mining providing jobs at a time when attractive alternatives were lacking, the women deplored the kind of work they were compelled to do and thanked their lucky stars that it was available.

> It was hard! hard! and there were times when I was near collapse, but if I think about it now, thanks to the mines, I could survive. Because at least there was a place where I could work.[34]

Mining songs, reflecting the hard lives of miners and their desire for recognition, emphasized that miners were human beings making a contribution to society with needs not so different from those of other people. Some verses stressed the risks and tribulations of the lives of female miners, and their hope in vain for release from them.

> Don't take me
> down as an *atoyama;*
> Surely you wouldn't sacrifice
> my freedom for the wagons.[35]

The women thought their role was unique and their lives quite different from those of women in other occupations. Thus, they did not expect their interviewers to fully grasp their predicament. One woman summed up one session of exchanges with Morisaki in these words:

> So the coal mines are terrible places. Just from what I've told you, you wouldn't understand. Well, somehow you may have got some inkling. But don't hesitate to come to talk to me again. Because there are things I might remember.[36]

She did remember other things to back up her statement that the mines were terrible places and, in her next interview, gave evidence that suggests the horror of working within earshot of dynamite blasts; with constant threats of flooding, roof falls, and abusive supervisors; and wearing inadequate protection against the moisture, heat, and soot.[37]

Gender differences and inequities

Regine Mathias has identified a deterioration in the situation of workers in the coal mines with the "rationalization" that followed World War I. This deterioration, she points out, affected women more than men.[38] Inequities already significant in the burdens and rewards of work underground thus became worse as "modernization" proceeded.

Despite these inequities, the retired women emphasized that they made a greater contribution to the welfare of their families and the mining community than did the men as the result of greater devotion to their work.[39] Though it is impossible to prove that the women worked harder than the men, their recollections give considerable evidence that they did. (And they did work longer hours.) There is little evidence, on the other hand, that the men appreciated their contribution. And, in fact, most of the women's testimony to Idegawa suggests that they did not.

As noted earlier, remuneration for women was never as high as for men in the Japanese collieries, though some women claimed that they *earned* as much (i.e., worked as hard). Sumiya's data for wages in several Nagasaki Prefecture mines in the 1880s show that wages for women varied between 60 and 70 per cent of those for men.[40] Sumiya also finds that for men who did hauling work, the pay in this period was virtually the same as for hewers.[41] In other words, discrimination in pay was based on gender. Yasukawa Junosuke, with what may be false precision, found that for female underground workers, wages were 64.4 per cent of those for men in 1926.[42] But according to Morisaki, women's wages were only 50 per cent of men's about the time of the attempted exclusion of women from the coal mines in 1928.[43] In road construction work during the Depression (circa 1929), one woman reported that the carrying of infill material—no doubt done mainly by women—earned 75 *sen* per day, while the men doing the cutting and filling earned about two-thirds more.[44] Most of the evidence points to the conclusion that women's wages had *dropped* relative to men's with the advance of the capitalist economy.

But there were variations, and some women proudly proclaimed that their incomes were higher than those of other women.

> Whether underground or on the surface, I was the best earner among the women. If it was tamping the dynamite into the holes, where others got 60 *sen*, I got 72 *sen*. Or I would dig the red clay for packing [dynamite sticks] with a mattock. Even at the same jobs, I would choose the hardest work with the best pay. The faces in the down-drifts were called Peninsula Faces, and [usually] only Koreans worked them, but I always went for the down-drift.[45]

The Amazon claimed that she put out twice as many wagons as other women, and hence, she should have earned much more than most. But she also complained that she did not receive her fair share of the wages. Moreover, "though my share was more, my husband, unfairly, spent it liberally as if it was his own," she moaned.[46] Even in relatively good times, the women usually had to be satisfied with whatever money was left over in the pay packet after the men had paid part of their debts. Another woman reported:

212   *Common seams, common attitudes*

> Even that money [my share], before it came into my hands, was collected by my husband. That happened many times. Eventually the foreman [*rōmu*], feeling some sympathy for me, caught my husband going to borrow money [against my wages] and gave him a good hiding.[47]

This woman "lucked out" when she got into a different kind of employment in the 1930s:

> The best thing was that my husband couldn't collect the money. For me to receive all the money that I earned … that really impressed me! When we were at the mines, since we'd borrow enough to balance the budget, on real paydays we saw little money and we'd have to borrow the difference [between expenses and pay] again. So we did it over and over. And the old man would sometimes make off with it like a hyena.[48]

Only rarely were mine wages paid separately to a man and his mate. And such cases were likely to have occurred after the turn of the century at the larger mines, where the wages were no longer "divvied up" by gang bosses but paid directly to workers.[49]

Changing rewards

By 1930, extensive mechanization had begun, and the women who managed to retain their jobs underground were making more money than before. But they were not enjoying significantly improved conditions of work. Moreover, in cases where they worked independently of their husbands, they had only modest discretionary funds. One recounted:

> I shared half of the money for the coal with the *sakiyama*. This was money for house-keeping. I also took out stone and put in timbers. I put aside the money for timbering as a nest-egg.[50]

It could not have been much consolation to the women that they could save money because they were not required to pay for a miner's uniform[51] as the men were often required to do at the larger mines.

At this time, there was still a smaller wage differential between male and female underground workers in coal mining than for workers in other industries such as textile mills. "The fact that underground work was heavy labor and was carried out by men and women working in teams, was probably one reason for the relatively high female wage and the relatively small gender-related wage differential," Mathias says. Coincidentally, she argues that colliery management kept male wages low by relating them to the low wages of female labor.[52] It would seem that factors such as the relative inelasticity of the labor market in the coal industry and the partial isolation of that market from the wider labor market outside north Kyushu kept both male and female wages low. But in underground work, female labor was paid comparatively well relative to male labor, if not well in relation to the cost of living.

Mathias also claims that "the labour movement in the coal-mining district of Chikuho (after 1918) demanded in its programme equal pay for equal work, but as female labour was hired because it was cheap there was little chance of realizing such claims."[53] Unfortunately, she gives us no evidence of such a demand, though the women's claims regarding the value of their labor would certainly have supported more adequate compensation.

Far from improving, the conditions of work for women seem to have deteriorated up to 1930, causing the government to initiate rudimentary schemes for the "protection" of female workers. One result was the legislated exclusion of women from underground work, which was implemented reluctantly and inconsistently by the larger companies and ignored by the smaller ones.

"Work-Sharing" and the division of labor

In spite of discrepancies in the rewards for their labor, most women spoke of the work being shared equally with the men. One woman remembered a rather loose work routine, at least for the men.

> The work was half and half [*gobun-gobun*]. But the *sakiyama* would dig enough and leave it for the next morning. Then whether the wagon came or not, when he'd done enough, he'd go out just like that.[54]

Leaving the coal for the next day seems to have been possible in the exceptional circumstances where the *atoyama* was not expected to get out all the coal that had been dug before she went out or where an amount over and above that needed to fill the available wagons was left. But such leftover coal could be subject to pilfering by others, and the practice could not have been common.

Couples who practiced real teamwork underground were uncommon, and marital friction would seem to have been the norm. Although one woman says that it was usual for a mother to go down later in the morning than her husband, after she had prepared the children for school or day care, several others indicated that they were expected to take as little time as possible for chores before the "real work." Another woman recalled that her husband would show concern only when she was stretched to the limit.

> Only when I slouched down, thinking that I could go no further, did he say, "Take it easy for a bit!" And he gave me a big summer orange.[55]

Even such a small gesture of solicitude on the part of the male partner would seem to have been unusual. And cooperation was more often the result of necessity than empathy where survival was "the name of the game."

It was common for the women to work extra hours in order to load enough wagons to generate an income that would sustain their families, no matter how

214 *Common seams, common attitudes*

few hours their mates worked to hew an amount of coal that they considered sufficient.[56] The Japanese Cricket told how her husband would make sure she stayed behind to load if he went out early.

> When there was lots of coal and I'd opted for two wagons, he'd sound me out: "Are you going to stay in and load them?" You could see that all he wanted was to go out early. "I'll go on ahead and get supper ready."[57]

Her husband, it will be remembered, was an inveterate idler, not one likely to help with the housework.

Work was "geared to the *sakiyama*," Mashio notes.[58] The importance of the *sakiyama* was symbolized by the fact that the *atoyama* not only took down enough drinking water for both herself and the *sakiyama* but often carried his lunch box and spare points for his mattock as well as other tools. Though the work of the hauliers might be more demanding than that of the hewers, the *atoyama*'s work was usually considered less important—as suggested by the fact that Korean males were often assigned to it.[59]

The movement in the 1920s away from a perceived equity in the treatment of women was accompanied by an attempt on the part of the men to assert their importance and authority in the work of hewing and to downgrade the value of the hauling. Although several of the women said that men were the boss in the mines, others tended to challenge the validity of the men's claims to prestige and esteem. Almost invariably, the husbands of the latter women were idlers (*sukabura*) and gamblers who dissipated the family income and left the wives to sustain the children and maintain the household. Several women expressed admiration for their husbands' mining skills but contempt for their indulgence and profligacy outside of work. One woman admired her father's leadership as a gang boss but complained that he was in constant trouble with the police over gambling and was an "inveterate brawler."[60] The women particularly castigated the men's tendency to shirk a full day's work underground, and were eager to affirm that their own contribution to the work was important and valuable.[61]

The women's capabilities

The claim of some mining women that they were as strong as the men and could do everything that the men did was one that the men could not always refute. One woman asserted:

> Although we were only young women, we could all do the work of carrying the *sena* on our own, and were physically strong. In mining work, we could do everything as if there was no difference between men and women. So we young women were aware of our abilities. We would tackle anything with confidence, welcoming challenges. … We made mistakes, but our attitude was, "I won't be beaten!"[62]

The Amazon claimed to actually be stronger than her husband. He was unable to push two empty wagons in tandem, whereas, to his chagrin, she regularly pushed two.[63] According to the Cricket, men did not have the patience or tenacity to carry the *tebo* in low shafts where "you just had room to crawl on your knees."[64] The women often claimed to have done everything that the men did, including lifting iron framing beams into place while standing on wagons in the tracked tunnels at larger mines.[65] The Goddess of the *Sena* was not atypical in claiming superior skill and talent to that of her husband. And, "I could do everything without losing out to a man," Strong-as-an-Ox recalled.[66]

One can imagine how galling it would be for a *sakiyama* to have a woman work with him if he could not hew enough coal to match her hauling capabilities. The Amazon bragged:

> I was faster than an incompetent *sakiyama*. He would get behind with the digging. Borrowing a mattock, I would help him dig.[67]

She also pushed and restrained heavily loaded *sura* on the slopes, worked and moved efficiently in the narrow tunnels, and carried loads on the surface that men would not carry. "In female *sumo*, I would have been a *yokozuna*!"[68] Though few female miners would have claimed the rank of grand champion at mining, many thought as she did: "There were any number of mines where I could work."[69] Shindo Toyo finds the essence of the women's confidence in their survival in the coal mines as successful competitors with the men.[70]

Standing up to the men

The differences in the physiological burdens on coal-mining men and women were highlighted by the Two-Wagoner, who complained that men did not understand the needs of women.

> Women have their burdens [*gō*]. We do our work no differently than men, but although you [sometimes] forget that you are a woman, in the darkness your breasts swell, or the monthly troubles come. [Pause] Men don't understand, but our body plays tricks on us. Women resent it.[71]

One could argue, of course, that because men did not have to endure such physiological burdens, they should have been able to work more consistently than the women.

Although aware of physiological differences, coal-mining women occasionally expressed a belief in equality between the sexes.

> It's right for women to stand up to men. What's reasonable is the same for both, and they both have the same hole in their arse. So men and women must be the same. And women should speak straight out [like men].[72]

216 *Common seams, common attitudes*

This retired miner's belief in equality was reinforced by the postwar democratic ethos, but her life story suggests that some mining women had a strong sense of their rights long before the Asia-Pacific War.

There are many accounts by retired female miners of women standing up to men, above and below ground. Maki decided that because her father-in-law had abused his position in the household by attempting to molest her, she would smoke in the house, regardless of the correct behavior for daughters-in-law.[73] The story of the "Ball-Crusher" is told with some relish by one of Morisaki's interviewees:

> She could lift big rocks and other things that men couldn't lift, higher than eye level. The sweat would cover her body and drip from her thighs. It was marvelous. … And even a young man would be amazed at the sweat dripping *poto poto* under her short miner's skirt. No sooner had she yelled, "What the Hell are you looking at?!" than she'd put down the rock and grab the young fellow's balls with all her might. Not being able to catch his breath, the fellow would crawl out of the mine and fall down with a thud. Then everyone would make a comic story out of it in the bath-house. They'd say not to tangle with that ball-crushing woman![74]

Many of the women took delight in the prodigious strength of such a female miner and laughed at the discomfort of a weaker male.

But only a few female miners were in a position to assert themselves physically at the expense of their male coworkers. According to Strong-as-an-Ox, women had "no rights" at the mines,[75] and female miners often used the Japanese saying, "Women have no homes in their three lives" (*Onna san kai ni ie nashi*). The saying meant that as daughters, wives, and mothers, women could not call their homes their own. Nevertheless, many hassled, pilloried, and manipulated their husbands for some customary rights to which they felt entitled. In a few cases, they may have enjoyed a modicum of prestige as the result of recognition of their substantial contribution to the family welfare, though this contribution was more often downplayed than recognized and rewarded. And their work left them little energy to assert rights that were not sanctioned by custom.

There was, of course, discrimination based on appropriate roles for men and women in the mines. This was most clearly illustrated when, in a conspicuous exception, a woman was recognized as being capable of doing a man's work. In such a case, her competence was likely to be acknowledged not with quiet respect but with ribald humor. The ability of the Amazon to put heavy wagons back on the track after derailing was recognized by her overseer:

> You seem to have been born without a dangler! Take your husband's and let it dangle![76]

Most often, mining women accepted their well-defined roles. But the retired women showed an appreciation of the heavier burdens on women. Maki asserted:

Atoyama, sakiyama—there was no difference in their work underground. [Above ground] we gave birth to children and reared them. We prepared their food. We patched their clothes with the needle. There was hardly any time for the woman to sleep. When the man came out of the pit, the damn fool took on airs and did nothing but drink *saké*, gamble, and play with women.[77]

Another woman recounted:

It was not a world in which you could go to the shop and find everything, and prepare food or do the washing while watching television. You had to sew clothes for the kids. You had to make the fire for cooking and carry the water for the washing. And on top of this, if you didn't go down the pit to work, you couldn't eat. Coal-mining women did two or even three people's work.[78]

And they had to do all this without much help from their husbands, while nonetheless trying to satisfy their mates' sexual needs. Yet, as one woman noted, "To treat women and children well was shameful in a man."[79]

Superstition and credulity

Even in the matter of which gods to worship, custom gave the women very little choice. They had a limited proprietorial interest in the Goddess of the Mines.

The God of the Mines was female, but she didn't get her hair dirty. It was said that if a woman combed her hair underground, she'd burn with jealousy, and would remove her supporting hand from the roof, so that it'd come down. Perhaps it was a superstition, but though some would put make-up on their necks, no one would dare to comb their hair.[80]

Another woman remembered reverently thanking the goddess for saving her husband and others when the ventilation pump broke down.[81] But others showed little interest, let alone any credulity, in such deities.[82] One noted that her husband used superstitious beliefs as a means of getting out of work.

When he was about to go to work, if a dog barked he'd pray at the household altar, and if the sound of his hands clapping was off, or the children wailed, he'd blame that or anything else [and not go to work]. Since he was always finding excuses like that, things to blame were bound to run out. When I stared at him and asked what he was going to say today, he couldn't think of anything to blame, and was so mad that he took the day off anyway. It was ridiculous![83]

Such observations led this woman and others to see the banality of many superstitions and to question the way in which men tried to use them. The skepticism of

218 *Common seams, common attitudes*

these women about the superiority of men (*their* men, at least), though perhaps tinged with postwar philosophical iconoclasm, suggests a latent ability to see through the paternalism and superstition that permeated prewar thinking as well as the ideals superimposed on Japanese society by males.

Accepting their lot

As we have seen, some women liked mining in spite of its hardships. One woman pointed out:

> In the mines, at rest time, people who liked each other would come together and, putting out our *okazu* in the middle, we'd enjoy eating. While working away, we would sing. The best times were when we were working. ... Not everyone understands the pleasures of working underground.[84]

But most found that the work and the competition underground made life difficult. Given the intense competition for wagons and right-of-way on the haulageway tracks, it was "just like in a war," one said, where "the tendency was for the first off the mark to triumph."[85] Kawajima Taka recalled:

> We all suffered when we worked in the coal mines. And it wasn't just minor suffering. I can laugh while talking about it now, but I can't forget the pain I felt at the time.[86]

It is amazing that most women could maintain an aura of cheerfulness in these circumstances. But few had the sense of satisfaction that accompanies true happiness. Although the women could joke about sexual encounters and enjoy the banter, affairs could lead to conception and pregnancy and thus even more unwanted burdens.[87]

If the women worked as hard as they could but still could not make enough to live comfortably, they felt that was "the way of the world." At the time of the Rice Riots in 1918, Maki's family was often so short of food that her mother had to collect wild grasses to supplement a meager meal of beans without salt (which they could not afford). Living in the north-east, Maki could not remember "a single time when she ate a meal of pure rice." Yamamoto Sakubei says that at a time when other men needed 2,580 calories a day for normal sustenance, miners working underground needed about 3,000.[88] The women's calorific needs could not have been less; indeed, they were probably more. But often their calorific intake must have been below even minimum requirements.

Another result of living near the margin was that most male miners would not even try to save money. According to one woman, "river-dwellers," miners, and boat people who lived and worked on or near the Onga River "did not use money kept overnight."[89] (The common Japanese characterization of poverty, *yoigoshi no zeni wa nai*, meant that today's income could not last until tomorrow.) Yamamoto Sakubei remembers that at some times, even in a family not burdened by a heavy drinker, there might not be enough money for food. "If there wasn't enough money for tomorrow's rice, it was no use lamenting. Since I worked as hard as I could, if that didn't give me enough for rice, it wasn't my fault, but someone else's, I thought."[90] By the 1920s, some male miners were organizing against those responsible for their inadequate incomes and bad working conditions, the operators of the mines. But among many there still persisted a belief that fate had condemned miners to a miserable life.

> It was a life of poverty. A friend from my time at Kami-mio Mine said, "Poverty doesn't disappear. One always carries on the poverty of one's parents," and in that I have been most filial. I have faithfully maintained the tradition of poverty.[91]

The women thought that, with poverty and danger their constant companions, they had no choice but to carry on in the face of adversity. Most assumed that if incomes and conditions were not what they should be, there was no alternative but to work harder and endure, even if borrowing more money was the immediate expedient. The shortage of jobs outside of coal mining in the Chikuho region gave them little alternative but to accept their fate. Jobs on public works, which were sporadic and migratory, did not favor workers encumbered by families and required flexibility in routines. At least mining companies housed their workers, however inadequately. In exchange for this small measure of stability, the women often accepted the limitations of their "*kagirareta sekai*" (constricted world) and avoided comparing their lives to those of people in other sectors of society. The miners' poverty was not the result of an unwillingness to try to better themselves or of passive acceptance of an avoidable fate. The circumstances of their lives tended to oblige them to endure penury and "make the best" of their position at the bottom of the social scale rather than to seek an upward mobility that was not open to them. There was, of course, a heavy psychological price to pay for their unfortunate situation.[92]

Fear

Part of that psychological price was the trauma that the women felt when reentering the mine after terrible accidents. Even if disasters did not affect their own families directly, the women's constant fear that such things could happen to them was stressful and debilitating. Although a few survivors took the only course they knew of to escape life in the mines and chose to emigrate, most felt they had no recourse but to return to the pits after dreadful accidents. Mashio tells of the fear that coal miners felt particularly acutely after disasters but which they also experienced to some degree throughout their working lives.

> Maki San escaped the disaster of fire in the vertical shaft. But it was not a unique event. At the pit mouth [she would ask herself], "Ah! Will I be able to come up to the surface safely today?" and she would stop to look at the sky.

220 *Common seams, common attitudes*

> [Maki said] "Even if such things happened, one had to eat. Since underground [work] earned the most money, there was nought for it but to go in. In the coal mines, if you were seized with fear, that would be the end of it; you couldn't work."[93]

Though the surviving women generally endured long working lives underground, many more quit at younger ages as the result of accidents, illness, or sheer exhaustion. One of Morisaki's interviewees speaks of a 50-year-old male being too old for mining.[94] On the other hand, there were many older women and men who were obliged to "go down the pit" in recurring situations of labor shortage. Mashio writes that there were any number of men over 50 working in the Joban mines in the interwar period (1919–1937),[95] when the average life expectancy for Japanese workers was not much over 50 years and no company or national pensions were available.

In accepting their fate, some of the women came to believe that severe tests made them better able to carry their burdens. One woman said that the trials and tribulations of mining life tended to make women stronger.[96] Others recalled that their determination to persevere was keen. Just as cold showers in winter for English private school boys were presumed to "build character," the heat of the deeper mines was felt to have tested the women's character. Most were not found to be wanting. Rupture tests used in modern mechanical engineering laboratories, where loads are increased until the test sample breaks, are not the kind of tests to which human beings should be subjected. But these women were put through similarly severe tests. Although we only have a couple of examples of the burdens of coal mining life severely bending or warping the spirits of the women, their burdens were indeed great and their endurance admirable, if not miraculous.[97]

No place to call "Home"

Many of the women had come to the coalfields hoping that their families could earn enough money to accumulate savings sufficient to allow them to return to their "native villages" (*kokyō*), where they could somehow reestablish themselves as farmers in the life that had sustained their families for generations. They had ventured into the unknown territory of the coalfields much as *dekasegi* workers had left their homes for other occupations in other regions of Japan,[98] expecting to return after their ordeals. But, with some dismay, most migrants found that, far from building up nest eggs for the future, their families were hard-pressed to sustain even a minimal standard of living and frequently went further into debt to their gang bosses, thereby becoming virtually enslaved. As they lost hope of ever returning to their rural homes, they became resigned to the fact that they had no chance of reverting to farming and had instead become miners—not a temporary job choice but an involuntary commitment to hazardous and physically taxing work.

Separated from their mainly rural, agrarian homes, many Japanese miners, particularly female hauliers, felt nostalgia for their more genuine homes of the

Common seams, common attitudes 221

past rather than the hastily built mine camps.[99] One male miner, Hanada Katsuki, composed a somewhat prosaic but trenchant poem concerning the ambivalence that many miners of either gender must have felt about their new "homes."[100] Kawajima Taka, a major contributor to Idegawa Yasuko's book, expressed a yearning to return to her Miyazaki home in much the same words as the poem.[101]

However, there are few elegiac recollections of childhood on the farm or romantic expressions of nostalgia for rural homes among the reminiscences of the retired female miners, though their use of onomatopoeia and vivid description suggests no lack of poetic capabilities. But Idegawa was sensitive to the loss expressed by Taka San, even while admitting to a presumption that, having shared her working life with people who were still her friends at the mine, Taka must somehow feel that this was her "real home." Taka herself stated, "When all's said and done, this (the housing at the abandoned mine) is the right place for me. I want to die here." Yet she also acknowledged, "Even now, I am still overcome with regret that I could not (go back to my real home)." Other female miners hint at a sense of deprivation at being prevented from being buried at their birthplaces. If they had lost their family home in the villages, they could not usually be buried there. Taka San, however, had surreptitiously arranged for a burial plot in her Miyazaki village. The removal of her remains to the distant village surprised Idegawa, who wondered how Taka's attachment to the Chikuho region, symbolized by the long-term registration of her residence in the mining village, could be broken with such apparent ease.[102]

Some women admitted that their ties to their home villages had been cut. On the other hand, their ties to the mining camps could be tenuous, even after some time there.[103] There was very little to engender comfort and content in the coal-mining camps, and the feelings of familiarity associated with the concept of "home," which are common in mining towns in other countries,[104] seem to have been absent in most of the colliery dormitories and row houses of Chikuho.

Women invariably left for the mines accompanying their parents or mates, usually as the result of a loss of their family's ability to sustain themselves on the farm. It was the push of poverty combined with the pull of supposedly better jobs that drove people to the mines and kept them there. One woman recalled that poverty made her an easily exploitable worker.

> My name soon became known as [that of] a woman *sakiyama*, and any number of employers wanted me. If one thinks about it, it was nothing to boast about. That's how poor I was. I had to work harder than the best of them. … If they weren't poor, what woman would work to get herself filthy at the bottom of a coal mine?![105]

Bankrupt tenant farmers sought work in the coal mines. There they often worked with criminals and those evading justice, many of whom had earlier been part of a pool of surplus or marginal labor in the agricultural sector.[106] Wives went with husbands and daughters with parents because they would not be hired separately at the mines. Daughters would rarely be sent to such rough places alone, unless it was to marry a miner whose prospects were thought (often mistakenly) to be promising. Their parents were often ignorant of actual conditions at the mines in the way that many parents who sent their daughters into the care of the supposedly kind *mamas* in "teahouses" or brothels in the cities and towns were ignorant of actual conditions in those places.

With no real option to return to their rural life, many miners must have felt rootless in a society that highly valued a sense of place and belonging. Their rootlessness could not have been compensated by feelings of security in their indentured state. Even the assurance of continuous work in good times often turned sour.

> When the mines flourished, no matter where you went, you could easily get work. The men would be full of confidence. But just see what happens when the mines fail! However much [the blade] glitters, even the framer's axe will be useless.[107]

The coal-mining economy echoed the cyclical economy of the nation, and miners thought that because people died of all sorts of causes, one might as well die earning good money when one could. Although the women remembered some facets of their exploitation clearly, they expressed little interest in analyzing the exploitative system itself. Sometimes they recalled the "good times" when work seemed readily available.[108] But, in more difficult times, when they absconded with the hope of improving their lot, the working conditions at new mines rarely met their expectations and often were as bad as those they had fled.[109]

The mining women of the Chikuho region were tied to their husbands as well as to their jobs. Married women obtained their jobs by virtue of their husband's employment with a gang. If a woman's husband was killed or died of an illness, the company felt little or no obligation to the widow.[110] Then the gang boss could only make use of her by marrying her off to another miner. Being widowed did not free a woman to go looking for either a job or a husband. Not only was it difficult to remove herself (or to be removed) with her children and possessions from her accommodation but she had little prospect of being hired as an individual at another mine. A widow's lack of job prospects elsewhere was symptomatic of the companies' desire and ability to prevent an open labor market.

Taka San's yearning for her rural home was interpreted as a yearning for "freedom" by Idegawa.[111] This concept of freedom implied a rejection of the miserable working and living conditions at the mines, the antithesis of real freedom. Many coal-mining women may have been persuaded at some stage in their working lives to accept the fact that it was unlikely that they would find a better way of life before their retirement. Others saw their hopes for freedom slowly dwindle as they became inured to the terms of their indentures and as the number of their dependent children and their unending debts increased.[112] Idegawa captured their predicament:

The pitifulness of their writhing in an attempt to survive, their expressions of defiance, the desperation with which they expended their energy; these female miners truly lived their lives like the proverbial loach in the cooking pot.[113]

Sexual abuse

Coal-mining women were not only victims of the exploitative production system but were subject to sexual exploitation by overseers and male co-workers. This exploitation could take the form of everything from mild harassment and demeaning attention to seduction and violent assault. Some of the women seem to have considered the attempts at seduction just one of the facts of life. Although I have seen no reports of rape by overseers, it undoubtedly was occasionally perpetrated by them against young unmarried women who could be separated from their families.

The women were not always passive victims of unwanted male attention. Although they did not deliberately provoke such attention, when offered favors, some women took advantage of them. The Slashed Auntie received favors from the wagon distributor without, apparently, doing him favors in return, demonstrating a degree of independence and even of combativeness. On the other hand, she quoted the verse of a song that suggests that submissiveness would go a long way to securing needed wagons from the *nori–mawashi*. The wagon distributors, often reflecting the attitudes of company men and overseers, could be fickle. And an unscrupulous wagon distributor had the power to induce naïve or weaker women to "curry favour with him." One young girl was perplexed when she was confronted with unexpected advances.

> When you said to the *saotori*, "Send me a wagon," he'd reply, "Can I do it? If you let me do it, I'll send you one."
> "Let you do what?" I was completely naïve.[114]

This woman no doubt learned quickly from older women what demands could be safely met and how to evade others in noncompromising ways. Another remembered:

> The *saotori* always distributed the wagons according to his inclinations, sending them first to women he liked, the conceited fellow. In my young girl's heart, I just thought he was impudent. And I thought I'd like to get even with the *saotori* and outwit the bosses.[115]

Had she been aware of the nature of the favors that the *saotori* expected in return for his indulgence, she might have realized that the situation was more serious than she surmised and that it would be risky to try to "get even" with him. But, abandoning the innocence of their youth, she and her mates managed to punish the overweening fellow. (See the story of the Indomitables in Chapter 6.) Retaliation

224   *Common seams, common attitudes*

against the arrogance and arbitrary action of the underground overseers, however, was not commonly available to the women as a weapon or even a threat, and not many of them would have found much humor in the way they were teased and harassed on a regular basis. If some were able to shrug off sexual innuendo and evade the overseers' demands with aplomb, others were no doubt vexed and frustrated by what they thought of as unwanted but unavoidable importunities.

The overseers and foremen were in a position to use sanctions against female miners who did not please them and who refused to submit to sexual advances or toady to demands for greater production. Unfavorable responses could result in a cudgeling or beating or perhaps in less violent penalties. The women must have resented any recurrent abuse. One song went:

> *When he took advantage of her, one of the*
> *kogashira fellows*
> *Said he would give her the best faces.*

"Since even a slightly better face was desirable, no matter what you thought about it, you couldn't just ignore it," the woman who cited this verse said. But the women didn't always yield.

> Although they were always saying things in jest like, "How about doing it with me?" they couldn't just use force on the women to do as they liked.[116]

Sexual exploitation in the coal mines seems to have been less common than in the textile factories, where the supervisors could take advantage of young single women without fear of reprisals from male family members or friends working nearby.[117] But it occurred nonetheless.[118] On the other hand, Maki, who also spoke of men in positions such as that of the *kogashira* taking advantage of *atoyama*,[119] said that "There was no suffering when we were young. When there was a woman of marriageable age, it was quite exciting."

> As one got older, you'd make fun of the men. You'd be pulling the *sura* in your short skirt. If you caught someone staring up from below the *sura*[-dumping] platform, you'd yell, "You don't need to look sneakily from down there! If you give me an offertory, I'll let you worship everything!" So in that way we enjoyed whatever erotic banter there was to enjoy.[120]

Such a peeping Tomohisa might be described as an "underseer" and was not likely an overseer or company man, who had more opportunity to see what he wanted by coercion rather than by stealth—which is not to say that mining companies used sexual coercion as a weapon in personnel management. Sexual assaults by underground supervisors were likely to cause problems that the company could not easily resolve. Nevertheless, there is little evidence that company management, if they were aware of it, took effective steps to prevent or even curtail everyday sexual harassment.

Among the miners themselves, some men used the variability of shift work to impose on women who might be vulnerable. Mashio records Maki's story of how her father-in-law invaded her sleeping quarters while her husband was at work on the night shift. "Nana was snoring, knowing nothing of what was going on." Maki managed to escape in bare feet, and to refrain from waking her mother-in-law, but she was not going to let that happen again. "If my father-in-law had been a widower, I thought, I wouldn't have stayed one more day." Her proposed solution was that her father-in-law go back to work and that they live separately, which was what eventually happened.

Mashio asserts that illicit familial relations of other types were not uncommon.

> This kind of story certainly is not unusual in the colliery dwellings. A younger sister gives birth to her brother's child, and there are even cases of a girl having [sexual] relations with her father.

A middle school student who in the postwar period gave birth to her miner father's child put it out to foster care and went to Tokyo as a maid. Maki commented:

> In this neighbourhood, there's no one who doesn't know about it. As long as there are males and females, such beastly mistakes will occur. If they seem to be common in the mining compounds, isn't that because the tenements are too small?[121]

But although the size of the tenement dwellings certainly meant that miners were living in close quarters, and flimsy construction ensured that they usually knew what was going on in their neighbors' units, there were of course other stimuli for erotic fantasies and resulting perversions arising from the nature of the miners' work and their insecure lives. It is impossible to confirm from the Chikuho women's accounts the real extent of incest in that mining region, but because of the similarities of Chikuho coal communities to Joban mining camps we can surmise that Maki's account and Mashio's comments would apply to northern Kyushu as well.

Their unnatural environment

The women were aware of ways in which the unpleasant environment underground affected them and their fellow workers. They do not, however, express great concern for the effects of coal mining on the surrounding landscape. *Bota yama*, the ubiquitous pyramid-like waste heaps, even when overgrown with foliage nowadays, may seem to modern eyes to be an unnatural feature in that landscape, but their looming black eminences were accepted by the women as an inevitable corollary of the everyday operations of the industry. Around the pit mouths, there was likely to be black and gray devastation, dead foliage covered by coal dust among the litter of rusted industrial debris. But there is no evidence that the surface plant and detritus of the collieries were seen as scars on the landscape. To the women, the smoke rising inexorably from the mine chimneys symbolized jobs and income, not harm to the air that they were forced to breathe. They rarely linked the difficulty of obtaining clean water to pollution caused by the mine workings. Their life of struggle to obtain a living no doubt inured them to the "incidental" environmental effects of mining. Some, however, seem to have looked forward to retirement when they could enhance their surroundings with modest gardens, no doubt as a contrast to the barren surroundings of the mining tenements and dormitories. One woman seems to have lived for the time when she could retire and grow flowers, selling them in the market. But another spoke of being *reduced* to a life of growing flowers,[122] perhaps as a reaction to the premature end of what she believed was a more productive and remunerative life. The women's occasional longing for their home villages may have involved nostalgia for a "purer" life in a relatively clean and green rural setting. It seems, however, that the proverbial Japanese love of nature was blunted among those who had very little chance to commune with it on anything like a regular basis.

Although preservation of the natural environment from the depredations of coal-mining enterprises was not a major concern of the women, they do give some hints as to the extent of the ravages that the industry wreaked on the north Kyushu landscape and on water resources. Most Japanese scholars who have dealt in one way or another with the history of coal mining in the Chikuho region have mentioned the subsidence of farm land due to subterranean mining.[123] Farmers who owned or rented land above extensive underground operations were often the victims of subsidence that resulted in the formation of pools or lakes or that made the land uncultivable in other ways. Natural justice does not make miners responsible for mining operations that were designed by mine management and engineers, of course. But it seems that in the eyes of farmers, if miners were not directly responsible for such calamities, they were at least the indirect agents of the farmers' misfortunes. Such feelings were reinforced by the generally bad opinion of miners, and particularly of *burakumin* miners, held by most of the rural population.[124] One woman recounted:

> The farmers were upset by the damage done when their fields subsided and water collected. But if they tried to go to the mines to collect compensation, they would be slaughtered [*kirikorosare*—by management thugs?], so they had to keep quiet. And many village people came to work in the pits.[125]

The retired miners made brief reference to other causes of environmental damage by coal mining in the north Kyushu region. One woman reported, for instance, that there were no waste heaps at Omuta because waste (*bota*) was dumped into the sea.[126] This waste from the long-lived and notorious Miike mines poisoned the Ariake Sea and, along with other poisons from such chemical factories as Minamata, turned it into a dead sea, a state from which it is still recovering. Other women noted that refuse from the coal mines was dumped into the rivers, which poisoned these bodies of water. It was only in the early 1970s, after many of these women had recorded their life experiences, that the full consequences of such waste disposal were beginning to be understood. Their suspicions, though, had been aroused earlier by simple observation. One pointed out:

> Sluicing coal is a way of taking the raw coal dug out from a rock waste site and running it through a trough where it's washed with water in order to separate the coal from the stone. As it's mixed around with a small, square scoop and passes through the trough, the stone sinks and only the pure coal flows to the end of the trough where it's collected. When the sluice water is flushed into the river, it quickly becomes a black, muddy stream.[127]

The rivers of north Kyushu, particularly the Onga River with its adjacent transport canal, had been the main arteries of the early coal transport system. But later, with the advent of the railways and the decline of rivers as transport arteries, they became receptacles for the waste and poisons of the industry, further downgrading their usefulness and increasing harm to the surrounding countryside.[128] Although the women were not particularly conscious of this damage, they were targets of a hostile attitude on the part of their rural cousins toward miners and the industry in which they worked.

Miners, too, could suffer from the consequences of pollution, particularly from inappropriate waste disposal, but also from other kinds of contamination. One woman told how a new source of drinking water had to be found when a miner who had lost his new wife committed suicide in a holding pond (*bakku*) used for drinking water, contaminating it perhaps spiritually as well as physically. The main source of the water, the neighboring Yamada River, was found to be polluted at the same time, and Mitsubishi had to bring water in from another river to provide a less contaminated supply.[129] Apparently, the managers of the mighty *zaibatsu* did not see fit to try to eliminate the source of the contamination of the Yamada River.

Perpetual night work

Of more immediate concern to the female miners than the surface environment were conditions underground. They spent most of their working lives in a world of eternal darkness, relieved only by the weak candlepower of primitive lamps and, eventually, of safety lamps and simple electric light bulbs strung along the tunnels and shafts. Working day shifts, they rarely saw the light of the sun at either end of their long hours of work. And when on night shifts, they were usually too exhausted and had too many family chores to relax in the sunlight during their time off. Some recognized the unnatural features of a life bereft of the benefits of sun and fresh air. One said:

> Miners like me all have skin the colour of dirt. Not the colour of [natural] faces. When the sun was shining, we were usually in the hole. When we

228 *Common seams, common attitudes*

> came up, it was night-time. We were moles. Our pallid faces were covered with coal dust, and you couldn't get it off by going just once to the baths.[130]

Such a life may not be natural for human beings, even if the women themselves, like the designers of underground shopping malls in modern Japan, came to no such conclusion.

Ishihara Osamu pointed out that both male and female operatives suffered malnutrition and loss of body weight as the result of night shift work in textile mills, printing shops, pharmaceutical factories, and iron works.[131] Though workers could recover *some* of their lost weight during subsequent day shifts, Dr. Ishihara's statistics showed that night work invariably weakened miners and made them vulnerable to disease and illness. He believed that no permanent damage would be done if the workers were able to fully recover from one set of night shifts but did not speculate on how long such a recovery would take. From prolonged night work, however, "The tendency was for the weight of workers to decrease gradually but steadily until the operatives 'were nothing but skin and bones.'"[132] The largest group of operatives doing night shifts were found in cotton spinning, and young women in the industry were suffering enervation with productivity hampered, a situation detrimental to personal and national well-being.[133]

Although Ishihara supposed that, among mature workers, the body might somehow recover a "balance" during day work, he argued that alternate night and day shifts were surely stunting the growth of younger women. "Not only do they not recover during day work, but since it interferes with development in the maturation stage of youth, they are in double jeopardy ... and such night work, over a long period, interrupts the very breath of life," he wrote.[134]

Because so many of the coal-mining women "went into the pit" at early ages, commonly between 14 and 16, they were subjected to many of the same effects of night work on young female textile workers. Certainly the relatively high incidence of deaths among coal-mining women from diseases like tuberculosis, silicosis, and other respiratory and digestive disorders suggests that weakened physiques could not stand up to the ravages of such diseases, and work in the dark had contributed to the women's weakened state.[135] Adaptation of young bodies to continuous work in the dark with inadequate artificial light may have been facilitated by forehand knowledge of working conditions; work routines better suited to human bodies than those in textile mills where machines set the work pace; and better food supplied by their families. But it is almost certain that the equivalent of continual night work in the mines, before the adaptation process could bring young bodies into a state of "balance," stunted the growth of young female miners in the same way, if not to the same extent, that Ishihara believed night work damaged the bodies of young textile workers. And similar effects on the bodies of mature miners, male and female, surely occurred even after the adaptation process had gone on for some years. Though the debilitating effects of working in the dark are hinted at by several of the retired female miners, most of them, having been "born to the work," were not likely to assume that human beings could not work at night or in the dark for long periods without suffering serious damage.

The "benevolence" of the bosses

It was traditionally argued that, in mitigation of the severity of his exploitation of coal miners, the gang boss was responsible for the health and well-being of the miners in his gang.[136] But even if his responsibility to his *male* gang members was taken seriously (and there is more than a little doubt on that score), his responsibility to the women was not. The harsh working conditions underground clearly had debilitating effects on them. Moreover, mining youths who remained at home with parents were expected to be looked after by their families when they were unable to work; the gang bosses appear to have exhibited very little concern and offered scant assistance in cases of illness or accident. Their responsibilities were limited when it came to caring for the young dependents and more mature women who were attached to the gang as appendages of the male members.

Although the *naya-gashira* contributed to the lives of female affiliates of his gang members by finding marriage partners for many of them, these liaisons, as discussed earlier, often turned out to be of dubious benefit to the bride. According to some wives, the "promising" mates whom bosses recommended often turned out to be lazy scoundrels, having worked hard only when they were young and, ironically, had fewer responsibilities. The boss had found partners for the men, of course, because their labor was needed and the company felt that it would be easier to retain them if they were married to a female miner. The role of the *naya-gashira* in making matches, however, was sometimes confined to sanctioning relationships that had been formed underground or on the surface. In many cases, the women had little cause to feel much appreciation or obligation to their bosses as go-betweens. The bosses exploited both marriage partners in ways that often, willy-nilly, turned the men into wastrels, the women into drudges.

As I have argued, female miners developed a strong sense of responsibility for their own and their families' well-being and worked hard to sustain their families, particularly in times of dearth. But if gang bosses showed any appreciation for the special contribution of the women to the process of "getting out the coal," there is negligible evidence of such appreciation in the recollections of the retired women. Rather, companies and gang bosses alike seem to have depended on the commitment of the women to the sustenance of their families in order to increase productivity and to keep miners on the job.

The women do not appear to have been aware to what extent they were being exploited by the gang boss system. One woman suggests that the company was the main exploiter, not caring how they worked or lived.[137] Another believed (at least in retrospect) that "the capitalists" were responsible for their exploitation.[138] But it was the gang boss who took a rake-off from the miners' wages at the larger mines in the days before the company began to pay wages directly,[139] and at the smaller mines throughout our period of study. Lack of knowledge of the size of the boss's cut seems to have minimized awareness among the women of his role in exploiting them.[140] By giving them loans against their wages, the boss may even have seemed to be a benefactor. Indeed, traditional Japanese scholarship presented the gang boss as just such a benefactor, aiding his gang members when they faced hardship,

230   *Common seams, common attitudes*

carrying them when they could not work due to accident or illness, tiding them over periods of unemployment due to layoffs or mine closures, and lending them the means to subsist when they arrived at a new mine.[141] But other than the loans for setting up housekeeping (*shitaku-gin*) and loans against future wages to sustain families that did not earn enough for sustenance in any one pay period, the women do not often mention the role of gang bosses as benefactors.

An exception to this lack of acknowledgment of any crucial role of the gang boss in their lives was the statement of Strong-as-an-Ox that when the "company man" ran off with the "separation fund" (such funds are not mentioned by others) in 1929, "All of us were dependant on the *ōnaya* [i.e., the gang boss]." She also mentions that loans could be taken out on the basis of the combined incomes of man and wife.[142] At this later date, however, the calculation of wages that formed the basis for the loans as well as the terms, if not the loans themselves, were almost certainly made by mine management and not by the *naya-gashira*. Coincidentally, the women do not mention unreasonable interest rates. In fact, the women's recollections suggest no awareness of interest being applied to the loans—only of the rollover of debts that kept them in constant anxiety about their ability to support their families. The woman who lost her husband, sister-in-law, and child within half a year recalled:

> My tears were consumed, our money was consumed, everything was used up, and a mountain of debt piled up. The only things remaining were the "mortuary tablet baby" and debts, and the maintenance of the family became a heavy burden on me.[143]

Where was the gang boss's assistance in this desperate situation?

Morisaki relates one woman's struggles to sustain her family when her husband was struck down by accident at the Meinohama Mine and she could not work underground because of illness. She does not mention any assistance from a gang boss. Previously a member of a gang boss's family, this woman was now the wife of a gang member and may have been reticent to borrow from the *naya-gashira* because of her family's earlier position. But she made no mention of aid from a gang boss when illness prevented miners from working and thereby earning enough to eat.[144] Hers would have been a classic situation demanding assistance if the gang boss had been fulfilling the duty implied in a new title: *seiwa-kata* (literally, caregiver) after the company had taken over his supervision of the underground work, relegating him to recruiting and provision of the miners' basic needs above ground. This woman's family had earlier repaid their loans at the behest of the company office at one mine (by selling off their tools to the pawnshop) and were forgiven their fees for sandals. It is inconceivable that the miners were not organized under gang bosses at this mine and had no one to ask for the medical assistance that the bosses were said to have customarily offered. But this woman had no way of finding the 20 *sen* she needed each day for medicine for herself and her critically ill baby. It had been a stroke of luck that took them to the Meinohama Mine, where her husband could work and they

Common seams, common attitudes 231

paid only a nominal fee for the medicine. It was a company supervisor, not a gang boss, who tried to persuade her not to go down the pit because of her poor health. But earning enough to feed her family was still her primary concern. After her husband was injured in a cave-in and, apparently, released from Meinohama before he could fully recover, they became indigent once more and she had to seek solace and assistance from relatives.[145] This was at the beginning of Showa (the late 1920s), and no gang boss is mentioned as assisting the family. Though the company at Meinohama seems to have been relatively benevolent, this contrasted with smaller companies that took no responsibility for the medical needs of the miners and left such burdens to gang bosses who claimed to care for their minions but seem to have regarded their obligations to ill and injured miners as strictly limited.

Far from guaranteeing the security and well-being of their labor force, the bosses, whether they were recruiters and deployers of gangs or company men overseeing the work, often prevented miners from enjoying the fruits of their labors. One woman recalled:

> Pick-up work was really fruitless. There were bad people who didn't pay our wages and ran away. When we all went after them, they'd turn around and threaten us, or tell us nice things to deceive us. … In the end, we were all taken in. Whether the owner was bad, or the overseer was bad, it always came to recriminations, and the matter was never settled. When somebody got angry, such fellows always used some big name [*erabutsu*] to get them out of it.[146]

The incredible brightness of being

Even though assistance from gang bosses and empathy from partners was unusual, several Japanese scholars agree that there was a certain "*akarusa*" in the women's overall attitudes. This word, which literally means "brightness," can be translated variously as "cheerfulness," "good spirits," or even "optimism." Although the women's moods may not always be obvious from the narratives recorded on the printed page, we can find evidence of this optimism sometimes contending with chagrin over the trials and tribulations of their lives. According to Shindo Toyo, who was well acquainted with some of the *burakumin* women who had worked underground, the typical spirit of *all* female miners is found in the words of one old woman who reflected on "the unbounded optimism (*soko-nuke no akarusa*) of colliery workers who had worked and survived, an optimism involving the confidence and strength of those who had competed with male workers and survived the work."[147]

"We were happy, weren't we? Even though we suffered so many hardships," one woman reminisced.[148] "In these words," Shindo believes, "are included both the happiness and the sadness of the female miners. What one feels when one meets many of these older women who have been miners is their boundless optimism and bravery."[149] But Shindo also quotes lines from songs that stress the bitterness and suffering of the miners of northern Kyushu.[150] Nevertheless, one

232 *Common seams, common attitudes*

woman reflected that, "When I was working, I put everything into it," using words that could be more literally translated to say that she worked "with bright earnestness *(shira shinken yatta)*."[151]

Morisaki wrote of the mining women: "Although their lives had deteriorated to the point where they weren't worth a mess of pottage, when you met them, you were overwhelmed by the intensity of their optimism *(akarusa)*."[152] This impression was strengthened by each one she met. Although some of Idegawa's interviewees did not share such optimism, they had been chosen for the particular difficulties with their husbands and for the harsh experiences in their working lives.[153] Perhaps we can accept the general validity of Morisaki's observation that, in spite of the harshness of their existence and a commonly felt fatalism, most mining women expressed an optimism and cheerfulness quite at odds with the actual conditions of their lives and work.

> The *atoyama* had worked and lived with the attitude of those who must live lives of sacrifice. They nevertheless had the desire to survive, and a disposition which sought self-assertion. Their whole lives, led at the extremes of labour which tended to obliterate any humanity, had [however] the potential to be positively validated on the basis of that labour.[154]

Although Morisaki seems to be saying that the work left little room for the expression of "higher" values of social justice and human compassion, she also suggests the beginnings of a consciousness of greater possibilities in the lives of these women. If this was indeed a class consciousness, and had the labor of women in the mines continued through the upheavals of the 1950s and 1960s, it might have resulted in a stronger labor movement and perhaps even the creation of a new society in northern Kyushu.

Notes

1 Idegawa, p. 60.
2 Morisaki, p. 22.
3 Ibid., p. 23.
4 Idegawa, p. 35. See also, p. 77.
5 Idegawa, p. 135.
6 Idegawa, p. 55. See also. Idegawa, p. 72.
7 Cf. Tsurumi, *Factory Girls*, pp. 92–4.
8 Commendations with bonuses for devotion to duty (hard labor in extra shifts) came later during the war mobilization of the 1930s. See Lewis, *Rioters and Citizens*, p. 211.
9 Idegawa, pp. 130–37, passim. This woman also speaks of the absence of any outside sources of encouragement but rather of the demand of her husband to forget about her blisters by concentrating her efforts on her work. Later, the only voice cheering her on was an internal voice telling her that only by her efforts could she feed her children and allow them to survive. p. 141.
10 See Fukamachi, *Tankō-Bushi Monogatari*. Retired miner Yamamoto Sakubei adduces a miners' song that, although stressing the difficulties of their working lives throughout, hints at the importance of coal to the national economy in one verse:

Miners! miners!
Don't belittle them;
The coal
Doesn't grow in the fields. (Yama ni Ikiru, p. 100)

11 Yamamoto, *Yama ni Ikiru*, pp. 97–8.
12 Idegawa, p. 158.
13 *Makkura*, p. 53
14 Idegawa, p. 26.
15 Idegawa, p. 56.
16 Idegawa, p. 29.
17 Shindo Toyo, *Chikuhō no Jokōfu-tachi*, p. 15.
18 Ibid.
19 Idegawa, p. 14.
20 Idegawa, p. 109.
21 Ibid., p. 73.
22 *Jizoku no Seishun*, p. 82.
23 Morisaki, p. 150.
24 Mashio, pp. 90–1.
25 Mashio, p. 15.
26 Shindo Toyo, *Chikuhō no Jokōfu-tachi*, p. 18.
27 Cf. Mashio, p. 12.
28 Cf. Idegawa, pp. 159–60.
29 Ibid., p. 110–11. For an outline of this system, not as extensive or effective in the collieries as the "*tomoko dōmei*" in metal mines, see Nimura, *The Ashio Riot of 1907*, pp. 39–40.
30 Idegawa, p. 18.
31 Ibid., p. 18.
32 Idegawa, pp. 18–24. See also, pp. 159–61.
33 Mashio, pp. 100–1.
34 Idegawa, pp. 140–1.
35 *Yama ni Ikiru*, pp. 99–100. The latter of these verses seem to make it a woman's song, although the word for miner (*kōfu*) in others is masculine in derivation. Shindo Toyo gives different verses of what may be more than one song. *Chikuhō no Jokōfu-tachi*, p. 15.
36 Morisaki, p. 18.
37 Ibid., pp. 18–21.
38 Mathias, "Female Labour in the Japanese Coal-Mining Industry," in Hunter, ed., *Japanese Women Working*, pp. 105–116.
39 Morisaki, p. 76.
40 Sumiya, *Nihon Sekitan Sangyō Bunseki*, p. 163, from Nagasaki Prefecture Mines Bureau, "*Kōzan Shiryō Shirabe*" (Survey of Mines Data). Sumiya says that the records of other coal mines in the Matsuura coalfield showed only minor variations in labor organization, and therefore, little variation in wage scales.
41 Sumiya, pp. 169–70. In the light of the women's descriptions of their relative abilities at hauling, I do not think it possible that the men earned more because they hauled more wagonloads, a possibility suggested by my mentor, Mark Selden.
42 Yasukawa Junosuke, "*Hisabetsu Buraku to Josei*," p. 209.
43 Morisaki, p. 183.
44 Idegawa, p. 149.
45 Idegawa, p. 115.
46 Idegawa, pp. 41, 45.
47 Idegawa, p. 158. There could not have been many overseers as sympathetic to the woman's cause as this foreman!

234 *Common seams, common attitudes*

48 Idegawa, p. 168.
49 Morisaki, p. 46.
50 Idegawa, p. 42.
51 Cf. Idegawa, p. 81.
52 Mathias, "Female Labour in the Japanese Coal-Mining Industry," in Hunter, ed., *Japanese Women Working*, pp. 109–10, 118.
53 Ibid., p. 115.
54 Morisaki, p. 76.
55 Idegawa, p. 126.
56 Nimura Kazuo, in conversation with the author in 1987, emphasized the relatively short working hours of Japanese male miners in apparent defense against overly generalized criticisms of the harsh degree of exploitation in the Japanese industry, but I have come to believe that his remarks could not apply to the women hauliers in coal mines who worked long hours under appalling conditions in order to sustain their families.
57 Idegawa, p. 81.
58 *Jizoko no Seishun*, p. 78.
59 Mashio, p. 81.
60 Morisaki, pp. 39–43.
61 Morisaki, p. 76.
62 Morisaki, p. 109.
63 Idegawa, pp. 42–3.
64 Idegawa, p. 79.
65 Morisaki, p. 95. This woman goes on to tell the parable of the Ball-Crusher, similar to a story told about a heroic textile worker. See Tsurumi, *Factory Girls*, p. 197.
66 Idegawa, p. 157.
67 Idegawa, p. 41. I have interpreted "*henna yoroke sakiyama*" as a contemptuous reference to incompetence because it would not have been much of a boast to be able to keep up with a foolish and/or disabled silicotic miner.
68 Idegawa, pp. 41–2.
69 Idegawa, p. 38.
70 Shindo, p. 18. See also Mathias, p. 107.
71 Idegawa, p. 134.
72 Morisaki, *Makkura*, p. 130.
73 Mashio, p. 114.
74 Morisaki, p. 95.
75 Idegawa, p. 152.
76 Idegawa, p. 42.
77 Mashio, *Jizoko no Seishun*, p. 120.
78 Idegawa, p. 39.
79 Idegawa, p. 64.
80 Idegawa, p. 28. It seems that the Goddess of the Mines had some Medusa-like characteristics. Because miners referred to the mines with the same term Japanese people use for mountains—*yama*—(probably because most mines were in the mountains), this Goddess may be the same as the Mountain Goddess, treated in the 1985 film *Himatsuri* as a symbol of sexuality by the ingenuous hero. The Japanese word *kami* is gender-neutral.
81 Idegawa, pp. 97–9.
82 Cf. Morisaki, pp. 78–9.
83 Idegawa, p. 163.
84 Morisaki, p. 75. This woman tends to remember the good times after 1930, not mentioning the attempt of the bureaucrats to exclude women from work underground. Concerning the exclusion, see Morisaki, *Makkura*, pp. 183–4.
85 Ibid., p. 34.

Common seams, common attitudes 235

86 Idegawa, p. 193
87 *Makkura*, p. 195. Cf. Shindo, *Chikuhō no Jokōfu-tachi*, p. 17.
88 "*Yamamoto* Sakubei *Zakki Chō* (Yamamoto Sakubei's Notebook)," in Ueno, ed., *Kōfu*, p. 184.
89 Morisaki, p. 175. See also Lewis, *Rioters and Citizens*, p. 204.
90 Yamamoto, *Yama ni Ikiru*, p. 40.
91 Ibid. Shinagawa Asayo said that her only inheritance from her parents was poverty. *Tankō Bijin*, p. 188.
92 Cf. Mashio, pp. 44–5.
93 Mashio, p. 106.
94 *Makkura*, p. 156.
95 *Jizoko no Seishun*, p. 114.
96 Idegawa, p. 110.
97 The 40-some interviews with retired female coal miners in Tajima Masami's *Tankō Bijin* support these conclusions.
98 Works in English by Otsuka Hisao and Irokawa Daikichi are referred to in a discussion of *dekasegi* by Patricia Tsurumi on pp. 191–2 of *Factory Girls*.
99 For the songs of female textile workers expressing a yearning for their rural homes, see Tsurumi, *Factory Girls*, pp. 101–2.
100 Shindo Toyo, *Chikuhō no Jokōfu-tachi*, pp. 39–40.
101 *Hi o Unda Hahatachi*, p. 6.
102 Idegawa, pp. 6–8 and 193.
103 *Makkura*, p. 112.
104 Ellison Robertson, who "was born in Sydney (Nova Scotia, Canada) and lived in most of the surrounding (coal) towns, though only in Sydney Mines long enough for it to feel like home," has written of "an unexpected depth of attachment and debt to my shabby home town." "Hearts and Mines," *Canadian Dimension*, vol. 34, no.5 (Sept/Oct, 2000), p. 38.
105 Idegawa, p. 163.
106 Cf. Lewis, *Rioters and Citizens*, pp. 199–200.
107 Idegawa, p. 50.
108 Cf. Mashio, p. 14.
109 Earlier material from Morisaki, pp. 84–7, 90–4.
110 One verse of the song given in Yamamoto, *Yama ni Ikiru*, p. 100.
111 Idegawa, p. 6.
112 Cf. the experience of the Japanese Cricket. Idegawa, pp. 63–85, particularly p. 73.
113 Idegawa, p. 210.
114 Idegawa, p. 198.
115 *Makkura*, p. 108.
116 Morisaki, pp. 177–8.
117 See Tsurumi, *Factory Girls*, pp. 165–7.
118 Cf. Sano Toshino's fear of seduction and escape from a *sakiyama* who claimed that the lamp's "carburization" was responsible for its sudden extinguishment before he tried to molest her. *Tankō Bijin*, p. 54.
119 *Jizoko no Seishun*, p. 88.
120 Idegawa, p. 198. See also, p. 101.
121 Mashio, *Jizoko no Seishun* pp. 113–15.
122 Idegawa, pp. 82–3. Morisaki, *Makkura*, pp. 164–5.
123 The photograph of the large pond created by the Hōjō explosion of 1914 is an extreme example of the subsidence created by mining activities. Orii Seigo, *Hōjō Daihijō*, p. 173. There are many materials dealing with such subsidence and the lawsuits arising from it in the library of the Ohara Social Problems Research Centre on the campus of Hosei University at Machida City, outside Tokyo.

236 *Common seams, common attitudes*

124 See Nakamura Masanori, *Rōdōsha to Nōmin*, p. 107.
125 Morisaki, p. 78.
126 Idegawa, p. 189.
127 Idegawa, pp. 50–1.
128 Cf. Kenneth Strong, *Ox Against the Storm,* passim, for Tanaka Shozo's campaign to counter the devastation wrought by the Furukawa Ashio mines in the Watarase River basin in the 1890s.
129 Morisaki, p. 139.
130 Morisaki, p. 189.
131 In Kagoyama Takashi, ed., *Jokō to Kekkaku*, p. 116–18. Ishihara was only able to gather data for two cotton-spinning mills, two printing plants, and one of each of the pharmaceutical and iron works, but it shows a consistent loss of body weight in each case, with the two spinning mills (where more women than men worked) showing losses of 154 monme (577.5 grams) and 170 (637.5) after seven days of night work.
132 Tsurumi, *Factory Girls*, p. 172, citing Ishihara in Kagoyama, *Jokō to Kekkaku*, p. 180.
133 *Jokō to Kekkaku*, pp. 116–118, 180–1.
134 Ibid., p. 180.
135 See Chapter 3, Working Conditions, for incidences of diseases and deaths due to diseases.
136 Cf. Oyama, *Kōgyō Rōdō to Oyakata Seido*, pp. 30–33.
137 *Makkura*, p. 47.
138 *Makkura*, p. 185.
139 Nakamura suggests that the wage packet was still being distributed by the gang boss at the beginning of the Taisho period (after 1912), but that the boss's own remuneration was strictly regulated and paid to him directly by the company. Nakamura, *Rōdōsha to Nōmin*, pp. 140–1. It is hard to believe that the *pin-hané* (rake-off) would not continue, perhaps in disguised forms, even at mines where the gang boss was no longer the main purveyor of labor.
140 The "hierarchically organized system of exploitation and oppression" in which the exploitation of one element of the working class by another is a feature of "the interposition of parasites between the capitalist and the wage-labourer" is described aptly by Karl Marx in *Capital*, vol. 1., p. 553. Marx reveals the way in which the real authors and agents of the exploitation can be obfuscated.
141 Cf. Oyama Shikitaro, *Kōgyō Rōdō to Oyakata Seido*, pp. 24–5, 30–3, where Oyama indicates that the benefits of the system to gang members at coal mines may have been less and the exploitation more severe than in other sectors of industry.
142 Idegawa, pp. 147–9.
143 Idegawa, p. 106.
144 Morisaki, pp. 42–59.
145 Morisaki, pp. 60–3.
146 Idegawa, p. 51.
147 If such optimism extended to the *burakumin* among the female miners, it would support my assumption that prejudice and discrimination against outcastes were not as severe as in other communities.
148 Shindo, *Chikuho no Jokōfu-tachi*, p. 18. Shindo evinces what may be a traditional Japanese reticence in attributing quotations to specific sources. This one comes from *Makkura*, p. 195. In Mathias's article, the sentence is translated, "Ah, we had a lot of fun, but it was also very hard sometimes!" In Hunter, p. 114. Unfortunately, it is difficult to know who should get credit for the translation in the Hunter book.
149 The cheerfulness is reflected in the faces of most of the 46 female miners photographed in retirement by Tajima Masami in *Tankō Bijin*, though some suggest that they had been asked to smile for the camera.
150 *Chikuhō no Jokōfu-tachi*, pp. 18–19.

151 Idegawa, p. 103.
152 *Makkura*, p. 196.
153 *Hi o Unda Haha-tachi*, passim. Some miners' songs may seem to indicate a fondness of male miners for their partners, but even the women interviewed by Morisaki refer more often to feelings of solitariness and vulnerability than to companionship and affection.
154 Morisaki, *Makkura*, pp. 196–8. My brother, Neil Burton, pointed out that Morisaki's ideology, arising from her own life experience, seems to have influenced her interpretation of the philosophy of the mining women and led her to be surprised at some of its features that do not seem peculiar in the light of behavioral and attitudinal studies of other social groups in the working class. If their philosophy has some universal characteristics, I would think that its study would be even more worthy of attention by others.

Afterword

> A woman can't work for herself. She's always working for someone else. Giving her all (*enyakōra*) for her husband, her children, or her parents and brothers, if she decides she'll do whatever is necessary, she can endure anything. It makes her very strong.[1]

The Japanese coal-mining women did not think of themselves as working and suffering for the good of the company or the nation nor for their own benefit but rather for the welfare of their families, particularly their offspring. Their working lives illustrate exploitation in a most extreme form. That they were not always aware of the many ways in which that exploitation debilitated their bodies and constrained their spirits did not make it any less onerous.

Coal-mining men rarely pushed themselves to the same extent as the women, but all coal miners had to work hard in order to subsist. The recollections of retired Japanese female miners, like the novels about the lives of British miners (*The Stars Look Down* by A. J. Cronin) and of French miners (Zola's *Germinal*), cannot but arouse sympathy for those who toiled in the bowels of the earth. These workers provided the sources of energy for the industrialization of their respective countries and (indirectly in some cases) comforts for others that they usually did not enjoy themselves.

Although this study has largely confined itself to the working lives of the women, perhaps enough material has been adduced to suggest significant differences in the nature of the work and of the attitudes of the two genders and to illustrate a pervasive paternalism by management and in the relations between the men and women underground. It is hoped that students and scholars might be inspired to make further comparisons to clarify the varying nature of gender relations in this sector of the working class in the later period before and since the Asia-Pacific War.

Clearly, the belief of the female miners in the value of the work that they had accomplished during their lifetimes gave them a sense of self-worth and self-esteem. The title of Idegawa's book, *Hi o Unda Haha-tachi* (Mothers Who Spawned the Fire), suggests not only their role in fostering the daughters and sons who became the indispensable workforce in the post-1930 coal-mining industry but also their role as the producers of the raw material that powered the modernizing industries of early twentieth-century Japan. Although the women themselves seem only vaguely aware of the importance of coal in the industrialization process, their role in gathering and hauling the "stone" (*ishi*) from the coal face to the galleries or to the surface, and sometimes even farther to the transportation centers from which it would be distributed to the ports and factories, was enormously important.

It might be thought that women involved in such arduous toil in their hours of employment and in their time spent caring for children and husbands would become dulled to the details of their work and cynical about the relationships involved in it. But their testimony shows that many, if not most, of the female miners took their work seriously and attempted to excel at its technical requirements. They also believed that work itself was valuable and life-affirming, and they tried to maximize the output of coal, if only to earn the income that sustained their families. Many managed to do their work with an element of cheerfulness and esprit de corps, while others, perhaps less adept or physically endowed for such work, refused to succumb to despair and strived to keep up with their sisters. That life in the *Makkura* (Pitch Dark) underground did not give them a gloomy attitude is, if not a tribute to the indomitability of the human spirit, at least testimony to the tenacity and faith of one section of the Japanese working class.

Laboring in abysmal conditions underground and enjoying few amenities above, it is amazing that the women did not become embittered about their existence. On the contrary, some found solace in the belief that their basic needs had been met; they had not craved luxuries. They claimed to have eaten well enough in good times and to have had their share of pleasures as well as pain. But most seem to have resigned themselves to a life of hardship while enjoying very few benefits from their work. Such attitudes echo a stereotype of the Japanese woman as resigned to her Fate, one determined by an essentially male, paternalist culture. Yet their gratification at having survived, their sense of accomplishment in getting out the coal and raising their children, their satisfaction at not being bested by the working conditions or by their menfolk, and their appreciation of the value of hard work formed the rudimentary basis of what might have become a class consciousness had they been able to benefit from modern organizational and bargaining weapons. Their only real weapons, however, were the strength in their arms and backs, their mining tools, and their skills, persistence, and dedication. (Their wit, percipience, and poetic sensitivities remained unfocused but latent instruments for betterment.) A more developed class consciousness might have persuaded them that their contributions to the industry could include not only productive manual labor but also the shaping of the mode of production and the amelioration of the conditions under which they worked.

Labor history tells us that workers, women in particular, can tolerate a great deal of suffering before they refuse to cooperate with a system that exploits them, as long as their primary needs are being sustained. Some women (and men), not knowing the limits of their endurance, may even break down physically or emotionally (or both) before they reach a point at which they give cogent voice

240　*Afterword*

to their dissatisfaction and mount some form of resistance. As long as the coal-mining women were able to sustain their families and envision a future for their children even marginally better than their own, they were likely to confine themselves to grumbling to their associates or to suffering in silence, directing their frustration inward rather than lashing out at management or at the bosses or taking it out on their husbands who might be unleashing their own frustration on their wives. In their thresholds of tolerance and recalcitrance, Japanese women are probably not essentially different from their "sisters" in other countries. Social norms, however, have at times required them to accept a larger measure of harsh treatment and abuse, and to limit their reactions to more subtle ones, than in some other societies. The limits imposed on the rebelliousness and resistance of the women in the coal mines, in the face of severe exploitation and repression, seriously impeded their desire and ability to express their aspirations. Although such infringement of what might be considered natural rights was not out of line with prevailing attitudes in Japan, it brings into question any claims of "modernity" for the social milieu in the coal-mining camps.

Notes

1　The "Floating Leaf," in Idegawa, p. 110.

Glossary

Note: The explanations of technical terms are mainly derived from Kaneko Useki, *Chikuhō Tankō Kotoba.*

Time periods

Tokugawa: 1601–1868
Meiji: 1868–1912
Taishō: 1912–1926
Shōwa: 1926–1989

Terms and definitions

agari-zaké	"coming-up *saké*," prepared by the wife to begin the husband's evening relaxation after coming out of the pit
ashi-naka	"part-feet;" half-soled sandals worn by hauliers; also called *tsuma-waraji*
atomuki	"rear guard" or "back-lookers;" underground hauliers; usually called *atoyama*
atoyama	"mine back-up;" the people, usually women, who did the hauling from the face underground; also called *atomuki*
bakku	dunking tubs in the Joban coal mines; the word was perhaps derived from the English "bucket," but the pools used for collecting run-off water in Joban and Chikuho mines were also called *bakku*
bara-kago	very large, bottomless basket used to measure the output of coal at the pit mouth
battera	large bamboo baskets mounted on runners to slide up and down slopes from the faces; the origin of wooden *sura*
bentō	boxed lunch eaten away from home
bota	waste rock in a coal mine
bota-yama	"mountains" of coal waste, symbolic of the Chikuho mines
burakumin	people labeled as outcastes in the Tokugawa period and still so called after their nominal "liberation" in the Meiji period, when they continued to live in the villages (*buraku*) that had been designated for them earlier

242 *Glossary*

dekasegi	"going out to work"; sojourners or migrant labor, used to characterize much of the labor force in pre-1945 Japan
dongorosu	canvas sack used as a cushion under the hips of a recumbent miner attacking a narrow seam, or as protection for shoulders or hips by a woman haulier
ebu	basket into which the *atoyama* raked the coal at the face for transfer to the larger carrying containers; also, *ebi-joke*
furoshiki	square of cloth used for wrapping and carrying things in transit
futon	quilts used as bedding
gamé	tin teapot used by miners, hence *gamé-tsuki ni iku*, to seek a job providing a teapot (ie, one in the mines)
gangan	crude stove for heating and cooking, made from half of an oil barrel with grate over the fuel and holes for air circulation
gichi	"powder dummies" put into the drill holes behind dynamite sticks to prevent the force of the blast coming back into the room
haikyū-sho	"distribution center," or company store, that handled "rations" or supplies for the miners, often "running up a tab" that would be partially paid with a miner's wages
hako	"wagons" or cars running on rails in the galleries in the coal mines; called "trucks" in American mines, corves or "tubs" in British mines
hamba	"eating place," or dormitory where bachelor miners were fed, usually called *ōnaya* in Chikuho; gang bosses in other regions were usually known as *hamba-gashira* rather than *naya-gashira*
harai	bigger "rooms" made possible by advanced methods of timbering, usually in thicker seams at the largest mines; several or even many teams would work in such rooms
hiban	person who looked after and distributed lamps, either underground or at the lampisterie above ground, and who also watched for dust and smoke as signs of danger
hitoguri	dispatcher responsible to the gang boss for getting miners to go down for their shifts; also *kurikomi*
hito-saki	mining team, usually comprised of one *atoyama* and one *sakiyama* and assigned to one face
ishi	"stone," or coal, in common parlance in Chikuhō
jimusho	"office" or aboveground, onsite administrative center of the mine
kakari	person in charge; various designations were used (*jinji kakari, romu kakari, genba-kakari, kōnai-kakari, tori-shimari*) for company supervisors of different aspects of the work
kaki-ita	rake, originally a "board," with which the *atoyama* gathered up the coal from behind the hewer
kanba	"accounts office," originally the office at the pit mouth where coal was "purchased" from the miners and dispatched to market or storage but later the office that handled miners' pay and, in most cases, provisions, deducting their cost from wages or putting wages toward miners' expenses and debts

Glossary 243

kanekata	galleries or mezzanines forming the main haulageways
kantera	miner's lamp, initially a saucer filled with oil and lit by a wick, often held with chopsticks between the teeth, and later a glass canister with a metal top and base, similarly held in the mouth by a metal handle when the *atoyama* was pushing *sura* or wagons in the tunnels; later, safety lamps (*anzentō*) similar to Western ones
kata	shafts sloping upward from the galleries in a deep mine, also called *nobori*, or "ascents"
kataire-gin	"recruiting money" received by the miner on signing up for work, not always repayable in early years but later indistinguishable from repayable *maegashi-kin*
kentan	"coal inspection," usually of coal in wagons at the pithead
ketsuwari	removing themselves, without notice, from the mining camp; absconding; running away
kirichin	payment for mining output, usually referring to the contract price per wagonload (of coal)
kiriha	face from which the miner took the coal; also used to designate the "room" in which hewing took place
kogashira	the "little boss" who supervised work underground on behalf of the *naya-gashira*
kogata	"minor people;" gang members owing loyalty to the *oyakata*, or boss
konaya	"little dormitory," or rowhouses for mining families at mining camps
koro	rails in the form of a wooden ladder placed on slopes to make footholds for the *atoyama* or guideways for the *sura* in the mine
kuragae	layered wooden lunchbox with separate compartments for rice and supplements; also, *kuragai*
kurikomi	dispatcher, charged with getting the miners to work
kyūsai-kai	relief societies; management body offering minimal relief to miners suffering from accident and illness
mabu-beko	"miner's skirt;" the short skirt worn by Chikuhō women working underground in the period of this treatise; derived from an old word for mine (*mabu*) and a dialect word for loincloth (*heko*)
mabu-jiban	"miner's shirt;" work shirt with Western-style sleeves
maegashi-kin	earnest money paid (by the recruiter on behalf of the gang boss) to a worker to induce him to come to the mine, repayable over time from the miner's (and his family's) wages
maito	dynamite
makiage-ki	winding gear, lifting coal out of a vertical shaft
naya	mine residence, a contraction of *nagaya*, meaning tenement or dormitory; written with Chinese characters, which suggests a building for warehousing things—in this case, people
naya-gashira	gang boss, literally, "head of the dormitory," or lodge boss (Nimura); he was essentially a labor contractor who recruited, fed, and housed his gang members as well as gave them work assignments; also, *tōryō*

244 *Glossary*

nori-mawashi	wagon distributor, or person who "rode around" on the wagons, leaving empty ones at the headings to the face; also *saotori*
noson	quitting and coming out of the pit early, usually associated with male "laziness" by the women
nusuto-bori	illegal, or "robber," mine
omiai	first meeting of a prospective bride and groom in an arranged marriage, often equivalent to an engagement among miners
ōnaya	"big dormitory" for unmarried miners; managed by the gang boss
oroshi	"descents," shafts sloping downward from the galleries
oyakata	"father figure" to gang members; a term for the *naya-gashira*, nominally responsible for the members' welfare
renai	love affair or love match
romu	"work manager" who supervised work for the company
sakiyama	"mine fronters;" the men who worked at the face, hewing the coal from the underground seam
saotori	wagon distributor, derived from the operator of the swinging pole used to lever water from a well pool and, initially, coal from a shallow mine
sasabeya	underground "office," or hut, from which overseers managed the mining work in a big mine and, in some cases, in which they allowed miners to gather for a quick smoke
seiwa – kata	one who "cared for" miners; another name for a gang boss
sena	coal baskets carried from the face on a yoke over the shoulder by the *atoyama*
sentan-fu	sorters, usually women, who cleaned and sorted the coal at the pithead
shichū	framing timbers
shikuri	framers, usually men, who fitted the timbers to make supports for the roof or walls of shafts in the coal mine
shitaku-gin	"preparation money," to allow a miner and his family to purchase necessities and to set up housekeeping at the mine, repayable to the gang boss or, later, to the wage-paying company
shōchū	low-grade distilled spirits, cheaper than *saké*
shumoku	short, angled stick used by the *atoyama* to steady herself against the slope while balancing the yoked *sena* over her shoulder
sukabura	"idler," usually masculine
sura	"box" that the *atoyama* hauled up and down the slopes from the face to the wagon galleries; from the Chinese, but possibly also adapted from the first two phonemes in the Japanese pronunciation of the English word "sleigh"
tabi	traditional canvas covering worn on the feet, particularly by Japanese workmen
tankō	coal mine; also called an *ishiyama*, or "stone mountain"
tanuki-bori	shafts sunk from the surface following an exposed coal seam, in the manner of "badger holes"; called *tanoki-bori* in Chikuhō after the dialect word for badger

Glossary 245

tatami	tightly woven rush mats used as flooring in Japanese dwellings
tebo	single basket of coal carried on the back with straps slung over the shoulders in the manner of a rucksack
tebo-karai	"carrying the tebo," one of three main ways of getting coal from the room to the wagons, along with *sena* and *sura*
tenugui	standard Japanese hand towel, used also as a head covering by women in the coal mines
tokushu buraku	"special villages" for outcastes; to distinguish them from ordinary villages (*buraku*)
tokushu naya	"special dormitories" for outcastes at coal-mining camps
tōryō	original mining bosses who contracted to do mining work in all or parts of the mine and who recruited and housed the necessary labor; later indistinguishable from the *naya-gashira*
tsuma-waraji	"better-half straw sandals," worn by the (mostly female) hauliers; they had only half soles for the toes and ball of the foot, which gave the workers purchase on the slopes and ladders, while the heel was left bare; also called *ashi-naka*
tsurubashi (or *tsuruhashi*)	miner's pick, with wooden handle and long pointed head, refittable with new points in the Showa period (after 1926)
uke-zura	*sura* "received" or balanced on the *atomuki*'s head as she backed down the slope to the wagons
waku	"frame" of timbers, predominantly pine, to support the roof
waraji	straw sandals
yama	"mountain," signifying one with a coal seam or a coal mine in it, or simply a coal mine
yamashi	contractor for all or part of a mine, usually providing the necessary labor and selling the product to the mine owners
yoki	axe of the framer or "timberman," usually honed to razor sharpness

Bibliography

Allen, Matthew, *Undermining the Japanese Miracle: Work and Conflict in a Coalmining Community*, Cambridge University Press, 1994.

Allinson, Gary, *Japanese Urbanism: Industry and Politics in Kariya, 1872–1972*, University of California, 1975.

Aso Hisashi Den Kanko Iinkai, ed., *Aso Hisashi Den* (The Life of Aso Hisashi), Aso Hisashi Kanko Iinkai Kai, 1958.

Berger, Stefan, Croll, Andy, and LaPorte, Norman, eds., *Towards a Comparative History of Coalfield Societies*, Aldershot, UK: Ashgate Publishing Ltd., 2005.

Bowen, Lynne, *Three Dollar Dreams*, Lantzville, BC: Oolichan Books, 1987.

Burton, W. Donald, "The Origins of the Modern Japanese Iron and Steel Industry, with Special Reference to Mito and Kamaishi, 1853–1901," PhD dissertation, London University, 1972.

Burton, W. Donald, "Peasant Struggle in Japan, 1590–1760," *The Journal of Peasant Studies*, vol. 5, no. 2 (Jan. 1978).

Colligan-Taylor, Karen, "*Barukoku bararage*: A Prayer for Rain," *Bulletin of Concerned Asian Scholars*, vol. 26, nos. 1 & 2, Jan.–June 1994.

Cronin, Arthur J., *The Stars Look Down*, London: Victor Gollancz, 1969.

DeVos, George, "The Relation of Guilt toward Parents to Achievement and Arranged Marriage among the Japanese," in Takie Sugiyama Lebra and William P. Lebra, *Japanese Culture and Behaviour*, rev. ed., pp. 80–101. University Press of Hawaii, 1986.

Emi Suiin, "*Ashio Dōzan Kōfu no Hanashi*" (Concerning Miners at the Ashio Copper Mine), *Taiyō*, vol. 4, no. 25 (Dec. 20, 1898).

Endicott, Stephen L., *Bienfait: The Saskatchewan Miners' Struggle of '31*, Univ. of Toronto Press, 2002.

Fukamachi Junsuke, *Tankō-Bushi Monogatari* (The Story of Mining Songs), Fukuoka, Kaichosha, 1997.

Gardner, A. Dudley, and Flores, Verla R., *Forgotten Frontier: A History of Wyoming Coal Mining*, Boulder, CO: Westview Press, 1989.

Gier, Jaclyn J., and Mercier, Laurie, *Mining Women: Gender in the Development of a Global Industry, 1670 to 2005*, New York: Palgrave MacMillan, 2006.

Hane, Mikiso, "The Coal Miners," in *Peasants, Rebels, and Outcastes: The Underside of Modern Japan*, pp. 226–45. New York: Pantheon Books, 1982.

Hane, Mikiso, *Peasants, Rebels and Outcastes: The Underside of Modern Japan*, New York: Pantheon Books, 1982.

Hanley, Susan B., and Kozo Yamamura, *Economic and Demographic Change in Preindustrial Japan, 1600–1868*, Princeton University, 1977.

Bibliography   247

Hidemura Senzo et al., eds., *Hizen Sekitan Kōgyō Shiryō-shu* (Compendium of Documents on the Coal-Mining Industry of Hizen), Bunken Shuppan, 1977.

Higashisada Nobumasa, "*Chikuhō Sekitan Kōgyō ni okeru Kindai-ka Katei*" (The Modernization Process in the Chikuho Coal Industry), in Ogino Yoshihiro, ed., *Senzen-ki Chikuhō Tankō-gyō no Keiei to Rōdō* (Management and Labour in the PreWar Chikuho Coal-Mining Industry), pp. 1–36. Kyoto: Keibunsha, 1990.

Hirokawa Sadahide, "*Hokkaido ni okeru Tankō Rōdōsha no Keisei to 1907 nen no Hokutan Sōgi*" (The Organization of Colliery Workers in Hokkaido and the 1907 Struggle at Hokutan [The Hokkaido Colliery and Steamship Co.]), *Nihonshi Kenkyū*, no. 114 (Sept. 1970).

Holland, John, *The History and Description of Fossil Fuel, The Collieries, and Coal Trade of Great Britain*, London: Frank Cass & Co., 1968.

Hosoi Wakizo, *Jokō Aishi* (The Pitiful History of Female Factory Workers), Iwanami, 1954.

Howard, Irene, "Home Brew," *Highgrader Magazine* (Canada), vol. 5, issue 3, May/June, 1999.

Hunter, Janet, ed., *Japanese Women Working*, London: Routledge, 1993.

Idegawa Yasuko, *Hi o Unda Haha-tachi* (Mothers Who Spawned the Fires), Fukuoka City: Ishobo, 1984.

Iida Kenichi and Kuroiwa Toshiro, eds., *Saikō Yakin Gijutsu* (The Technology of Mining and Metallurgy), vol. 20 of Nihon Kagaku-shi Gakkai, ed., *Nippon Kagakugizyutusi Taikei* (History of Japanese Science and Technology), Daiichi Hoki Shuppan KK, 1965.

Ikeda Yoshimasa and Sasaki Ryuji, *Edo Makki kara Meiji Jidai made* (From the End of Edo to the Meiji Period), *Kyōyōjin no Nihon Shi* (The Educators' Japanese History) series, vol. 4, Shakai Shiso Sha, 1967.

Imano Takashi, "*Aso, Kama Senseki Sha no Seiritsu Katei*" (Aso and the Process of Formation of the Kama Cokeite Co.), in Ogino Yoshihiro, ed., *Senzen-ki Chikuhō Tankō-gyō no Keiei to Rōdō* (Management and Labour in the PreWar Chikuho Coal-Mining Industry), pp. 37–83. Kyoto: Keibunsha, 1990.

Ishihara Osamu, "*Kōfu no Eisei Jōtai Chōsa*" (Survey of the Health Conditions of Miners), in Sumiya Mikio, ed., *Shokkō oyobi Kōfu Chōsa* (Survey of Workers and Miners), pp. 169–204. Koseikan, 1970.

Ishihara Osamu, "*Jokō no Genkyō*" (The Current Situation of Female Workers), in Kagoyama Takashi, ed., *Jokō to Kekkaku* (Female Workers and Tuberculosis), pp. 77–198. Kosei-kan, 1970.

Ishimoto, Baroness Shidzué (Kato Shizue), *Facing Two Ways: The Story of My Life*, Stanford University Press, 1984.

Iwaya Saori, "Work and Life at a Coal Mine: The Life History of a Woman Miner," in Wakita Haruko, Anne Bouchy, and Ueno Chizuko, eds., *Gender and Japanese History*, vol. 2., pp. 413–48. Osaka University Press, 1999.

John, Angela, *By the Sweat of Their Brow: Women Workers at Victorian Coal Mines*, London: Croom Helm, 1980.

John, Angela, *Coalmining Women*, Cambridge University, 1984.

Josei-shi Sogo Kenkyu-kai, ed., *Nihon Josei-shi* (History of Japanese Women), vol. 4 (Kindai), Tokyo: Daigaku Shuppan-kai, 1982.

Kadogawa, *Kanwa Chū Jiten* (Dictionary of Chinese Characters as used in Japanese), Kadogawa Shuppan, 1976.

Kagoyama Takashi, ed., *Jokō to Kekkaku* (Female Workers and Tuberculosis), Kosei-kan, 1970.

248 Bibliography

Kaneko Useki, *Chikuhō Tankō Kotoba* (The Terminology of the Chikuho Coal Mines), Meicho Shuppan, 1974.

Kato Shizue (Baroness Ishimoto Shidzué), *Facing Two Ways*, Stanford University, 1984.

Kobata Atsushi, *Nihon Kōzan Shi no Kenkyū* (Research on the History of Japanese Mining), Iwanami Shoten, 1968.

Konoe Kitaro, *Chikuhō Tankō Shi* (History of the Chikuho Collieries), Fukuoka: Nakamura Kinkoko, 1898.

Kozan Konwa Kai, ed., *Nippon Kōgyō Hattatsushi* (History of Japanese Mining), vol. 2, Hara Shobo, 1993, originally published 1932.

Kyoto Daigaku Bungaku-bu Kokushi Kenkyu-shitsu, ed., *Nihon Shi Jiten* (Dictionary of Japanese History), Osaka: Sogensha, 1954.

Kyushu Sangyo Shiryo Kenkyu-kai, ed., *Kōfu Taigū Jirei* (Examples of the Treatment of Miners), Meiji Bunken Shiryo Kankokai, *Fukkoku Han* (reprint edition), no date; originally published by the Noshomusho Kozankyoku (Mines Bureau of the Ministry of Agriculture and Commerce) in 1908.

Lahiri-Dutt, Kuntala, and Macintyre, Martha, eds., *Women Miners in Developing Countries* (Pit Women and Others), Aldershot, UK: Ashgate Publishing Ltd, 2006.

Lebra, Takie Sugiyama, and William P. Lebra, *Japanese Culture and Behaviour*, University Press of Hawaii, revised edition, 1986.

Lewis, Michael, *Rioters and Citizens: Mass Protest in Imperial Japan*, particularly Chapter 4, "The Coalfield Riots: Riots as Labor Dispute," pp. 192–241. University of California Press, 1990.

Makabe Tomoko, *Picture Brides* [*Shashinkon no Tsumatachi*]: *Japanese Immigrant Women in Canada*, translated by Kathleen Merken, Ontario: Multicultural History Society of Ontario, 1995.

Makabe Tomoko, *Shashinkon no Tsumatachi* (Picture Brides), Miraisha, 1983.

Marx, Karl, *Capital*, vol. 1, Moscow: Foreign Languages Publishing House, 1961.

Mashio Etsuko, *Jizoko no Seishun: Onna Atoyama no Ki* (Youth Underground: The Record of a Female Haulier), Chikuma Shobo, 1979.

Mathias, Regine, "Female Labour in the Japanese Coal-Mining Industry," in Janet Hunter, ed., *Japanese Women Working*, London: Routledge, 1993.

Matsumoto Kichinosuke, *Chikuhō ni Ikiru: Buraku Kaihō Undo to tomo ni Gojūnen* (Living in Chikuho: 50 Years with the Buraku Liberation Movement), Kyoto: Buraku Mondai Kenkyu-jo Shuppan-bu, 1977.

Matsuoka Koichi, "*Takashima Tankō no Sanjō* (Dreadful Conditions at the Takashima Mine)," in Ueno Eishin, ed., *Kindai Minshū no Kiroku*, (Records of the Modern Masses), vol. 2, (*Kōfu*—Miners) 2, pp. 416–19, Shinjinbutsu Oraisha, 1971.

Miike Tanko Rodo Kumiai, ed., *Miike Nijūnen* (Twenty Years at Miike), Rodo Junposha, 1967.

Morisaki, Kazue *Makkura: Jokōfu kara no Kikigaki* (Pitch Black: Interviews with Women Miners), Riron-sha, 1961.

Morris-Suzuki, Tessa, *The Technological Transformation of Japan*, Cambridge University Press, 1994.

Murakushi Nisaburo, *Nihon Tankō Chin-Rōdō Shiron* (Treatise on Wage Labour in Japanese Coal Mines), Jichosha, 1976.

Murakushi Nisaburo, "*Tokugawa-ki Sekitan-gyō ni okeru Gijutsu Keiei Chin-rōdō*," (Technology, Management, and Wage Labour in the Tokugawa Period Coal Industry), *Keizai Shirin*, vol. 512, no. 1.

Nagahara Kazuko and Hirota Masaki, eds., vol. 4 (Kindai), *Nihon Josei Seikatsu Shi* (History of the Daily Lives of Japanese Women), Tokyo Daigaku Shuppan-kai, 1990.

Bibliography   249

Nagaoka Tsuruzo, "*Kōfu no Shogai*" (A Miner's Life), in Ueno Hidenobu, ed., *Kindai Minshū no Kiroku*, (Records of Modern People): Vol. 2, *Kōfu* (Miners), pp. 237–48. Shin Jinbutsu Orai Sha, 1971.

Nagatsumi Junjiro, "*Ōshū Taisenji ni Okeru Waga Kuni no Tankyō*" (Condition of Our Collieries During World War I), in Nihon Kagaku Shi Gakkai, ed., *Nippon Kagaku-gizyutusi Taikei*, (Historical Outline of Japanese Science and Technology) vol. 20, pp. 276–77. Daiichi Hoki Shuppan KK, 1965.

Nakamura Masanori, ed., *Gijutsu Kakushin to Joshi Rōdō* (Technological Innovation and Female Labour), Tokyo: Kokusai Rengo Daigaku (The United Nations University), 1985.

Nakamura Masanori, *Rōdōsha to Nōmin* (Workers and Cultivators), Shogakkan, 1987.

Nakamura Masanori, ed., *Technology Change and Female Labour in Japan*, Tokyo: The United Nations University at Tokyo University, 1994.

Nakatomi Hyoei, *Nagaoka Tsuruzō Den* (Biography of Nagaoka Tsuruzo), Ochanomizu Shobo, 1977.

Newsome, Eric, *The Coal Coast*, Victoria, BC: Orca Books, 1989.

Nihon Kagaku Shi Gakkai, ed., *Nippon Kagaku-gizyutusi Taikei* (Historical Outline of Japanese Science and Technology) vol. 20 (*Saikō Yakin Gijutsu*—Mining and Metallurgical Technology), Daiichi Hoki Shuppan KK, 1965.

Nimura Kazuo, *Ashio Bodō no Shiteki Bunseki* (Historical Analysis of the Rising at Ashio), Tokyo: Tokyo University Press, 1988.

Nimura Kazuo, *The Ashio Riot of 1907: A Social History of Mining in Japan*, Durham, NC: Duke University Press, 1997.

Nishinarita, Yutaka, "The Coal-mining Industry," in Nakamura Masanori, ed., *Technology Change and Female Labour in Japan*, pp. 59–96. Tokyo: The United Nations University Press, 1994.

Nishinarita Yutaka, "*Sekitan Kōgyō no Gijutsu Kakushin to Joshi Rōdō* (Technological Innovation in the Coal Industry and Female Labour)," in Nakamura Masanori, ed., *Gijutsu Kakushin to Joshi Rōdō* (Technological Innovation and Female Labour), pp. 71–105. Tokyo: Kokusai Rengo Daigaku (The United Nations University), 1985.

Noshomusho, Shoko Kyoku, ed., *Shokkō Jijo* (Factory Workers' Conditions), Meicho Kanko Kai, 1967, first published 1903.

Ogino Yoshihiro, ed., *Senzen-ki Chikuhō Tankō-gyō no Keiei to Rōdō* (Management and Labour in the Pre-War Chikuho Coal Industry), Kyoto: Keibun Sha, 1990.

Ogino Yoshihiro, "*Taisen Zengo ni okeru Kaijima Tankō-gyō no Rōshi Kankei*" (Labour-Management Relations in Kaijima's Coal Operations Around the Time of the First World War), in Ogino, *Senzen-ki Chikuhō Tankō-gyō no Keiei to Rōdō* (Management and Labour in the Pre-War Chikuho Coal Industry), pp. 85–108. Keibun Sha, 1990.

Orii Seigo, *Hōjō Daihijō* (The Hojo Disaster), Tokyo: Asahi Shimbun Sha, 1979.

Oyama Shikitaro, *Kōgyō Rōdō to Oyakata Seido* (Mining Labour and the Gang Boss System), Yuikaku, 1964.

Patrick, Hugh, ed., *Japanese Industrialization and its Social Consequences*, University of California, 1976.

Price, John, "Postwar Industrial Relations and the Origins of Lean Production in Japan (1945–1973)," PhD dissertation, University of British Columbia, 1993.

Robertson, Ellison, "Hearts and Mines," *Canadian Dimension*, Winnipeg MB, vol. 34 no. 5 (Sept/Oct, 2000).

Romu Kanri Shiryo Hensan Kai, ed., *Nihon Rōmu Kanri Nenshi* (Japanese Labour Management Annual Statistics), Nihon Rōmu Kanri Nenshi Kanko-kai, various years.

250 Bibliography

Rodo Undo Iin Kai, ed., *Nihon Rōdō Undō Shiryō* (Historical Materials Pertaining to Japan's Labour Movement), 5 vols., Tokyo: Daigaku Shuppan Kai, 1968.

Saegusa Hiroto, ed., *Nihon Kagaku Koten Zensho* (Classics in Japanese Science), vol. 9, no. 3 (*Saikō Yakin*—Metallurgy), Tokyo: Asahi Shimbun-sha, 1942.

Sakamoto Yuichi, "*Chikuhō Sekitan Kōgyō to Hisabetsu Buraku*" (Persecuted Villages and the Chikuho Coal Industry), *Buraku Mondai Kenkyū*, no. 140 (Aug. 1997).

Saxonhouse, Gary, "Country Girls and Communication among Competitors in the Japanese Cotton-Spinning Industry," in Hugh Patrick, ed., *Japanese Industrialization and its Social Consequences*, pp. 97–125. University of California, 1976.

Schwieder, Dorothy, *Black Diamonds: Life and Work in Iowa's Coal Mining Communities, 1895–1925*, Ames: Iowa State University Press, 1983.

Scott, J. W. Robertson, *The Foundations of Japan*, London: John Murray, 1922.

Shimazaki Toson, *The Broken Commandment* (Hakai), translated by Kenneth Strong, Japan Foundation translation series, Kokusai Koryu Kikin, University of Tokyo, 1974.

Shimonaka Kunihiko, ed., "*Nihon Zankoku Monogatari*" (Tales of Japanese Inhumanity), vol. 5, "*Kindai no Ankoku*" (The Modern Dark Ages), Tokyo: Heibonsha, 1960.

Shindo Toyo, *Chikuhō no Jokōfu-tachi* (Female Miners of Chikuho), Kyoto: Buraku Mondai Kenkyu-Sho, 1974.

Shinmura, Izuru, *Kōjien* (Compendium of [Japanese] Terminology), Iwanami Shoten, 1960.

Smith, Thomas C., *Political Change and Industrial Development in Japan*, Stanford University, 1955.

Smith, W. Donald, "Digging Through Layers of Class, Gender and Ethnicity: Korean Women Miners in Prewar Japan," in Kuntala Lahiri-Dutt and Martha Macintyre, eds., *Women Miners in Developing Countries*, pp. 111–129, Aldershot, UK: Ashgate Publishing Ltd, 2006.

Smith, W. Donald, "Gender and Ethnicity in Japan's Chikuho Coalfield," in Stefan Berger, Andy Croll, and Norman LaPorte, eds., *Towards a Comparative History of Coalfield Societies*, pp. 204–18. Aldershot, UK: Ashgate Publishing Ltd., 2005.

Smith, W. Donald, "The 1932 Asō Coal Strike: Korean-Japanese Solidarity and Conflict," in *Korean Studies*, no. 20 (1996).

Smith, William Donald III, "Ethnicity, Class, and Gender in the Mines: Korean Workers in Japan's Chikuhō Coal Field, 1917–1945," PhD dissertation, Washington University, 1999.

Sone, Sachiko, "Coalmining Women in Japan: Cultural Identity, Welfare, and Economic Conditions on the Chikuho Coalfield," PhD dissertation, University of Western Australia, 2001.

Sone, Sachiko, "Coal Mining Women Speak Out: Economic Change and Women Miners in Chikuho, Japan," in Jaclyn J. Gier and Laurie Mercier, *Mining Women: Gender in the Development of a Global Industry, 1670 to 2005*, pp. 153–170. New York: Palgrave MacMillan, 2006.

Sone, Sachiko, "Exploitation or Expectation?" in *Critical Asian Studies,"* vol. 35, no. 1 (2003).

Sone, Sachiko, "Japanese Coal Mining: Women Discovered," in Kuntala Lahiri-Dutt and Martha Macintyre, eds., *Women Miners in Developing Countries*, pp. 51–72. Ashgate Publishing Ltd, 2006.

Soseki, Natsume, *Kōfu* [*The Miner*], translated by Jay Rubin, Stanford University Press, 1988.

Statham, I. C. F., *Coalmining*, London: English Universities Press, 1951.

Strong, Kenneth, *Ox Against the Storm: A Biography of Tanaka Shozo,* Vancouver: University of British Columbia Press, 1977.

Sumiya Mikio, "*Naya Seido no Seiritsu to Hōkai*" (The Rise and Fall of the *Naya* System), *Shisō*, no. 434 (Aug. 1960).

Bibliography 251

Sumiya Mikio, *Nihon Chinrōdō no Shiteki Kenkyū* (Historical Research on Japanese Wage Labour), Ochanomizu Shobo, 1976.

Sumiya Mikio, *Nihon Sekitan Sangyō Bunseki* (Analysis of the Japanese Coal Industry), Iwanami Shoten, 1968.

Sumiya Mikio, ed., *Shokkō Oyobi Kōfu Chōsa* (Survey of Workers and Miners), Kosei-kan, 1970.

Tagawa Shi-shi Hensan Iinkai, ed., *Tagawa Shi-shi* (History of Tagawa City), vol. 2 (*chūkan*), Gyosei Shuppan, 1976.

Tajima Masami, *Tankō Bijin* (Coal Mine Beauties), Chikushi Shokan, 2000.

Takematsu Teruo, *Kōnai Uma to Bafu to Jokōfu: Jizoko no Kiroku—Juso* (Pit Ponies, Drivers and Female Miners: Underground Record—The Curse), Soshisha, 1982.

Tanaka Naoki, *Kindai Nihon Tankō Rōdōshi Kenkyū* (A Study of the History of Labour in the Collieries of Modern Japan), Sofukan, 1984.

"*Tankō Kōzan ni okeru Hamba Seido*" (The Hamba System at the Coal Mines), in Nihon Romu Kanri Nenshi Kanko-kai, ed., *Nihon Rōmu Kanri Nenshi*, vol. 1, 1962.

Tazaki Nobuyoshi, "*Josei Rōdō no Shoruikei*" (Classification of Female Labour), in Nagahara Kazuko and Hirota Masaki, eds., *Nihon Josei Seikatsu Shi* (History of the Daily Lives of Japanese Women), vol. 4 (*Kindai*), pp. 163–97. Tokyo: Daigaku Shuppan-kai, 1990

Tsurumi, E. Patricia, *Factory Girls: Women in the Thread Mills of Meiji Japan*, Princeton University Press, 1990.

Ueno Eishin, ed., *Kindai Minshū no Kiroku* (Records of the Modern Masses), vol. 2, *Kōfu* (Miners), Shinjinbutsu Oraisha, 1971.

Wakita Haruko, Anne Bouchy, and Ueno Chizuko, eds., *Gender and Japanese History*, Osaka University Press, 1999.

Yamamoto Sakubei, *Chikuhō Tankō Emaki* (Picture Scroll of the Chikuho Coal Mines), Fukuoka: Ashi Shobo, 1985.

Yamamoto Sakubei, *Yama ni Ikiru: Ji no Soko no Jinsei Kiroku* (Living at the Coal Mines: A Record of Life Underground), Kodansha, 1967.

Yamamoto Sakubei, *Yama no Shigoto* (Work at the Mines) and *Yama no Kurashi* (Life at the Mines), Fukuoka: Ashi Shobo, 1976.

Yamazu Naoko, "*Miike Tankō no Saitan Rōdō*" (Mining Labour at the Miike Coal Mines), in *Mitsui Bunko Ronsō*, no. 8, 1974.

Yasukawa Junosuke, "*Hisabetsu Buraku to Josei*" (Women and the Outcaste Villages), in Josei-shi Sogo Kenkyu-kai, ed., *Nihon Josei-shi* (History of Japanese Women), pp. 185–222. Tokyo: Daigaku Shuppan-kai, 1982.

Yasuzo Ryusei, "*Hayashigatani Sekitan-zan Kenka no Tenmatsu*" (Particulars of the Dispute at the Hayashigatani Coal Mine), in Kyodo Tagawa and Tagawa Kyodo Kenkyu-kai, eds., *Tagawa Shi*, no. 23 (Oct. 1964).

Yokoyama Gennosuke, *Nihon no Kasō Shakai* (The Lower Classes of Japan), Iwanami, 1949.

Yoshida, Kayoko and Miyauchi, Reiko, "Invisible Labor: A Comparative Oral History of Women in Coal Mining Communities of Hokkaido, Japan, and Montana, USA, 1890–1940," in Jaclyn J. Gier and Laurie Mercier, *Mining Women: Gender in the Development of a Global Industry, 1670 to 2005*, pp. 136–52. New York: Palgrave MacMillan, 2006.

Yoshimura Sakuo, *Nihon Tankō-shi Shichū*, (A Japanese Coal-Mining History Memoir), Ochanomizu Shobo, 1984.

Index

abortion, prohibitions on 94
accidents in coal-mines 75–8; causes of
74; flooding 64
adornment 142–3
agari-zaké 112, 150
age and marital status 14, 16–18
akamari strokes 67
alternative employments 6, 96, 99, 191,
210; in "tea-houses" or brothels 209–10
ashi-naka sandals 139
Asahara Kenzo, 195, 196
Ashio Copper Mine 116, 168, 170
assei-yama 183–4
atomuki 14, 19, 38, 54
atoyama 14, 29, 31, 35, 57, 87, 232
attitudes toward child labor 100–1

bakku 141, 227
bara-kago 33
bathing conditions 149–50
battera 36
behavior modification 185–6
benevolence of bosses 229–31
bento 135–6
blasting 54–56
braking wagons 42
brutality as management strategy 183–4
burakumin; baths for 149–50;
discrimination against 8–9, 22–4

capabilities, women's 214–15
carbon monoxide poisoning 2, 70
casualties, in Japanese mines 75, 77, 86, 87
cave-ins 75–8
chauvinism 117–18
Chikuho coal mines 11–14
child labor; in coal mines 98–9; attitudes
toward 100–1

childcare, facilities 5, 95, 132, 137;
minders 208
clothing 137–9
coal dust and soot 66–7, 68–9, 73
coal miners 5; characterization of 3;
origins of 17–19; reputation of 2
company store 150, 173
concept of belonging, to home 220–2; and
burial places 221
conflict; reproduction and 118–20; rivalry
and 165–6
convicts and culprits at coal mines 8, 138,
170, 191, 192
cooking 131–5
courting and marriage 103–6; go-betweens
103, 105–7, 110, 229
cradling 30, 52
credulity 217–19

daibassha carts 35
daily routines; adornment 142–3; bathing
148–50; cooking 136–7; early in morning
129; eating underground 143–4;
evening tasks 151–2; fetching water
132–4; hygiene and sanitation 141–2;
improvements 129–31; inadequate
clothing 137–39; late in the evening
145–9; long shifts 144–5; straw sandals
139–41; surroundings in twilight 152–4
darkness in the mine 62–3, 227–8
Daté waistband 139
deaths; in Hojo mine 73; in other mines
70; in Mitsubishi Mining Company 73
digestive disorders 67
disasters, Japanese coal mines 74
discrimination; against *burakumin* 8–9, 22;
racial and social 22–4
discriminatory regimes 188

disease, respiratory, 67–8, 228; rheumatic, reproductive and sexually transmitted, 67–8
disparity, gender 19–20
divide-and-rule methods 22–3, 192
divisions and solidarity 191–2
domestic violence 119–20
drilling 55
dust-filled tunnels, smoking in 81–2
dust-laden air 68–9
dynamite; dangers of using 78–80; preparation and use of 56; for tunneling 54, 55

eating underground 143–4
electric lighting in mines 62
emissions, gas 68–72
encephalomalacia, softening of the brain 80
endurance, limits of 209–10
"Enquiry Into the Development of Mines" 16
environment, unnatural 225–7
equal-allocation system, wagons 45–6
eta-buro baths 148, 150
evening bath 148–50
evening's activities and duties 145–8
explosions; fire and 68–74; Hojo mine 72, 73; Takashima Mine 82

Factory Law of 1911 99
family production system 2–4, 6, 16, 19, 28, 76, 84, 101–2, 111–12, 122, 137, 208
fear 219–20
feisty termagants 166–7
fires 2; and explosions 68–74; gas 69, 75
food 136, 144–8, 151, 168, 174, 196; calorie requirements 218; Korean 24, 190; prices 147, 193–4
framing 50–4
Fukuoka Mines Administration 74, 86
funerals and burials 82, 116–7

gamé teapot 136
gang boss, as middleman 229–30; his rake-off 174, 229; subservience to 173–4
ganzume rake 20
gas emission 68–9
gas fires 69–74
gender differences and inequities 210–12
gender disparity 19–20
getten frustration 117–8
gichi powder dummies 55
grime 64–8, 142

hamba-seido 5, 174, Notes 42 p.26 and 67 p.199
haulage ways, framing/timbering in 51–4
hauling 28–39; in cramped quarters 31; at pit mouth 33–4; with *sena* 31–3; with *sura* 36–9; with *tebo* 35–6
heat 62–7
hewing 30–1; in cramped quarters 31; by women in *mabu-beko* 140
hiding runaways 177–8
hitosaki teams 29. 92
Hojo Mine 47, 72, 73
hours of work 2, 45–9, 96, 127, 131; flexibility in 137, Note 83 p.156; and gender disparity 19; to load wagons 44
housing 13, 17, 119, 127–9; for *burakumin* 22; modest improvements in 5, 129–31
hygiene and sanitation 141–2

Igisu Mine 183, 188
illegal mining operations 62, 96, 175
indebtedness 49, 121–2, 170–6, 182, 189, 208, 220–2, 230
indignities, self-esteem and 206–8
independence for women, limits on 3, 109–10
Indomitables, the 164–5
inequities, gender differences and 210–12
infant mortality 94
Ishihara Osamu 67–8, 75, 77, 135, 228
Ishimoto, Baroness Shidzue, and poor facilities 134; appraisal of "low-lifes" 138

Japanese Coal Mines; accidents and rates of injury in 87; causes of injuries in 1924–1926 74; disasters, before 1930 74
Joban mines 12, 53, 64, 67, 82, 103–4, 130–2, 152, 174, 220, 225
job classifications 9

Kaijima mines 74; day-care at 95; punishments at 181; relief schemes at 85–6
Kaijima Tasuke, and his regional *zaibatsu* 85
kane-nokoshi savings 151
Karatsu region coal mines 11–14
kataire-gin recruitment loans 49, 170–2
kentan inspections 47
ketsuwari, indirect resistance 175–80, as political action 182
kōnai bijin mine beauties, Note 62 p.124, 206
kōnai kaburi head covering 139

254 Index

Korean miners 9, job assignments 214; nos. of 23; suppression of and relations with Japanese miners 191–2; wages of 22; wives of 9; women 24
Koyanose mines 65
kuragae lunch boxes 136

loads, in *sena* 31–2; in *tebo* 35; in *sura* 36–7
long shifts 49, 144–5, 152, 213
love matches 105–6
lynchings 180–2

mabu-beko skirt, sewing 138
Machida fire 72–3
machismo 84, 110–18, 119–20, 163, 175, 180
marital friction 121–2
marital struggle 111–13
marriage; courting and 101–4; loose bonds of 107–9
Matsumoto Kichinosuke 20–1
medical facilities 76, 84–5, 92 Note 158, p. 202
Meinohama Mine 77, 230
menstruation 19, 141
methane gas leakage 2, 69–70, 73
Miike Mine 12, 16, 23, 54, 92, 93, 134, 147–8, 170, 226
miners as social outcasts 138, 184–6, 188–91, 221, 226
Mining Law of 1905 99
miscarriages 64, 92–4
Mitsubishi Mining Company 12, 23, 73, 81–4, 134, 150, 188, 227
Miyoshi Mine 45, 71, 178, 183, 189
mutual aid 163–4

Nakama coal mine 65
Natsume Soseki, and recruiting at Ashio 168
naya-seido 5, 85, 127
Nishijin Mine 19, 69
Nishikawa Mines 183
nonpunitive damages 80–3
number of women in mining 13–14

organized resistance 193–6
oshidashi-ban, pushing-out priority 45
Otsuji Mine, women demonstrate at 195

paternalism 3–4, 6–8, 16, 20, 71–2, 76, 79–81, 85–6, 129–30, 147, 153, 168–71, 214, 229–31
partners, choice of 104–6
perpetual night work 227–8

piecework wages and deductions 46–9, 79, 86, 168, 229
pillar-and-room system 54
pillaring and robbing 29
pit ponies 41–2
polluted water 65, 134, 227
poverty, shared 84, 151, 162, 204, 218–19, 221
power of bosses 184–5
proletarians, subdued 166–7
prototype, single mother 96
punishment, for absconding 178; for undercover recruiters 168–9; (in)appropriateness of 180–2
pushing wagons 41–4
"putting in the boat" procedure 42

racial discrimination 20–4
reactions to bondage 208–9
recruitment, by subterfuge 168–9; continual recruiting 168–9
regulatory regimes 188–9
relief programs 85–6
Rengeji Mine 70
reproduction and conflict 118–20
revelation, of one husband's pathology 114–16
rewards, changing 212–13
rice, foreign 147
Rice Riots, of 1918, 193–6
ridiculing staffers 186–7
rivalry and conflict 165–6
robbing methods 29

sakiyama 19, 23, 54; loading responsibilities of 35; an unskilled one 56
sanitation, hygiene and 141–2
sasabeya underground offices 81–2, 203
savings 5, 19, 151, 220; compulsory 172–3
schooling 97–8; of *burakumin* 98
self-image 205–8
sena 31; hauling with yoked 32; at pit mouth 33
sexual abuse 3, 223–5
sharing, food 4, food and clothing 160–2; Fate 161–2
shikuri framers 14, 50
sibling responsibilities and rivalry 5, 95, 97, 98, 166
sieving at pit mouth 34
single mother prototype 96
smoking underground 81–2
social discrimination 20–4
solidarity, divisions and 191–3

Index 255

sorting and transporting 57
straw sandals 139–41
strikes 6–7, 148, 182; women's role
   in 165, 194–6
subdued proletarians 166–7
Sugitani Mine 70, 189
Suiin, Emi 168
superstition 217–18
supervision 2, 40, 160, 184, 230; by
   kogashira 54, 137; by foremen (*romu*
   or *kakari*) 54, 56, 70, 141, 164–5, 176,
   205, 224
sura, filling under low roofs 38; forms
   of 37; hauling with 36–9; removable
   boards of 50
syphilis 68

Tagawa mines, conveyors at 57; ideal
   mining unit at 17, 94; nos. of *burakumin*
   at 21–2; vulgarities of women's
   language at 186
Taisho Mine 195
Takashima Mine 65, 74, 82, 106, 108, 183
   Note 64, p. 156
tanmake eczema 68
tanuki-bori mines 28, 33, 65, 96, 154
tebo, hauling with 34–6, 63, 84, 93, 100, 215
termagants, feisty 166–7
timbering or framing 28, 50–3
tonbo frames 52
transporting, sorting and 57
treatment for injuries 84–5
tsuma-waraji sandals 139
tsumiage-ban loading priority 45
tsurube balance pole 12

tsuya head-covering 139
Tsuya, Matsumoto 44, 93
tuberculosis (TB) 68
tunneling 28, 50–4

Ube coalfields 11–12
uchi-kowashi house-wrecking 193–4
uke-zura received on the head 38, 39
underground miners in major
   coalfields, 15
unnatural environment 225–7

voices of mining women 7, 9, 10, 203

wages 4, 16, 19–20, 94, 134; demands for
   increases 195; for child-minders 100,
   137; for tunneling and framing 53–4;
   gender disparity in 211–12; in company
   scrip 173; loans against 170–3, 212,
   229; payment of 146–8, 152–4, 230–1;
   and quotas 47; and Rice Riots 194; to
   burakumin and Koreans 22
wake-ban equal allocation (of wagons)
   45–6
water, availability of 132–4
widows 6, 54, 73, 109–10, 206, 222
woman-and-man frame, 52–3
work load 49, 96, 127, 137, 217
wagons 34 availability of 43–5; loading
   and spreading 40; obtaining and pushing
   out 41–4; size and capacity 43; wagon
   trains 41, 42

Yamada mines, conflict at 185
Yamada River pollution 134